THE CHINA NEXUS

PRAISE FOR *THE CHINA NEXUS*

"*The China Nexus* is one of those rare books that very clearly records the political environment in China over the past thirty years. Benedict Rogers, from the perspective of a Westerner and in a very detailed manner, documents this authoritarian country's political orientation and agendas through his personal experience. It is often very difficult to comprehend the society of an authoritarian regime like China through its history, its ideology, and the Communist Party's behaviour. While almost 20 percent of the world's total population belongs to that society, the West has in effect a very limited, and often distorted and illusory understanding, of it. Benedict Rogers went to China for the first time when he was a teenager. In *The China Nexus*, he connects his experience of the past thirty years with political events in China and covers almost all the political topics, ranging from Tibet and Xinjiang to Hong Kong and Taiwan. His concrete, authentic, and reliable narrative provides readers with the precious possibility to understand China. Now that there is open confrontation between China and the West once again, Benedict Rogers' comprehensive account is an invaluable source of knowledge that helps us understand today's world in its whole complexity."

—AI WEIWEI, artist and activist

"This outstanding book by one of Britain's foremost and most knowledgeable campaigners on human rights in China and Asia as a whole is an excoriating and comprehensive denunciation of the appalling and increasingly harsh abuse of its citizens by the Communist regime in Beijing. It should be read by everyone concerned about the challenge of sharing our planet with Communist China in the years ahead."

—LORD PATTEN OF BARNES, the last governor of Hong Kong

"Benedict Rogers has done the world an extremely important service by documenting and exposing the repression of the Chinese Communist Party and the Xi dictatorship in his new book, *The China Nexus*. Through fifty trips to China and eighty interviews with exiles, dissidents, and even the Dalai Lama himself, Rogers takes us forensically through the crimes of the Chinese Communist Party to the indisputable conclusion that the Chinese government must face international justice for these crimes. There are very few people in the world who have the experience, knowledge, and authority of Rogers on China, and this book is a must-read for anyone who wants to know what's really happening there."

—BILL BROWDER, author of *Red Notice: How I Became Putin's No. 1 Enemy* and *Freezing Order: A True Story of Russian Money Laundering, Murder, and Surviving Vladimir Putin's Wrath*

"Benedict Rogers, the dedicated founder of Hong Kong Watch, is a serious China watcher. Here he documents the crackdown on the pro-democracy movement in Hong Kong and the steady dissolution of the rule of law there, setting it against the backdrop of the grievous human rights abuses in China, including the slow genocide of the Uyghurs. He argues that the 'golden era' of relations between the UK and China is now over, and that this emergent superpower is a growing challenge to the democratic world. A powerful and alarming analysis."

—BARONESS HELENA KENNEDY, KC, director of the International Bar
Association's Human Rights Institute

"The Chinese Communist Party has a formidable foe in Benedict Rogers, just as the Chinese people have no better friend. His heartfelt, deeply researched, and powerfully argued book should be essential reading for anyone seeking to understand the threat we face—and what we must do to protect ourselves."

—EDWARD LUCAS, *The Times*

"I know Benedict Rogers and hold in high regard his work to help protect the people of Hong Kong from tyranny and the loss of their traditional freedom. His book also covers the plight of the Uyghurs, the Tibetans, and others who are being persecuted at this very moment. I hope his book will be read by all who yearn for freedom and the rule of law in China, and who wish to understand what has happened and is happening in that country today."

—SIR MALCOLM RIFKIND, former British foreign secretary

"Benedict Rogers knows the Asia Pacific well and has been in the vanguard, campaigning for freedom, security, and human rights. His strong sense of conscience drives his dialogue with UK parliamentarians, promoting understanding and action for those whose voices are so often silenced by authoritarian regimes. *The China Nexus* will be a textbook for all who value the importance of freedom and human dignity at the forefront of UK–China discussions."

—CATHERINE WEST, member of Parliament of the United Kingdom

"Benedict Rogers has worked tirelessly and bravely to defend the rights and freedoms of those people in China unable to speak for themselves because of the Chinese Communist Party's brutal repression. His book is another act in his brave defence of freedom. It should be read by all those active in government and politics who seek meek accommodation with this brutal regime in the hope of stronger business ties. Appeasement of such dictatorial regimes didn't work in the 1930s and doesn't work with the CCP now. This book shows us why, from genocide in Xinjiang to forced labour in Tibet and from the persecution of Christians to the tyranny in Hong Kong, the brutality grows. How many times must we relearn the lesson that freedom comes at a price? This book shows us what happens when we turn away in the free world."

—SIR IAIN DUNCAN SMITH, member of Parliament of the United Kingdom

"Riveting reading. When the Chinese government decided to extinguish the possibility of independent thought in Hong Kong, Benedict Rogers was the first foreigner they targeted. On Beijing's orders, Rogers was expelled by the Hong Kong police and, more recently, threatened with arrest for 'jeopardizing state security.' Why is he so feared in China's halls of power? What makes him particularly dangerous to the regime? Look no further than this extraordinary book. *The China Nexus* blends deep research, epic sweep, and beautiful writing to give us a harrowing account of the Chinese Communist Party's totalitarian quest to re-engineer human society. Now more than ever, we need a book like this to remind us that a war of ideas is underway, and while the stakes are nothing less than the future of the world, a single defender of freedom can make all the difference."

—IAN EASTON, author of *The Final Struggle: Inside China's Global Strategy*

"Benedict Rogers' credentials as a human rights campaigner are impressive. In this book, he takes us through the intriguing story of where his commitment comes from. At the heart of his campaigning are the spreading tentacles of the Chinese Communist Party, which he has experienced at first hand. It is this immediate experience that gives *The China Nexus* its humanity and fascinating insights into how the dictatorship operates. Rogers has the kind of curiosity which leads him to run down the memorable details that bring this story to life. The net result is a compelling book that will be of great interest to anyone seriously concerned with the consequences of the world's largest dictatorship."

—STEPHEN VINES, author of *Defying the Dragon:*
Hong Kong and the World's Largest Dictatorship

"Benedict Rogers offers an interesting book of facts. Facts represent truth, and the truth will set us free from illusions about China today. It recounts his thirty-year-long direct personal experience of the Chinese Communist Party regime, but more importantly, it tells the story of brave Chinese peoples. The reader finds a broad analysis of inhumane treatment, persecution, and discrimination of Uyghurs, Tibetans, Christians, political dissidents, and Falun Gong practitioners, as well as the exploitation of workers, the abuse of human rights and freedoms in Hong Kong, and Beijing's support for the dictatorship in North Korea and the military junta in Myanmar. In spite of all this suffering and darkness, one can see clear signs and sources of hope. We need to work with the courageous people and youth across China and in the diasporas, supporting their quest for freedom and their desire for dignity. The diverse peoples of China have suffered too long and sacrificed too much. But their future is born through sacrifice, as this book shows."

—JAN FIGEL, former deputy prime minister of Slovakia,
former European Union commissioner, former EU special envoy
for freedom of religion or belief outside the EU

"At a time when Xi Jinping is extending his repressive rule in China, this chilling book is a timely and important reminder of the brutality of Xi's Communist Party—at home and also abroad, where the world is only now beginning to wake up to the party's routine bullying and interference. Benedict Rogers has been watching and chronicling the rise of China for thirty years, and doing so with a passionate commitment to the cause of human rights. He has witnessed those rights systemically crushed, from Xinjiang to Tibet and Hong Kong. His study of Communist Party thuggery is tempered by sadness—for the Chinese people, and for the fading dream of a more open and free China. There are few people better equipped to highlight the oppressive reality of Xi's China, and the urgent threat this poses to individual rights and to liberal democracy."

—IAN WILLIAMS, author of *Every Breath You Take: China's New Tyranny*

"The world must wake up to the challenges it faces from the Chinese Communist Party regime. In this carefully researched and engaging work, author Benedict Rogers lays out the diabolical character of this regime by examining its repression at home and aggression abroad. Rogers has had an eyewitness view of CCP atrocities and crackdowns through years of travel and residing among China's peoples, with whom he forged deep friendships. The chapters on China's dissidents, Uyghurs, Tibetans, Hong Kongers, persecuted Christians, victims of forced organ harvesting, and those now threatened in China's neighbours all draw on Rogers' personal experiences and interviews of scores of experts and exiles, including the Dalai Lama. This valuable book gives the reader a graphic view of the geopolitical, as well as human rights, threats posed by this emerging superpower."

—NINA SHEA, director of Hudson Institute's Center for Religious Freedom

"In this compellingly personal book, Ben explores the many injustices of the Chinese Communist system through stories, anecdotes, and conversations involving everyday people in China. Shining through these pages is the reality that a different path for China is possible. This book is frank and realistic about horrific crimes and yet still leaves the reader with an abiding sense of what can be achieved through a thoughtful and principled response."

—GARNETT GENUIS, Member of Parliament, Canada and
Member of the Interparliamentary Alliance on China (IPAC)

"*The China Nexus* documents the beautiful journey of its pure-hearted author to help the many people disempowered by the Chinese Communist Party. His book covers a wide range of issues, from Hong Kong and Taiwan to the persecution of Christians and Tibetan Buddhists. His efforts led to the China tribunal, which exposed the horrendous crime of harvesting organs from Falun Gong practitioners, Uyghurs, and other prisoners of conscience. I will always be grateful for Benedict Rogers's kindness. He is a selfless gentleman who has devoted years of his life to fighting for people who are marginalized and persecuted in different parts of the world."

— ANASTASIA LIN, actress, Miss World Canada 2015, human rights advocate

THE CHINA NEXUS

Thirty Years In and Around the Chinese Communist Party's Tyranny

BENEDICT ROGERS

FOREWORD BY LORD ALTON
PREFACE BY NATHAN LAW 羅冠聰

The China Nexus, Thirty Years in and Around the Chinese Communist Party's Tyranny © Ottawa, 2022, Optimum Publishing International and Benedict Rogers

First Edition

BRITISH NATIONAL BIBLIOGRAPHY (CIP)

Benedict Rogers, 1974
The China Nexus, Thirty Years in and Around the Chinese
Communist Party's Tyranny I. Title

ISBN 978-0-88890-326-6 (Hardcover)
ISBN 978-0-88890-327-3 (Paperback)
ISBN 978-0-88890-328-0 (ePub)

Printed and bound in United Kingdom

For information on rights or any submissions, please e-mail to Optimum:
deanb@opibooks.com

Optimum Publishing International
Dean Baxendale, President
www.optimumpublishinginternational.com www.chinanexusbook.com
Twitter @opibooks | Instagram @opibooks

OPTIMUM
PUBLISHING
INTERNATIONAL
LONDON I MONTRÉAL I TORONTO

For all the peoples living under the Chinese Communist Party regime's repression or threat in China, East Turkistan, Tibet, Hong Kong, Taiwan, Myanmar (Burma), North Korea, and beyond.

For freedom.

CONTENTS

FOREWORD

BY LORD ALTON OF LIVERPOOL

My reading of Benedict Rogers' important manuscript has been against the sombre backdrop of war in Europe and the challenge increasingly posed to liberal democracies by new authoritarians—not least by those who lead the Chinese Communist Party (CCP). As *The Times* wryly remarked, Vladimir Putin and Xi Jinping have been "cementing an alliance to make the world safe for autocrats," signing a declaration that in achieving their objectives there would be "no limits" to their friendship.

Xi Jinping has boasted that "the East is rising and the West is declining"—although when he and Putin met on February 4, 2022, to agree to the timing of Russia's illegal invasion of Ukraine, they gravely underestimated the will to defend our values and way of life, represented by the heroism of President Volodymyr Zelensky and the people of Ukraine.

Although it is true that non-democratic countries outnumber democracies for the first time in two decades—what President Biden has called "an inflection point"—and we have grown lazy and complacent in contesting the erosion of the rule of law, human rights, and democracy, nevertheless, Churchill's contention that democracy remains a better form of government than any of the alternatives is a belief shared by millions across the planet.

And the wake-up call in Ukraine has stirred many out of their apathy.

It is into this dangerous moment that Benedict Rogers' timely critique speaks. He comes to his task with a long track record in fighting for human rights including in establishing Hong Kong Watch, and as an advisor to the Inter- Parliamentary Alliance on China (IPAC), which is rapidly reframing the global China debate.

Like the "Tank Man"—the unidentified Chinese man who stood in front of a column of tanks leaving Tiananmen Square during the massacre of pro-democracy protesters in Beijing on June 5, 1989—Benedict Rogers metaphorically, but equally defiantly, stands in front of the same tanks, painstakingly describing to his readers the depredations which have marked the decades since 1949 when the CCP took power.

The past informs the plight today of over one million Uyghurs in Xinjiang, where a genocide—the word used by Britain's former foreign secretary, now prime minister, Elizabeth Truss MP—is underway.

The past informs an understanding of the incarceration of dissidents, academics, journalists, pastors, and lawyers today.

It informs the lamentable destruction of democracy in Hong Kong and the daily attempts to try and subjugate Taiwan's twenty-three million people.

Capturing Taiwan and its free people will enable it to dominate the Western Pacific and the South China Sea, using the new Russia-China alliance to make these territorial, military, and economic gains.

We too easily forget what the regimes of both those countries have done in the past—with too little study of the horrors of either Stalin's famines, gulags, and purges, or the Cultural Revolution and the Great Leap Forward, which put Mao Zedong ahead of the other mass murderers of the twentieth century.

Executions, famine, deaths through forced labour, mass deportations, forced sterilization, and coercive abortion—the horrors and appalling outcomes of its one-child policy and social engineering—purges of opponents, incarceration for dissent, or unwillingness to comply with a brutal ideology: these are all the hallmarks of the CCP.

The historian Frank Dikötter estimates that at least 2.5 million people were summarily killed or tortured to death during the Great Leap Forward alone, and that it "motivated one of the most deadly mass killings of human history."

Millions more were fatalities of the Cultural Revolution, when Mao's Red Guards were given a free hand to kill, torture, and abuse anyone who was said to be an enemy of the Revolution.

And what has happened in the past in Tibet—and the destruction of culture, language, religion, and ethnicity—also informs the present.

Even the same Party chief in Tibet, Chen Quanguo—having established a draconian security apparatus in Tibet—became the mastermind behind today's concentration camps in Xinjiang and the enslavement of a people.

In March 2022, I participated in the wreath laying at Westminster Abbey to mark the sixty-third anniversary of the Tibetan uprising. I have visited Tibet and Western China and once hosted a visit to Liverpool by the Dalai Lama. He says that "Tibetans were not only shot, but they were also beaten to death, crucified, burned alive, drowned, mutilated, starved, strangled, hanged, boiled alive, buried alive, drawn and quartered, and beheaded."

Read that description alongside the report of the United States Holocaust Memorial Museum's Simon-Skjodt Center for the Prevention of Genocide: "To Make Us Slowly Disappear."

Or the report of the independent Uyghur Tribunal headed up by Sir Geoffrey Nice, KC, which describes monstrous crimes against humanity.

Beginning with discrimination against the mainly Muslim Uyghurs, it escalated with intense surveillance, mass detentions, forcible sterilization and insertion of IUDs, forced migration, kidnapping of Uyghur children (abducted from their parents and placed in state institutions), accompanied by terrible violence, torture, and killing.

Both Nice and the Holocaust Museum found evidence of "coercive interventions of the Chinese government to prevent sizable numbers of Uyghurs from coming into being," suggesting that the deliberate goal is "to biologically destroy the group, in whole or in substantial part."

Nice's Tribunal concluded that this is genocide.

The increasingly neglected story of Tibet—deliberately airbrushed so as not to disrupt trade deals with the CCP—should have been a terrible warning about what would happen to the Uyghurs.

But it ought also to be a warning to any nation which believes it will be safe from comparable vicissitudes. Millennials and generation X need to hear this story and, indeed, learn about the struggles of the last Cold War—lest the freedoms and liberties which are often taken for granted slip through our hands. They need to know about the vicious retaliatory sanctions against brave countries like Lithuania, which dared to open a Taiwan office in Vilnius.

And it's not just about the loss of freedom and democracy—it's about sovereignty, the right to self-determination, identity, and what Rabbi Jonathan Sacks once described as "the dignity of difference." It's about the defence of universal norms which have benefited humanity, exemplified in the great charter of the 1948 Universal Declaration of Human Rights—the antidote to the ideology of Mao and his acolytes.

It is also about our appalling dependency on the CCP and the clarity of their strategy in comparison with any coherent approach by the U.K.

The CCP has a clear strategy of undermining resilience and security; promoting dependency; acquiring intellectual property and data; and destroying competitiveness through slave labour in everything from green energy to surveillance equipment made in places like Xinjiang and then used to collect data up and down the length and breadth of the U.K.

By contrast, in letting the CCP acquire the U.K.'s largest-selling silicon chip factory, allowing it to penetrate our telecommunications and nuclear energy sectors, we have been betrayed by unprecedented levels of entryism—jeopardizing both industry and security. And we allowed China to join and then exploit its membership of the World Trade Organization—foolishly believing that more trade—on their terms—would lead to internal reform. It has merely increased the appetite of the crocodile.

Paradoxically—or perhaps intentionally—the CCP has been the biggest beneficiary of the COVID-19 pandemic.

I extracted from a very reluctant U.K. government an admission that they had bought one billion lateral flow tests from China.

They subsequently confirmed that they purchased 24.1 billion items of personal protective equipment—with China recorded as the country of origin—at a phenomenal total cost of £10.9 billion. That's about the equivalent of the entire (reduced) British Overseas Aid budget.

It is also money that might have been used to support developing nations now dependent on the CCP's Belt and Road programmes which increasingly take on the appearance of colonialism.

Belt and Road indents developing nations and turns them into vassal states. Nations like Sri Lanka, Kenya, Uganda, Montenegro, Laos, and Kazakhstan have found themselves crippled by debt, and reliant on the CCP. Reports detail abandoned railways and half-built bridges, with China's "debt traps" schemes costing countries billions. This is not China's Marshall Aid programme or U.K. development aid. This is about predatory loans and bringing countries into the CCP's sphere of influence. In Africa, one in five infrastructure projects are funded by China with one in three built by Chinese companies.

Then we are surprised when Commonwealth countries in hock to the CCP vote in the General Assembly of the United Nations at the behest of CCP cadres.

We see the same attempted systematic appropriation of international institutions—including the World Health Organization and even the UN Human Rights Council. We see it in the infiltration and financial dependency of British universities. We see it in the presence of CCP agents inside Parliament and political parties.

If the West wants to protect itself, it must face up to the reality of the CCP's history and its future intentions. Charles Moore is right that we must respond to "a regime entirely controlled by a totalitarian party trying to take control of the world."

In its selective view of the past, the CCP repeatedly tells the story of the deplorable nineteenth century opium trade between British India and Qing China. Not only do they omit to describe how even in the 1840s many in Britain opposed it—Gladstone, a fierce critic of the Opium Wars, describing it as "infamous and atrocious"—but that when comparable analysis of the CCP's contemporary actions and atrocities occurs, those who write about it or speak out are brutally silenced. Hong Kong's textbooks can no longer mention Tiananmen, and even works of art commemorating CCP victims have to be destroyed.

Think of the young woman journalist Zhang Zhan, who went to Wuhan to establish the facts about the origins of COVID-19. For doing so she was given a prison sentence of four years and, after continuing to protest from within prison, and with her health deteriorating, she has been subjected to forcible feeding.

Think of Liu Xiaobo, the Chinese writer and dissident, and Nobel laureate, who died in 2017, after serving four prison sentences, and who said, "There is no force that can put an end to the human quest for freedom."

Think of Hong Kong's arrested lawyers such as Martin Lee and Margaret Ng (both given suspended prison sentences); think of young jailed pro-democracy campaigners such as Andy Li, Joshua Wong, and Agnes Chow; or the imprisoned newspaper owner Jimmy Lai. Think of defiant women like the brave Grandma Wong, arrested for contesting menacing intimidation and brutal suppression of human rights and challenging trade based on slave labour.

Think of the people I met in Taiwan, in 2019—people like Lam Wing-kee and the wife of Li Ming-che. Lam had been imprisoned in China for selling books—including the banned *1984*—and Li, a Taiwanese pro-democracy activist, had been arrested in 2017 while on a visit to China. He remained incarcerated until his release in April 2022.

As Benedict Rogers asks, is it any wonder the people of Taiwan—a territory which has never been part of the People's Republic of China—live in dread of a military invasion by the CCP, an apprehension underlined by Putin's illegal seizure of the sovereign state of Ukraine?

Of course, the tragedy is that if "one country, two systems" had not been destroyed in Hong Kong, it could have offered hope to Taiwan.

Instead of which, it demonstrates the deceit of the CCP in upending international treaties.

It is why I have urged the U.K. government to lead other democracies in acting together to recognize Taiwan, "turning the tables on the CCP's bullying posturing."

Over the past forty years in Parliament, I have repeatedly raised these issues—not because I hate China: quite the reverse. I love China and its people and admire its many qualities. What I loathe is the ideology which has oppressed and broken the lives of wonderful people. But the writing is on the Great Wall of China for that ideology, and increasingly it is being contested.

The CCP's decision to impose sanctions on me and six other parliamentarians was designed to try and silence us. It hasn't. Nor has it lessened my love of the people of China. It has merely re-enforced my determination and that of countless others to keep speaking out.

And, like Tank Man, in this important book, and through his campaigns with Hong Kong Watch, Benedict Rogers has demonstrated that countless voices ultimately become a cacophony—a cacophony for change.

I hope that all who want to stand with the people of China in their struggle will read it.

David Alton
House of Lords, London
March 2022

PREFACE

BY NATHAN LAW

How does it feel to say a seemingly eternal goodbye to your home? Have you imagined a life without it?

It has been two years since I fled Hong Kong. I had lived there for two decades, yet it took me just a few days to finalize the decision to leave. I had no choice. The implementation of the National Security Law—a law that abuses the vaguely defined term "national security" and criminalizes free speech and peaceful protest—changed everything. I would have faced decades of jail time if I had stayed.

In recent years, hundreds of Hong Kongers have been put behind bars because they protested against the government, even in the most civilized and peaceful ways. Joshua Wong, Lester Shum, Chu Hoi Dick, Jimmy Lai . . . the list goes on, and many of them are my friends who stood shoulder to shoulder with me when we were protesting on the streets. The fact that I am now wanted by the government not only deprives me from the chance to go back to Hong Kong, but also makes it dangerous to communicate with my friends in need. The authorities forced us to sever our ties, in order to protect activists within reach of their persecution.

When you are living in exile, no matter how much work you have done and recognition you have earned, the hollowness of guilt and pain creeps into your mind. You are able to speak to journalists and politicians, to speak at rallies and events, and to write this Preface to raise awareness, while others are spending time in jail. Many of them have no idea when they could get out—they have been there for more than a year without a proper trial. The very idea of being an activist, to empower and energize the crowd in order to advance society, comes to an existential crisis when the activist is stuck in a mud of grief and powerlessness.

This is the state of mind that we, who are forced to leave home—the place we love and have dedicated so much of our lives to protect—face on a regular basis. Each of us has different stories of trauma and courage based on what we have been through in the rhythm of the deterioration of freedom. These stories should be written, spread, and remembered. It completes our existence that we are not leaving for nothing, and it lessens our pain when we see in the eyes of our fellows, who are so strong and brave, that speaking up for them is a form of refuge and commitment.

As we remind everyone about what is happening in Hong Kong, we must encourage others to think. Who are we? Who are the people to be remembered? What are the issues that have an impact on me so that I should pick up a book and read? This is definitely a deeply personal question, but also has its public aspect—as a citizen of any country, it requires our action together. If you are a British citizen, the historical ties between the U.K. and Hong Kong may give you incentive to care about the city's democratic movement. If you are a U.S. citizen, the threat of the rise of authoritarianism may make you rethink how to stop the aggression of the Chinese Communist Party (CCP). Besides these arguments, the stories of fighting for freedom are among the most important notions that we must not forget and should continue to learn.

Benedict Rogers' book tells the tales of a range of people who have similar experiences of sorrow and loss, yet also suffer with courage shaped by the pursuit of what genuinely constitutes a free and open society. In the current dictatorial state of the People's Republic of China (PRC), human rights defenders face severe attacks and are silenced. They are beaten, jailed, or even disappeared. Some of their footprints are deleted from the Internet fully controlled and censored by the CCP, and their mere existence magically vanishes within the boundary of the "Great Internet Firewall." They all have different aspirations and demands, but they face the same source of repression that also suppresses the rest of the Chinese population.

Freedom fighters who dare to speak up against the CCP should be remembered, especially to the people who care about freedom and democracy. In this comprehensive book, Benedict Rogers successfully encapsulates the core of their beliefs, and captures the essence of why these voices matter to the world. If we forget their stories, we are unable to understand what the CCP is destroying; if we don't know what the CCP is trying to destroy, we do not know how to react when these intrusions come to our doorstep, which is already happening. If we are unable to react when our freedom and democratic way of life slip through our fingers, the understanding of the world that we know will have collapsed, and may never be recovered.

Freedom is not free. Sometimes it is costly. It is costly to maintain it, and it will cost you much more when you try to retake it after it is lost. The first step of stopping complacency is to learn the stories of people who are resisting the rise of authoritarianism. It is never too late to pick up a book and delve into their world.

Nathan Law
May 2022

INTRODUCTION

As the plane took off from Hong Kong's Chek Lap Kok airport and I looked out of the window at the sheer beauty of that dynamic city—ranging from the skyscrapers and tower blocks to the lush, hilly green islands amidst the shimmering sea, with ships and boats dotted around this major global trading centre—a lump formed in my throat and my eyes welled up. The thought sunk in that, in all likelihood, I would never be able to return to the city that had once been my home, where I had begun my working life—at least until there is a change of regime in Beijing.

It was October 11, 2017, three years before the imposition of Beijing's draconian National Security Law on Hong Kong and just over twenty years after I had moved to Hong Kong for my first job as a fresh graduate. A couple of hours earlier, I had landed for what was intended to be a private visit to meet old friends and new contacts, to learn about their latest concerns about the situation in the territory.

I had not been planning any public appearances, speeches, or media interviews and was not intending to "pick quarrels or provoke trouble" (a criminal offence in China). The worst I would have done—from the Chinese Communist Party's point of view—is perhaps to have written an op-ed and maybe a short report that only a few people would have read.

I joined the line for immigration, and when it was my turn I approached the immigration desk in the usual way, and presented my passport. The young female immigration officer typed my details into the computer.

Suddenly, her face and body language changed. A look of fear came across her.

"I will have to call my superior," she said nervously.

Her supervisor came, looked at the computer, and then politely told me that there was a problem. I was taken aside to an office in a corridor behind the immigration counters. But before they could take me in for questioning, there was a moment of farce. The office was locked.

"Please wait here, while I try to find the key," he said.

I was left alone in the corridor for several minutes. Of course, I could not have gone anywhere, but I was able to make two calls—one to the British Consulate-General, and one to another key contact. The immigration officer then returned, and we were joined by several other officials. I was questioned, asked to provide my hotel booking, and then informed that they had orders from Beijing not to permit me to enter Hong Kong. They were denying me entry.

A very key contact offered me the support of a very prominent lawyer, who would come to the airport to represent me. The lawyer called me during my interrogation and asked me to enquire with the immigration officers whether, if he came, they would allow him access to me. They said they would—if he arrived in time. A few minutes later, they escorted me to the plane. He called me just as I was boarding to tell me he had arrived at the airport, but it was too late.

The fact that I feel I should not name those who tried to help me says so much about the climate of fear that has engulfed Hong Kong since that incident. They are household names, yet both now are serving sentences for their peaceful pro-democracy activities, and I certainly do not want to add to their woes.

I was marched to the plane, surrounded by half a dozen or more immigration officers. As we left the immigration office for the journey to the van to be driven across the tarmac, and then up the gangway to the plane, I joked with their superior, pointing at the crowd of uniformed officers that had formed a circle around me as I walked, asking, "Are they all for me?"

She returned my smile, and said yes, they were all for me.

At the gate, after all the other passengers had boarded and before I—a "pariah," *persona non grata*—was permitted on board, I turned to the one remaining immigration officer who was guarding me. He was the last person I spoke to as I walked up the gangway to the plane; indeed, the last person I spoke to in person, face to face, and on the ground in Hong Kong.

"Is this the death of 'one country, two systems'?" I asked. "Does this mean 'one country, one system'?"

He looked at me pleadingly. "Please, I am just doing my job. I can't comment," he replied.

"I know. And thank you for treating me well," I said, for they had handled my deportation with typical Hong Kong courtesy.

But having been deported from Myanmar twice (I try not to make a habit of it), I could not let the unreasonableness of the system go unchallenged, so I said, "This is a sad day. It's sad for me personally, but even sadder in terms of what it represents for Hong Kong."

With a little glistening hint of emotion in his eyes, my one remaining companion before boarding the plane—a Hong Kong immigration officer—replied, "Yes. It is a sad day." The Hong Kong officials, I felt, did not enjoy deporting me, but were just following orders.

Little did I know what would then follow in the subsequent years in Hong Kong and China. That tiny incident was just an *hors d'oeuvre*. The total crackdown, police brutality, and dismantling of every basic freedom in every space in the city is truly shocking. Most of my friends from Hong Kong today are now in prison, on trial, keeping their heads down, or in exile.

It is fair to say that, in my case, I had received some prior warning that a problem might arise.

A couple of days before flying to Hong Kong from Bangkok, where I was attending a conference, a British MP—who was also a friend of mine—telephoned me. He said he had been contacted by the Chinese Embassy in London and had reason to have real concerns for my safety.

I listened in astonishment as this elected representative in my own country's legislature told me that the Chinese Embassy had found out about my intended visit, and had asked him to urge me not to go. Through a series of calls and text messages, I learned that the embassy was furious about my visit, and warned that if I proceeded I might find myself denied entry.

Apparently, the Chinese Embassy seem to have significantly overestimated my own importance.

I serve as deputy chair of the U.K. Conservative Party Human Rights Commission—which, in reality, is a small, hugely under-resourced and entirely voluntary group consisting of MPs and activists aimed at highlighting international human rights concerns. Its influence comes solely from its ability to conduct inquiries, publish reports, and put in a huge amount of time and energy to getting the word out, but it is one of many voluntary Conservative Party groups and certainly does not speak for, or represent, the Party as a whole, let alone the government. Indeed, we speak independently and occasionally at odds with the government.

In the Chinese Embassy's mindset, however, "Party" and "government" are one and the same, as they are in Xi Jinping's regime. Moreover, members of the "Party" toe the line—and can be pressured or punished if they fail to do so. The embassy had got it into its head that I was travelling to China as a representative of the Conservative Party as a whole, and therefore the government. On that basis, such a visit, which had not been cleared with Beijing, was unwelcome. They also thought I had plans to visit Hong Kong pro-democracy activists Joshua Wong, Nathan Law, and Alex Chow, who had been recently jailed and for whom I had campaigned.

I asked the MP to reassure the embassy that I was travelling entirely as a private citizen, not on behalf of any official organization; that I was willing to give a guarantee that I would not give any speeches or interviews while in Hong Kong; and that I had absolutely no plans to visit any prisons.

The embassy official responded by text message to the MP. He wrote the following: "Thank you, Sir, for your important information. Do you know WHEN he is travelling to HK and WHOM he plans to visit/meet there. If he were to meet with some particular political figures, it still would be unwelcome to say the least, given his deep-seated bias on the developments of HK. The advice is NOT travelling to HK to engage in activities disrespectful of rule of law, or judicial independence of HK, interfering into HK affairs [or] for that matter China's internal affairs. Pls do pass on the message."

I reiterated my assurance that I very much respect the rule of law and Hong Kong's judicial independence. The message came back, via the MP: "I still have to ask you to strongly advise Mr. Rogers against travelling to Hong Kong. I am afraid if he insists on travelling, he will not be able to enter."

With these messages, I sought advice from some experienced and wise friends in Hong Kong itself, the British consul-general, and several senior British political figures, including the last governor of Hong Kong, Chris Patten.

Without exception, everyone gave me the same message: this is an attempt by the Chinese Embassy to intimidate you into not going, but it is likely to be a "bluff." The chances are, on arrival in Hong Kong, you will be able to enter, because Hong Kong's autonomy under "one country, two systems"—although being eroded—is still intact, and Hong Kong immigration would not want the embarrassment of refusing entry. But, in the event—unlikely, they thought—Beijing intervened directly in Hong Kong's immigration, the world should know, because it would be an outrageous breach of Hong Kong's autonomy. So the only way to find out was to go.

I agreed, and so I went. It turns out, Beijing was more serious than anyone had thought.

In the melee of it all, I managed to alert a key contact who put a plan in place. By the time I landed back in Bangkok—where I had flown from and was sent back to—I was inundated by media enquiries.

For more than six hours I sat in transit in Bangkok airport giving interviews by phone to the world's media—Hong Kong newspapers, BBC, CNN, the wire services—ensuring, from time to time, I recharged my mobile phone battery and was in a Wi-Fi zone. Attempting to eat was futile; when I eventually sat down and ordered a dish and a drink, I could barely lift the food from my plate to my mouth without my phone ringing again.

I then boarded a flight back to London. After the day I had had, all I wanted was a glass of wine, so when the drinks and dinner trolley came round, I requested one. To my astonishment, I was told that it was not permitted. I enquired why, as I was a frequent traveller on that airline and had never been refused before. The answer came: "You were deported from Hong Kong, and it's the airline's policy not to serve alcohol to deportees." I went to sleep instead.

When I landed home in London, the frenzy began again. I went into the BBC within hours of landing, and a few days later, the incident was raised in both Houses of Parliament. The foreign secretary—who was Boris Johnson at the time—had issued a statement, and the Chinese ambassador had been summoned. A media, political, and diplomatic incident had occurred.

I was probably the first foreigner—certainly "Westerner"—to be so publicly denied entry to Hong Kong—which brands itself "Asia's world city"—though the precedent was set and I was followed by others, including the executive director of Human Rights Watch, Kenneth Roth; the American journalist Michael Yon; the American scholar and photojournalist Dan Garrett; the Japanese city councillor Kenichiro Wada; and the expulsion of the *Financial Times'* Asia editor, Victor Mallet.

Almost exactly a year later, I sat on a panel at the Conservative Party Conference in Birmingham, alongside the father of Hong Kong's democracy movement, Martin Lee; one of the Umbrella Movement organizers, Benny Tai; and Nathan Law, who had been both the youngest elected legislator in Hong Kong and one of the city's first political prisoners. Just as we were drawing to a close, I was invited by the chair—a courageous MP, Fiona Bruce, who at the time chaired the Conservative Party Human Rights Commission—to give some closing remarks.

Partway into my brief comments, in which I emphasized that I am pro-

China as a country and it is because I love China and the peoples of China that I oppose the Chinese Communist Party (CCP), a Chinese woman in the second row sprung into a furious rage. Kong Linlin, a reporter for CGTN, a Chinese state media organization, literally screamed at me for several minutes with a venom I have never experienced before.

"You are a liar," she yelled.

"You are anti-China. You are trying to destroy China."

When a young Hong Kong activist, Enoch Lieu, approached her—with remarkable calm, composure, and courtesy—to ask her to resume her seat, she slapped him several times. Her final slap was caught on camera and the video went viral, causing worldwide news.[1] She was arrested and subsequently charged with, and convicted of, common assault. Of course, the Chinese Embassy was furious at her arrest and did everything possible to subvert the course of justice.

I have also received dozens of threatening letters, postmarked and stamped from Hong Kong, through my home letterbox, and my neighbours in the quiet London suburb where I live have received letters telling them to monitor my movements. The first such letter had my photograph, taken from the Internet, at the top and the words "Watch him!" It went to all my neighbours.[2]

My mother has received letters asking her to tell her son to shut up,[3] and at least four British MPs have, on four different occasions, been asked by the Chinese Embassy to silence me. An attempt was made by an imposter to resign my membership from the Conservative Party on my behalf, and I have been told that the Chinese ambassador to London at the time, Liu Xiaoming, called the Conservative Party specifically about me. Not long after that call took place, I was removed from the Conservative Party's official candidates list. Make of it what you will.

On a visit to Canada in November 2021, I received a blank email from a fake email address in my name, with the subject line "See you at the Sheraton." I had been booked to stay at the Sheraton in Vancouver a few days later, and had some meetings arranged there. Immediately I sought security advice. My initial instinct was not to give in to what was clearly an attempt to intimidate me, and so I resolved to proceed with my plans. But I was then told by an experienced Canadian ex-police officer that Vancouver is so infiltrated by the CCP that it is now, in his words, "ground zero," and that I should take this threat seriously. If I were in London; New York; Washington, D.C.; Paris; or even Ottawa, he said, I would probably not need to worry, but in Vancouver, I was far from my political and security contacts and very close to the CCP.

I had no idea how whoever was behind this email knew where I would be staying—it could have been through an email hack, but it could just as easily have been from a leak from one of my chain of contacts in Vancouver, or—as several Canadian security experts told me—it could have been that the Chinese regime had a friend in the hotel who had recognized my name, such is the level of infiltration. I had a couple of meetings arranged at the Sheraton with Hong Kongers who I knew did not want to be exposed, so more for their sakes than mine, I changed hotels. When I told Hong Kong-born Canadian MP Jenny Kwan about this, she looked horrified. "I would have done the same," she said.

Then, in February 2022, the website of the organization I co-founded and lead, Hong Kong Watch, was blocked in Hong Kong. A month later, I woke up one morning, opened my email, and found an attached letter from the Hong Kong Police Force, followed by an email from the Hong Kong National Security Bureau, informing me that our website posed a serious national security threat to China, we were required to take down the entire website, and that failure to comply might result in me, personally—as co-founder and chief executive—facing a fine of HK$100,000 (US$13,000) and anything between a year and three years or life imprisonment.[4] We made sure this became headline news a few days later, broken by *The Times*[5] and the BBC[6] and followed by others, and Liz Truss, then the British foreign minister and now the prime minister, and others spoke out in support of us. Threatening a foreign national and a foreign organization on foreign soil might be consistent with the extraterritoriality clause in the National Security Law which Beijing imposed on Hong Kong, but it is outrageous and unacceptable.

By comparison with the atrocities that people living under the CCP's rule endure, these little anecdotes are hardly worth mentioning, except as a reminder that the behaviour of the Chinese regime is not simply confined to repressing its own people, but extends to attempting to silence its critics well beyond its borders. The regime's ridiculous attempts to pressure me only make me laugh and redouble my determination to continue to speak out against the brutal regime in Beijing. It is astonishing to me that a dictatorship that purports to be a superpower could be so worried about the activities of one activist in London as to go to the lengths it has. It is a sign of the regime's insecurity. But while it is laughable, the underlying issue—the long arm of Beijing extending into our democracies: in our universities, our economy, our businesses, our energy sector, our arts, our critical natural infrastructure, and our politics—should be taken seriously.

For thirty years I have worked in and around China.

I first went at the age of eighteen—three years after the 1989 Tiananmen Square Massacre—to teach English for six months in Qingdao, a city on the east coast of China in Shandong Province, famous for the best beer in China. I went back as a student to teach in a hospital during the summer holidays in 1995 and 1997, pursued a master's degree in China studies at the University of London's School of Oriental and African Studies, and completed my dissertation on the Chinese government's policy towards religion, for which I interviewed prominent house church leaders such as Allen Yuan Xiangchen in Beijing, and the retired head of the official State-approved church, known as the "Three-Self Patriotic Movement," Bishop Ding Guangxun (or KH Ting) in Nanjing, among others. And I began my career as a journalist and human rights activist in Hong Kong, where I lived for the first five years after the handover. It was my first job after graduation.

I have slept on the Great Wall of China, walked at midnight under the moonlight through the Forbidden City in Beijing, climbed Taishan, been cormorant fishing on Lake Erhai in Dali, crossed the border from Yunnan Province into Myanmar several times, and been chased by the Chinese police in Liaoning Province near the North Korean border.

For twenty-five years I travelled in China regularly, from Beijing to Kunming; from Shenyang to Shenzhen; from Qingdao to Dali; from Shanghai, Hangzhou, Suzhou, Guangzhou, and Nanjing to Dandong, Guilin, Yangshuo, and Ruili; and, of course, Hong Kong. Since 2017, I have known that I cannot go back to China, and so my work has been confined to international advocacy, trying to awaken hearts and minds to the ever-growing dangers that the CCP regime poses.

A regime that declares war on values of universal human rights, democracy, freedom, and the rule of law; tears up an international agreement registered as a treaty at the United Nations; commits genocide and crimes against humanity with impunity; and threatens its critics abroad with real aggression is surely not a regime that any liberal, open, democratic society can regard as a friend. And a regime that props up and covers for brutal neighbouring dictatorships such as the totalitarians in Pyongyang and the criminal military junta in Naypyidaw is not one that can be a trusted partner.

For some time I wrestled with the question of whether to write this book. In my head was an idea, but I know that there are so many books on China. The market is saturated, and I questioned what I could add.

Kai Strittmatter's *We Have Been Harmonized: Life in China's Surveillance State*,

Ian Williams' *Every Breath You Take: China's New Tyranny*, Desmond Shum's *Red Roulette*, Roger Garside's *China Coup: The Great Leap to Freedom*, David Eimer's *The Emperor Far Away*, Joanna Chiu's *China Unbound: A New World Disorder*, Elizabeth Economy's *The World According to China*, among others, all inspired, informed, and engaged my attention.

So, too, did specialist books on the CCP, the Uyghurs, Hong Kong, Tibet, and other aspects, including, but not limited to, Richard McGregor's *The Party: The Secret World of China's Communist Rulers*, David Shambaugh's *China's Leaders: From Mao to Now*, Peter Mattis and Matthew Brazil's book on the United Front entitled *Chinese Communist Espionage: An Intelligence Primer*, Rush Doshi's *The Long Game: China's Grand Strategy to Displace American Order*, Robert Spalding's *Stealth War: How China Took Over While America's Elite Slept*, Clive Hamilton and Mareike Ohlberg's *Hidden Hand: Exposing How the Chinese Communist Party Is Reshaping the World*, as well as books by Sean Roberts, Darren Byler, Gardner Bovingdon, and Geoffrey Cain on the Uyghurs; and Stephen Vines, Michael Sheridan, Anthony Dapiran, Jason Ng, Louisa Lim, Karen Cheung, and Mark Clifford on Hong Kong.

Dissident memoirs such as those by Ai Weiwei, Joshua Wong, Nathan Law, and others are also superb. These are all books I can only commend and do not seek to replicate. And there are others I have not mentioned. So this little attempt of mine is only intended as an addition, an appendix, and a salute to these. As such, I do not rehearse China's history in this book, because so many other books tell that story. My focus is its present, and its future.

Furthermore, I know full well the biggest critique that will come from the CCP's social media trolls, known as "wumaos," and from kowtowers and appeasers is that I have not been on the ground in China or Hong Kong for the past few years. That is undeniable. But that is not because I have not wanted to visit. It is because the regime does not want to let me in. What does it have to hide? What does it not want me to see? Those are the questions.

For a long time I put off writing this book. But in the end, I was persuaded by friends, by events, and by my courageous publishers that it should be written.

A book that first and foremost looks at the fundamental questions of our relationship with China.

A book that says we should love, engage, and, as much as possible, help and partner with the peoples of China, but oppose the CCP regime's mendacity, brutality, inhumanity, and criminality—and know the difference.

A book that is absolutely not a memoir or an autobiography, but nevertheless draws quite extensively on my own life experiences in China and Hong Kong, life in advocacy for human rights in China and Hong Kong, and, in a tiny way, life on the receiving end of the CCP's bullying, alongside my friendships with many activists from among the peoples of China and Hong Kong who endure levels of intimidation I can only imagine. I draw on my own experiences not because they are particularly unique, but in order to help bring the issues alive and remind you that this is not some abstract challenge taking place far away, but a topic of concern to us close to home, wherever you are in the world.

More importantly, this is a book in which those personal journeys provide merely a backdrop, a tangible hook, an introduction, and a bit of colour to the much more important big, fundamental issues of what we can do, how we can deal with Beijing, and whether we can reshape our entire policy and relationship. When those thoughts began to percolate, this book began to take shape.

The book charts the changes in my own personal attitudes, in parallel with the changes in China. Until Xi Jinping's rule began in 2012, it was my view that while the CCP regime was always repressive, there were plenty of reasons for cautious optimism about China's liberalization. As the country opened up economically, it would relax politically. And I could see that for myself. I met with Chinese human rights lawyers, civil society activists, bloggers, citizen journalists, and religious adherents in Beijing and in China's other cities, who, within certain red lines, had some space to operate. I was hopeful that, however falteringly, the space would expand and China would become freer.

Over the past decade, as Xi Jinping's leadership has heralded an ever-increasing intensification of repression, all that space that I witnessed for myself has disappeared—and many of the people in those sectors have literally disappeared with it. Watching this largely from afar in recent years, my own views have changed as dramatically as China's situation. An old adage says, "when the facts change, I change my mind." The CCP proffers little or no hope of reform, and represents an increasingly dark and dangerous future. Hope must lie in the peoples of China, and the prospect that one day they may find a way to achieve fundamental change in the way they are governed.

China has been a link in so much of what I have done for all of my adult life. Even in my work in Myanmar, North Korea, East Timor, the Maldives, Pakistan, and other parts of Asia, the elephant in the room that I could not ignore for long was China.

In recent years, I have become more vocal and active in my criticism of Beijing's regime, in various capacities—as co-founder, chair, and chief executive of Hong Kong Watch; as senior analyst for East Asia at the international human rights organization Christian Solidarity Worldwide; as deputy chair of the Conservative Party Human Rights Commission; as a member of the advisory boards of the Inter-Parliamentary Alliance on China, the China Democracy Foundation, and the Stop Uyghur Genocide campaign; and as an "ambassador" of Tories for Tibet. That is why this book includes a chapter on the free world beginning to wake up, and the emergence of a worldwide human rights movement for all the peoples suffering under the Chinese regime's repression.

So if it is the nexus in my life, think how much more it is a nexus for the big geopolitical questions of our time. It is not a question to be shunted away, or ignored. Those who demand "nuance" or recognize the "complexity" of the subject have a point, but they risk selling their souls. Yes, there is a complexity involved in getting the policy response correct. And no, I do not believe we can "disengage" from a regime that rules 1.4 billion people and is the world's second major economic, political, and military superpower besides the United States. The question for me is not whether to engage, but how to engage. And we must do so, recognizing that there is little that is complex or nuanced about the character of the CCP regime. It's clear as day, for all to see. It is a mendacious, untrustworthy, corrupt, barbaric, brutal, inhumane, repressive, criminal, insecure dictatorship. The question is, what do we do about it, both in the interests of the peoples of China whom I have come to know and love and our own freedoms which I cherish. That is the question this book aims to ask, and at least begin to attempt some answers.

This book coincides with the "Silver Jubilee" (if one can stomach calling it that) of Hong Kong's handover to China twenty-five years ago. It also marks— barring unforeseen eventualities—the beginning of the second decade of Xi Jinping's rule, which represents, to some degree, a return to the politics of personality cult and lifetime dictatorship, abolishing term limits and ending the collective leadership that has ruled China for the past forty years. And it comes two years after the seventieth anniversary of the invasion of Tibet and the centenary of the founding of the CCP, three years after the seventieth anniversary of the founding of the People's Republic of China, twenty years after I left Hong Kong, and thirty years since I first went to China

It is a book about China, my love of the country as a whole, and my horror at the regime's rape and abuse of this land. It begins—following an account of my time in Qingdao—with Hong Kong, because for this book, for me, and for so many, that great city is an entry point to a wider and richer—and, sadly, very tragic—story. Yet in saying that, I am very mindful of Hong Kong's distinctiveness, its autonomy, and its separate culture and identity, which I defend passionately. Recognizing that distinctiveness, deep down, I also know that Hong Kong's future is interlinked with the future of every other opponent of Beijing's regime. So this book tries to chart, at least as an introduction, the struggles of the Uyghurs, Tibetans, Taiwanese, Chinese Christians, Falun Gong practitioners, Chinese civil society, lawyers, dissidents, bloggers, and every critic of the corrupt and brutal rulers who live in Beijing's Zhongnanhai. And to show that as I sat eating dumplings or noodles or rice in Qingdao, Beijing, Kunming, Shanghai, Suzhou, Nanjing, or Hong Kong with dear friends, it was their liberation and dignity that I sought and respected, and still do. And if they are to succeed in their struggles, they must stand together. The CCP regime is the "nexus" that unites them all—and me—against it.

In 1949, Chairman Mao Zedong declared that the Chinese people had stood up. At the heart of this book is this intrinsic message: being pro-China and pro-CCP are two entirely different things. I am deeply pro-China. But I am deeply hostile to a regime that beats up, tortures, and jails my friends, either in breach of an international agreement or in violation of international law governing crimes against humanity and genocide and other atrocity crimes. And I believe the time has come to stand up for the peoples of China.

The very reason I speak out for human rights is because I want the peoples of China to live in freedom and be treated with dignity. It is the CCP, not its critics, that is anti-China. The sooner people absorb that message, the better. And the sooner the rest of the world stands up and stops kowtowing to the tyrants in Beijing, the better. I hope that in telling my story and, more importantly, the testimonies of my Hong Konger, Uyghur, Tibetan, Chinese, and other friends—from across political, faith, ethnic, and other perspectives—we might build a connection against the one cause which we oppose: authoritarianism. Let us all work for a free China, which would make a free world a bit easier.

This book starts with my time in Qingdao, and then my early years in Hong Kong, and my many happy memories of travels throughout China. It tells the story of the peoples I have been privileged to meet—and love. But it is not a book about the past. That is merely the backdrop. It is primarily a book about the present and the future—for China and for us all. And for freedom.

CHAPTER 1

FROM DUMPLINGS WITH EVERYTHING TO ALICE IN WONDERLAND:

SIX MONTHS TEACHING IN CHINA

"While his parents are alive, the son should not go abroad to a great distance," Confucius is alleged to have said. But, with great wisdom, he added: "If he does go on a long journey, he must tell his parents the definite place he is going to."

My adventures in China began in 1992 when, at the age of eighteen, I flew to Beijing, to begin almost six months of teaching English in the coastal city of Qingdao, famous for the best beer in China. It was as part of my "gap year" between school and university. I chose China because, though my family was very well travelled, it was the one country that none of them had ever visited. I broke Confucius' first rule, but I kept the second and went with my parents' full support.

I was accepted by GAP, a British organization (now known as Lattitude Global Volunteering) that runs "gap year" projects around the world. At the time, it was led by retired Brigadier John Cornell. Out of one hundred applicants for twenty places, I was selected, and assigned to Qingdao. I was paired with another young student, but on the day of departure, September 2, 1992, at Heathrow Airport, as all the other gap year students met up with their pairs, he didn't show up. The project manager was called to the information desk on the loudspeaker, and when he returned, he headed directly to me to inform me that the student who had been paired with me had become so scared of travelling that he had a breakdown and would not be coming. I would be going to Qingdao solo.

We flew on a Pakistani International Airlines (PIA) flight via Karachi, with the Pakistani cricket team on board. When we arrived in Beijing, all our luggage was stuck in Karachi. We found the PIA office in the Beijing airport and asked them for help. "What do you want me to do about it?" asked a grumpy airline official. "Get our luggage here," we replied. The next flight from Karachi to Beijing was three days later.

We had three days of "orientation" in Beijing, staying at Beijing Polytechnic University, before being dispatched to our different cities. Being the only one who would soon be venturing alone to an unknown city in an unfamiliar culture, the rest of the team—especially the girls—made a point of looking after me while we were together.

We visited the main tourist sites—the Forbidden City, the Ming Tombs, the Great Wall—and, because I needed a change of clothes, I bought a T-shirt with Chinese calligraphy on it that said "If you have not been to the Great Wall, you are not a real man," a quote from Mao Zedong. A few years later, I actually slept under the stars on the Great Wall of China, so I guess by then my masculinity was confirmed.

On my first morning in Beijing I awoke at 6 a.m. to the sounds of bustling street life—bicycle bells, market stalls, and the loud guttural, hawking noise of people spitting. I came to learn that the latter is a feature of daily life in China—so much so, I thought, that if phlegm was a valuable commodity, China would have become a great economic power long ago.

We observed elderly Chinese sitting out in the streets late at night playing mah-jong, and others enjoying open-air dancing in the streets.

We were introduced to different varieties of Chinese food, from Beijing roast duck to Cantonese dim sum, bamboo shoots, sea cucumber, and snake. I also learned to use my chopsticks to eat fried egg and pick up peanuts.

One day we were taken to the Friendship Store—a special shop for foreign tourists—where, to my amazement, I saw a Chinese man, Mr. Wang, wearing a T-shirt with a British Conservative Party logo and the slogan "JM 4 PM," a reference to John Major's campaign for re-election as prime minister. Mr. Wang, it turned out, had a friend studying in Oxford at the time of the 1992 British General Election, and had given him that T-shirt. To my even greater surprise, Mr. Wang added, "I want to set up a branch of the Young Conservatives in Beijing." I am not sure Deng Xiaoping, China's paramount leader at the time, would have approved, and Mao would have turned in his grave.

After our orientation in Beijing, we all went to the airport to fly out to our different designated destinations. My flight was the last. One by one I waved goodbye to my new comrades flying off to Nanjing, Hangzhou, Fuzhou, and Guangzhou in pairs. I then waited to board my flight to Qingdao and suddenly realized I was alone. I didn't speak Chinese, I was far from home, and I had just left school. But I was encouraged by an American I met on the flight, who said, "If I was going to live in China, Qingdao would be the city I would choose. You are very lucky to be going there." He was right.

In my six months in Qingdao, I made many friends and had so much fun. I taught English in two schools, six days a week—three days in the city's most academic school, No. 9 Middle School, and three days in No. 29 Middle School, a vocational school specializing in training students for the tourism and hospitality sector. The motto of No. 9 Middle School, emblazoned on the wall of the main building, was "Be United, Decorous, Diligent, and Rigorous"—in English. No. 29 owned a hotel where students put into practice what they had learned in class, and where I lived, in one small bedroom. It was called, appropriately, the Espero Hotel, or sometimes Hope Hotel—and, incongruously, had some association with Esperanto. When I arrived late at night from Beijing, I caused the hotel staff, who were lined up to greet me, great amusement when I took a step backwards and promptly tripped over my luggage which had been left behind me unbeknownst to me. I fell flat on my back, but it helped break the ice immediately.

Each morning I woke to three different sets of sound: first, the news from the BBC World Service on my radio; next, the noise of people in the public bathroom opposite my room, brushing teeth, spitting, and vomiting; and finally, following shouts from outside, the Chinese national anthem and a harsh voice shouting instructions, as the school's students gathered for their morning flag-raising ceremony and exercises.

For my first week I was free, as my classes had not begun, so I explored the city. Qingdao (which means "green island") is a beautiful coastal city built originally by the Germans when they occupied it as a treaty port from 1898 to 1914. The historic heart of Qingdao still looks more like Bavaria than China, particularly the Protestant church and the Catholic church downtown, and the scenic Badaguan area where the old German governor's mansion sits. Apparently, when the Kaiser heard about the cost of the mansion, the governor who built it was immediately recalled.

On my second night in Qingdao, I experienced a Chinese banquet for the first time. The Municipal Education Bureau hosted this dinner to welcome me. Around the table were the Bureau's director, two officials, and the head teachers of the two schools. One of the head teachers was an interesting character with a somewhat sinister grin and villainous voice who kept flaring his nostrils, rolling his eyes, laughing wickedly, and speaking in a serpentine tone.

"Don't be lonely—we are your friends," he declared, encouraging me to "eat more, drink more, eat as much as you like, drink as much as you like." That wasn't difficult, because the dishes kept coming, and in front of me were three glasses—one for wine, one for beer, and one for Maotai, a Chinese rice wine liquor—which were refilled as soon as they were empty.

Toasts were frequently proposed, with the word *ganbei*, which literally means "empty glass" but is often interpreted simply as "cheers." As the visitor, I observed my Chinese hosts and tried to follow their example, so when I saw them knock it back in one, I would do the same. But halfway through yet another drink, *ganbei* was spoken, and I didn't pay attention. One of the Chinese officials, rather red in the face under the influence of alcohol, saw me knock it back in one and said to me in English: "No, Ben—this time, not 'bottoms up,' only 'cheers!'" He explained that as the guest of honour, what I did required everyone else to follow, but they all wanted to slow down as they had consumed rather a lot already. I had just thought I was to follow them.

Conversation at the banquet was interesting, and ranged from the history of Qingdao, to Margaret Thatcher, to Hong Kong. One of the officials told me that the Chinese government was "looking forward to being able to lower the standard of living of the Hong Kong people" but that John Major was respected and Margaret Thatcher was very popular in China. He appeared astonished when I told him I had ventured out unaccompanied to explore the city that day—presumably, he had expected me to stay in my room all day, not moving without approval or a companion.

As I walked the streets of Qingdao those first few days, I observed various fascinating behaviours. There seemed to be a lot of old men standing with one trouser leg rolled up and one leg held high up against a lamp post, watching the world go by in what looked a most uncomfortable position. Plenty of other elderly people were out doing tai chi. Little children did not wear diapers, but instead had a little slit in their shorts, from which they just peed happily in the street.

Towards the end of my first week, before starting teaching, it was Chinese

Teachers' Day—an important celebration in China—and No. 9 Middle School had arranged six buses to take teachers to Laoshan, a nearby mountain famous for its natural spring water. I was invited to join them. We climbed to the top, to the alleged "entrance to Heaven," and then took a cable car back down. We then began an immense banquet, with speeches by the head teacher and his two deputies and the Party Secretary. Two local fishermen came in wanting to talk to me, because they were fans of English football and wished to toast Paul Gascoigne, Gary Lineker, and the rest of the England team.

When I walked into my first class, I greeted my students with "Good morning" but was met with silence. Surely they have enough English to understand a greeting, I thought, as I had been assured they were not total beginners. I repeated it, but still there was silence. Then one bright spark at the back responded, in excellent English, with "Actually, it's good afternoon." He was right.

I spent my first lesson with each class in both schools introducing myself, talking about life in the United Kingdom, and getting them to introduce themselves. This took most of the entire lesson, because there were—in most classes— between fifty and sixty students. The introductions became a bit repetitive, because they all followed a formula: "There are four people in my family—my mother, my father, my brother, and me. My father is a worker. My mother is a worker, too. My brother is a student." People were "workers" whether they worked on a factory floor or in a bank. The fact that most of them had siblings surprised me, but I then learned that China's one-child policy was not introduced until the early 1980s, after they had been born.

One day, I came into class and found the students in silence slowly massaging their eyelids to music. I asked the teacher what they were doing, and she looked as if I had asked a silly question. "Eye exercises," she said. "Don't you do eye exercises in England? Students must protect their eyes." Apparently, it had been ordered by Mao Zedong, who had been concerned that so many people required spectacles.

Another day, I had a bad cold, and the teachers at No. 29 Middle School were greatly concerned. I assured them it would soon pass and I would eat lots of oranges for vitamin C, but they insisted I see the school doctor. Expecting to be given something simple as a cure, I was surprised to receive five different boxes of tablets and ointments, with instructions on what to take and when. On closer inspection, the main ingredient of most of them was snake bile.

I was delighted to receive a bicycle after a few weeks, which I used to get to No. 9 Middle School and to explore Qingdao more. But it was not a very reliable bicycle, and I often had to deal with loose breaks or punctured tires. One day, having been to the market to buy fruit, I crashed into an elderly cyclist, sending apples, oranges, bananas, and my books from school scattering across a major intersection on one of the busiest roads in the city, causing the traffic to screech to a halt.

Many of the students and some of the teachers became real friends. The students were more or less my age, and some of the younger teachers were only a few years older. The authorities had a rule that staff and students of the schools were not allowed to invite the foreign teacher to their homes. Several people ignored that, but always secretly. I received plenty of invitations each week to go to dinner in friends' homes, but only on the condition that I told no one. One amusing but awkward dimension of this was that I received repeated invitations to learn how to make Chinese dumplings. Each time I accepted the invitation, and had to pretend that I had never done it before and was a total novice—whereas, in reality, I had been given a dumpling-making class in another home just the previous week. I literally had dumplings with almost everything.

One particular teacher whose family I visited regularly was a remarkable young woman who spoke superb English, with a strong American accent, even though she had never been out of Shandong Province. She had learned her English through having a wide range of American friends, and as such had not only an impressive command of the language, but also a great understanding of Western culture and humour. She had a large collection of Western films and programmes on video, and so during my first few weeks I watched the BBC's production of *Jane Eyre* and several episodes of *The Cosby Show* with her. Later on, we watched the Bush-Clinton-Perot presidential debates. My mother asked me to thank her—with appropriate irony—"for introducing Chinese culture" to me.

One evening, I arrived at her home for dinner with her family, as I did at least once a week. She met me at the door and with a straight face said, "Ben, I know that this might not be too comfortable for you, but my mother was at the market today and dog was on sale for a very good price, so we're having dog for dinner tonight. We've never had dog before as a family—it's not a northern dish. So we thought we'd try it. I hope you don't mind." I braced myself. The meat was served, and I politely ate it. "How is it?" she asked. "Good," I said politely. We enjoyed the rest of the evening, but then as she showed me to the door at the end she asked, "Did you believe it was dog?" I replied that I took her word for it. "Nah," she said with a cheeky grin. "It was pork!"

Of course, I engaged in the obligatory karaoke sessions with some friends, because throughout China karaoke is hugely popular. I am an atrocious singer but was persuaded by one family that befriended me to sing "Jingle Bells" in a karaoke bar, and then we all sang "Edelweiss" together.

Some people came to visit me at the Hope Hotel. One, a Chinese man who wore a French beret and had a little moustache, was an interpreter at the Institute of Oceanography and also worked as an English teacher at a night school. He dropped in one evening and after we chatted for a while, he casually asked, "May I use your bathroom?" Of course, I said, assuming he simply wanted to use the toilet. "Thank you. I think I'll take a bath," he replied. With that, he turned on the taps, stripped off, and bathed. Most Chinese homes have only showers, not bathtubs, so for him, taking a bath in a tub was a rare luxury.

About a month after I arrived in Qingdao, all the GAP volunteers were gathering in Shanghai, and so I prepared to travel to China's most populous city by train. In the years since I was first there, China has built the world's largest bullet train network. As *The Economist* put it in 2017, "less than a decade ago China had yet to connect any of its cities by bullet train. Today, it has 20,000 km (12,500 miles) of high-speed rail lines, more than the rest of the world combined."[1] As a friend pointed out to me, the equatorial circumference of the world is 24,901 miles, so China's high-speed rail track covers the equivalent of half the globe. Much of this rail track has been built in Tibet[2] and Xinjiang, and is associated with the bloody repression in those two regions, used both to bring Han Chinese workers into the areas and to transport Uyghur slave labour to other parts of China.

But in 1992, the pre-bullet train era, the journey from Qingdao to Shanghai took twenty-four hours, and getting a ticket was almost impossible. China's trains were divided into four classes: "soft sleeper," "hard sleeper," "soft seat" and "hard seat." I always preferred hard sleeper, because it was less expensive than soft sleeper, but perfectly comfortable. Soft sleeper was a closed compartment shared with three others, whereas hard sleeper was an open carriage with rows of bunks. I managed to get a hard sleeper ticket to Shanghai, but coming back, I had to endure twenty-four hours on a hard seat—which meant sharing uncomfortable seating with people spitting, smoking, eating sunflower seeds and oranges, and scattering the floor with peel.

In Shanghai, we walked down the Bund, Shanghai's famous street on the banks of the Huangpu River, and discovered East Nanjing Street, one of the city's main shopping areas. We stayed at the Conservatory of Music, which was built in 1927, but closed during the Cultural Revolution. It reopened in 1979, and the British violinist Yehudi Menuhin visited soon after and invited eleven-year-old violinist Jin Li to study in Britain. According to my guidebook, "the kid enthralled audiences in London in 1982 with his renditions of Beethoven." The accommodation was basic, but it was fun to be woken at 6 a.m. each day by the sound of choral practice, scales, and trumpets.

The only other travel I did from Qingdao at that time was a visit to Suzhou and Nanjing. Suzhou was described by Marco Polo as "the Venice of the East" due to its canals, bridges, and gardens. Marco Polo apparently also said, "In Heaven, there is Paradise. On Earth, there is Suzhou and Hangzhou." I cycled around the city and visited some of the wonderfully named gardens, including the Garden for Lingering In, the Garden for Cultivation, the Garden for Retreat and Reflection, and the Humble Administrator's Garden, as well as the North Pagoda, the Twin Pagodas, and the Temple of Mystery.

In those days in China, people would quite regularly approach me in public, simply because they wanted to practise their English. Foreigners outside the major cities of Beijing and Shanghai were rarer then than today, and the Chinese Communist Party's repression and nationalism were less intense, so Chinese people seemed genuinely to want to befriend a Westerner. Sitting in one street restaurant in Suzhou, I was approached by a slightly eccentric Chinese man who was reminiscent of Inspector Clouseau from the *Pink Panther* films. He asked where I was from, and when I told him, he was delighted. "Ah, from England. My girlfriend is in England, at Oxford University," he said. But then, pointing at the woman with him, added, "But shh! My wife! Ha ha!"

After a visit to Nanjing, where I saw the Sun Yat-sen Mausoleum, the old city wall, and a Confucian temple, I returned to Qingdao—on a hard seat. What was even worse was, it was an "unreserved hard seat," which meant, because the train was so overcrowded, I had no seat. The train departed late at night, and so I curled up on a newspaper on a part of the floor that was not covered in phlegm, vomit, chicken bones, orange peel, sunflower seeds, and worse things, in the corridor next to the boiler, in between carriages. But Chinese people can be extremely kind, and at 8 a.m. a couple whom I had met in the station came and found me and invited me to join them as a seat had become available. I shared their breakfast of beer and chicken, and they taught me some Chinese.

"There is nothing more terrible above or below than a foreigner speaking

Chinese," says an ancient, and probably fair, Chinese saying. At that time, I had only a few phrases, self-taught from a phrase book or picked up from teachers and students in Qingdao, but I had not taken any formal classes. And to be honest, everywhere I went there was always someone who spoke good English, and people eager to practise.

But I was keen to make an effort to learn more. The biggest challenge I found was the tones. Mandarin Chinese is a tonal language with four tones, and if you get the tone wrong, you change the entire meaning of what you are saying. For my first few weeks in Qingdao, I was constantly saying what I thought was "Excuse me?" in shops, to female shop assistants, and being either ignored or met with a blush and a giggle. No wonder. I learned from a teacher at No. 9 school that I was using the wrong tone for *qingwen*. Instead of saying "Excuse me," I was actually saying "Please kiss me." Sadly, they never did!

People would ask me what I was doing in China, and I proudly replied, "*Wo shi yingyu laoshi.*" But I emphasized the ending of *laoshi* too much, putting a tail on it when I should have used a hard ending, and saying *laoshe* instead. And so instead of informing them that I was an English teacher, I was declaring "I am an old English snake." Happily, I never combined my two mistakes in one sentence.

I persevered though, and within a few weeks, I was able to order a beer (*Wo yao mai yi ping Qingdao pijiu*) and say that I had eaten enough (*Wo chibaole xiexie*)—two very useful phrases to know.

One day, walking down the street towards a group of giggling school children of about eight years old, I saw them pointing at me and saying "*Meiguoren, Meiguoren*" ("American, American"). I gave them a big smile and, to their complete shock, said, "*Wo bu shi Meiguoren. Wo shi Yinguoren*" ("I am not an American. I am an Englishman").

Another time, some people in Zhongshan Road in Qingdao mistook me for a famous Canadian who lives in Beijing, speaks fluent Chinese, and has a television show in China. He is known as *Da Shan* (literally, "Big Mountain"). They pointed at me and said, "*Da Shan,*" and mischievously I replied, "*Nimen hao. Wo shi Da Shan*" ("Hello. I am Da Shan"), to their amazement.

When the vocabulary was lacking, gesticulation helped. In a restaurant with foreign friends one time we had forgotten the Chinese words for pork, beef, and chicken. So we made the appropriate animal sounds—oinking, mooing, and clucking for the waitress—and drew pictures of pigs, cows, and chickens. The waitress understood immediately and seemed to enjoy the entertainment.

A source of much amusement to me, though, were the mistakes in some of the English signs in public places in China. A no-smoking sign in an underground market in Qingdao was accompanied by these words: "For safely sake, No Firing." In Shenzhen, the economic boom town bordering Hong Kong, a public toilet contained this announcement: "Civilized and hygienic toilet." On a train were four hilarious notices: "Don't put yourself out of the window," "Don't thpow [throw] something out of the train," "Don't put something dirty on the floor," and "No srit" (meaning "No spitting"). People generally observed the first two, but ignored the latter two.

Western pop music was becoming popular throughout China at this time, though much of it somewhat out of date. In 1992, the Carpenters' "Yesterday Once More" was played everywhere, in shops and restaurants. When my students first asked me to sing it for them, I had to admit that I did not know it—which was unbelievable to them.

My students and I exchanged tongue twisters. I taught them "Peter Piper Picked a Peck of Pickled Peppers," and they taught me a Chinese equivalent. I recited both of these at No. 9 school's Arts Festival—in front of two thousand students and staff in Qingdao's People's Hall—to overwhelming applause.

Most of my students had English names, but those who did not asked me to give them one. Most had run-of-the-mill names like John, James, Martin, Alice, Jane, and Wendy, but there were some who had decided to be quite inventive. I had two boys who sat next to each other in class, one called Fish and the other Cooker, and two girls called Moon and Star. There were also Robin Hood, James Bond, George Barton, Sandy Clark, London, Washington, and Erebus. One boy translated his Chinese name into English and was Stonecliff.

They decided to give me a Chinese name, too. I was offered several. One suggestion was Li Jia Cheng, which means "great achiever" but is also the Mandarin name of Hong Kong's biggest tycoon, Li Ka Shing. Someone else offered You Cai (a Chinese vegetable). The one I ended up using was a translation of my surname, which in Chinese becomes Luo Jie Si. I am told that *luo* is a real Chinese surname which also means "to gather," and *jie* means "hero" or "distinguished person"—so, apparently, it means a "hero who gathers other heroes." It's preferable to using the sound of my first name, Ben, which in Chinese means "foolish."

I learned to write my name in Chinese characters, and from there began to learn other characters. The first Chinese sentence that I mastered, I wrote on the blackboard, slowly and carefully, during one lesson, to hearty applause. I gradually learned more and after a while was able to address letters to other parts of China myself.

In my teaching, I used various word games and texts to liven up the class. One activity was to invite everyone to write a description of themselves, and then gather them in and read them out, with the students having to guess who wrote each one. Some of the responses were amusing: "I am a boy. I'm not tall. I'm clever and loving. I'm very honesty"; "I am not tall. Sometimes I am clever"; "I'm very tall. I'm very bad"; "The others say me: 'thin.' I think me 'No.' The others say me 'foolish.' The others say me 'clever.' I say 'No no no.' The others say me: 'Your hair is white. I say 'Yes'"; "I am very like singing, but nobody like listening. Then I am singing with myself." I wrote my own, too, which I threw into the mix—"I am tall, have curly hair, wear glasses, speak English quite well, and have a long nose." It took them a surprisingly long time to guess.

My interactions with people were surprisingly relaxed. Among the teachers, we were always joking. One teacher asked me if I would like him to find me a Chinese girlfriend, and when I said—knowing that we were both just bantering—that I wouldn't mind, he pointed at a rather unattractive, plump woman teacher in her fifties. "Ah," she cried, and poured a bucket of water over him. All in jest.

In the hotel, a couple who spoke no English would always greet me in Chinese warmly as *pengyou* ("friend"), and one day, the husband turned up with bottles of beer to share, proclaiming in Chinese "Friends drink beer."

And I experienced more acts of kindness than I can ever describe. I remember one bitterly cold winter's day—with a temperature of minus five—I was wearing jeans but not the long johns I usually wore, because they had burned on the radiator. One of my closest friends—a student—asked me, "How many pairs of trousers are you wearing?" When I told her only one, and explained what had happened to my long johns, she was horrified. The next day a package arrived at my room. Inside was a brand new pair of long johns and a note from my friend. "You were so cold yesterday. When I told this to my mother, she said your parents and your sister aren't here now, but we are your friends. We should take care of you. She said if one day I go abroad or any other place, she will feel deep anxiety about me. If she know I felt cold or hunger she will feel sad. So she bought a new trousers for you. Because we are good friends. And some medicine for you. Hope you will feel better tomorrow." The next day, another friend asked me if I still just had one pair of trousers on. When I started to say "No, our friend so kindly . . ."

the friend who had delivered this act of kindness looked at me, put her finger to her lips, and said, "Shh!"

Halfway through my time in Qingdao, I had an idea. I asked No. 9 Middle School if we could do a school play, in English. The idea had to go not only to the head teacher, but also to the Party Secretary. They had never done a school play before. After I submitted my proposal—to do *Alice in Wonderland*, with a script I wrote from a copy of Lewis Carroll's novel I found in a bookshop in Qingdao—it was approved. I did the casting and the directing. I found a medium-sized female student to play Alice. I found a very short female student to play Alice at the point in the story where she shrinks. But we had a challenge as to whom to cast for the part where Alice grows enormously tall. I raised the question, and all the students looked at me and grinned. There was only one option, only one person significantly physically taller than the others, and that was me. So the play was given a pantomime element, with me in drag playing Alice for that part of the story.

We also had a very amusing, if slightly irritating, student playing the White Rabbit. "I don't want to wear a tail. Do I have to wear a tail?" she asked. I conceded that maybe she didn't have to wear a tail. "Do I have to hop? I don't want to hop," she whined. "Okay," I said, "you don't have to hop." But when she moaned about wearing rabbit's ears or dressing in white, I drew the line and insisted she must. "You're the White Rabbit. Yes, you have to wear white and you need to wear rabbit's ears."

With hindsight, given some of the bizarre—and horrific—behaviour of the Chinese Communist Party regime today, perhaps the choice of *Alice in Wonderland* as a school play in Qingdao was somewhat prophetic and prescient. Sadly, today it is more a case of "off with their heads" than White Rabbits. Yet, whatever the strength of my antipathy towards the regime, my love for China has never dimmed, shaped as it was by those formative months in Qingdao.

One of my closest friends was a remarkable elderly man whose English was the best of all the school's teachers, yet he had never been to university. With extraordinary courage and ability, he had taught himself English secretly during the Cultural Revolution by listening to foreign radio—in the full knowledge that if caught, he could have been killed. We would meet often for Laoshan beer and Chinese food in his home, and he would tell me, privately, what he really thought of the Party. He told me to call him "Mr. Three Ears," which was the meaning of his name.

So, too, would another teacher, who spoke bravely of his dream of democracy for China. He once told me he wanted to translate Jeffrey Archer's novel *A Matter of Honour* into Chinese and asked if I could request Lord Archer's permission. I did, and the author replied, saying he was "very impressed" by the initiative but was unable to give permission "because it has already been published in China."

And yet another, who was infused with love of liberal democracy. Yet she also spoke depressingly about the prospects for change. This was just three years after the Tiananmen massacre of 1989. "We cannot change the system," she said. "We are helpless. If the students try again, the government will only respond in the same way again."

It was these friends who sowed the seeds in my own heart of a lifelong desire to see the peoples of China free. But I also encountered others, who showed flickers of a desire for freedom but ultimately toed the Party line—sort of.

In a market one day, I met Mr. Ma of the People's Construction Bank of China, and we got into conversation. He claimed to have been a student leader in Shanghai in the 1989 protests, but said that he now believed the government's line about what happened. "I don't believe so many people were arrested—certainly in Shanghai it was not bad," he argued. It had all been exaggerated by Western media.

Mr. Ma also toed the line on Tibet. "Every Chinese person, from the top to the bottom, believes that Tibet is part of China. It always has been, and it always will be. It should not be a separate nation. The West is not very clever about it. The Tibetans were slaves until the People's Liberation Army liberated them." His view was similar on Taiwan. "There are not two Chinas. There is just one."

However, he also insisted on his desire for democracy. "In thirty or forty years, China will be the strongest economic power in the world, and it will be a democracy. We will have democracy in China sooner than you think."

Most of the time I did not feel the repression of the Chinese Communist Party. My interactions with people were generally friendly and relaxed. But as American academic Perry Link famously described, the regime is like an "anaconda in the chandelier"—it is there all the time, observing, and occasionally it drops on you.

I caught glimpses of this. One day at No. 9 school, I was in an office waiting to go to my next lesson. I asked the teacher what this particular room was. "This is the office where the students come to be criticized. The teachers in this office are in charge of the students' thinking. This is the political education office," she said. "If a student thinks wrongly, he or she must be criticized." She then informed me that students would soon be going to the countryside for "physical labour," which she termed "re-education." Another teacher, overhearing our conversation, interjected: "So-called re-education," which drew a rebuke from this apparatchik: "No, not 'so-called.' It is re-education." I felt a chill in my spine.

I was once invited by a Mr. Lu to give a talk to a night school English class about life in England. But he emphasized, "Not politically, though." When I finished the talk and invited questions, Mr. Lu told the students, "Not politically, though." When I asked what jobs the students in the night school had—for they were all adults—he said, "In China, there is no unemployment at all. Socialism is a very great system." I bit my lip and stopped myself from responding: "Not politically, though."

Others were also quick to shut down any sensitive conversation. When I asked three students who came to chat to me whether they were looking forward to Hong Kong's handover to China in 1997, they replied, "We don't like politics." I had not intended the question politically as such, but it was clear it was a topic with which they did not want to engage. When I asked others—more open to talking—the same question, they said they weren't bothered. "It's at the other end of China; we will probably never have the chance to go there anyway, as it's so far. Why should we care?" came the reply.

But some people did want to talk. One teacher, who had spent a year in Britain, told me she admires Christianity and wants China to become more like Britain, in terms of democracy and freedom. Another told me how she dislikes the term "liberation" to describe the Communist revolution in China. "Life is probably better now than it was before, under Mao. But we are not 'liberated.' We are not free. Why can't we have the freedom to say and do what we like? Why?"

There was one scene in the English teachers' office at No. 9 Middle School that will always stay with me. Every city in China has a People's Congress. Every work unit—school, factory, company—has a representative. The school was "voting for" their representative one day. A teacher with whom I often discussed politics came up to me that day and clapped his hands: "Democracy has come to China," he said. "Vote for Mr. N. I shall vote for Mr. N." At that point the aforesaid Mr. N stood up, bowed, and gave a mock victory speech. "Thank you, thank you. I will serve all of you and do my very best for you." It was all in jest, and amazing to see people mocking the system so openly.

In Shanghai, I was approached by a man out of the shadows in a park at dusk, who asked to talk. He told me he had learned English himself, by listening to the BBC World Service. The people, in his view, feel cheated by the government. He complained about pay levels, the fact that a waitress earns more than a university professor, and that the government often blocks foreign broadcasts. He said China would have been better off with the Kuomintang, who fought the Communists in the 1930s and 1940s before fleeing to Taiwan. Then he paused. "There is someone lurking behind that bush. I think it could be a plain clothes policeman. They are often here. I had better go." With that, he left.

I heard occasional examples of the anaconda moving into action. On Christmas Eve, some of the foreign teachers at one of the universities in Qingdao organized carol-singing. As they went round the student dormitories, the students joined in. Before long, the campus was filled with song and was lit up by candles. Security became alarmed, because it brought back memories of 1989, and called the police, who broke it up. Even worse, the Chinese husband of a British teacher—who worked in Xi'an and had returned for Christmas—was interrogated, because, as an outsider, he was suspected of inciting this unrest, even though he had nothing to do with it.

I celebrated my first-ever Christmas and New Year away from home, in Qingdao, in 1992. On Christmas Eve, we had a party at No. 9 Middle School, after which a group of friends staggered to the Haitian Hotel in Qingdao for bowling. As the evening became more raucous, we all descended into song, mindful of Confucius' saying: "How to play music can more or less be known. At the start of each of the pieces, the cadence should be bold, unrestrained, and exuberant; as it proceeds, it should be serene, harmonious, and resonant. And then let it be resounding and linger in the ear, and thus on to its conclusion." Whether we were at any moment serene is for others to judge—we certainly greeted every passerby with an exuberant "Merry Christmas" through the streets of Qingdao.

Christmas Day itself was spent teaching at No. 29 Middle School, filmed by Qingdao Television in action. We had a party and the students had gone to great lengths to prepare. They had a huge Christmas tree, well decorated; one student dressed as Father Christmas; and we played games and sang songs. I taught students Christmas songs, including John Lennon's "Happy Xmas (War Is Over)"—though, regrettably, I didn't have the courage to play them the next song, "Power to the People."

Students presented me with cards and presents which were overwhelming.

My teaching was almost over, and my bond with them was so strong none of us wanted it to end. "We don't want to say 'goodbye.' We will miss you forever. Please don't forget that you have many friendly Chinese friends. We hope you will come back to Qingdao again. Please remember 'You are always welcome,'" read one card. "Christmas is a time of joy and beauty and a time to wish pleasant things for wonderful people like you," read another. Yet another read, "Dear Ben: You left your hometown and came to China to teach us English. Your lessons bring us joy. I wish you to spend a happy Christmas in China. Wish you to get on well with your study and work when you go back to England."

We ended Christmas Day by going carol-singing around the Hope Hotel—which, it seems, the residents enjoyed—and then walking to the beach, watching the waves hit the sand. A week later, the round of partying continued as we saw in the new year—1993—with parties in all classes in both schools. As one teacher put it, "We're having a great get-together." We certainly were.

During a farewell dinner in a restaurant in Qingdao with a trio of friends, I went to the bathroom. When I emerged, all the lights were off. Before I could enquire, one of them said, "Please don't put the lights back on—not yet." There were sounds of sniffling and wiping of eyes. When I did turn the lights on, there were tear-stained cheeks all around.

I walked all my friends home and, when it came to the last, believe it or not, we skipped down the street holding hands singing "There were three in the bed and the little one said, roll over." The next day, I decided to delay my departure. I knew that spending deeply quality time with people with whom I had become friends was infinitely preferable than visiting tourist sights.

I had planned to leave Qingdao just after New Year's Day, to travel across China, to see the Terracotta Warriors in Xi'an and various other sights. But my friends told me, "If you stay on until our end-of-term exams, we could play with you." I made up my mind, and shortly before I was due to leave, as I met with some of my closest friends, I was hit with an emotion I did not expect, and a bond I hadn't anticipated. I changed my travel plans.

When I eventually left Qingdao, several friends came to see me off. It was early in the morning, but they did not care. As we waited for check-in, one of them said, "Make us laugh, Ben."

With a smile, I said in my very poor Chinese, "*Zenme shuo?*"—which means "How to say?" I said it in a slight Qingdao accent, which sent them into hilarious laughter. I promised I'd see them again. They watched as I departed.

For many years after that first stint in Qingdao, I corresponded regularly by letter with many of my Chinese friends. Many of the letters I received were deeply moving.

"Dear Ben: It's snowing outside. A very heavy snow. It can already cover the ground. It's a great pity that you aren't here or we can go outside and leave our mark everywhere. It's the very weather to sing 'Edelweiss,'" wrote one friend. "I can't face the fact that you've already gone. You're not here?! I always ask the same question: Has Ben already gone? It cannot be true! . . . But I believe that while there is friendship, there is hope. Yes?"

The same friend in another letter wrote, "Yo dude! Today is the day all the students back to school to do some cleaning and have a meeting. I bought many books today. They are *Gone With the Wind*, *The Portrait of a Lady*, *Emma*, and *Vanity Fair*. Ah, they are heavy! But I like them very much. Especially *Gone With the Wind*. We'd better not read a book which has been translated into Chinese, yes?!"

Another friend wrote, "Dear Ben: Today I received your letter. It almost make me cry. I really miss you . . . I know that you like laughing. But also know that the feeling for you is very important. I still remember those days, we laughed a lot together. So when I remember you I will laugh. Sometimes my parents ask me 'why are you laughing?' because at that time I'm alone. Is it very interesting? I've almost finished the book you gave me, *Robinson Crusoe*. I like it very much. Though it's a little difficult for me, I want to try to finish it."

She added: "I will tell you a good news. In the Qingdao evening newspaper I found an article of you, it's a student of No. 29 wrote. It said you had already gone, the students missed you very much, they cried. I read it and moved deeply. You left a deep impression on us. In our minds you are a kind teacher to us. You are a good friend of us. Also you are a funny boy, because you can make me laugh. We are the best friends of you in China."

I returned to Qingdao several times in subsequent years. My Qingdao friends told me I was *ban ge Qingdaoren* (half a Qingdao person) and I learned to say *Qingdao shi wo di er ge jia* (Qingdao is my second home). In 1995, and again in 1997, I spent almost two months of my summer holidays as a university undergraduate teaching English to doctors and nurses in a hospital in Qingdao. I lived in the hospital, and made many friends among the hospital staff who attended my classes.

I also spent time with my old friends from No. 9 and No. 29 Middle Schools, students who had graduated from school and were at university, and teachers still teaching.

Since my first stint in Qingdao, two things happened at university that changed my life. I became a Christian, and I had become actively involved in human rights campaigning. In 1994, I met Baroness Cox, a tireless and courageous human rights advocate and member of the British House of Lords, and she invited me—a young undergraduate—to travel with her to the war-torn Armenian enclave of Nagorno Karabakh, the scene of years of brutal conflict between Armenia and Azerbaijan. I travelled with her, U.S. Congressman Frank Wolf, and others on a cargo plane loaded with humanitarian aid. A ceasefire had just been signed, but as I lay awake at night in my half-bombed-out hotel in Stepanakert, I could still hear sporadic sniper fire on the frontlines. I had written an article about the visit for my university newspaper, and brought it to share with friends in Qingdao. To my surprise, one of them said he wanted to translate it into Chinese and publish it in the local newspaper. A few days later it appeared in the *Qingdao Daily*.

I did not proactively share my new Christian faith with people in Qingdao, but I attended packed church services at the State-approved Three-Self Patriotic Movement Protestant church in the city. Sometimes people asked me about religion. A sixteen-year-old student asked me, as we walked down the street after swimming in the sea, whether I believed in God. I said I did, and another friend, a doctor, who was with us, said, "I would like to believe, but I am a member of the Communist Party Youth League, and so I am not allowed to." On another occasion, a doctor—who was a Party member—pointed out the spires of two churches from the roof of the hospital, and asked if I was a Christian. Three days later, in the middle of my evening class, he suddenly asked if he could come with me to church. To my surprise, he then asked me to tell the class something about the Bible. The class was an informal conversation class, known as "English Corner," and was run by the hospital's Communist Party Youth League. I took the precaution of asking the class whether they wanted me to talk about the Bible, and was met with an enthusiastic "yes." Most of them had never read it, so I shared what I knew.

Despite these positive examples, I caught a glimpse of the restrictions on religious freedom. One Christian friend—the daughter of a senior general in the People's Liberation Army—told me that those who go to the State-controlled churches have to register. "The government controls you. They know who are Christians," she said.

At one of the weekly English Corner gatherings, I was asked my views about Margaret Thatcher, John Major, Chris Patten, Chairman Mao, and Hong Kong. The conversation seemed surprisingly open until a Communist Party Youth League leader calmly but firmly suggested we talk about "tourism, everyday life, and other things!" We were clearly approaching a red line.

One family I had dinner with brought up Hong Kong and said they liked what Chris Patten was trying to do to strengthen democracy, and that they disliked the Communist Party. "We like Chris Patten—but Beijing doesn't!" one of them said.

Another friend agreed. "What Chris Patten was trying to do for Hong Kong was right. He was trying to safeguard their freedoms," he said. "I am Chinese, and I am happy that China and Hong Kong are reunited, but I know my government, and I fear for the people of Hong Kong. Patten must be a good man. The fact that the Chinese government criticized him so ferociously means he must be a good man. But if you are surprised by the language used by the Chinese government about Patten, a foreign politician, think what they can do to me, an ordinary Chinese citizen. I am old. I don't want to go to prison. If I go to prison at my age, I know I would not survive."

Many people spoke along similar lines to me privately. A few, though, were bold in standing up to the system. One young friend, in his thirties, expressed his concerns about China's future to me, and described how he had challenged his boss, a die-hard communist, about the Cultural Revolution and the Great Leap Forward. His boss denied that there had been any starvation, famine, injustice, or persecution, and argued that these were lies from Western media. My friend responded by pointing out the lies and propaganda from the Chinese Communist Party's newspapers. I asked if that was not dangerous for him. "That is what all my friends are worried about. They all say they won't raise their heads above the parapet, they'll leave it to someone else. But if we all do that, who will stand up to them?"

Despite the restrictions on freedom of expression and religion in those years, almost everyone I met emphasized how much better life was compared with the Cultural Revolution years of the 1960s and 1970s. One teacher told me that had I been in China fifteen or twenty years earlier, we would not even have been able to talk to each other, let alone discuss politics. In 1975, I was told, a teacher was swimming near the pier in Qingdao and she saw a rare foreigner. All she said was "hello," and he replied with the same greeting and walked on. The next day, she was summoned to the police station, forced to write a full confession on what was discussed, and cautioned never to converse with a foreigner again. In contrast, I could meet Chinese friends in their homes, receive them in my room, go out to restaurants with them, and engage in some deep conversations.

I was told a joke by one doctor. George Bush Sr., Mikhail Gorbachev, and Deng Xiaoping were walking along the road and, in front of them, blocking the way, was a donkey. They all agreed they needed to get the donkey to move. Bush offered the donkey U.S. dollars to move, but it refused. Gorbachev threatened to fire nuclear warheads, but it refused to budge. Deng said, "If you don't move, I will lead you down the path to socialism," and the donkey ran away. One of the other doctors, overhearing this, said, "That donkey didn't like socialism, and we Chinese don't like it either!" You would be unlikely to hear such open expression in Xi Jinping's China today.

When I left, the doctors and nurses presented me with a book of handwritten messages from them. I share some of the messages, not because of what they say about me but because they illustrate the depths of friendship I received.

"Ben, you are really a good teacher. And also a good partner. Please don't forget I'm waiting for you to co-operate at another English Party. I believe that all of us want to say we love you, Ben."

"Ben—I consider you are really a good teacher and a honest person. They say 'a friend in need is a friend indeed.' I want to be your friend indeed. Friendship forever."

"Ben: you are my teacher and friend. You are one of the most excellent youths I know. You love life, love your cause, love friends, most important you love China. Although time is short, but from you, we know English people cherish profound feeling of friendship for Chinese people. We love you, I never forget you, never forget Great Britain."

"Time goes so fast. This summer is the shortest season in my experience. Thank you Ben. You opened a window for us, a window to the world, a window to beautiful human nature. Chinese is a shy, reserved nation. We are not good at expressing emotion. But now, I believe, all of us want to say: Ben, we love you! Do not forget China. Here is your second home. We are waiting for you."

And, amusingly, this message, from the doctor who organized my classes and translated for me when needed:

"Dear Ben: I'm really very pleased to work with you. I hope we can fulfill our dream—you become the prime minister of Great Britain, I become a famous scholar, and one day I can receive an invitation from the prime minister to visit London. I wish you good luck!"

I knew a bond had been made—between me and these friends, and me and China. I just didn't anticipate that my friendship with the peoples of China would result, three decades later, in such enmity between me and their atrocious rulers.

CHAPTER 2

ONE COUNTRY, TWO SYSTEMS

THE FIRST FIVE YEARS ON THE GROUND IN HONG KONG

In the early hours of July 1, 1997, the last governor of Hong Kong, Chris Patten, sailed out of the city with the Prince of Wales on the Royal Yacht Britannia, having handed sovereignty over the territory to the People's Republic of China. At the handover ceremony a few hours earlier, in his final speech, he famously declared, "Now, Hong Kong people are to run Hong Kong. That is the promise. And that is the unshakeable destiny."

Earlier in his remarks, Chris Patten said, "History is not just a matter of dates. What makes history is what comes before and what comes after the dates that we all remember. The story of this great city is about the years before this night, and the years of success that will surely follow it."

In an acknowledgment that the way Britain colonized Hong Kong—a result of the Opium Wars—was far from ideal, he noted that Hong Kong's relationship with the United Kingdom "began with events that, from today's vantage point at the end of the following century, none of us here would wish or seek to condone." Despite that, Hong Kong's story was one to celebrate. "What we celebrate this evening is the restless energy, the hard work, the audacity of the men and women who have written Hong Kong's success story—mostly Chinese men and Chinese women. They were only ordinary in the sense that most of them came here with nothing. They are extraordinary in what they have achieved against the odds."

In an important nod to the values that have shaped Hong Kong, he added, "Our own nation's contribution here was to provide the scaffolding that enabled the people of Hong Kong to ascend: the rule of law; clean and light-handed government; the values of a free society; the beginnings of representative government; and democratic accountability. This is a Chinese city, a very Chinese city with British characteristics. No dependent territory has been left more prosperous, none with such a rich texture and fabric of civil society—professions, churches, newspapers, charities, civil servants of the highest probity, and the most steadfast commitment to the public good."

And, in an expression of hope for the future, he argued, "I have no doubt that, with people here holding on to these values which they cherish, Hong Kong's star will continue to climb. Hong Kong's values are decent values. They are universal values. They are the values of the future in Asia as elsewhere, a future in which the happiest and the richest communities, and the most confident and most stable, too, will be those that best combine political liberty and economic freedom as we do here today."

Two months after Chris Patten sailed out of Hong Kong, I flew in. Five years after my first adventure to Qingdao, and with several visits to China in the intervening years, I had completed my master's in China Studies at London's School of Oriental and African Studies (SOAS) and was embarking on my career.

Ever since my first time in Qingdao, I had a fascination with and love for China. As an undergraduate, I founded a China Society to raise awareness and understanding about this great nation, inviting speakers on different aspects of Chinese history, politics, arts, and culture. In my room in my hall of residence, I had a Chinese teapot constantly filled with jasmine or green tea. There was no doubt about my eagerness to get back out to China as soon as I graduated.

My dream job was in journalism covering China. Initially, I assumed that would take years to reach, and that I would have to begin like most people do in journalism, working in local or regional press and climbing the ladder. One couldn't simply become a foreign correspondent in Beijing—a fresh graduate needed to first earn their spurs reporting on court hearings or cats stuck up trees for the *Bournemouth Echo*, the *Birmingham Mail*, or the *Salisbury Journal*. A lucky, talented few—very few—are taken on as graduate trainees on national newspapers, but even they spend the first few years doing the photocopying and monitoring the wires.

But I got lucky. As I scoured the jobs sections of newspapers, I saw an advertisement for the post of editor of a business journal called *China STAFF*. It focused on human resources management in China, and its readership was primarily foreign enterprises. I did not have much interest in, and certainly no experience of management or business, but I saw the words "China" and "journal" and applied.

China STAFF was one of a stable of publications owned by a legal publishing house in Hong Kong called Asia Law and Practice, a subsidiary of the international financial publishers Euromoney/Institutional Investor. After submitting my application, I travelled back to China to conduct research for my master's dissertation on the Chinese regime's policies towards religion, and spend a couple of months teaching in Qingdao. While there, I received a message from Asia Law and Practice, inviting me to Hong Kong for an interview. I flew down from Nanjing in late July 1997, just a few weeks after the handover.

I had the interview, both with the managing director and the managing editor, who then took me for lunch at the Foreign Correspondents' Club—an institution of which I subsequently became a regular member. At the end of lunch, the managing editor said to me, "Come back at 5 p.m. to collect the reimbursement for your flight. I think it is very likely that we will offer you the job. If we do, will you accept?" Thinking on my feet, keen but not wanting to immediately commit myself without a little bit of further thought, I replied, "If you offer me the job, I think it is very likely that I would accept." The prospect of working in Hong Kong at this historic time just after its handover to China, combined with working on China itself, was too good an opportunity to pass up, and so a few weeks later—after a brief sojourn back home in the U.K.—in September 1997, I found myself on a flight to Hong Kong.

For almost three years, I worked at *China STAFF*. Although I had the grand title of "editor," the truth is I was the only full-time journalist on the publication. We had a designer and a sales team, but in terms of editorial content, it was me, aged twenty-three. My role was to think of the content, commission some experts and freelancers, and write some articles myself. And it was—in its niche—a highly respected publication. For human resources directors and managers in foreign enterprises, employment lawyers, consultancies, headhunters, think tanks, and academics specializing in this field, it was the "go-to" journal. Moreover, the topic was broad, covering all the challenges—and opportunities—of managing a workforce in China, from labour law and compensation and benefits, to cross-cultural communication, training, and leadership development. The first edition I edited had as the front-page headline "Foreign firms face slim odds in wave of labour disputes." In my second edition, we included a feature on business and human rights, with an interview with John Kamm, the American businessman who devotes much of his time to negotiating the release of political prisoners in China. And another edition led with the headline "Crackdown rumours persist as headhunters tackle China," a story I wrote about rumoured restrictions on foreign recruitment firms in China. Later, we featured stories on child labour, corruption, sex discrimination, and the dangers of doing business in China.

The founder and chairman of Euromoney had developed a strict editorial style guide. Early on in my career in the company, I received, along with all other employees across the world—thousands of us—a one-sentence email from Padraig Fallon, which is embedded in my mind to this day: "Anyone convicted of using the word 'ongoing' will soon be outgoing."

To this very day, I have been petrified of using the word "ongoing."

I managed to get one edition banned in China. I interviewed the Mainland Chinese labour rights activist Han Dongfang, who had become a trade unionist and a Christian, participated in the Tiananmen Square protests, spent two years in jail, was released on medical grounds to the United States, fled to Hong Kong, and ran a hotline and radio phone-in show for labour rights in China. A far cry from firebrand leftist unionists in the West, Han was a mild, moderate man who simply sought decent working conditions for labourers in China.

Han, a railway worker raised by his mother living on thirty renminbi (at the time around US$4) a month, described to me the appalling working conditions in some factories in China. Labourers working sixteen-hour days, subjected to beatings if they did not perform, living in crowded, unhygienic basic conditions. He told me of one worker who telephoned him from a shoe factory in southern China, claiming he had been falsely accused of stealing. "The boss fired him and forced him to crawl out of the factory [on all fours] like a dog, in front of several hundred workers."

In the interview, we discussed what the conversations he has with Chinese workers who phone in to his shows mean. "These are not conversations with intellectuals, economists, experts," he said. "It is not about figures. It's about real life. Economic success is about individuals' lives. If you ignore individuals' lives and only talk about figures, you are lying to yourself." What truth there is in that.

The interview was not the cover story, but it was halfway through that edition, with his photo and this headline: "'One day the workers will take to the streets,' warns labour dissident." In the interview, Han warned that "labour issues are a time bomb which will explode one day." He noted that "in China, law on paper is one thing, law in practice is quite another."

He went on to say this: "The people . . . will not stand up—until the day they cannot keep quiet anymore. Then they will definitely go to the streets, without notice to anybody. It will suddenly happen. I cannot see fundamental reform of the system coming from government. They cannot make the investment needed; they cannot stop the corruption by themselves. We will have more State-owned enterprises close down, more corruption, and the workers will become more angry. All of this will push the workers forward until they explode. The government still does not allow the workers to have representatives to make peaceful negotiations, indoors not in the streets, so you cannot imagine what will happen."

The mailing house that was used to send copies to subscribers in the Mainland usually took the magazines across the border before posting them. That meant, they were checked by customs. Normally, the content was uncontroversial enough to be waved through, but clearly this edition—and the article's headline, complete with Han's photograph—caught customs officers' attention. It was blocked. Seasoned reporters say that if you're a decent journalist, you need to get banned by the Chinese regime at least once.

In that role, I travelled frequently in China—not just to Beijing, Shanghai, and Guangzhou, but to other cities, too. I returned to Qingdao, where I visited the Haier factory and wrote a case study on the transformation of that remarkable enterprise, as well as a profile of the Huadong Winery and the Qingdao International Golf Club. I wrote case studies on Canadian Airlines and French building materials producer Lafarge, visiting its cement plant near Beijing. I spoke at the China Business Summit and the World Economic Forum: all throughout the Asian financial crisis and the "bird flu" crisis, which was, with hindsight, a precursor and warning of SARS and COVID-19 to come. I also travelled internationally, once to the International Bar Association's conference in Barcelona, and once to the Asian Development Bank's (ADB) conference in Chiang Mai, Thailand.

On the first day of the ADB conference, two colleagues and I went to the conference centre to register. There were no taxis available, but plenty of tuk-tuks—the motorized auto rickshaw cycles common in Thailand, India, and Bangladesh. The three of us, in our suits, squeezed in, with at least one of us hanging out of the side. As the international bankers and politicians rolled up in their limousines, we three scruffy, sweaty, dishevelled journalists emerged from our smoke-belching tuk-tuk. Euromoney has always been cost-conscious, so our bosses would have been proud of us.

We took tuk-tuks each day that week, and one evening, I was due to attend a reception hosted by the mayor of Chiang Mai. I arrived late, as I had to attend a previous function first, so as I pulled up in my tuk-tuk at a grand mansion, I asked the driver to drop me at the gate. He failed to understand, and so drove right through the main gate and up the driveway to the house. I assumed that the formalities would have concluded and that I could slip quietly into the reception, so I paid him and got out. However, at the entrance, I was met by a flash from a photographer assigned to take pictures of every guest, and then, as I came up the steps, a very smart gentleman stepped forward and held out his hand. "Good evening, sir. I am the deputy mayor of Chiang Mai," he said. I hope he was impressed that I was supporting the local economy and culture by travelling by tuk-tuk.

These were remarkable opportunities for a fresh graduate. During my time at Asia Law and Practice, I established the *China STAFF* Human Resources Awards of the Year—which became the "Oscars" of the human resources management sector in the region. And I led an editorial team that produced a remarkable book, *The Life and Death of a Dotcom in China*—a business guide written in the form of a novel.

The Life and Death of a Dotcom in China, published in 2000, was an idea conceived by long-time China resident and former Reuters bureau chief Graham Earnshaw, my colleague Chris Hunter, and myself one evening over dinner in Shanghai. It was a successor to the very successful book *The Life and Death of a Joint Venture in China*, published by the same company a few years previously. The concept involved Graham, with input from Chris and myself, preparing a fictional narrative, which we then gave to experts—lawyers, consultants, tax specialists, investors, and Internet entrepreneurs—to write their respective chapters drawing on their expertise but using our storyline.

Graham, Chris, and I sat in M on the Bund, a wonderful restaurant which looks out across Shanghai's historic waterfront to the business district, Pudong, on the other side of the Huangpu River, and created the central characters and thread of the story together. It revolves around an entrepreneurial team that starts a new online business selling Mao memorabilia—MaoPortal.com—and it charts their journey through securing investment from venture capitalists and then working with lawyers and consultants to get the business off the ground. The book opens with the following scene:

"Call me Jackal," he said, and grinned.

The scene was the 198th floor of Get-Rich-Quick Square in Hong Kong. Their first meeting with venture capitalists—the seed money round. Jackal loved the way the announcement of his name startled people, knocked them slightly off balance, especially when accompanied by the grin. His boss, Jefferson, sitting beside him, was also uncomfortable with this introductory approach, but there was nothing he could do about it. His English name, after all, was Jackal. It was quietly pleasing.

The other people around the long boardroom table identified themselves. There were three staff from the venture capital firm, two men and a woman, all in starched clothes with neat, tidy hair. No nonsense. Then there was Jefferson Huang, CEO of MaoPortal.com, and his team: Jackal, MaoPortal's marketing manager; Miracle Liang, the Chief Operating Officer; and Stanley Chen, acting Chief Financial Officer.

Later on in the first chapter, we describe the idea of MaoPortal.com. Jefferson Huang recalls that his uncle, Lao Zhang, is the director of the Number Two Mao Memorabilia Factory.

"Why don't we put his Mao stuff online? We can sell the badges and all the other Mao stuff produced by the Number Two Mao Memorabilia Factory . . ."

Miracle considered the idea. "Mao commerce," she mused. "Mao mail."

"Mao dating!" continued Jefferson. "Maostrology! My Mao!! We'll call it . . ."

"MaoPortal!" they both said together, and laughed.

It was well received. The senior vice president of Sohu.com said the book "takes you inside the hearts and minds of Internet investors and entrepreneurs"; the chief operating officer of Sina.com described it as "a gripping tale of life in the Internet world in China"; and I&I Asia's Jonathan Hakim said it was an "excellent insight into the dotcom gold rush in China." I never would have imagined we would have had such fun putting this book together.

Alongside my job, in my spare time, my human rights activism took shape in Hong Kong. As a student, I had been inspired by a human rights organization called Christian Solidarity Worldwide (CSW), and got involved. When I moved to Hong Kong, CSW asked me if I would start a branch there, and so I did—from one corner of my bedroom in the flat I shared in Happy Valley.

My focus at the time was not so much human rights in China, but rather other parts of Asia. I started travelling to the borders of Myanmar (Burma), became involved in the struggle for East Timor alongside exiles in Macau, and began to learn more about North Korea. I got involved in assisting refugees fleeing persecution from Pakistan, Sierra Leone, and Sudan, and helping them in their applications to the United Nations High Commission for Refugees (UNHCR), which has an office in Hong Kong. Although Hong Kong has no asylum system itself, it was one of the few places which allowed visas on arrival, so there was a steady flow of people coming to Hong Kong to apply to the UNHCR.

Two Pakistani Christians I came to know were arrested one night for over-staying illegally. They called me from the police station in Tsim Sha Tsui, with one request: the food in the police station was grim, they said, so could I bring them some McDonald's.

After confirming with the police that this was permitted, I rushed off to buy some hamburgers, and brought them into the station. The duty officers insisted on searching the burgers—layer by layer, bun, pickle, fries, and all—before per-mitting me to hand over the bags of strip-searched McDonald's meals through the bars of the cell to the two detainees.

My two friends were then transferred to Victoria Prison, but released when I agreed to be their sponsor, on the condition that they would report to Immigration once a week. If they failed to do so, I would be liable for a fine. I worked late into the night for many days writing letters and sending faxes to the UNHCR in sup-port of these two Pakistanis, and when their visas expired, I rallied church leaders, political figures, and the media to lobby the Hong Kong government to extend them. Finally, we succeeded, and their visas were extended. In the end, however, UNHCR rejected their case three times and they returned to Pakistan.

Hong Kong, at the time a remarkably open and free city, became both a base for me to begin to be involved in the struggles for human rights elsewhere in Asia, and also a place to raise awareness—in churches, civil society, and media—for people facing persecution in the region. I organized talks at the Foreign

Correspondents' Club, contributed to Hong Kong's media, spoke in churches, and led protests through the streets of Hong Kong for East Timor and Myanmar. At the height of the crisis in East Timor, I led a march through the streets of Wanchai and Central and a press conference at the Foreign Correspondents' Club, against Indonesia's atrocities. I regularly visited the East Timorese diaspora in Macau, and led groups from Hong Kong churches on humanitarian visits to the Thailand-Myanmar border, and to East Timor. I organized human rights conferences in Hong Kong and worked closely with Hong Kong's remarkable champion of the poor, Jackie Pullinger-To, whose story is told eloquently in her memoir, *Chasing the Dragon*. I spoke at a church run by an incredible pastor who ministers to street sleepers, prostitutes, drug addicts, and Triads in Yau Ma Tei. And I became good friends with a couple who had been the first British family to legally adopt in China and had fought a long legal battle to adopt a blind orphan from Jinan in Shandong Province—a case which subsequently forced a change in Chinese and British adoption laws and opened the way for others. Little did I think, then, that one day, I would have to advocate for the rights of Hong Kongers themselves.

In 2000, I moved from Asia Law and Practice to join one of Hong Kong's two English-language daily newspapers. Previously known as the *Hong Kong Standard*, and owned by Sing Tao Holdings, the paper was being relaunched and rebranded under new leadership. Positioning itself as a quality tabloid—quality in content, tabloid in size—it was called the *Hong Kong iMail* and was intentionally pro-democracy and pro-freedom, and critical of both the Hong Kong government and Beijing. I was taken on initially as a business reporter, writing a weekly management page, but within a few days of joining, the editor, Andrew Lynch, called me into his office and said he thought I had potential to be the newspaper's editorial writer, writing the daily editorials, as well as an occasional column in my own name and general features.

The very first editorial I wrote was on August 19, 2000, the day of Al Gore's speech to the Democratic Convention in which he was formally hailed as their presidential nominee. Andrew said, "We'll do Gore." I asked what our line on Gore should be; he leaned back in his chair for a few moments and then said, "I don't like Gore." I paused, waiting further instruction, and he waved me away with a cheery "Off you go. Go and write it."

I read the transcript of Gore's speech, complete with lines indicating audience response, and began the editorial with "The delegates at the Democratic convention chanted, 'Go, Al, go.'" I then outlined a critique of Gore, and ended with this line: "Maybe the American people will tell Mr. Gore where to go in November." I filed it, and later that night got a note from Andrew congratulating me on the start of my editorial-writing career.

From then on, I wrote the editorials every day. Most days, the topic and line to take either was decided in conversation with Andrew as brief as the one about Gore or, on occasion, left entirely to me. Only on major set-piece stories such as the Budget, the chief executive's Policy Address, or some other historic events did we have an editorial meeting to discuss in depth.

One day in October 2000, Hong Kong's Catholic coadjutor bishop at the time, who later became cardinal and bishop emeritus, Joseph Zen Ze-kiun, spoke out boldly against Beijing's criticism of Rome's decision to canonize 120 new saints from China. That Sunday, I called Andrew to ask what he might like me to write as the editorial.

"Do the bishop," he said.

"Okay," I replied. "What's our line on the bishop?"

"Our line is what it always is: we're for what's good; we're against what's bad," said Andrew. "On this occasion, we're on the side of the church. In fact, we're on the side of the angels."

And so I wrote the editorial that night about the man who later became one of my heroes and friends:

> As Beijing's crackdown on religious groups—Catholic, Protestant, Muslim, and Falun Gong—intensifies, how easy will it be for the government to make life difficult for any religious leaders in Hong Kong who fall out of line? Although there is no imminent threat to religious freedom here, menacing words from Beijing make one consider such questions. Whatever happens, Bishop Zen was right to speak out as boldly as he did. Hong Kong is fortunate to have leaders like him, who are prepared to speak out and defend their beliefs.

Over the two years I spent at the newspaper, I wrote a variety of columns and features in my own name, on a range of subjects close to my heart, including human rights in China, the crisis in East Timor, and a fascinating encounter with a taxi driver in Singapore, who extolled the virtues of Lee Kuan Yew, "the Master."

I wrote two pieces mocking the then secretary for security Regina Ip and one proposing that the former head of the civil service Anson Chan, a leading pro-democracy voice, be made Hong Kong's chief executive.

I met Hong Kong tycoon Eric Hotung twice, and interviewed him once about his life, career, and philanthropy. On the first occasion, I presented him with an article I had written about East Timor, a cause he had taken up.

Eric Hotung looked at the article I handed him. And then he looked at me.

"Do you know Mr. Li Ka Shing?" he asked."

"Not personally," I admitted.

A look of disappointment momentarily appeared on his face. But then he called his secretary in and told me, in front of her, that he had "an open door" to me whenever I wanted to see him.

"Whenever Mr. Rogers calls, put him through," he told her in front of me.

I also interviewed lawyer-turned-author Gordon Chang about his book *The Coming Collapse of China*.

And I wrote a piece calling for democracy in China, in which I described meeting a survivor of the Tiananmen Square massacre:

> The world should be careful not to forget the dark side of China. Earlier this month I was in Beijing. It was, I believe, my 21st visit. I met a man who had been a student protestor in Tiananmen Square on June 4, 1989. He told me that he just escaped with his life. A tank came up behind him and his two friends with no warning, and no sign of stopping. His friends pushed him out of the path of the tank. But they themselves were not so lucky. This man witnessed his two friends being crushed by a tank.
>
> It is essential that we do not simply consign the Tiananmen massacre to history, for it symbolizes the continuing struggle for freedom and against corruption today. If we forget 1989, we lose all sense of value and meaning.
>
> This man now runs a small business, and is doing well. But he told me that on October 1, China's National Day, while others were celebrating the mainland's successes, he and his friends—veterans of the Tiananmen protest—wept. "The Chinese government does not rule," he told me. "It conspires to stay in power."

I concluded the article with these words to China's then president Jiang

Zemin: "If he really wants to leave a great legacy behind, Mr. Jiang should take the boldest step of all. Mao Zedong founded the People's Republic. Deng Xiaoping opened up the economy of the People's Republic. Mr. Jiang should bring democracy, accountability, and legitimacy to the People's Republic."

Such an article—as well as my columns about Regina Ip and others in the Hong Kong government—would be a crime under today's draconian National Security Law in Hong Kong. But twenty years ago, I was able to write for the city's media freely—and the worst that happened was Regina Ip informally complaining about me to my editor when they met at a drinks reception.

I wrote a profile of George W. Bush's nominee to be U.S. ambassador to China, lawyer Sandy Randt, whom I knew when I was at Asia Law and Practice because I edited his book on doing business with China. I had last seen him at an Election Day breakfast hosted by the American Club, where we gathered to watch the results, and he had cheered each state that turned Republican red and booed each time a state turned Democrat blue. As I wrote in the profile, "it was clear that he was more than a Republican voter—he was an activist." He was also an old university friend of the president's, and presumably his enthusiasm for the result may have been because he knew something that we did not about his next potential job offer.

And on a less politically controversial note, I got to know the inspiring Harilela family.

Possibly the wealthiest and most influential Indian family in Hong Kong, the Harilelas have at least 115 family members in total—and sixty-five of them live together in an extraordinary mansion in Kowloon Tong, divided into forty separate apartments. Every Sunday, all family members gather.

I was invited to dinner with the Harilelas twice, once to a farewell for an American diplomat, and once to a simple family gathering. The family had such charm and, despite their wealth, a complete lack of ostentatiousness. Dr. Hari Harilela described to me how they built their business, rising from real poverty in the 1920s when they first arrived in Hong Kong to a thriving business today. Dr. Harilela built the business, he said, on his father's principle: "Don't be greedy, and don't cheat. Make your profit, all you want, but don't cheat."

Perhaps my favourite column was one titled "Extraordinary man you find in ordinary places." In 2001, I had the privilege—as a result of my advocacy work for East Timor—of hosting Xanana Gusmao, the leader of East Timor's resistance who went on to be his country's first president and then prime minister. His wife, Kirsty Sword-Gusmao, and their newborn baby, Alexandre, came with him. In between our meetings, we sat down in McDonald's in Pacific Place. Kirsty wanted a banana for Alexandre, so I offered to go and find one. I turned the episode into an entertaining column which began as follows:

> The check-out lady at "Great" supermarket in Pacific Place looked at me in total amazement as I put one banana on the counter, gave her a dollar, and held out my hand for the 20 cents change. It was the first time in Hong Kong that I have ever been given change for a dollar. She probably wondered what planet I was on, coming to Great and spending 80 cents. But she did not know just *who* that banana was for.

I described my friendship with Xanana and Kirsty, and then an amusing encounter as we were leaving McDonald's:

> As we were about to leave, someone whom I had met before came up and greeted me. With Xanana out of earshot, he whispered: "Isn't that that East Timorese politician?" Yes, I said. He looked at me with an expression of complete astonishment. "Well what on earth is he doing in McDonald's in Pacific Place, Hong Kong? And, moreover, what are you doing with him?"
>
> I explained briefly my role, and told him of my success in finding a banana for Alexandre. His eyebrows rose to new heights and I left him, his mouth wide open and a perplexed look on his face. This person was amazed because, as he himself said, most visiting political leaders stay in the presidential suite in the Grand Hyatt, drive around in limousines with heavy security, fly in and out in helicopters, and are followed by a fleet of servants. Instead, with Xanana it was taxis and McDonald's and a young reporter at his side.
>
> No one who meets Xanana Gusmao can fail to be charmed. His charisma is great, his past history is impressive, his transformation from poet to guerrilla fighter to international statesman is extraordinary, and his presence on a platform is big. But he has something that many political leaders in the world today have lost. He has great humanity.

For most of my time with the *Hong Kong iMail*, the newspaper lived up to its proclaimed values, and gave me an extraordinary free rein to use my platform in the newspaper to champion causes. Our editorial line was unashamedly pro-democracy.

But then suddenly things changed. In January 2001, the fund managers Lazard Asia, which had bought Sing Tao from Sally Aw Sian in 1999, decided to accept a HK$356 million bid for its stake by the tobacco tycoon Charles Ho, owner of Hong Kong Tobacco and Global China Technologies. Mr. Ho had business interests in the Mainland and ambitions to expand further into China.

Mr. Ho did not do anything to change the newspaper immediately, but a few months later, in a night of the long knives, he sacked the editor and many of the senior journalists. More than eighty out of the 140 or so staff were laid off, receiving a letter sent by DHL on a Saturday morning. No one, including the outgoing editor, had any idea of the plan until it hit them.

The newsroom was filled with security guards and officious human resources staff watching employees closely as they cleared their desks. Management cancelled the work visas of foreign staff fairly swiftly, and handed them a document titled "How to Leave Hong Kong." It was, one friend of mine said, almost as if a banner had been hung from the ceiling saying "*Gwailos* (foreigners), go home."

A new editor, a Hong Kong Canadian called Tim Jim, was brought in, and from that moment, the writing was on the wall. His first words to us in the newsroom were, "We can no longer be so bold in our content, though we should continue to be bold in our design. Lots of colour, graphics, pictures—really jazz it up and make it exciting. We have to compete with television. And remember, we now subscribe to Xinhua." Almost every day he liked to remind us that "the days of colonial rule are over." He also compared himself to New York Mayor Rudy Giuliani walking through the rubble of the World Trade Center in the aftermath of the 9/11 terrorist attacks. Given that this was just twelve days after that horrific tragedy, it seemed horribly inappropriate. He told us that if we were short of content, we could use articles from *Psychology Today*.

It was a surprise to me that I had not been axed along with the others, but I knew that my days were numbered—my own conscience would not allow me to remain. I immediately told the new editor that I would no longer write editorials if I was to be required to write pro-Beijing propaganda. He offered me a seat.

"Ben, I was young and radical once," he said patronizingly.

He then proceeded to regale me with the history of his career as a young reporter. Some of his friends had been imprisoned by the British; he witnessed police using batons to beat protesters; and the disparity in pay between foreign journalists and local Hong Kong reporters was huge. All of this was probably true, but of what relevance to my concerns? Furthermore, I was on a local salary, not an expatriate package.

"I often wondered why Westerners get paid more than locals," he said. He left a long pause. And then he concluded, "The reason is that Chinese eat rice and foreigners eat steak, and as steak is more expensive than rice, foreigners have to be paid more."

My head was spinning. However, he did go on to say some things which gave me a flicker of hope. "Democracy and freedom—it's our birthright," he declared. "I would not allow anyone to tamper with that."

Good, I thought. I pressed him for a commitment that we would continue to write editorials "in the public interest" and hold the government accountable, and after three attempts at clarification, I secured his agreement on these basic principles. He added—and I was ready to accept this—that he did not want us to just criticize, but wherever possible offer ideas and solutions as well. And nor should we criticize for the sake of it—if the government does something good, we should be willing to give praise. I had no difficulty at all agreeing with that—indeed, that had always been my position.

But, I soon discovered, Mr. Jim flipped and flopped. No sooner had he gone from anti-colonialism to pro-democracy but he then declared that in every sphere of life, including human rights, China was now "pretty good—not perfect, but pretty good."

He then made my eyebrows rise even higher when he announced that he wanted the *Hong Kong iMail* to become a more conservative, pro-establishment newspaper—"the voice of the establishment." Well, which is it, I asked—the establishment or the public interest? "The two need not be contradictory," he replied. I resolved to stick with the public interest.

With Mr. Jim, one could never be sure what would come out of his mouth next.

"We should not be positioned as the wife of the *South China Morning Post*, but as the concubine of the *South China Morning Post*," he said. "And we should not cater to those anti-government people who sit around on Lamma Island smoking marijuana." They had never been our target audience, I pointed out.

Ultimately, he summed up his position by saying, "What we should really write about is how to make money. That is all this city is interested in." When asked about the sacking of the political editor, he reportedly told staff that the newspaper would be repositioned as a business newspaper, and that politics and business have nothing to do with each other so there was no need for a political editor. Hong Kong, he claimed, was not a political city—a remark that would be dramatically proven wrong in subsequent years. "Politics all comes from Beijing now," he added—a remark that history shows was all too prophetic.

Five days after the change of editorial leadership, a column appeared in the newspaper with Charles Ho's byline. Mr. Ho had never before written a column in the newspaper, and while as the proprietor he had the right to do so, his interest should also be declared and his piece should be consistent with our editorial standards. It turned out it was a two-part series, and in the first piece his position as proprietor was not mentioned, though it was in the sequel. It was essentially a copy and paste of a report by a law firm funded by Mr. Ho, setting out ideas for developing Hong Kong as an international financial centre. It might have merited a genuine op-ed commenting on it, but not a serialization of such a technical document—and certainly did not deserve his byline. It was a flagrant abuse of the opinion pages to promote Mr. Ho's ego.

I continued to write editorials for a few weeks, deliberately trying to slip pro-democracy themes in to test the waters and see what I could get away with. Many of these editorials—including some very critical of the establishment—were published, and I am unsure whether that was because Mr. Jim was not actually reading them or whether he was allowing them through in order to present the semblance of independence for the newspaper.

In October 2001, I wrote an editorial about Tung Chee-hwa's fifth and final Policy Address of his first term. The first two paragraphs read as follows:

> Chief Executive Tung Chee-hwa yesterday demonstrated a masterly ability to say absolutely nothing. His final Policy Address of his first term was long on talk, and extremely short on policy. It was an extraordinary mixture of repetition, prevarication, and statements of the blindingly obvious.
>
> Mr. Tung devoted much of his speech to summarizing his previous four Policy Addresses. He said that an important factor in building a knowledge-based economy is "the possession of creative ideas." Yet there was little sign that he himself possessed any.

These paragraphs were published unchanged, but my concluding paragraph was altered. The original read as follows: "The one saving grace of Mr. Tung's speech this year is that he did not say anything really wrong. It was evasive and meaningless, but not actually damaging. But if he serves a second term, he should put the Policy Address to better use than he did yesterday's."

When I opened the newspaper the next morning, the final lines had changed: "One saving grace of Mr. Tung's speech this year is that he did not say anything really wrong. And at least his efforts to relieve hardship through job creation, rates cuts, and extra tax deductions will give a boost to those struggling to make ends meet at this difficult time."

In addition to trying to hold the line in editorials and columns, I wrote two emails to friends describing the changes at the *Hong Kong iMail*. They were intended to be private and confidential, but instead they ended up being circulated.

The British and Australian consuls-general received the emails, Hong Kong's radio station RTHK quoted from them, and the Freedom Forum quoted them on its website.

One of Democratic Party Chairman Martin Lee's staff wrote to me, saying, "I am so glad that you remain steadfast in the guard for our democracy and human rights. It is not easy in times like this. I hope things will change for better soon. And please know that there are people who appreciate your work very much and stand behind you, though silently."

Another person I did not know—a Superintendent Khan—telephoned me in response to my columns generally, saying, "There are very few people in the Hong Kong media who dare to speak the truth, and you're one of them."

A public relations consultant wrote, "Your voice is refreshing and your friendship enjoyed. Here's to extending both."

Mr. Jim was made aware of my emails, but said nothing to me—presumably, he did not want a martyr for press freedom.

A friend at the *South China Morning Post* wrote this to me: "It is a pity what's happened. It is bad news to you and others at the *Hong Kong iMail*, but also bad news for us, and in fact everybody. I would say this is also the root evil of the Hong Kong press: that its fate is determined by profits alone—not news. It is reasonable for bosses to be concerned about profit. But in Hong Kong, profitability is the only criteria. And sometimes one has to wonder why the managers can exonerate themselves so easily when the companies are not turning the profits as they expected. This is in a way amazing because such privilege is almost unique to the business world in Hong Kong."

The unravelling of *Hong Kong iMail* was not the only example of the decline of press standards. In contrast to what happened to the press two decades later, the erosion of press freedom in the first five years after the handover was not due to direct intervention by Beijing, or even the Hong Kong authorities, but self-censorship—a desire on the part of proprietors and some editors to ingratiate themselves with Beijing. One small example was when Disney's chief executive Michael Eisner visited Hong Kong, and dismissed reports that Disney might open a park in Mainland China as "erroneous." He admitted that it was a possibility for the long term, but there were no immediate plans. I wrote a story for the *Hong Kong iMail* headlined "Disney opening may be delayed." The *South China Morning Post*, incredulously, spun it as "Mainland may get Disney.

The *South China Morning Post*'s editorial line was already weakening even when I was in Hong Kong. Whereas my editorials tended to express a view, theirs were largely—in the words of a friend who worked for the newspaper—a summary of the story. And sometimes they were fawning to Beijing. In September 2001, for example, Beijing announced that Hong Kong and Macau media would be able to open bureaus in the Mainland. The *South China Morning Post*—one of the very few that already had Beijing, Shanghai, and Guangzhou bureaus—claimed that Beijing's decision "to open the Mainland's doors to members of the Hong Kong and Macau media represents a significant shift in policy and, undoubtedly, a growing acceptance of scrutiny by news organizations." In my view, welcoming scrutiny was not something on Beijing's mind.

Indeed, the *South China Morning Post*'s China editor, Willy Wo-Lap Lam, was the best example of this. He had written countless columns of the regime in Beijing, upsetting the newspaper's pro-Beijing proprietor at the time, Robert Kuok. The editor demanded that his op-eds be pre-screened before being sent to the opinion pages, and then informed him that he was being replaced as China editor by Wang Xiangwei, a former journalist at the State-run *China Daily*, the regime's mouthpiece. Willy—whom I came to know quite well—resigned in November 2000, setting out in detail what had happened in an article in *The Wall Street Journal* titled "Why I Left the South China Morning Post."

One of the few bold voices in defence of Hong Kong's freedoms was the Chinese-language *Apple Daily*, founded by the entrepreneur Jimmy Lai. Twenty years later, the newspaper was forced to close and Jimmy and his senior editors were jailed, but when I lived in Hong Kong, the pressure was already beginning but in a more subtle way. I did not know Jimmy at that time, though I came to do so later in life, but I knew some of his key aides and friends. They told me that Hong Kong's pro-Beijing businesses and tycoons were boycotting *Apple Daily*, refusing to advertise in the newspaper. Li Ka Shing, owner of Cheung Kong Holdings and Hong Kong's richest man, was one of the first to pursue an aggressive commercial boycott of the newspaper, and in July 2001—two decades before the newspaper was eventually shut down—HSBC withdrew its advertising. The White House and U.S. State Department were concerned by the implications of this for press freedom, and in its 2000 Country Report on Human Rights Practices in Hong Kong, the State Department noted that "several property developers significantly reduced their advertisements in the [*Apple Daily*]" because it had offended Beijing. The report claimed that there was a growing belief in Hong Kong that if newspapers are seen to be "too antagonistic to China or powerful local interests," advertising revenues fall.

Apple Daily's director of corporate accounts, Mark Simon—one of Jimmy's key aides—told me that, at that time, the interference was not directly from Beijing, but from Hong Kong's tycoons kowtowing to the regime. "There seems to be a belief among those who ban us that there is some sort of reward for this from up north. But most sinologists will tell them that it's meaningless," he said. He expressed concern about the impact of such behaviour on Hong Kong's image. "There are people who are looking for faults in Hong Kong," he argued. "This is exactly the kind of fault that they will find. The handlebars are there [to make it an issue in U.S.-Hong Kong relations]—it just needs somebody to ride it. There are people out there who watch Hong Kong and pay attention. Hong Kong seems to forget that these people pay attention." The situation would deteriorate beyond all expectations two decades later, but the seeds of trouble were already evident in the first five years after the handover.

In an editorial on China's National Day 2001, I argued that Hong Kong "appears to have lost its nerve." I added:

> A major problem in Hong Kong is the insidious self-censorship and second-guessing that goes on. Beijing itself has behaved with remarkable restraint since it assumed sovereignty in 1997. It is unlikely that Beijing really cares who says what in Hong Kong, as long as the Special Administrative Region (SAR) does not destabilize the rest of the coun-

try. But too many people in the SAR have sought to ingratiate themselves with the Central Government by silencing critical elements, and that is at the root of Hong Kong's decline. We have lost our guts.

The past four years are littered with a trail of examples of bowing to Beijing before Beijing has even expressed a view . . .

If Hong Kong is to rediscover itself and build a new future, we must show more courage. We must think for ourselves, instead of looking to Beijing for answers. We must be willing to exercise the "two systems," whilst recognizing that we are "one country." We must come up with solutions, develop a vision, and speak up for Hong Kong. If we do that, we will have more to celebrate at future anniversaries.

By the time I resigned from the *Hong Kong iMail* and prepared to return to the United Kingdom, it was clear that some storm clouds were on the horizon for Hong Kong. Karl Kwok, chairman of Wing On Company International, was predicting then that by 2047, the cut-off date for "one country, two systems," Hong Kong and neighbouring Shenzhen, across the border, would merge into one metropolis, directly governed by China. The Economist Intelligence Unit's Asian chief economist Ken Davies expressed concern about a lack of "strong, clear, and above all credible long-term vision" for Hong Kong. The fact that Hong Kong's leaders were not democratically elected by universal suffrage, he said, was part of the problem. "Without political leadership, the best to be expected is honesty, efficiency, and competence," he argued, but it leaves policy-making as "reactive rather than proactive." George Soros called on Hong Kong to "lead the way" by introducing democracy, saying that "advances in democracy will send a positive signal to the markets." He warned that China's economic growth could not continue without political reform. "China's opening has to go beyond markets, and involve freedom of speech, free flow of information, and free discussion. Without it, China cannot continue to flourish," he argued. The *Hong Kong iMail* carried the story as its lead, but the *South China Morning Post* had nothing more than a photograph of Mr. Soros with two short paragraphs about an idea he proposed for international aid funding. Talk about burying the story.

There were other controversies and scandals during my time in Hong Kong.

Pollster Dr. Robert Chung, an academic at Hong Kong University, who carried out opinion polls on the popularity of Chief Executive Tung Chee-hwa, claimed he had come under pressure from senior academics and from Mr. Tung's special advisor, Andrew Lo, to stop conducting the polls when Mr. Tung's ratings slipped. An investigation was carried out by an independent panel and, while it appeared complex, it seemed that Dr. Chung's charges contained some truth. Ying Chan, director of the Journalism and Media Studies Centre at the university, said that Vice Chancellor Patrick Cheng, whose rebuttal of the allegations was unconvincing, "failed to demonstrate unquestioned integrity." Andrew Lo was described by the judge who led the inquiry as a "poor and untruthful witness." A motion in the Legislative Council calling on Mr. Tung to sack Mr. Lo was only defeated by one vote.

Then there was the controversy around legislative councillor Gary Cheng, from the pro-Beijing Democratic Alliance for the Betterment of Hong Kong. A few weeks before the 2000 Legislative Council elections, it was revealed that Mr. Cheng had failed to declare his interests in a public relations consultancy of which he was the majority shareholder. Worse, though, was the fact that he had leaked confidential government and Legislative Council documents to some of his clients. His clients included major Hong Kong companies such as the Kowloon-Canton Railway Corporation, Towngas, and Li Ka Shing's Cheung Kong Holdings. However, because the Legislative Council Ordinance stipulates that a candidate can withdraw before, but not after, the close of nominations, he fought the election despite intense pressure to withdraw, and he won re-election. He did then, however, have the decency to resign.

In a taste of the crackdown to come, in November 2000, the Hong Kong government undertook the unusual step of proposing a motion in the Legislative Council asking legislators to endorse the Public Order Ordinance, an archaic colonial law that imposes strict requirements and restrictions for protests and demonstrations. Used in later years to prosecute many of Hong Kong's pro-democracy protesters, the government in 2000 was clearly getting ready. As Martin Lee said at the time, "I have never come across any government anywhere in the world which asks its legislature to say that an existing law is good and therefore should be preserved." Motions are tabled to amend laws or introduce new laws, not endorse existing laws. "If the law is good," said Mr. Lee, "you will never have to go to your legislature for endorsement."

Since the handover, Hong Kong has been served by a series of inept chief executives and governments. The current administration is by far the worst, but even in those early years, decisions were taken that were concerning. Michael Suen, who served as Secretary for Constitutional Affairs, proposed, for example, that the 2002 election for chief executive—an election consisting solely of 800 predominantly pro-establishment voters who made up the Election Committee—be held on a Thursday instead of a Sunday, which was the norm. When asked for an explanation, to everyone's amazement, Mr. Suen explained that Sunday might not be convenient for some Election Committee members because they may have to go out of town on business or "to play golf." Such extraordinary pandering to the desires and pleasures of Hong Kong's elite illustrated what a farce Hong Kong's electoral system is.

China's president at the time, Jiang Zemin, made it clear in those early years that Beijing's understanding of "one country, two systems" was rather different from how Hong Kongers, the United Kingdom, and the rest of the world interpreted it. In a speech on the first anniversary of Macau's handover, in 2000, he emphasized "one country" more than "two systems," and inferred that "two systems" related more to the economic than the political realm. "The main part of the country sticks to the socialist system, while Macau [and Hong Kong] retains the capitalist system," he said. With hindsight, this was perhaps an early warning of the fact that for Beijing, Hong Kong's "high degree of autonomy" did not mean freedom and democracy.

Mr. Jiang lost his temper with Hong Kong journalists on occasion. In October 2000, as Tung Chee-hwa visited Beijing, Hong Kong's press pack called out to President Jiang asking whether he supported a second term for Mr. Tung. He replied "good" in Cantonese, but then journalists asked whether that meant it was already a done deal and that the Election Committee's vote was just a formality. Screwing up his face into a most furious contortion, Mr. Jiang pursed his lips, jabbed his finger, and shouted, "I'm angry!" He then added ominously, "I'm anxious for you all, really!"

A friend of mine who was an experienced journalist who had been covering China since the 1970s told me later that night over dinner: "That's it—this is the beginning of the end for the Communist Party." I queried him, and he explained: "The emperor never loses control in front of his people. Jiang—the 'emperor'— has just lost it. Big time. Such an outburst indicates a serious loss of control, a weakness, a fear in the Party leadership. The whole thing will unravel." My friend did not put a timescale on it, and two decades later, it is Hong Kong's freedoms that have unravelled with the Communist Party remaining in power, but there may be some truth in what he said. Clearly, the Party—then, and even more so now—is insecure.

Among the political figures I got to know during my time in Hong Kong was Christine Loh, a legislator until 2000, leader of the Citizens Party, and founder of a think tank Civic Exchange. In more recent years, she appears to have taken a very different track, serving in government and compromising with Beijing in a way which makes most of her former democratic colleagues profoundly uncomfortable. But in the days when I knew her, she was a key ally for me on East Timor and on wider human rights issues, and a valuable source of ideas and analysis. I recall one conversation in which she summed up Hong Kong's problems:

"People don't dare to speak out. Everybody is afraid of upsetting somebody else. That prevents us from having a good look at the real problems," she said. "Off the record, people will complain. But on the record, nobody says anything."

She urged Hong Kongers from all parts of society to contribute ideas, and not simply look to government for solutions. "Part of Hong Kong's problem is that we don't feel very sexy," she added. "We think the world thinks Shanghai and Beijing are sexy, and we have a low sex drive at the moment. We don't feel sexy because we have forgotten what drives us. What drives us is the rule of law, which is broad and deep."

She also commented on a problem that was widely perceived at the time but was proven by events two decades later to be a fallacy: that Hong Kongers avoid anything "political." In her analysis of the 2001 Policy Address, she wrote, "Economic and social policies are political decisions although Hong Kong often deals with them as if they have nothing to do with politics. 'Politics' is often narrowly defined in this town, confined to electoral/party politics, constitutional reform, or Hong Kong's relations with Beijing. The aversion to politics is a legacy of Chinese culture and colonialism. Few people have experienced meaningful participation. Disagreeing with authority is seen as risky. Opposition is never seen to be loyal. To date, politics has not been seen as something people want to get into."

Joshua Wong, Nathan Law, Agnes Chow, Edward Leung, Ray Wong, Joey Siu, and many others who had just been born when she made those remarks were to prove her completely wrong.

Two years before I left Hong Kong, I was in a taxi in Gloucester Road in Wan Chai. The driver asked me when I came to Hong Kong, and I told him I had arrived in September 1997.

"Oh, what a pity," he said. "You missed the handover."

I nodded.

"Even worse, you missed Chris Patten," he continued.

"Yes, I know," I replied.

"Worst of all, you missed Chris Patten's daughters," he declared with a big grin.

The tear-stained faces of the last governor's daughters as the family left the city in 1997 were indelibly etched in the minds of many Hong Kongers. Perhaps one of the reasons Beijing loathes Lord Patten is the fact that, in contrast to all his successors governing Hong Kong under Chinese rule, he was able to walk down the street to buy his favourite egg tarts, go shopping and meet people, and be confident that he would be greeted with warmth and affection.

Despite the clear problems that were already apparent in those first five years after the handover, overall, Hong Kong's freedoms were largely intact. As Lord Patten said in his inaugural Paddy Ashdown Memorial Lecture in 2020, which I helped establish through Hong Kong Watch, as Hong Kong teetered on the brink, during those early years, "Things were not going too badly. A school report might have said, 'could do even better, could do a lot worse.'"

The scandals I have mentioned above were exposed; independent inquiries held; and, unlike in Mainland China then or Hong Kong today, people could speak out and protest. Each year for the time I lived in Hong Kong, I joined hundreds of thousands of others on June 4 in Victoria Park for a candlelit vigil to commemorate the Tiananmen Square massacre of 1989. In 1999, the tenth anniversary of the massacre, the former student leader Wang Dan, who had been released and was in exile in the United States, appeared on a screen to address the crowd and was then linked up by telephone with his mother in Beijing, in an emotional conversation heard by everyone gathered. For twenty-two years, the vigils continued unhindered, but by 2020, under the auspices of COVID-19, and by 2021, due to the draconian National Security Law, they had been made illegal and the organizers are now in prison.

In one editorial I wrote, "To fail to remember the June 4th massacre would be to abdicate ourselves from any vestiges of morality. It would also be against our self-interest. The moment we forget the sacrifice of the students made in Beijing, we lose our will to defend the freedoms we have." Tiananmen, I argued, "should never be forgotten"—to drop Tiananmen from our memories would be to "drop our conscience." The spirit of Tiananmen "should continue to burn brightly in Hong Kong for as long as we want 'one country, two systems' to survive." At the time of writing those words, I had little understanding for just how prescient they would be.

For five years, I roamed around Hong Kong freely. I hiked along the Peak, walked in the New Territories, and took weekend visits to Cheung Chau, Lamma, Lantau, and the other islands and periodic forays to Macau. I was invited out on occasions by wealthier expats for "junk trips" in the harbour, where I learned to water-ski. I adored the city and its nearby islands, and enjoyed a mix of work, social life, and rest. I worshipped at St. Andrew's Church, on Nathan Road, in Tsim Sha Tsui, Kowloon, but also visited other places of worship around the city, including Community Church Hong Kong, which met at the time at the summit of Central Plaza, the skyscraper owned by property tycoon Thomas Kwok. To pray and praise the divine while virtually touching the clouds was sublime.

As a member of the Foreign Correspondents' Club, I regularly went for drinks or dinner at the club—either with or alongside the great Clare Hollingworth, the doyenne of war correspondents. And in that club, with which I took lifetime membership, I found inspiration from her and others.

When I left Hong Kong in the autumn of 2002, after five years in the city, I genuinely felt, overall, that "one country, two systems" was working well. It was not perfect, but given that Hong Kong had been handed over to Chinese sovereignty, I was grateful that day-to-day freedoms were reasonably intact. Was it fraying and under pressure? Clearly so, as this chapter outlines. But were there structures, institutions, systems, and people in place to hold it, more or less, intact at that time? Yes. Civil society was active, the media was bold, academia was free, places of worship were unhindered, protests could be held, and the legislature was still partially elected, with a vocal, vibrant, and active democracy camp.

Did I agree with a visiting delegation of members of Parliament from the House of Commons Foreign Affairs Committee who called, in November 2000, for the implementation of universal suffrage for elections for chief executive, as promised under Hong Kong's Basic Law? Of course I did, and I wrote about it in the *Hong Kong iMail*.

Did I agree with their conclusion that democracy "is both a basic human right for the people of Hong Kong and the strongest defence against unwelcome intervention by the Mainland"? Strongly so.

Did I share their concern about self-censorship in the media, the negative influence of newspaper proprietors' business interests in China, and their statement that "a free press remains vital to Hong Kong's future as an international centre"? Absolutely I did.

But as I left Hong Kong in 2002, did I have any inkling of the disastrous fate that awaited the city two decades later?

Not at all.

I left after five very happy years with, despite concerns, hope in my heart.

Events two decades on—detailed in a later chapter—would severely challenge that hope.

CHAPTER 3

CHINA'S CRACKDOWN AFTER A DECADE OF OPENING

THE SHRINKING SPACE FOR LAWYERS, CIVIL SOCIETY, MEDIA, AND DISSENT

Whenever I was in Beijing, my absolute favourite activity was to go, after a day of meetings, to dinner with friends—or sometimes alone—in a beautiful restaurant in an old Chinese courtyard house on the edges of the Forbidden City.

After dinner, often around midnight, I would walk in the moonlight along the walls of the Forbidden City, with the canal waters lapping on the other side, soaking in the ancient history.

I would then walk through the final ramparts of this ancient fortress, past People's Liberation Army (PLA) sentries, and out under the Gate of Heavenly Peace—Tiananmen—under the portrait of Mao Zedong into a floodlit, empty, and silent Tiananmen Square.

As I did so, I could feel the spirits of those who had gone before me. And as I shielded my eyes from the midnight floodlights and moonlight, I could feel in my own spirit the voices of those who had died in 1989 crying out, "Stand up, speak out, never forget."

I walked that path often—and I heard those voices every time.

Before I changed jobs in Hong Kong, I made a particularly special visit to Beijing. It was my last business visit to Beijing with Asia Law and Practice and so, knowing that in my new job my business travel into the Mainland would be less frequent—and unsure when I might return to Beijing—I stayed on for a weekend. I asked friends if we might do something memorable. They suggested we sleep on the Great Wall of China. That sounded memorable enough for me.

We trouped off to a remote part of the Great Wall, a non-tourist spot several hours outside Beijing. We had dinner in a simple village restaurant. Unfortunately, in the middle of dinner, some form of food poisoning, or a virus, hit me, and I was violently sick. But I kept going, and we slept on the Wall under the stars, in the open air but near enough to the turrets in case it rained.

On my final visit to Mainland China before leaving Hong Kong for good, I decided to visit Confucius' birthplace in Qufu, and to climb Taishan, the mountain which Chairman Mao walked up and declared at sunrise that "the East is red!"

During my five years in Hong Kong, I travelled in Mainland China widely, both for business and pleasure. One Chinese New Year, I went to Guilin and Yangshuo, in the Guangxi Zhuang Autonomous Region, famous for the mountains surrounding the Li River, scenery which has given inspiration to many traditional Chinese landscape paintings. Guilin, which literally means "Forest of Sweet Osmanthus" as a result of the preponderance of sweet osmanthus trees, is now quite a large city, albeit surrounded by breathtaking beauty. Yangshuo, on the other hand, is—or certainly was when I visited twenty years or so ago—a smaller town, full of backpackers, but relatively unspoiled.

In Yangshuo, I hired a bicycle and went out each day cycling in the Chinese countryside. On one occasion, I almost got stranded, as I was far out on a country lane in the middle of nowhere, miles from the nearest village or town, and the chain on my bicycle fell off. Anyone who knows me well will confirm that I am no handyman, and I did not know how to fix it. I tried, and ended up covered in black oil. Except for some oxen in the paddy fields, there was no other living being in sight. Just at that moment, however, a motorbike came towards me, and stopped, astonished to see a Westerner in the middle of a country road. Within seconds, the chain was back on and I set off again, grateful for the kindness of strangers.

At Easter in 1999, I went to Kunming, in Yunnan Province, and on to the charming town of Dali, on the shores of Lake Erhai. In Dali, I hired a boatman to take me out on the lake, ate fresh fish on an island in the middle of the lake, went cormorant fishing, and climbed Cangshan, the local mountain. I celebrated Easter at the Dali Church of Christ, a State-sanctioned Three-Self Patriotic Movement (TSPM) Protestant church, which was packed. I also met the amazing Mr. He Liyi, from the Bai ethnic minority, in the little café that he founded in 1996 called "Mister China's Son Café." In his seventies, Mr. He was quiet and unassuming, sitting in the corner watching television and smoking a pipe. He smiled, but did not initiate a conversation. Eventually I asked to see his books, and we got talking.

Mr. He had written an autobiography about his experiences of life in the 1950s and 1960s—the Great Leap Forward and the Cultural Revolution—titled *Mr. China's Son: A Villager's Life*. He wrote it in English, despite never having left his native Yunnan Province until 1988, when he won a scholarship to attend a BBC English Language Summer School. Somehow, the book ended up in the hands of an international publishing house, and in 1993, it was published in Europe.

In 1956, Mr. He had been selected to work as an interpreter for a special committee—the Research Institute for National Minority People's Social History—established by the Beijing-based Academy of Social Sciences. Because he was ethnic Bai who spoke his local ethnic language, as well as being fluent in Mandarin and having studied English in college, he was instructed to translate English materials into Chinese for research purposes, or to accompany experts into the mountains to interpret for them in their conversations with local Bai villagers.

"I rejoiced over the change," he writes. "I had been working in a government office building where an eight-hour day seemed like a sixty-four-hour day. But as soon as I was transferred to do a translator's job, my workday passed by like eight minutes. Opening my dusty boxes, I brought out my books. I began to think, I began to plan; I was going to use my English again."

In pursuit of his English language study in the 1950s, Mr. He writes, "I abandoned all other trivial pursuits. I had only one goal, and that was to lay siege to the English language and recapture my lost territory as soon as possible. I made this poor and mountainous corner my permanent home and the English language my daily bread."

However, in the summer of 1957, Mr. He recalls, "a great political movement known to the world as the Struggle Against the Rightists started all over our country." It followed the campaign initiated by Mao Zedong to "Let a hundred flowers blossom and a hundred schools of thought contend," which was initially interpreted as a new dawn of free expression. However, it turns out it was a trap to expose critics of the regime, and quickly led to a policy of "drawing a clear line between sweet-smelling flowers and poisonous weeds."

Mr. He was an immediate target in this new struggle, both for his love of English language and because, as he recalls, his family had been classified as part of the "landlord" class. He was labelled an Anti-Party Rightist and tortured, beaten, imprisoned, stripped of his job, and constantly harassed. He was accused of having made criticisms of the Soviet Union, and of being someone who "loves the enemy, America!" Mobs told him, "You hate our Party! No mistake—you are just the rightist we are all trying to search for!" He was sent off to a re-education-through-labour farm, where he was detained and forced to work until 1962.

In 1979, as China under Deng Xiaoping was just taking the first tentative steps towards opening to the world, Mr. He's wife sold her fattest pig to buy him a shortwave radio, and he spent every possible spare moment listening to the BBC and Voice of America, in order to recover and improve the English he had learned in the early 1950s. In 1985, his first book, a translation of Chinese folk tales titled *The Spring of Butterflies*, was published on the international market, and eight years later, *Mr. China's Son* was released. I bought a copy of both books, and in his autobiography he inscribed this message, on April 3, 1999:

> Dear Ben,
>
> Thank you very much for coming to honour our 3 year-old baby café. In a way my life story looks like a "window." You'll "see" and learn what on earth happened to my family and myself sometime before and after my country became Communist in 1949. I hope you'll enjoy reading it. Have a great trip! Your Bai friend, He Li-Yi.

Mr. He also wrote his *Rules for Being Human*, which he displayed in the café. They are as follows:

1. You will receive a body. You may like it or hate it, but it will be yours for the entire period this time around.
2. You will learn lessons. You will be enrolled in a full-time, informal school called "life." Each day in this school you will have the opportunity to learn lessons. You may like the lessons or think them irrelevant or stupid.
3. There are no mistakes, only lessons. Growth is a process of trial and error experimentation. The "failed" experiments are as much a part of the

process as the experiment that ultimately "works."

4. A lesson is repeated until learned. A lesson will be presented to you in various forms until you have learned it. When you have learned it, you can then go on to the next lesson.

5. Learning lessons does not end. There is no part of life that does not contain its lessons. If you are alive, there are lessons to be learned.

6. "There" is no better than "here." When your "there" has become a "here," you will simply obtain another "there" that will, again, look better than "here."

7. Others are merely mirrors of you. You cannot love or hate something about another person unless it reflects to you something you love or hate in yourself.

8. What you make of your life is up to you. You have all the tools and resources you need. What you do with them is up to you. The choice is yours.

9. Your answers lie inside you. The answers to life's questions lie inside you. All you need to do is look, listen, and trust.

10. You will forget this.

The humour, wisdom, insights, courage, and linguistic ability of Mr. He are truly inspiring. I went to his café each day that I was in Dali, to sit and chat and learn from him. And throughout China, in different ways, I have encountered similar characters—those who have suffered much, with immense—though quiet and humble—courage and dignity, and with much to teach us all.

Unfortunately, not all my travels in China were as beautiful and inspiring as my times in Dali and Yangshuo. In Shanghai, for example, I was mugged in a very sophisticated way. I wrote about it in the *Hong Kong iMail*, but, unfortunately, the headline was potentially misleading: "Innocence Lost in Nanjing Road."

That was in June 2001, and by then I had been travelling in and around China for nine years. I had learned over the years that it was not at all unusual for a stranger to come up to a foreigner and genuinely wish to practise their English. It happened to me often, and on the vast majority of occasions it was sincere and innocent. But on this occasion in Nanjing Road, I was too trusting—and naive.

It was midnight, and I was walking back to my hotel after enjoying dinner with a friend overlooking the Bund and listening to jazz in the Peace Hotel. The jazz band in the Peace Hotel in 2001 looked like the same band that was highly popular in that hotel in the 1920s—the musicians looked ancient, and they played old tunes, painfully out of tune. The drummer crouched over the cymbals looking as if he were about to die at any moment, if he wasn't dead already.

With this entertainment still playing in my head, I strolled down Nanjing Road—Shanghai's main shopping street—feeling carefree. A young Chinese man approached me, and started to tell me about a new bar. I indicated that I was not interested, and I was suspicious that he might be a pimp. I kept walking, but he was persistent.

"A positive attitude is the fountain of success," he said.

He certainly had that, and I admit I found this rather endearing.

"Are you American?" he asked.

Not wishing to be rude, I told him I was British, and almost immediately he responded by saying, "I am going to Wales in September. I am going to work in a laundry."

By this point my intrigue got the better of me.

"Will you come and have a cup of tea with me? I want to learn about Britain before I go there," he asked.

I hesitated. It was late at night and I was tired. It sounded unwise. But then I thought, "Why not? What harm is there in a cup of tea?"

So we went into a tea house, and he took me into a private room. This made me feel slightly concerned, but he seemed harmless.

He said he would order some snacks, and I said no, just tea, because I had already eaten. But he insisted, promising it would just be a few snacks. A plate of vegetables arrived, and a bowl of peanuts. We agreed we would split the bill.

To my surprise, a little later a large fish was presented on a plate. I reminded him that I had already eaten, and it was 1 a.m. by this point. But he had not eaten, he said, and invited me to share the fish with him. He offered me a beer, and told me about his visa application process for Britain.

He was a likeable, intelligent, and entertaining young man, and we had an enjoyable and interesting conversation. My earlier suspicions had disappeared and I felt relaxed. At 2 a.m., we requested the bill.

The waiter came into the room, and closed the door—an act which I noticed. He then put the bill on the table. I read it. It was 2,700 renminbi yuan—which is approximately £300, or $420.

"There must be some mistake," I said.

But there was no mistake. The young man made a feeble pretence of looking surprised while the waiter explained it was the cost of the private room, the fish, and the late service—none of which I had asked for.

The waiter offered a special reduction—to 1,600 yuan, or just under £200 or $250. But that still meant I would have to pay 800 yuan (if my young friend stuck to his side of the agreement to split the bill). I resisted. Then the waiter made a grab for my wallet. I hung onto it, but the atmosphere was turning nasty and the waiter became increasingly menacing. I sensed that if I did not pay up, I might not get out in one piece. I put the money on the table and ran for it.

I later learned that this experience is well known. These young, intelligent Chinese people who speak good English are often part of an organized under-world, using their wit and charm to lure foreigners to restaurants which charge a vastly inflated price—which they receive a cut of. I was told that I was lucky it was in Shanghai, not Guangzhou or Shenzhen where I may well not have escaped unharmed.

On a more amusing note, an old university friend came to visit me in Hong Kong, and we decided to travel to Qingdao together. We booked a hotel and decided to share a room. On arrival, the porters took our luggage to our room, and I realized I had no change on me with which to tip them, so I asked my friend—who did not know China and was unfamiliar with Chinese currency—to give them something. Their reaction was hilarious. Upon receiving a note each from my friend, the two porters stared at us in disbelief—and some disgust—and walked out of the room backwards, very slowly. After they left, I, somewhat bemused, asked my friend what he gave them.

"I gave them each one of these," he said, holding up a one *jiao* note. It's about the equivalent of ten cents—more insulting than throwing a dirty sock at them.

I now understood their reaction and so, a little later, summoning up my best Mandarin, I went to find them, apologized, explained that my friend didn't know Chinese currency, and gave them something more appropriate for their efforts. They laughed and were delighted.

On that visit to Qingdao with my university friend, we had another close encounter with the Chinese criminal underworld. We went to a bar in an old German colonial mansion in Badaguan, with a Canadian friend called Douglas. It was a wonderful place, with wood-panelled walls, antique furniture, and beautiful paintings.

Douglas mentioned in conversation that he speaks Spanish, and the bar-maid evidently overheard this. A little later she approached us and asked, "You speak Spanish?" Douglas confirmed that he does, and she explained that she had a Chinese customer who needed his help. He had received a fax in Spanish which he could not understand. As Douglas spoke both Mandarin and Spanish, he was happy to help.

My other friend and I watched as Douglas was taken over to a corner where four men in raincoats were sitting playing cards, shrouded in smoke. He was with them a long time. When he returned, he looked pale and suggested we leave immediately. We asked what it was all about, and he explained that the fax was from a bank in Bolivia confirming the transfer of millions of dollars to a private account. How many Chinese businessmen have bank accounts in Bolivia, and why?

After I left Hong Kong in 2002, I continued to travel in China throughout the following decade or more. In particular, in my work with Christian Solidarity Worldwide, I travelled often to Yunnan and to the China-Myanmar border, and once to northern China to the border with North Korea, topics which will be covered in later chapters. I also travelled several times to research and document the human rights situation in China, in particular with regard to freedom of religion or belief. For obvious reasons, I cannot go into much detail about these visits, but I never experienced any problems and, to my knowledge, nor did anyone I met. I was never stopped, questioned, interrogated, restricted, or hindered. And while I was never under any illusions about the dangers and repressive nature of the Chinese Communist Party, I was hopeful that as the economy continued to grow and open, society and even politics might further liberalize.

One sign of some openness in China at the time was the existence of an English-language bookstore called the Beijing Bookworm. Admittedly, its clientele were mostly expats or very internationalized Chinese, and it steered clear of any topics directly confronting the regime, but it held regular events with speakers on subjects that were somewhat sensitive, and sold international books that were uncensored. I was invited to give a talk at the Beijing Bookworm on the human rights crisis in Myanmar in about 2006. Sadly, in 2019, the bookstore closed down after fourteen years.

On one visit, not long before Xi Jinping became general secretary of the Chinese Communist Party, I met a group of Chinese human rights lawyers for dinner in a restaurant in Beijing. I was struck by how open and relaxed they were. They told me that within certain limits—and they knew what the red lines were—they were able to defend clients, including religious practitioners and labourers, and defend cases of land rights and property disputes. They knew they were monitored, and periodically subjected to low-level harassment and intimidation, but generally—with some exceptions—they were still able to conduct their work.

They were part of the *weiquan* ("rights protection") lawyers network that had emerged in China in the early 2000s. Teng Biao was one of the earliest promoters of this movement, as a lawyer and lecturer at China University of Political Science and Law in Beijing. In 2003, he became deeply involved in the case of Sun Zhigang, a migrant worker who died from physical abuse in detention in Guangzhou under what was known as "custody and repatriation," an administrative procedure established in 1982 which allowed the police to detain people if they do not have a residence permit (*hukou*) or a temporary living permit (*zanzhuzheng*), and return them to the place where they could legally live or work.

"I wrote an open letter to the National People's Congress to challenge the constitutionality of the regulations and the 'custody and repatriation system,'" Teng recalls. In 2003, "custody and repatriation" was abolished, following Sun's death and Teng's protests. "That was regarded as the start of the *weiquan* movement," Teng claims. "A group of lawyers and human rights defenders tried to use the constitution, laws, and the legal system to promote human rights and the rule of law in China." In the early 2000s, there were, Teng estimates, perhaps only twenty or thirty human rights lawyers throughout China. By 2015, there were several hundred or perhaps even a thousand.

Teng himself took on controversial and dangerous cases, defending Falun Gong practitioners, Tibetans, Uyghurs, and underground Christian churches; defending free speech and religious freedom; and fighting forced evictions, forced abortions, and the death penalty. Among the most high-profile cases, he became involved in providing counsel to the blind rural rights advocate Chen Guangcheng, dissident Hu Jia, and religious freedom defender Wang Bo. He co-founded China Against the Death Penalty as well as the Open Constitution Initiative in 2003, advocating for stronger constitutional protection of human rights.

The movement grew, Teng believes, because, at the time, the Chinese Communist Party was developing a new narrative around "rule by law" and was interested in strengthening the legal profession. More people were qualifying as lawyers; at the same time, the Internet, social media, and the growth of the market economy, in Teng's view, "provided more space for civil society." Compared with both the Mao Zedong and the Xi Jinping eras, "we did have some space" during the early 2000s, Teng argues. "We were able to challenge government officials, we encouraged people to participate in local elections as independent candidates, we organized protests and demonstrations, and we were very active on social media, both *Weibo* and Twitter and Facebook. Even after Twitter and Facebook were blocked in 2009, it was not difficult then to use a VPN and other software to circumvent the 'Great Firewall.' Looking back, it's amazing that we had that space to develop human rights activism."

Nevertheless, there came a point where the regime would no longer tolerate Teng's activities. "I continued to write papers and articles, many of which were very critical of the Communist Party. So I was seen by the government as a dissident. I had moved from a scholar, to a human rights lawyer, to a political dissident," Teng recalls. "Because of my dissenting human rights activities, I was disbarred and put under house arrest from time to time, and fired by my university. My passport was confiscated, and I was even kidnapped by secret police three times, and detained and tortured."

In 2012, Teng co-founded the New Citizens Movement (*Zhongguo Xin Gongmin Yundong*) together with fellow legal scholar Xu Zhiyong, but the following year, while he was in Hong Kong as a visiting scholar, many of his fellow rights activists associated with this movement were arrested. "It was quite clear that if I went back to the Mainland, I would definitely be arrested, so I decided to stay on in Hong Kong for a few months. I then received an invitation from Harvard Law School, and in 2014, I went to the United States—just two weeks before the Umbrella Movement in Hong Kong. In 2015, my wife and daughter were smuggled out of China and joined me."

Nicola Macbean, a lawyer and anthropologist by training, has been at the forefront of engagement with China since the 1980s, and has in-depth, first-hand experience of both the opening and the more recent crackdown. As director of the Great Britain China Centre—a non-departmental public body sponsored by the British Foreign, Commonwealth & Development Office— she spent more than fourteen years pursuing exchanges with China in various policy areas, particularly the rule of law, in an era when, she said, "China was hugely interested in how others did things. It was the era of reform and opening, and there was enormous interest in understanding legal systems and principles."

In 1992, for example—when I was teaching in Qingdao—the Great Britain China Centre hosted the first visit by a Chinese delegation from the Institute of Law, to look specifically at human rights. "It was quite significant," Macbean recalled. "There was a recognition and awareness of international law, the role of lawyers, civil society, an interest in juvenile justice, women's rights. We later provided a summer school for young women in China in 1994, in preparation for the World Women's Conference of 1995, for example."

The delegation visited Northern Ireland during The Troubles, several years before the Good Friday Agreement, because, in Macbean's view, "if we are to engage with China, we must be honest and open about the challenges we face in our own country."

In 1995, Macbean left the Great Britain China Centre and in 2002 she established The Rights Practice, a non-governmental organization (NGO) focused on "bridging the gap between human rights law and everyday practice," and built on the work she had already been doing with Chinese lawyers.

"In the early years, what we were trying to do was to bring about systemic change in the criminal justice system in China," she recalled. "We were trying to help Chinese lawyers and scholars think through how to bring about fresh thinking and reforms. We worked closely with academics and universities, because they had an important role in providing research and policy recommendations to the government. We would discuss juvenile justice (which is not so politically sensitive), pretrial detention, combating torture, the death penalty—and we found people genuinely wanting to make changes. And we saw some policy reforms. Our approach was open and collaborative, largely through workshops and problem-solving, trying to move away from the sterile forums where people talk past each other. For a few years, it was really interesting. But it was only possible when we had a champion—a professor, a senior lawyer—in China, committed to change."

However, the Chinese Communist Party was getting nervous about just how much open exchange of ideas there was and just how wide the space for human rights defenders, civil society activists, citizen journalists, bloggers, religious believers, and dissidents had become.

By 2005, according to Macbean, it was "beginning to get harder" to engage in the ways that had been possible a few years earlier. "We still had opportunities, but we were meeting more resistance. The environment for engagement was becoming more difficult. Officials didn't want foreigners telling them what to do. The atmosphere had moved away from that initial curiosity and desire for reform."

Although, as this chapter will later describe, the crackdown has intensified very severely during the past decade of Xi Jinping's leadership, the early signs were there during the second term of Hu Jintao's presidency.

Charles Parton, a former British diplomat who specializes in China, believes that in the 1990s and early years of the twenty-first century, there was "an implicit deal to focus on building the economy, as the Party was recovering from all the trauma of Tiananmen." Under that unspoken "deal," people were allowed "much more space than before." It followed a traditional pattern that can be seen throughout the Communist Party's history, of loosening and tightening. "By the time of Hu Jintao, there were those in the Party feeling that the opening up was becoming a bit dangerous, that there were elements rising which could threaten their long-term control and survival," he explains. Xi Jinping, Parton adds, has simply been "an accelerator."

Macbean believes the Beijing Olympics in 2008 were "one catalyst for the crackdown," with increasing talk of *weiwen* ("stability maintenance"), but the so-called Arab Spring in the Middle East at the end of 2010—especially Tunisia's Jasmine Revolution which led to the ousting of long-time president Zine El Abidine Ben Ali in January 2011—and other "colour revolutions" marked a real turning point.

"China's leaders were looking around the world, seeing civil society being politicized—not just across the Arab world but also in Georgia, Ukraine, and elsewhere—and this, to them, was a warning sign that if they did not control those who had the capacity to organize and articulate ideas, criticism, [and] dissent, they could face the same challenge," says Macbean.

"Those who have been detained in China in the past decade are often those who were particularly good at articulating problems—those who led the complaints about shoddy construction standards in the aftermath of the Sichuan earthquake in 2008, for example, or those who led public fury at the cover-up of the rail crash in Zhejiang in 2011, which killed at least thirty-two and injured 192. There were quite a lot of protests, strikes, labour unrest, disquiet, and criticism of the government in the early 2000s," she adds.

Under Jiang Zemin and in the first part of Hu Jintao's government, there was, Macbean notes, "a bit more tolerance, a bit more of a sense of trying to 'manage' discontent." The government would let people express grievances—and this was sometimes for positive reasons. "It could be helpful for government to gather information about what people did not like, so that they could respond and put things right. Even when a detainee died in police custody in Yunnan in 2008, and it was claimed that it had been a game of 'hide-and-seek' that went wrong—when it was obvious that the man had been beaten to death—the response from Beijing was to beef up inspections of detention centres, investigate, regulate," she recalls.

"In 2008/09, lawyers would be talking about these issues publicly, on Weibo, on the Internet. They sought to use scandals, cases of abuse strategically as a way to challenge the system," says Macbean. "But it was also challenging the whole basis of the Party's control. Lawyers and liberals were hugely enthusiastic—but the authorities were one step ahead of them."

Arguably, this all culminated in the Charter 08 movement led by dissident and writer Liu Xiaobo. In December 2008, at least 303 Chinese activists, including Liu, issued a petition calling for greater respect for human rights and democratic freedoms in China. In its preamble, Charter 08 referenced the fact that it was a hundred years since China's first Constitution, and that it coincided with the sixtieth anniversary of the promulgation of the Universal Declaration of Human Rights, the thirtieth anniversary of the birth of China's Democracy Wall at which dissident Wei Jingsheng published his "Fifth Modernization" calling for democracy, and the tenth anniversary of China's signing of the International Covenant on Civil and Political Rights.

"Having experienced a prolonged period of human rights disasters and challenging and tortuous struggles, the awakening Chinese citizens are becoming increasingly aware that freedom, equality, and human rights are universal values shared by all humankind, and that democracy, republicanism, and constitutional government make up the basic institutional framework of modern politics," Charter 08 declared.[1] "A 'modernization' bereft of these universal values and this basic political framework is a disastrous process that deprives people of their rights, rots away their humanity, and destroys their dignity. Where is China headed in the 21st century? Will it continue with this 'modernization' under authoritarian rule, or will it endorse universal values, join the mainstream civilization, and build a democratic form of government? This is an unavoidable decision."

The Charter 08 manifesto noted that "the 'Reform and Opening Up' of the late 20th century extricated China from the pervasive poverty and absolute totalitarianism of the Mao Zedong era, and substantially increased private wealth and the standard of living of the common people." It acknowledged that "individual economic freedom and social privileges were partially restored, a civil society began to grow, and calls for human rights and political freedom among the people increased by the day. Those in power, while implementing economic reforms aimed at marketization and privatization, also began to shift from a position of rejecting human rights to one of gradually recognizing them."

However, although China had signed up to some important human rights treaties and promised a "National Human Rights Action Plan," the Charter noted that "this political progress has largely remained on paper . . . The ruling elite continues to insist on its authoritarian grip on power, rejecting political reform. This has caused official corruption, difficulty in establishing rule of law, the absence of human rights, moral bankruptcy, social polarisation, abnormal economic development, destruction of both the natural and cultural environment, no institutionalised protection of citizens' rights . . . and the continuous surge of resentment."

To resolve these tensions and decide "the future destiny of China," the Charter's authors outlined an explicit demand for fundamental freedoms; human rights; principles of economy, democracy, and constitutionalism; and more detailed proposals for what this would look like, including separation of powers, legislative democracy, judicial independence, and human rights guarantees.

The "spring" we had begun to see did not last. Rapidly, the Chinese Communist Party cracked down on the Charter 08 organizers, detaining Liu on December 8, 2008, and formally arresting him the following June for "inciting subversion of state power." On Christmas Day 2009, he was sentenced to eleven years' imprisonment and two years' deprivation of political rights—the latter sentence being ironic, given that he had been demanding political rights denied to China's peoples. The following year, Liu was awarded the Nobel Peace Prize, becoming the first Chinese to receive the award while in China and only the third recipient to be honoured in this way while still in prison. Seven years later, he died of liver cancer, arguably killed by the regime which denied him the right to travel overseas for medical care and only permitted him hospital treatment belatedly.

From 2008 onwards, according to Macbean, controls tightened. "We started to see people who were talking about grievances silenced on social media, no accountability for these disasters—and, ultimately, the response was to stop information coming to light, restrict the Internet, and silence discussion of politically sensitive issues," she recalls.

On November, 15, 2012, a transfer of power began. Xi Jinping assumed office as general secretary of the Central Committee of the Communist Party of China. Four months later, on March 14, 2013, he became president of the People's

Republic of China. As China's sixth leader since the Revolution—following Mao Zedong, Hua Guofeng, Deng Xiaoping, Jiang Zemin, and Hu Jintao—there were hopes that he might be the man who would liberate the country politically. It soon became apparent that not only was that not the case, but that Xi would take China backwards politically and in terms of human rights. Chinese dissident Yang Jianli, founder of Initiatives for China, told me in 2016 that "this is the darkest moment for Chinese human rights in years."

Xi Jinping's first speech to the Politburo as the Communist Party's new general secretary, in January 2013, gave an indication of his ambitions. Xi said, "Most importantly, we must concentrate our efforts on . . . building a socialism that is superior to capitalism and laying the foundation for a future where we will win the initiative and have the dominant position." As Charles Parton points out, Xi specifically uses the word in Chinese, *douzheng*, which means "struggle" or long hard fight, with the goal of gaining *youshi* ("superiority" or "dominance") over the West. No one could accuse him of hiding his plans. The problem was that the rest of the world either did not pay attention to his statements or did not take them seriously. A decade later, we are learning he meant what he said.

The clear turning point was the issuance of the now notorious Document No. 9, alongside two other key documents, prepared even before Xi assumed office and enforced six months before he took power.

Six key documents are essential to understanding the regime's thinking.

The first is the Communique from the Sixth Plenum of the 17th Central Committee of the Chinese Communist Party, in November 2011, which revealed the Party's plans to tighten control over culture, religion, literature, education, the media, the Internet, and society. It strengthens the Party's role in the cultural sphere and charts a much more ideologically oriented path. It is worth noting that Xi Jinping was in charge of drafting this document, which Parton believes "sets out all the forms of tightening that were to occur later."

The second is the above-mentioned and most important Document No. 9—also known as the "Communique on the Current State of the Ideological Sphere"—released in April 2013, which contains explicit proscription of seven acts; namely, promoting Western constitutional democracy, promoting "universal values," promoting civil society, promoting neoliberalism, promoting "the West's idea of journalism," promoting "historic nihilism, trying to undermine the history of the CCP and of New China," and "questioning reform and opening and the socialist nature of socialism with Chinese characteristics." A direct rebuke of

Charter 08 and, in Parton's view, "a complete rejection of universal values set out in the UN Declaration of Human Rights, of which, it should be remembered, some of the principal drafters were Chinese."

The third is Document No. 30, released a year after Document No. 9. It bans the teaching of liberal values in universities and schools. "Never let textbooks promoting Western values enter into our classes," education minister Yuan Guiren said. "Any views that attack or defame the leadership of the party or smear socialism must never be allowed to appear in our universities."[2]

The fourth is China's National Security Law, introduced in 2015, which the UN High Commissioner for Human Rights at the time, Zeid Ra'ad Al Hussein, said has "extraordinarily broad scope" with vague wording that leaves "the door wide open to further restrictions of the rights and freedoms of Chinese citizens, and to even tighter control of civil society."[3]

The fifth key document is the new law governing foreign NGOs, in force from January 2017. The law gave the police unprecedented powers to restrict the work of foreign organizations in China, and limit the ability of domestic groups to receive foreign funding or work with foreign organizations. Foreign NGOs are required to have a Chinese government organization as a sponsor, be registered with the police, and come under the supervision of the Public Security Bureau. Police are empowered to arbitrarily summon representatives of foreign organizations, seize documents, examine bank accounts, and revoke registration. Organizations deemed to be "splitting the state, damaging national unity, or subverting state power" can be shut down by the police, and its staff detained; barred from leaving China; or deported. As Lu Jun, a social activist now in the United States, put it, "The real purpose of the foreign NGO law is to restrict foreign NGOs' activities in China and to restrict domestic rights NGOs' activities by cutting the connection between [the two]. They consider foreign NGOs and some domestic NGOs as a threat to their regime."[4]

And the sixth key document that completes the framework for the crackdown in recent years is the "Outline of Patriotism Education in the New Era," which emerged in November 2019. In an article in *Standpoint*, Parton describes this document as "Xi's manifesto for totalitarianism," with education as "the main tool for achieving it."[5] In the "Opinion on Deepening the Reform and Innovation of the Ideological and Political Theory Courses in Schools in the New Era," issued in June 2019, the Party outlines in detail how the education system—from primary schools, to high schools, to universities—should be guided "to form feelings of loving the party . . . loving socialism . . . loving the collective," so that they can "sincerely support the party's leadership."

Jerome Cohen, one of the world's leading experts on Chinese law, believes Xi Jinping is taking the Communist Party "back to Stalinism." Cohen, a professor at New York University, first began studying China in 1959 and first visited in 1972, when he met Premier Zhou Enlai. In 1977, accompanying Senator Ted Kennedy, he met Deng Xiaoping. Speaking to me from his home in New York, he compares Xi with Stalin rather than Mao Zedong. "There can be no dissent, no collective leadership, and there is total repression. A totalitarian system now exists, with the fear that it inculcates in people. The leadership is not subject to normal criticisms even within its own elite," he argues. "There are some comparisons with Mao— the personality cult, the one-man management, the emphasis on ideology, but he is very different from Mao."

Mao, Cohen notes, "stirred up revolution in his own people, and tried to destroy his own Party because he had lost control of it. Mao created chaos for ten years." Xi's aims are the exact opposite of this. "He is creating the stability of the graveyard. He is not stirring up the masses; he is afraid of the masses being stirred up."

In Cohen's view, Xi "evokes the historical memory of Qin Shi Huang Di, the first Chinese emperor, and the adoption of legalism and harsh punishment for anybody who dissents." He "pretends to be a Confucianist," and revives Confucianism in order to fuel nationalism. "But he is not a Confucianist by any means. If Xi Jinping were a Confucianist, he would listen to his father's advice. Xi Zhongxun wrote that the Party must always allow differences of opinion—and if they do not, then the Party will never achieve its goals. Xi Jinping talks about what a great man his father was, and he wants to build more museums to his father, but he ignores his father's basic wisdom. That is not very Confucianist. He is a legalist."

Fairly quickly, the policies outlined in the key documents mentioned above took effect and the space that had existed for human rights lawyers and defenders, civil society, bloggers, citizen journalists, and dissidents rapidly disappeared—as did individuals, too, literally.

On July 9, 2015, for example, the regime launched a major nationwide crackdown on lawyers and their associates and assistants which became known as "709." Between July 9 and 16, over 120 lawyers were summoned by the police for questioning, and while most were released within hours, thirteen lawyers and legal assistants were jailed. At least eight were charged with subversion, including the prominent lawyers Wang Yu and Li Heping. All were initially held under a form of secret detention, where they were held incommunicado and denied access to legal representation. In total, according to the China Human Rights Lawyers Concern Group, over 317 people were affected by the crackdown, twenty-one of whom were formally arrested and charged.

But Teng Biao emphasizes that the crackdown did not stop with those arrests. "Scores were detained or disappeared for many months or even years. Some are still in prison, like Chen Wuqian, facing subversion charges and severe sentences. And since then, more than seventy human rights lawyers were disbarred."

Lawyers who have been released report having been violently stripped, shackled, and threatened, or kicked, punched, and forced to sit in a chair which would not let their feet touch the ground for up to twenty hours a day, causing extreme pain; others were force-fed medicine and deprived of sleep.

Indeed, according to the Network of Chinese Human Rights Defenders (CHRD), torture is widespread and systematic, including "violent assault, deprivation of proper medical treatment, solitary confinement, deprivation of food . . . and extended shackling of hands and legs."[6] A culture of impunity prevails. In 2020, Safeguard Defenders said that "the torture of detainees by Chinese police and state security remains endemic and goes virtually unchecked and unpunished because of China's failure to make proper legal reforms—reforms that they are required to make because they ratified the UN Convention Against Torture."[7]

In June 2019, lawyer Wang Quanzhang's wife saw her husband for the first time since he had disappeared in 2015. However, she said that he had "completely changed—he was thinner, had lost a tooth, and he seemed to have lost his mind." She wrote, "Quanzhang raised his head and looked me in the eye. His expression was still dull and wooden. He sat there and watched me cry as if I were a stranger and not the wife whom he hadn't seen for four years."[8]

In many cases, torture occurred under a measure known as "residential surveillance at a designated location" (RSDL): itself essentially a form of enforced disappearance, well documented in a report called "The People's Republic of the Disappeared." Individuals typically have no access to legal counsel and no contact with family members: police do not even have to tell their families where they are. RSDL exists outside the detention system and beyond any "normal" oversight or supervision. Under Article 73 of the Criminal Procedure Law (CPL), an individual can be held in a police-designated location for up to six months under

RSDL—although, in practice, they can be held for even longer.

China's most famous lawyer, Gao Zhisheng, disappeared on August 13, 2017, and, at the time of writing, has not been heard from since. "Even his family, his wife, his daughter, and son don't get information from him," Teng notes. "They don't even know whether or not he is still alive."

In 2019, two years after his disappearance, Amnesty International wrote to the Chinese regime demanding answers. "He has been subject to enforced disappearance, raising fear of torture and other ill-treatment," the organization said.

What is especially shocking is that this is the eighth time in twelve years that Gao has "been disappeared." That phrase might look like a grammatical typo, but it is now an established expression in China among lawyers and activists. People don't "disappear"; they are "disappeared" by the regime.

In 2001, Gao was recognized by China's Ministry of Justice as one of the country's top ten lawyers. But his relentless defence of China's persecuted religious minorities—Christians, Falun Gong practitioners, and others—and his courageous open letters to China's leaders appealing to them to respect human rights turned the Chinese Communist Party and its repressive apparatus against him. His law firm was shut down, his licence to practise law was revoked, and he began a cycle of arrest, imprisonment, disappearance, and torture that has continued—with periodic intervals of release—for more than a decade.

In 2006, Gao was charged with incitement to subvert State power. He was given a probation period of five years, during which he was forcibly disappeared at least six times. On one occasion, he was held incommunicado and tortured for six weeks.

In April 2010, Gao disappeared again while visiting his in-laws in Xinjiang. In December 2011, State media reported that Gao had violated the terms of his probation and had been sent to prison for three years. Following his release in August 2014, his wife reported that Gao had been kept in solitary confinement without sufficient light, had lost almost twenty kilograms in weight, and was suffering from malnutrition. Three years later, he was disappeared once more.

In 2016, while recovering from his ordeal in prison, Gao continued to challenge authorities by writing a forty-page document detailing human rights abuses and related social issues in China. In what is believed to be the first comprehensive human rights commentary written by a human rights lawyer still living in China, Gao argues that the situation in China has deteriorated to an unprecedented level. It is, he claims, the "harshest and most brutal political oppression since the end of

Mao Zedong's rule."[9] It was released to the world by three human rights organizations—CSW, together with China Aid, and the Human Rights Foundation—three months after he was disappeared again.

Teng Biao believes Gao was targeted for such severe treatment because he is "the bravest Chinese lawyer." In defending the most sensitive cases, Gao was "very, very outspoken and did not compromise. That's why he was so brutally treated."

In 2017, I had the privilege of meeting his daughter, Grace Gao, when she visited London. In 2009, Grace—together with her mother and brother—managed to escape from China, and she now travels the world courageously speaking out for her father and for human rights in China. "I find myself in a position of picking up the mantle and becoming a human rights defender like my father," she has said. "Truth is power and I will keep speaking it until my father is free."[10]

Gao's family were wise—and fortunate—to have been able to flee China. Not all relatives of lawyers and dissidents are able to. Many human rights defenders face not only the terror of imprisonment and torture, but also the harassment of their spouses, siblings, children, and parents, who endure midnight knocks on the door, persistent threats, constant surveillance, evictions, discrimination at school or university, and detention. Bao Zhuoxuan, the son of lawyers Wang Yu and Bao Longjun, for example, was originally detained with his parents on July 9, 2015. Together with two friends—Tang Zhishun and Xing Qingxian—Bao managed to escape to Myanmar (Burma) but, as Professor Eva Pils, an expert on Chinese law at King's College London, put it, they were "forcibly retrieved back to China from the border region" and he was then held under the strictest surveillance.[11]

In detention, medical treatment is often denied. On April 27, 2016, for example, Zhang Qing, wife of Guo Feixiong (sometimes known as Yang Maodong), a human rights defender and writer, wrote an open letter to the United Nations High Commissioner for Human Rights in which she said that her husband, who has been detained four times since 2005, is seriously ill. "Guo Feixiong's body has been seriously ravaged," she wrote. "He suffers from bleeding in multiple places. I believe that his situation is life-threatening, but he is not receiving the medical examination and treatment that he needs. I am very worried . . . The Chinese government uses prison to not only deprive him of his freedom, but also directly damage his health, letting him face life-threatening risks. His request for a medical assessment and treatment was rejected."[12]

In January 2022, Zhang Qing died from cancer in exile in the United States, and Guo was disappeared after requesting permission to leave China to visit his critically ill wife and children before her death.[13] This is just one of many examples of the regime preventing activists seeing critically ill or dying loved ones.

Of course, the crackdown has not only been against lawyers. "China is the biggest jailer of bloggers and writers," says Teng Biao. "At least 500 or 600 activists or dissidents are in prison now. And these are only the ones recorded, those who are famous—it does not include those human rights defenders not known by the media, nor does it include Falun Gong practitioners, Uyghurs, or Tibetans."

CHRD reports that at the end of 2019, there were 1,106 known cases of "arbitrarily detained prisoners of conscience—individuals in police custody for defending or exercising human rights."[14] From 2017 to 2019, the United Nations Working Group on Arbitrary Detention issued ten opinions that declared twenty human rights defenders had been arbitrarily detained in China. "The Working Group noted in May 2019 that in its 27-year history, it had adopted 89 opinions in relation to China; 82 of the cases found the deprivation of liberty to be arbitrary," CHRD note. Such deprivation of liberty may, under certain circumstances, constitute "crimes against humanity," the Working Group further noted.

Among those arrested recently are activist Chen Bing, sentenced to three-and-a-half years' imprisonment in April 2019 for commemorating the Tiananmen Square massacre; Huang Qi, founder of the human rights website 64 Tianwang, sentenced in July 2019 to thirteen years' imprisonment for "leaking state secrets"; Qin Yongmin, sentenced in July 2019 to thirteen years in prison for "subversion of state power"; journalist Sophia Huang Xueqin, detained in October 2019 for writing about China's #MeToo movement and the protests in Hong Kong; and Cheng Yuan,/ Liu Dazhi and Wu Gejiangxiong, known as "The Changsha Three," detained on July 22, 2019, and held incommunicado without access to lawyers. They were not even dissidents, but civil society activists working for a group called Changsha Funeng, which defended the rights of disadvantaged persons, including the right to health and non-discrimination.

One of the most chilling aspects of Xi Jinping's crackdown is the use of forced televised confessions—a step backwards to Cultural Revolution–era tactics. One of the first to be subjected to this was the Hong Kong-based Swedish national Gui Minhai, who was abducted by Chinese agents from Pattaya, the seaside resort in Thailand, in October 2015. Gui, one of the Hong Kong booksellers who ran the Causeway Bay Books, reappeared in January 2016 in China on State television, "confessing" his involvement in a fatal traffic accident that allegedly occurred more than a decade earlier, and denouncing Sweden, the country which had given him citizenship. He was then held mostly incommunicado in Ningbo, including spending two years in prison and then a few months in some form of house arrest. Swedish diplomats negotiated his release in 2018, and were with him on a train to Beijing when he was abducted again. Two years later, he was sentenced to ten years in jail, for "illegally providing intelligence" to "overseas" parties—a far cry from a traffic accident.

Lawyer Zhang Kai, who had defended Christian churches against the removal and destruction of crosses, was forced to confess on television in February 2016, before his release on bail. He had been detained on August 25, 2015, and accused of "disturbing social order," stealing, and spying, among other crimes. During six months' detention under "RSDL," Zhang was denied contact with his family and his lawyer, but in his televised confession he was filmed admitting to "disturbing social order," "endangering State security," and behaving in an unprofessional manner.

British businessman Peter Humphrey and his wife spent two years in prison, where he was twice forced to record a televised confession which was broadcast on State media. "I was placed into a metal chair with a locking bar over my lap, wearing handcuffs and the orange prison vest, inside the steel-barred cage," he claims.[15] "They drugged me, and CCTV journalists then aimed their cameras at me and recorded me reading out the answers already prepared for me by the police. No questions were asked," he continues. His confession was broadcast on CCTV, before his case had even come to trial.

Humphrey was subjected to a catalogue of abuse: an overcrowded cell, poor sanitary conditions, meagre food rations, sleep deprivation, separation from family, denial of legal representation or consular access for part of the time, and denial of medical treatment for cancer. "The aggregate of these different types of duress adds up to what the UN would describe as torture," he says.

Swedish activist Peter Dahlin was taken in January 2016, in Beijing, and detained for just under a month before being forced to make a televised confession. Working at the time for the Chinese Urgent Action Working Group, Dahlin was accused of being a threat to China's national security.

Dahlin first went to China in 2004, travelling around the country by train as a backpacker for four months after university. "In those days, there was, relatively, more personal freedom. People could talk, at least privately, and I met a number of really interesting people just randomly," he recalls. "One of them was a guy who had been a pilot for a Chinese airline, had been in Germany for training, and had written a personal blog—one that almost no one would read—declaring his belief in multi-party democracy. When he came back to China, he was fired and banned from most jobs other than street cleaning and driving a cab. His story, and those of others I met, left a mark on me."

Dahlin returned to Sweden to take up a job in government, but in 2007, he returned to China, with the intention of working for a small NGO called the Empowerment and Rights Institute. "When I arrived, however, there was not much of an operation at all, and the woman running it had to flee to Canada not long afterwards. But I got to know a few Chinese human rights lawyers, and together, we decided to start a new NGO, to strengthen civil society capacity," he told me in an interview from his new base in Madrid. "We did not really have a name because we knew we could never be public, but it grew over the course of eight years. By the time it all ended in 2016, we were operating across most of Mainland China, in almost every province. We had eleven legal aid stations, as well as our urgent action work supporting human rights defenders facing persecution. It was a pretty sizable operation, and we managed to keep it quiet for a long time. But of course, it also meant basically living in hiding. Almost none of the people we were working with even knew I existed. We had a good risk assessment system."

That risk assessment system endured until 2015—but when the 709 crackdown on lawyers began in 2015, Dahlin knew that the net might close in on him. "Many of the lawyers who were targeted in 2015 were working with us, so, obviously, we realized that the authorities were monitoring us and that the noose was getting tighter," he said.

In early January 2016, Dahlin was due to travel to Thailand for a holiday with his family. But at his girlfriend's insistence, he brought forward the plans due to concerns that they were being monitored and planned to fly out at midnight on January 3. "It had become clear in the previous two weeks that I might not be able to return, so I started preparing. We shredded documents and I carried the waste paper from the shredding machine in sports bags, covering up everything, packing everything up, preparing for the worst," he said.

That night, two hours before he was due to leave for the airport, Dahlin and his girlfriend had just enjoyed their last home-cooked meal in the traditional Beijing courtyard house they shared near Xihai Lake when about twenty Ministry of State Security agents "charged in and started banging on the door."

Dahlin opened the door, to be confronted with a stream of strong lights, film cameras, and the entire courtyard filled with security agents. "They told us that my girlfriend and I were being detained on charges of endangering State security," he recalled.

Dahlin was taken into RSDL, in a location that he subsequently discovered was the same facility where Canadian Michael Kovrig was held. "The roads were closed off by the police, we sped through at about 200 km an hour, and we arrived around 1 a.m. at this facility in the south of Beijing. After twenty-four hours' detention, I was called into an interrogation room," he said.

Held for just under a month, Dahlin was subjected to psychological torture, including sleep deprivation. "You do one interrogation session every night, strapped to a 'tiger chair' (an instrument of severe torture) for six hours, and it is always at night, when you are supposed to be sleeping. Then you spend the other eighteen hours sitting in a suicide-watch padded cell designed for minimum stimulation," he recounted. "You stare at the grey wall, you are not allowed to move around the room, you cannot see anything outside the windows. And although there are two guards watching you at all times, noting any move you make, they are not allowed to speak to you. You start wishing for the interrogation, just to have some communication with another human being."

Dahlin believed—as a foreigner who was well known to the diplomatic community, and with a rare medical condition—that they would not physically torture him, and so he was determined not to provide any information that could endanger others. "I refused to let them decrypt my computer drives, and I did not give them access to my emails, because I knew that there was enough information to put away 1,000 people. We had been working at that point with thousands of people, so there was no way I could ever give them that information. If I did, my colleagues would be screwed for life," he explained. "So instead, I tried to paint a picture for them that was as wide as possible but empty—giving no details, no specifics, no names, claiming that I was just an administrator. I could not lie directly—especially when they did a lie detector test—but I could be as vague as possible in order to protect people."

One day, Dahlin's interrogators brought in a female reporter and cameraman from CCTV. "They did not tell me it was for television. They told me simply that they wanted to record a video to show to the judges," he recalled. "Up until then, I had already written almost daily confession letters. They set everything up, they gave me the lines I had to read, and basically we began acting out this play, with the journalist asking me the questions that had been scripted and me giving her the scripted answers. Behind us were about a dozen people from the Ministry of State Security. It went on for hours, with them directing me what to say, what tone to speak in, what speed to speak with. I only found out once I had been released and deported that it had been broadcast as a 'confession' on State television."

Dahlin's organization, Safeguard Defenders, has published two books on China's use of forced televised confessions—*Scripted and Staged: Behind the scenes of China's forced televised confessions* and *Trial by Media*. Typically, Dahlin explains, confessions fall into three categories—"defend," "deny," and "denounce." The person giving the statement must defend the CCP, deny any mistreatment, and denounce their own "crimes" and the regime's critics.

In November 2018, Humphrey and Dahlin filed a complaint to Britain's broadcasting regulator, Ofcom, about the U.K. licence of CCTV and its international arm China Global Television Network (CGTN), which had just built a large new European headquarters in London. In his complaint to Ofcom, Humphrey writes, "CCTV was working in active collusion with the police and the Chinese state."[16] In 2011, Ofcom had ruled that Iran's *Press TV* was in violation of Britain's Broadcasting Code for airing a forced televised confession and Press TV's licence in the U.K. was revoked. It was this precedent that prompted Humphrey to file a seventeen-page complaint with Ofcom, detailing fifteen violations of the Broadcasting Code by CCTV. Angela Gui, daughter of abducted publisher Gui Minhai, and Simon Cheung, a former employee of the British Consulate-General who had been arrested in China, filed similar complaints to Ofcom subsequently. In 2020, Ofcom found China Global Television Network (CGTN) guilty on *all counts* and revoked its broadcasting licence in the United Kingdom.[17]

At the end of 2019 and the start of 2020, a new virus began to spread across China and then around the world. The origins of COVID-19 are still being debated, but the causes of the pandemic are not in doubt: the mendacity and repression of the Chinese Communist Party are, at least partially, directly responsible.

A study by the University of Southampton argued that if information had been shared and interventions made even "one week, two weeks or three weeks earlier, cases could have been reduced by 66 percent, 86 percent and 95 percent respectively."[18]

The Henry Jackson Society, a London-based think tank, concluded in a report titled "Coronavirus Compensation? Assessing China's Potential Culpability and Avenues of Legal Response" in April 2020 that the Chinese regime had "failed in its obligations" under the International Health Regulations (2005) to report "timely, accurate and detailed public health information" and, furthermore, that this may have been "a deliberate act of mendacity."[19] It argues that "as a direct consequence of the CCP's decision not to share information about the initial stages of the outbreak of Covid-19, the disease spread far faster than it would otherwise have done and reactions by countries globally were hampered." It goes on to note that "time and again throughout the early stages of the initial outbreak, Chinese authorities lied about the situation. They cracked down on doctors discussing the virus, and some were detained by the police." In other words, the regime repressed the truth instead of repressing the virus.

The tragic case of Dr. Li Wenliang is emblematic of the disastrous consequences of the regime's behaviour. On December 30, 2019, Dr. Li—a young ophthalmologist in Wuhan—sent a message to fellow doctors warning about a possible outbreak of an illness that resembled severe acute respiratory syndrome (SARS). According to the medical journal *The Lancet*, "Meant to be a private message, he encouraged them to protect themselves from infection. Days later, he was summoned to the Public Security Bureau in Wuhan and made to sign a statement in which he was accused of making false statements that disturbed the public order."[20] Along with seven others, he was detained for "spreading rumours." *The Lancet* reported that "in a video, he said he was asked to sign a statement agreeing to stop illegal activities or face legal punishment. Nevertheless, Li decided to speak out about his experience because 'I think a healthy society should not just have one voice.'" Tragically, he contracted COVID-19 himself and died on February 7, 2020.

Another doctor, Ai Fen, director of the Emergency Department at the Central Hospital in Wuhan, also disseminated information about COVID-19. In a media interview subsequently, she claimed she received a message from the hospital ordering her not to share information about the virus, and then she was summoned to a disciplinary committee and reprimanded for "spreading rumours" and "harming stability."[21] She subsequently was disappeared.

Citizen journalist Chen Qiushi began reporting from the streets and hospitals of Wuhan on January 23, 2020, but then was disappeared in February. The same happened to Li Zehua and Fang Bin. And former lawyer and Christian human rights defender Zhang Zhan, who posted videos and articles about COVID-19, was arrested and jailed in May 2020.

According to the human rights organization CSW, a source who must remain anonymous for security reasons said, "In early February [2020], when everyone in Wuhan tried to flee out [sic], human rights defender Zhang Zhan travelled the opposite direction towards Wuhan to report on the crisis. Her videos and articles were posted on Twitter and YouTube, both of which are blocked in China, and other social media platforms. She questioned whether the authorities' response to the epidemic infringed on human rights. She spoke up for Dr. Li Wenliang and questioned whether the severity of the outbreak had been covered up. She was deeply concerned about those ordinary, voiceless Wuhan citizens who face destitution, having lost livelihoods in COVID-19."[22] In prison, Zhang began a long hunger strike that has led to grave concerns about her health.

Zhang once worked as a lawyer, but her licence has been suspended due to her human rights activism. She was previously arrested in Shanghai in September 2019, and spent sixty days in detention for her support of pro-democracy protesters in Hong Kong. She suffered severe mistreatment during her previous detention, and was twice forced to be checked for mental health issues, for which she went on a four-day hunger strike. She also spent seven days in solitary confinement, during which her hands and feet were tied to the floor, making it impossible to go to the toilet.

She once wrote, "If all that remains in life is fear, then all I can do is to fight fear repeatedly until I cross it. Because if not, all emotions outside of fear are masks. If I were to face God, I would pray sincerely for [the perpetrators] and ask Him to forgive their sins, not because I'm a moral person. Rather, it's that I have to do it."[23]

The contrast between Zhang Zhan, Gao Zhisheng, Teng Biao, and other courageous activists in China, and the Chinese Communist Party is like night and day. The activists are armed with nothing other than good hearts; in some cases, a knowledge of the law and an ability to communicate well using various media—facing a regime with all the tools of torture and repression, the world's largest army and the world's second-largest defence budget. Yet it is Xi Jinping and his regime that seems to be in a position of fear and insecurity. As Teng Biao told me, "the Communist Party is facing a crisis—a political crisis, a conflict between the people and the government, and a loss of trust. More and more people do not believe the Party's propaganda. It likes to show that it is very powerful, very confident, but actually it has a sense of crisis. They worry about the political system."

Xi Jinping has ended term limits, so he could be in charge for life. He has abolished collective leadership and revived a cult of personality around himself that China has not seen since the Mao era. He has purged rivals, failed to name any successor, and added Xi Jinping Thought as an appendix to the Constitution itself. "No one in the Party seems to be able to challenge Xi Jinping," concludes Teng Biao.

While the Communist Party has always been repressive, the human rights crisis in China today is a far cry from the situation in the country when I used to walk through the Forbidden City in the moonlight and into the floodlights of Tiananmen Square. Today, China is engulfed in darkness—politically and spiritually—even if the economic lamps still blaze. And as Xi Jinping turns against private enterprise, even that is now in question.

Peter Dahlin believes that with hindsight, the Chinese Communist Party's era of relative relaxation in the 1990s and the first decade of the twenty-first century "was never intended to be permanent." The crackdown today, he suggests, "was always the intention of the Party" and that while it is partly due to Xi Jinping, it also represents the Party's mentality. "One of my ex-colleagues from China who knows the Party well believes that the decision to loosen up on personal freedoms over the 1990s and early 2000s was solely in order to strengthen the economic takeoff, and that it had always been the intention of the Party elders to clamp down once China reached a certain level of economic growth and strength. They want to reassert control. But Xi Jinping has sped up this process, as a result of his personal convictions. It was always going to happen; it has just happened faster because of Xi."

The father of China's democracy movement, Wei Jingsheng, agrees. "The Chinese Communist Party is a sinful system, and the disaster it has brought to China is getting deeper and deeper," he told me in a call from his home in Washington, D.C. "The so-called Chinese model has become very unstable—on the one hand, the Party is very corrupt, and on the other hand, people are very dissatisfied. The regime realized that you cannot control society if you only control politics and not the economy. So they face a choice: reform the system and establish democracy, or go back to the Mao Zedong era. The Party is afraid of losing power, and so Xi Jinping is reverting to Mao Zedong's playbook."

Although space for civil society has almost disappeared in recent years,

Dahlin believes it will never completely vanish. "They can imprison human rights defenders, torture them, but you can never kill off civil society completely," he argues. "You can marginalize it, drive it underground, but unless you want to cut off the country from the rest of the world completely, you cannot destroy it. It is much harder to run projects in China, it is more difficult to get funding to groups in China, and it is much harder to communicate with activists in China. People are more scared. But it is still possible to do something."

It is time for the rest of the world to wake up to the horror that is engulfing China and, in the words of the Chinese classic work the *Book of Han*, completed in AD 111 and so often quoted by both Mao Zedong and Deng Xiaoping, "seek truth from facts."

CHAPTER 4

CHRISTIANITY UNDER FIRE

THE INTENSIFICATION OF PERSECUTION OF CHRISTIANS

"Chinese Christians are like birds in a cage," explained the elderly pastor sitting next to me in his home in Beijing. "Within the cage, there is freedom to fly around. But if Christians escape from the cage in search of real freedom, they are hunted down, captured, and put in a smaller cage. Often their wings are broken."

That was how Allen Yuan Xiangchen, one of the best-known house church leaders in China, described the Chinese regime's approach to religion when we met in Beijing in 1997. The size of the cage may have varied over the years, according to political era and, to a certain extent, provincial authorities' attitudes, but ever since 1949, Christians in China have been caged, unable to fly freely.

I met Allen Yuan through serendipity. In preparation for this particular visit to China, for research into the state of Christianity in the country, I spoke with a number of experts and Chinese Christians. One exiled Chinese Christian gave me the names of several house church Christians she recommended I try to meet. Separately, Tony Lambert, a former diplomat and author of two excellent books on the topic—*The Resurrection of the Chinese Church* and *China's Christian Millions*—suggested Allen Yuan, but also recommended that I ask Pastor Yuan about another house church leader, Moses Xie.

On arrival in Beijing, I contacted some of my lower-key Chinese Christian friends. I decided to leave Allen Yuan until the end of the trip because I thought that, although he receives many foreign visitors, it was extremely likely that his home was monitored. Therefore, if I met him at the end rather than the beginning, it was less likely that my visit would be jeopardized and the security of others I met endangered if I was picked up.

I met with one couple, and a friend of theirs, for dinner in a restaurant one evening. They were wonderful—hospitable, generous, kind—and they invited me to their home the following evening.

When we met the following day, they told me that we would go to the home of the husband's parents. I had no idea who the parents were, but was happy to fit in with the plan.

We reached the apartment, and an elderly couple greeted us. As we began a conversation, it became apparent that the elderly man—the father of my new friend—was a very senior house church leader. Over dinner, the elderly man left the room briefly. As I had not yet caught his name, I took the opportunity to enquire.

"Xie Moshan," they replied.

Something in my brain clicked and I remembered Tony Lambert's request that I ask Allen Yuan about Moses Xie. Moses Xie, Xie Moshan, it could be the same person, I thought. And yet, conscious of sensitivity and security, I did not want to ask outright. So when he returned, I asked of the elderly gentleman before me this simple question, in Chinese:

"Do you know of someone who calls himself Moses Xie?"

With a smile, he said, "*Wo shi* Moses Xie"—"I am Moses Xie."

It was a spine-tingling moment. I explained to him that Tony Lambert had asked me to ask Allen Yuan about the health of Moses Xie, and there I was with Moses Xie before I had met Allen Yuan.

He smiled again.

"Would you like to meet Allen Yuan?" he asked.

I confirmed I would, and Moses Xie made the connection.

When I then met Pastor Yuan, he told me that the previous day he had baptized several hundred people. His church had hired a public swimming pool in a nearby park.

"Weren't you watched?" I asked.

He looked at me as if I had asked a silly question, which I had.

"Of course we were. The Public Security Bureau officers were all around," he replied.

I asked what happened.

"I used the opportunity to explain to the officers the meaning of baptism, why it is important, the meaning of the Gospel, and why they, too, needed it!"

In Pastor Yuan's home, I met other inspiring, courageous Christians who worked with him. One of them was an elderly lady named Mabel, in her early eighties, who told me that she made regular journeys to Tibet to encourage a tiny but growing group of Christians in Lhasa. She described how she takes the train from Beijing to Chengdu, in Sichuan Province, adjusts to the altitude, then flies to Tibet. I asked who goes with her.

"Usually no one," she said. "Most of the people I ask are too afraid to come."

Allen Yuan was one of the giants of the Chinese underground church. Together with Watchman Nee and Wang Ming-dao, as well as Samuel Lamb (Lin Xiangao)—whose huge rabbit warren of a "house church" in Guangzhou I was also privileged to visit—he was one of the unregistered church's most senior leaders and greatest heroes. In 1958, for example, aged forty-four, he was arrested—and imprisoned for twenty-two years. He was sent to Heilongjiang Province, near the Russian border, to labour in rice fields. In his testimony, which he gave me in person, he writes:

"During the Cultural Revolution I did not receive any letters from my family for ten years. It was extremely cold there in the labour camp, with hard work and a poor supply of food. But praise the Lord that I never once got sick in the 22 years there. Though I was thin, I came back alive whereas many died in between. For 22 years I did not have a Bible, nor did I meet with other Christians."

Despite such hardship, Pastor Yuan kept his faith throughout:

"Two songs continued to encourage me. One was from Psalm 27, and the other was 'The Old Rugged Cross.' We had to work nine hours a day and were allowed a break in the middle. Many would go to their cells to smoke during their break. As I did not smoke, I usually stood outside and sang those choruses again and again."

I asked if he had a message for the wider world.

He nodded.

"Many friends come and ask what they could do to help the Chinese church. The answer is in this one word: Pray!"

That was back in 1997, but his words are as relevant now as they ever were.

The attitude of the Chinese Communist Party towards religion has always been hostile. Ideologically, the Party is atheist, and demands absolute loyalty to its teachings. Inevitably, it is therefore suspicious of any alternative idea or belief that commands a following, and it is nervous of any large gathering of people that it does not control. However, its approach towards religion in general—and Christianity in particular—has varied, from control, co-option, and coercion to attempts at elimination, from some relaxation to outright repression.

When the Communist Party took power in 1949, it started to expel foreign missionaries. In 1950, the regime forced Protestant leaders to form the State-controlled Three-Self Patriotic Movement, based on the "three-self" principles of self-governing, self-supporting, and self-propagating. A few years later, Catholics were forced to establish an equivalent State-controlled body, the Catholic Patriotic Association, which was not recognized by the Vatican and was therefore out of communion with Rome.

Premier Zhou Enlai tried to be reassuring, presenting the new structure as an opportunity for co-operation, telling Christians, "You are theists and we are atheists, but we are not trying to open up a debate on atheism and theism with you. We believe that materialists and idealists can co-exist and co-operate with one another on a political level, and that we should practice mutual respect. It is our sincere hope that between us, we can follow a path of co-operation . . . Our principle is 'No commonality of views shall be enforced, but we shall respect one another and be flexible.'"[1]

But that persuasive approach did not last. Less than a year later, on April 19, 1951, the Party launched the Denunciation Movement, aimed at the churches. Leading Chinese Protestant Christians were forced to denounce former missionary friends and fellow Chinese Christians. The situation grew worse, and the Anti-Rightist Movement that followed the 1957 Hundred Flowers Campaign saw serious persecution of Christians. Many churches were closed down. In Beijing, sixty-five churches were reduced to four, and in Shanghai, only twenty-three churches out of 200 remained open.

This was just a precursor to the Cultural Revolution. From 1966 until 1979, Christianity in China was effectively banned. Churches were closed, Christians were sent to labour camps, and Bibles were burned. "For the 13-year period from 1966 to 1979," writes Tony Lambert, "institutional Christianity was completely eradicated in China."[2]

Bishop Ding Guangxun—who later became president of the Three-Self Patriotic Movement and its sister State-run organ the China Christian Council—was president of the seminary in Nanjing when the Cultural Revolution broke out. He told me when I met him in 1997 how Red Guards took over the seminary and gave him and his family four hours to leave their home. His home then became the headquarters of the Nanjing University Red Guards, while the seminary became the base of the local middle school's Red Guards. Bishop Ding was assigned to a class that was studying Mao Zedong Thought, and to a farm to do physical labour. "By all human reckoning, Christianity, perhaps for the fourth time in Chinese history, was breathing its last breath. What we were blind to was that when we were weak and dying, life was in the offing," he told a gathering in the Archbishop of Canterbury's Lambeth Palace in 1982.[3]

Indeed, while Mao and the Red Guards shut down institutional Christianity, courageous Chinese Christians secretly kept the faith. Pastors like Allen Yuan never accepted the Three-Self Patriotic Movement in the first place, as they rejected coming under the authority of the Communist Party. "Christ is the head of the church, no one else," Pastor Yuan emphasized to me. "Not even a pastor is head of his church." So how could an atheist state be?

In 1978, as China was recovering from the chaos and nightmare of the Cultural Revolution and beginning to open up following the death of Mao, Bishop Ding and other clergy were rehabilitated, and he was appointed president of the Three-Self Patriotic Movement and the China Christian Council, positions he held until his retirement in 1996.

Bishop Ding, who died in 2012, was a divisive and controversial character. For many in the unregistered house church movement, he was regarded as a sell-out, someone who was part of the Communist Party regime. He sat as a delegate in the National People's Congress from 1964 to 1993, and on its Standing Committee and Foreign Affairs Committee from 1983 until 1993. What was China's leading Christian doing sitting on such important Communist Party bodies?

On the other hand, some believe he was a moderating force with good motives who did what he could to speak out within the system.

In 1988, for example, he wrote a letter to the Religious Affairs Bureau, in which he said, "I feel that the government is really too involved in too many matters which belong to the church itself . . . We have seen Communist Party members taken out of the Religious Affairs Bureau and put into churches as atheistic church leaders."[4]

The following year, surprisingly and boldly, he described the student hunger strikes as a "patriotic activity," urged the government to "carry on a dialogue with the students as soon as possible," rejoiced that "Christians are making their presence felt in these demonstrations," and declared that "we wholeheartedly affirm the student demonstrations."[5]

Premier Li Peng—known as the "Butcher of Beijing" for having ordered the Tiananmen massacre—reportedly described Bishop Ding's remarks as counter-revolutionary,[6] although Bishop Ding denies this. "I do not think he made any comment," Bishop Ding told me. "At the time, many statements were made. I doubt whether he even noticed mine. If he did, my comments could not be described as counter-revolutionary. I was not speaking against the revolution or against the government. I was simply speaking in support of the students against corruption."

In July 1992, Bishop Ding again spoke out, calling for an end to the "wind of suppression" against unregistered churches. The following year, notably, he was not reappointed to the National People's Congress.[7]

Yet despite speaking out in support of the student protests, he was silent in the aftermath of the Tiananmen massacre in 1989. There are those who are profoundly suspicious that Bishop Ding was secretly a Communist Party member, a wolf in sheep's clothing. I put this question directly to him, and he denied it. "I have never been a member of the Communist Party, or any party, and I never will be," he told me. "I have never wanted to be, and I think the Party has never wanted me as its member. To be a Communist one has to be unreligious, atheist. So I cannot be a member. Even without such a stipulation, I would not want to be involved in Party politics."

When I met Bishop Ding in his home in Nanjing, he took a moderate view about the unregistered house churches. He told me he was "sympathetic to those Christians who don't like to come to the big churches. They prefer to read the Bible and pray together in a small group, in their home. I don't think we should compel them to disband and go to the official churches."

But, he defended the requirement that they should register. "The government has declared that home-church Christian groups can obtain registration if they fulfill six requirements. These six are very easy to fulfill: they must have a fixed meeting-place, a named leader, a committee, a regular legal income, and a set of bylaws about the organization," he said. "To join the Three-Self Patriotic Movement is not a requirement. Groups not affiliated to the Three-Self Patriotic Movement can be registered." And, he added, registration would be protection against persecution, because then such churches would be legal, even though—by his own admission—in some provinces, "ultra-leftist thinking" has led to continued repression. "That is what I object to. We should not be afraid to register. We would like every underground church to be above ground."

On the surface, Bishop Ding's position sounds reasonable—except for the fact that by registering, and providing all the information required, churches then open themselves up totally to the regime's monitoring, interference, and control. And, as events in the past decades or more have shown, being registered offers no protection whatsoever if the regime decides to crack down.

On December 4, 1994, 200 plain clothes police entered Gangwashi Church, one of the two largest State-approved Protestant churches in Beijing, and physically forced the pastor, Reverend Yang Yudong, from the pulpit. Yang was known as an evangelical within the State-controlled church, and had seen his congregation grow from 500 to 2,000. The authorities clearly disliked this, and replaced him with a hardline apparatchik called Reverend Yu Xin-li.

Meeting Reverend Yu as I did in Beijing in 1997 felt nothing like meeting a pastor. It felt much more like meeting a Politburo member. We sat in a large meeting room, with several other church officials present.

"You may ask me anything you wish," Yu said, but his expression looked uninviting, even hostile.

"But before you ask me questions, I want to know why the West constantly criticizes China," he added. "You always criticize China for human rights, religious freedom, Tibet. But you, in the U.K., you have your Northern Ireland problem and China does not comment on that."

Then, unprompted, he declared, "The Communist Party is the best party for China."

I was taken aback. I had not uttered a word, yet was confronted with this propaganda diatribe. I was told later by a trusted Christian friend who had worshipped at Gangwashi that Yu's lecture had not been for my benefit, but for the officials sitting alongside him, to prove to them his loyalty to the Party line.

Alongside the State-controlled church bodies, the Amity Foundation based in Nanjing provokes mixed feelings among many. In 1997, I visited its offices and printing press, which is approved to print Chinese-language Bibles. Working with orphans, the disabled, and the poor, and in rural development, the foundation claims to be a non-governmental organization, but operates strictly within the sphere of government control. One of its senior representatives whom I met on that visit was honest about both their mission and their limitations. "I believe everybody needs to believe something," she said, and people are searching for ideas to fill the void in their hearts left by the death of Marxism. "People are curious, and Amity's work is effective and makes people ask about our faith and the purpose for our work. But in China, there are restrictions. We cannot preach in public, only in the church. We can invite people to church, but we cannot preach outside the church."

Throughout the 1990s and the first decade of the twenty-first century, the picture for Christians in China was complex and varied. The expression "whatever you say about China is true somewhere in China" was an accurate one. In some parts of the country, there was some relaxation, while in other places, the situation for the church was more repressive. Much depended on the attitudes of the provincial authorities. In general, the authorities tended to turn a blind eye to small gatherings of Christians in apartments, but grew more alarmed by larger public worship outside the registered churches. Yet even in this respect, there were some unregistered churches whose presence and size were tolerated for a time. Shouwang Church in Beijing grew to a congregation of 1,000, Beijing's Zion Church attracted 1,500 worshippers, Living Stone Church in Guizhou reached 700, Early Rain Church in Chengdu had about 800 members, and Golden Lampstand Church in Linfen, Shaanxi Province reached 50,000 members. All these churches were, for a time, very visible—with either their own buildings or rented office space—and yet totally unregistered.

As with every other aspect of human rights, however, all this changed when Xi Jinping came to power. In April 2016, he made a speech to senior Communist Party officials at a meeting on religion, in which he said that "religious groups . . . must adhere to the leadership of the Communist Party of China." Party members must be "unyielding Marxist atheists" who "resolutely guard against overseas infiltrations via religious means."[8] Religious affairs, it appeared, was no longer going to be governed at a local or provincial level, but by the centre and from the very top.

One Chinese Christian interviewed for this book confirms this. "Religion is no longer a provincial or regional matter. Policy is clearly co-ordinated at the top level since Xi Jinping took power. And it affects every single house church today," he says. "I believe the regime did a 'SWOT' analysis of the strengths, weaknesses, opportunities, and threats the churches pose—they did their homework. Their main consideration was the potential threat to their power. Religion has always been regarded as a threat, particularly because of overseas connections and support which different religions—Christianity, Islam, Buddhism, Falun Gong—have."

One of the developments the Party appeared to have become concerned about is the fact that a growing number of their own members were embracing the Christian faith. In May 2015, the Party's Central Commission for Discipline Inspection published a newsletter that stated that some Party members had "turned to religion , . . attracting serious concern, to the extent that it now falls within the purview of disciplinary work."[9] That same year, Party authorities in Zhejiang Province warned that applicants for Party membership would be rejected if they were found to have "embraced religious beliefs," while existing members would be required to submit "a written promise rejecting religion beliefs."[10]

Perhaps the most striking and visible sign of the crackdown on Christians—which arguably is the most severe since the Cultural Revolution—is the destruction of thousands of crosses and hundreds of churches. The campaign began in Zhejiang in 2014 and 2015, but spread to other provinces as well. On July 24, 2015, Catholic bishop of Wenzhou Vincent Zhu Weifang led a protest outside government offices, and three days later circulated a public letter alleging that the authorities' campaign had become "a naked attempt to rip down the crosses atop every single church."[11]

Cross destructions were followed by church closures and demolitions. Most dramatic was the dynamiting of the Golden Lampstand Church in Shaanxi in January 2018, along with the forced closures of Living Stone Church in Guiyang in 2017, Zion Church in Beijing in October 2018, Early Rain Church in Chengdu in December 2018, and Shouwang Church in Beijing in January 2019, among many others. Some pastors were arrested, prosecuted, and imprisoned—notably Living Stone Church's pastor, Yang Hua, was sentenced to two and a half years in prison on January 6, 2017, and Early Rain Church's pastor, Wang Yi, and his wife, Jiang Rong, were arrested along with over one hundred members of the congregation in December 2018. A year later, the day after Christmas Day, Wang Yi was sentenced to nine years in prison.

Wang Yi, who was previously a legal scholar at Chengdu University and a pioneering attorney before founding Early Rain Church and becoming a full-time pastor, was a persistent critic of the Chinese Communist Party regime. In 2004, he was listed as one of the "50 Most Influential Public Intellectuals of China" by *Southern People Weekly*. The following year, he converted to Christianity and was baptized, and in 2006, together with other Chinese Christian human rights lawyers, he met president George W. Bush at the White House to discuss religious freedom in China. In 2008, he founded the church, and three years later was ordained as a pastor. Every year he held a service to commemorate the Tiananmen Square massacre, saying, "Many people ask us why we pray for June 4th as it is politics. I say I didn't see politics, I saw people being killed, an injustice, people being oppressed and suffering. In a politicized society, just maintaining freedom of conscience is already considered political."[12]

In the summer of 2018, Early Rain Church organized a petition in protest at the intensifying crackdown on Christians, and Wang Yi's signature was alongside the signatures of over 400 pastors from across China. On October 28 that year, he preached a sermon in which he said the regime was launching "a war against the soul," across Xinjiang and Tibet, and throughout China. But, he warned defiantly, "they have established for themselves an enemy that can never be detained, can never be destroyed, will never capitulate, nor be conquered: the soul of man . . . so they are destined to lose this war and are doomed to fail."[13]

Strikingly, in a speech to the Foreign Correspondents' Club in Hong Kong in March 2019, the United States Ambassador-at-Large for International Religious Freedom Sam Brownback used very similar language, arguing that "It seems that the Chinese government is at war with faith. It's a war they will not win. The Chinese Communist Party must hear the cry of its people for religious freedom."[14]

In an interview with me in January 2022, Ambassador Brownback shared the back story. "A day or two before I was going to leave Washington, D.C., for this visit, I was out jogging in front of the U.S. Capitol and the thought hit me: "China is at war with faith. It's a war they will not win." I stopped. My speech had been approved. I had been trying to give this speech for six months and several times it was turned down in the system, for different reasons: 'We're afraid of bad relations, you have to pull it' . . . Then, finally, they allowed me to go ahead; the speech was vetted, and it was all approved. But that line was not in it," he told me. "But I felt it was a line from the Holy Spirit. And so I added it without getting it approved in the Administration. As a former senator and governor, I am not used to having somebody else approve what I say, but I was a member of the Administration and I was supposed to. Anyway, I got to Hong Kong, I met the U.S. consul-general, I handed him the speech, and I said, 'Guys, I did not get that line approved and it's a real zinger.' But the consul-general said that it seemed fine. So I said, 'Okay, I have got his approval. I will go ahead and do it.'"

Ambassador Brownback arrived at the Foreign Correspondents' Club—a place I know well, as a former, and very regular, member—to find "everybody's nervous, like cats on a hot tin roof, fidgety. You could sure feel the tension in the room." That night, Ambassador Brownback had been invited to dinner at which thirty guests were expected. Only he and his host and one other guest showed up. "It was after my speech came out, and the rest were too scared that this could impact their business, their travel, their safety, so they did not want to be seen anywhere near me. But when I returned to Washington, D.C., the Secretary of State's senior advisors told me it was one of the best speeches of the Administration. I feel honoured to have given that speech because it opened up a new battle front that needed to be opened."

In December 2018, Wang Yi published a 7,300-word manifesto titled *Meditations on the Religious War*, and urged Chinese Christians to engage in civil disobedience. He accused the Communist Party of instituting "Caesar worship" by elevating Xi Jinping to the status of a Roman emperor or an Egyptian pharaoh. Such an ideology, he wrote, is "morally incompatible with the Christian faith and with all those who uphold freedom of the mind and thought."[15]

Anticipating his likely arrest and imprisonment, he also wrote an open letter, titled *My Declaration of Faithful Disobedience*, which he instructed his church to publish within forty-eight hours of his arrest. Wang Yi, along with one hundred church members, was arrested on December 9, 2018, and tried and sentenced a year later. In his letter he writes, "I believe that this Communist regime's persecution against the church is a greatly wicked, unlawful action. As a pastor of a Christian church, I must denounce this wickedness openly and severely."[16]

A former member of Guiyang's Living Stone Church, who wishes to remain anonymous, told me that the church was one of the earliest targets because it had grown so rapidly in a very short space of time, and that had alarmed the Communist Party. "It was a young church, founded only in 2009 with just four or five families—about twenty people. But within just a couple of years, it had grown to 700 people, and that drew the government's attention," he says. The church had purchased a venue and invested at least five million renminbi in the property. "It was probably the first time a house church in Guizhou had been in a position to afford its own property. It was quite a substantial amount of money, and it meant that the church had financial power and had become influential. That alarmed the government."

Initially, the authorities urged Living Stone Church to join the Three-Self Patriotic Movement but, as its former member told me, "most church members and the pastors could not accept this, so we refused several times. That's why the government then began to harass us, threaten us, try to destroy us. The harassment and threats began in 2013, and finally in December 2015, the church was closed down and the pastors and others were arrested and imprisoned."

Living Stone Church, like Early Rain Church in Chengdu, was targeted both because of its rapid growth, and because its pastors were influential in the house church movement. "The two pastors played a very active role in supporting the struggle of other house churches across the country, helping other Christians to face persecution," says one Chinese Christian friend. "They travelled all over the country, especially to rural areas, to support house churches."

Today, all those from Living Stone Church who were jailed have been released, and far from being cowed, they continue their activities, but in smaller groups. "The police continue to visit them constantly, and monitor them closely," a former church member says.

New regulations have also been imposed to tighten control of religious affairs. On February 1, 2018, revised Regulations on Religious Affairs—first introduced in 2005—came into effect. According to Christian Solidarity Worldwide (CSW), these regulations "strengthen state control over religious activities in China," close down the "grey area" in which unregistered churches had until then been tolerated in some areas, and increase pressure on unregistered churches to register or disband. According to China Aid Association, "non-government churches, called 'house churches,' have been outlawed completely. Many of them are ordered to join the official church system and submit to government censorship. Often, authorities inform these church leaders that their congregations are 'illegal' and accuse the Christians who attend these churches of various crimes."

Children are now prohibited from participating in religious activities. "No children under eighteen years old; no Communist Party member; no students at college, high school, or elementary school; no Youth League member; no military—these are known as the 'five forbiddens,' the categories forbidden from even coming close to a church building," says Bob Fu, founder and president of China Aid.

"Millions of Chinese Christian children have been forced to sign Communist Party forms renouncing their faith, falsely proclaiming that they were misled into believing Christianity," Fu adds. "Parents are threatened by the police, warned that their jobs, position, social benefits, even retirement benefits could be removed if their child doesn't sign a renunciation of their Christian faith. The same applies to teachers—they are banned from faith. Every church is mandated to install facial recognition cameras. Of course, there is the massive social credit system—being a Christian is a liability for your social credit, which can affect small, mundane activities, even including recharging your subway ticket card. It's crazy."

Churches have been prohibited from livestreaming services online, according to CSW, and, at the end of 2021, new guidelines were released to regulate online religious activity, banning foreigners from preaching online, prohibiting overseas organizations and individuals from sharing religious information online, and requiring Chinese organizations and individuals to seek a permit from the authorities to view online religious materials. The scope of these regulations is deliberately broad, including text messages, images, audio, and video messages—not only websites. There are still many unanswered questions, but overall, it is another bleak development in a series of new measures restricting religious freedom. We are already seeing Christians withdrawing from social media chat groups. Others are adopting a "wait and see" approach. The offline space has already been shut down; now the virtual space is being eliminated.

On top of this, State-controlled churches are under pressure to display portraits of Xi Jinping and Communist Party propaganda slogans alongside—or even sometimes instead of—religious images; sing the Communist Party anthem at the start of services; and install surveillance cameras at the altar to monitor worshippers. As China Aid notes, the regime "intends to bring Christianity under the full control of the government."[17]

The "most chilling thing," according to Fu, is a plan by the Chinese Communist Party for a new translation of the Bible. Another Chinese Christian, who wishes to remain anonymous, confirmed this. "The regime wants to have a different 'Chinese-style' theology, a CCP version of the Bible," he says. Wang Yang, chairman of the Chinese People's Political Consultative Conference, which oversees ethnic and religious affairs, has called for "a comprehensive evaluation of the existing religious classics, aiming at contents which do not conform to the progress of the times."

Two of the most recent threats to Christians, according to a Chinese Christian, are the targeting of Christian education—Christian schools or homeschooling—and the accusation of "terrorism" against some Christians. "Some Christians have been jailed for trying to give their children a Christian education. And some Christians have been accused of illegally possessing materials which promote terrorism, particularly materials in support of the Hong Kong pro-democracy protests. The regime is trying to frame Christianity as not a non-violent religion, and this is deeply disturbing."

One case that illustrates this is the arrest of Zhao Weikai, leader of Xuncheng Reformed Church in Taiyuan, Shanxi Province, in July 2021. Charged with "unlawfully possessing items that advocate terrorism or extremism," this Christian leader was denied access to his lawyers on the grounds that his case involved suspicion of "endangering national security." Two months previously, police raided Zhao's home without a warrant and confiscated his computer and books. Those close to him described the charge of advocating terrorism or extremism as "beyond imagination."[18]

Fu says the persecution of Christians is now "across the board, totally legalized and under one banner—what the Party calls the 'Sinicization' of religion." In the past, under Jiang Zemin and Hu Jintao, the situation varied, and while persecution was severe in certain regions, life for Christians in some other areas was more relaxed. "Hu Jintao and Jiang Zemin tolerated the existence of urban large Christian churches, even Wang Yi's Early Rain Covenant Church," says Fu. "But now, all these large churches have been declared illegal, and even the government-sanctioned churches are persecuted if they don't totally comply with the 'Sinicization' campaign."

One pastor, Fu notes, was sentenced to seven years in jail for refusing a Communist Party flagpole in the church car park, while another pastor from the State-approved church was sentenced to twelve years for a similar crime. Female Christian evangelists in Guizhou have been sentenced to twelve years in prison for setting up an offering box, while another Christian woman in Shenzhen has been sentenced to six years for producing audio Bible players in Shenzhen. Pastor Joseph Gu Yuese, a member of the National Standing Committee of the Chinese Christian Council, and chairman of the Three-Self Patriotic Movement in Zhejiang Province, was stripped of his position and title and detained on January 27, 2016. Pastor Gu—who led the largest church in Hangzhou, Chongyi Church, had written letters to the national Three-Self Patriotic Movement complaining about the destruction of crosses—remains under house arrest today.

Two days after Gu Yuese's arrest, another State-sanctioned church pastor, Li Guanzhong, was detained. On February 25, 2016, Pastor Bao Guohua and his wife, Xing Wenxiang, were sentenced to fourteen and twelve years' imprisonment, respectively, for "corruption" and "gathering people to disturb social order."[19] And on March 9, 2016, Pastor Zhang Chongzhu was charged with "stealing, spying, buying or illegally providing state secrets or intelligence to entities outside China."[20] All of these individuals had, in fact, been arrested due to their opposition to the removal and destruction of crosses. Indeed, according to China Aid, over 500 Christians in Zhejiang alone were detained, more than 130 beaten and assaulted, and over 1,000 punished in other ways for protesting against the cross demolitions.

On April 14, 2016, in Henan Province, it was reported that Ding Cuimei, wife of Pastor Li Jiangong, was buried alive while protesting against the destruction of a church. Three days earlier, six house church leaders were arrested in Xinjiang, charged with "gathering a crowd to disturb social order."[21]

The persecution has not eased since 2016. In its submission to the U.K. Conservative Party Human Rights Commission's inquiry into human rights in China in 2020, China Aid notes that whereas in 2017 it documented 1,265 cases of persecution, in 2018, it documented 10,000 cases. Similarly, whereas in 2017 it reported 3,700 Christians detained—of whom 650 were church leaders—in 2018, it reported 5,000 detained—of whom 1,000 were church leaders. "More than 1,000,000 people were persecuted in 2018, which is three-and-a-half times more than those recorded in 2017," China Aid claims. "More than 500 people were sentenced to prison terms, an increase of 44 percent from 2017."[22] And these figures only relate to Christians.

Far from slowing the repression, the COVID-19 pandemic only added to it. According to research by CSW, "even during the most severe period of the epidemic, demolition of crosses and the banning of the churches in various places never stopped."[23] On May 3, 2020, more than 200 police raided Xingguang Church, an unregistered church in Xiamen, Fujian Province, beating worshippers. Xu Wenping suffered broken ribs and chest and forearm contusions, and others sustained varying degrees of injuries. In Zibo, Shandong Province, Sun Feng was detained for twenty-four hours for a post on WeChat in which he said he would pray and fast for people affected by the COVID-19 outbreak. In January 2021, in Hebei Province, Catholic writer and activist Pang Jian was taken away by police when he went for a coronavirus test. Police subsequently sent a notice of detention and a notice of formal arrest to Pang's father, stating that he was detained on suspicion of "inciting secession." Pang had previously reported on forced demolitions of crosses and churches and evictions of Catholics in rural areas, and about the Catholic community in Hebei. He had also spoken to Hong Kong media about Hebei's underground Catholic church.

On January 4, 2021, the Party's Central Committee and the State Council announced measures to "push forward rural vitalization and accelerate the modernization of agriculture and the countryside." Bizarrely, these measures included "increasing efforts to combat illegal religious activities and overseas infiltration activities in rural areas and stop the use of religion to interfere with public affairs in rural areas in accordance with the law." These measures signalled a new wave of repression of Christians. In January 2021, three churches in Wenzhou, Zhejiang Province, had their crosses forcibly removed, and the following month, Sacred Heart Church in Yining, Xinjiang, was threatened with demolition.[24] Probably due to international pressure, it was not destroyed, but it cannot be used because, according to CSW, water, electricity, and other services have been cut off by the government.

In perhaps one of the most extreme illustrations of how desperate some Christian communities in China now feel, in 2019, Pastor Pan Yongguang and dozens of members of his church, Shenzhen Holy Reformed Church, fled China to South Korea's Jeju Island.[25] After years of harassment from the Chinese authorities and in the face of increasing pressure, according to CSW, the church members "felt they had no option but to uproot their lives and seek safety and freedom overseas." Church members who remained in China or were sent back by Korean immigration have, CSW reports, been placed under surveillance and interrogated by police, and at least one person who was denied entry to Jeju has been placed under "Residential Surveillance" and prohibited from leaving her home. Even in Jeju, there is evidence that the Chinese authorities are monitoring the church members closely.

At the end of 2021, the Chinese Communist Party escalated its repression of Christianity even further, with a clear instruction to all Christian pastors to preach sermons emphasizing loyalty to the Party and obedience to the Party leaders. Emanating from a National Conference on Work Related to Religious Affairs, held on December 3 and 4, 2021, and presided over by Xi Jinping, it called on everyone involved in religious activities to engage in more in-depth study of Karl Marx's texts on religion. According to *Bitter Winter*, Xi's speech has been described as the "Nine Musts," setting out nine requirements for religious leaders which will "become the program for every pastor and community."[26] In addition to preaching loyalty and obedience to the Party and studying Marx, Christian pastors and congregations are required to study the Party's teachings, pursue "Sinicization" of religion, and understand that "the main aim of each

Christian community is to rally Christian believers around the CCP." Those who deviate from the regulations must be punished.

In March 2022, pastors in the Three-Self Patriotic Movement church were ordered to study new directives on the "Sinicization" of religion, issued by the deputy minister of the United Front Work Department of the Chinese Communist Party's Central Committee, Wang Zuo'an, who is also director of the State Administration of Religious Affairs. In a follow-up to Xi's December speech, these directives state that the CCP will do what is needed to "strengthen the ideological and political guidance of religious circles," "improve the political consciousness of the religious circles," and "guide the religious community to support the leadership of the Chinese Communist Party and the socialist system, unite closely around the Party Central Committee with Comrade Xi Jinping at the core, and firmly follow the path of socialism with Chinese characteristics." It is necessary to "encourage religious circles to earnestly study Xi Jinping Thought on Socialism with Chinese Characteristics for a New Era, to study the history of the Party, the history of New China, the history of reform and opening up, and the history of socialist development in a targeted manner, and to carry out in-depth education on the theme of 'Love the Party, Love the Country, Love Socialism.'"[27]

"We never thought the day would come when we would see such persecution as we see under Xi Jinping," says Fu. "There are at least thirty to forty different government agencies involved. Xi has launched a 'war on faith,' and religion was declared a national security issue. Tibetans and Uyghurs have long been seen as a national security threat because of territorial issues, but I never thought the Communist Party would designate Christians as a national security threat."

Fu, a student leader in the Tiananmen Square protests in 1989, became a Christian and a house church leader after the June 4 massacre, and engaged in evangelistic activities on campus in Beijing. He even got a job teaching English at the Chinese Communist Party school. "That was my time as God's double agent," Fu jokes. "During the daytime, I was teaching Chinese Communist Party leaders, and in the evening, I was planting churches and holding Bible studies. I established an underground training centre for Christians."

Eventually, he and his wife were arrested and imprisoned for two months, and then held under house arrest, but they managed to escape from the country in 1996. "We were about to have our first child but were facing the possibility of a forced abortion, because of a lack of quota under the notorious family planning policy of the regime, so we fled to the countryside, escaped to Hong Kong, and eventually reached the United States on June 28, 1997, just three days before Hong Kong's handover."

In the United States, Fu began to receive faxes on a daily basis from Christians suffering in China. "You cannot just sit still and be silent. We were constantly thinking about the suffering in China," he recalls. "Sometimes on the phone, especially at night, I could hear children crying when a church was raided. People would call me: 'Pastor Fu, help us.' We could hear the police knocking on the door; breaking into a church; picking up Bibles, pews, offering boxes; and beating people up and yelling. We would feel that we were still there, living with them, and so I had to do something."

Fu wrote to the U.S. president, detailing the names of all the arrested pastors he knew of—at least eighteen individual cases. "To my surprise, I received a letter back signed personally by President Bill Clinton. Then I was invited by the Assistant Secretary of State John Shattuck to meet him." By 2001, Fu had formed China Aid, after being inspired by well-connected friends at a retreat in Maryland to establish an advocacy organization for religious freedom in China.

"There were some members of Congress and their staff at the retreat, as well as several Chinese dissidents—including Peng Ming, who was later kidnapped from Burma by the Chinese regime and sentenced to life imprisonment, and later found dead, and Dr. Wang Bingzhang, known as the 'father of modern Chinese democracy,' a Canadian Chinese dual permanent resident who was later kidnapped from Vietnam and is still serving a life sentence in a Chinese prison," Fu recalled.

"During the retreat—on 'Christian faith and the future of China'—we received news that five house church leaders had been sentenced to death, and numerous others had been arrested and sentenced to between four and fifteen years' imprisonment. That triggered the birth of China Aid. I was coached to write my first-ever press release by former *TIME* China correspondent David Aikman, and it became the front-page headline on the *New York Times, Irish Times*, and *Washington Post*. President George W. Bush paid attention to it, and my interaction with the highest levels in the White House began."

The Communist Party, Fu confirms, has always been atheist and "antagonistic towards Christianity," but Xi has intensified the repression to an entirely new level. "We have seen the passage of new regulations on religious affairs, religious personnel, and foreigners' religious activities, so they use the banner of law to legalize persecution," he said. "And the regime provides monetary incentives to people to report so-called illegal religious activities. People can receive up to 100,000 renminbi yuan for reporting religious activities in Guangzhou, for example. This is Cultural Revolution–style."

Another deeply disturbing development has been the successful coercion of the Vatican by the Chinese Communist Party regime, effectively buying Pope Francis' silence on the genocide of the Uyghurs, the dismantling of Hong Kong's freedoms, continued repression in Tibet, and the intensifying persecution of Christians in China. Despite being a pontiff well known for speaking out regularly on issues of justice, conflict, and persecution, praying for one part of the world or another most Sundays when he prays the Angelus from his window over St. Peter's Square, and in his "Urbi et Orbi" addresses at Easter, Christmas, and on other occasions, Pope Francis has almost never referred to the repression in China.

Apart from one exception—a fleeting mention of the Uyghurs in his book *Let Us Dream: The Path to a Better Future*, in which he name-checked them in the context of the need to see the world from the peripheries—the Pope has not spoken about the contemporary world's latest genocide. In the book, he speaks of places "of sin and misery, of exclusion and suffering, of illness and solitude," and says, "I think often of persecuted peoples: the Rohingya, the poor Uyghurs, the Yazidis—what ISIS did to them was truly cruel—or Christians in Egypt and Pakistan killed by bombs that went off while they prayed in church."[28] But that was all.

And while he has spoken in general terms of his prayers for the Church in China in annual statements ahead of the Day of Prayer for the Church in China established by Pope Benedict XVI and held each year on May 24, he has not spoken specifically about the increasing persecution. This is in stark contrast to other religious leaders, especially from the Jewish community which has led the way in campaigning for the Uyghurs, and indeed many in his own church, clergy and laity, who have been outspoken.

Myanmar's Cardinal Bo, for example, criticized the Chinese regime's handling of COVID-19 when the virus first broke out, writing in an opinion piece in April 2020 that "there is one government that has primary responsibility for what it has done and what it has failed to do, and that is the CCP regime in Beijing . . . It is the repression, the lies and the corruption of the CCP that are responsible."[29] He also called out the regime's "increasingly repressive nature," especially its "campaign against religion." On other occasions, he has condemned the Uyghur genocide, called for prayer for Hong Kong, and, in a statement on March 14, 2021, in his capacity as president of the Federation of Asian Bishops Conferences, Cardinal Bo called for an extension of the annual Worldwide Day of Prayer for the Church in China to a week of prayer for the peoples of China. In response to Cardinal Bo's call, a group of lay Christians from six continents, including prominent Catholics, came together to facilitate the Global Week of Prayer.[30]

So why are the Pope and the Vatican so silent?

In September 2018, the Vatican signed an agreement with the regime in Beijing in an attempt to "normalize" the status of the Catholic Church in China. Until this deal was agreed, the official State-sanctioned Chinese Patriotic Catholic Association was out of communion with Rome (although some individual bishops and clergy were recognized by both Rome and Beijing), while the "underground" Catholics, who refused to join the regime's church, remained loyal to Rome. Catholics who chose to stay in communion with Rome and worship in underground churches faced the risk of harassment, arrest, imprisonment, and torture.

So the desire to address this situation is not in itself wrong. Nor is Pope Francis' love of China as a nation and a people. As a Jesuit, he is inspired by the example of Matteo Ricci, the first European to set foot in the Forbidden City in Beijing in 1601 as an advisor to the imperial court. Ricci converted several Chinese officials to Catholicism, established the foundations of the Cathedral of the Immaculate Conception in Beijing, the city's oldest church, and adopted Chinese culture as his own. He learned Chinese, dressed in Chinese robes, and defended Chinese traditions and Confucian values.

Francis has spoken of his desire to be the first Pope to visit China, following in his fellow Jesuit's footsteps. But Ricci's accommodation of Chinese culture is not the same as the current Vatican's appeasement of the Chinese Communist Party. It ought to be possible to distinguish between the people and the Party, and indeed speak up for the human dignity and liberty of the people repressed by the Party.

The Vatican-China deal is problematic in four respects: secrecy, substance, timing, and impact.

Several years after the deal was announced, the text remains secret. If it is such a good deal for Catholics in China, are they—and the Church as a whole— not entitled to know what it contains?

What we do know is that it appears to include an agreement on the nomination of bishops. From now on, the Chinese Communist Party regime—an officially atheist outfit—will nominate candidates. Theoretically, the Pope has the final say. But given the reluctance of Rome recently to stand up to Beijing, is it likely that he would actually veto a nominee?

At least seven previously excommunicated bishops, appointed by the regime, are now back in communion with Rome, while at least two underground bishops, loyal to Rome, have been asked by the Vatican to step aside from their positions in favour of the regime's bishops.

In December 2018, Bishop Vincent Guo Xijin, underground bishop of Mindong, Fujian Province, was replaced by Monsignor Vincenzo Zhan Silu, one of the previously excommunicated bishops. Bishop Guo, who has been arrested several times, was reported to have disappeared soon after, believed to be on the run from the authorities. He was then demoted to auxiliary bishop, before—in January 2020—being forced by the authorities to leave his residence, which was shut down. This sixty-one-year-old prelate ended up sleeping in the doorway of his church office and only after an international outcry was he permitted to return to his apartment, but with the utilities cut off.

In June 2020, seventy-year-old Bishop Augustine Cui Tai, coadjutor bishop of the underground church in Xuanhua, was taken away again—having already endured thirteen years in detention.

In September 2020, in Jiangxi Province, dissenting Catholic priests were placed under house arrest—in breach of an agreement to protect clergy from coercion. Priests from Yujiang diocese, under surveillance, were forbidden from "engaging in any religious activity in the capacity of clergy" after they refused to join the regime's so-called "patriotic church," and Bishop Lu Xinping was barred from celebrating Mass.[31]

The underground bishop of Shantou, Monsignor Pietro Zhuang Jianjian, was also asked to make way for State-approved Bishop Giuseppe Huang Bingzhang. Even if rapprochement with Beijing is desirable, sacrificing those who have risked and suffered so much for so long for the church is not just a tragedy, but a scandal.

It should have been a precondition for any agreement that Catholic bishops, priests, and laity in prison should be released. Yet, to my knowledge, no such attempt was made, and an unknown number remain in jail.

The whereabouts and well-being of one of the most prominent imprisoned clergy—Bishop James Su Zhimin of Baoding, in Hebei Province, who has spent over forty years in prison—remain unknown. In 1996, while leading a religious procession, Bishop Su was taken into police custody and has not been heard of since. He had already been imprisoned for twenty-six years and severely tortured under Mao Zedong's rule. In July 2020, Congressman Chris Smith held a hearing in the United States Congress titled "Where is Bishop Su?"[32]

Just two months after the deal was announced, another bishop, Peter Shao Zhumin of Wenzhou, was arrested for the fifth time in two years. He was released later that month, but continues to face harassment. Father Zhang Guilin and Father Wang Zhong of Chongli-Xiwanzi diocese were detained in late 2018 and their whereabouts are unknown.

Even if the substance of the deal was more hopeful, the timing is wrong. If such a deal had been reached a decade ago, when—despite the regime's repressive nature—there were some signs of space expanding for religious freedom and civil society, it might have been more understandable. But this agreement has been announced at a time when, as has been outlined, Xi Jinping's regime has unleashed the most severe crackdown on religion since the Cultural Revolution.

While the Vatican's intention was presumably to better protect and unify Catholics, it has had the opposite result, leading to disunity in the Church and no improvement in religious freedom. In fact, life for Catholics in China has become worse. Many dioceses in China are without bishops, and some who have been loyal to Rome for decades have been forced to retire in favour of Beijing's appointees.

Despite all this, and although the agreement was provisional for a two-year period, the Vatican quietly renewed the agreement in 2020, with no public review, explanation, or transparency. Former U.S. secretary of state Mike Pompeo, in an article in the journal *First Things*, outlined the Chinese Communist Party's brutal repression and urged, "Now more than ever, the Chinese people need the Vatican's moral witness and authority in support of China's religious believers."[33]

Sadly, they are not receiving it. Instead, there are people in senior positions in Rome such as the chancellor of the Pontifical Academy of Social Sciences, Bishop Marcelo Sánchez Sorondo, who appear to admire the Chinese Communist Party. Bishop Sorondo has described the regime in Beijing as the "best implementer of Catholic social doctrine,"[34] and in 2017, hosted a conference on organ harvesting around the world and invited as the only speaker on China the former deputy health minister Huang Jiefu—one of those responsible for forced organ harvesting.[35] The Vatican resisted appeals to invite expert researchers on the subject to present their evidence. The only compromise was the fact that the Pope, to his credit, pulled out of an audience with the delegates, thus denying the Chinese officials their much-desired photo opportunity.

Secretary Pompeo ended his article with the words "the truth shall set you free." Those twin pillars of truth and freedom are directly threatened and undermined by the Vatican-China deal.

Christians in China are facing the most intense persecution in decades. And as Hong Kong's freedoms are dismantled, Christians in Hong Kong will face greater repression, too.[36] The city that was once the gateway to China not only for traders but missionaries is becoming a city where violations of religious freedoms need to be monitored. Freedom of worship may still be intact, but wider aspects of full freedom of religion and freedom of conscience are already threatened.

Consider the case of Protestant pastor Roy Chan, whose Good Neighbour North District Church was raided by police in 2020, in retaliation for his pastoral support for young pro-democracy protesters.[37] "Beat me, not the kids," Chan said at the time. And he was beaten—not just by the police but by HSBC which, under pressure from the authorities, has frozen the assets of the church, Pastor Chan, and his family.

Even before the crackdown in Hong Kong, a Hong Kong pastor, Reverend Ng Wah, disappeared in China in July 2015 and was prosecuted for printing Christian books. His colleague, Reverend Philip Woo, was summoned by the police in Shenzhen around the same time and ordered to stop preaching in Mainland China.

And despite the courageous example of Hong Kong's Bishop Emeritus Cardinal Joseph Zen, a long-standing outspoken critic of the CCP and champion of democracy, the Hong Kong Catholic Diocese is already showing signs of surrender. In 2020, when a group of lay Catholics tried to organize a public prayer campaign for the city—inspired by Cardinal Bo's call to pray for Hong Kong—the Diocese actively discouraged it. A few weeks later, Hong Kong's apostolic administrator, Cardinal John Tong, issued an instruction to clergy to "watch your language" in homilies, and the Diocese has since published religious textbooks with guidance on how Hong Kong students can "contribute to their nation"—a clear pro-Beijing slant. Whether it wants to or not, the diocese is undoubtedly feeling—or at least anticipating—the CCP's pressure.[38]

In January 2022, pro-Beijing newspaper *Ta Kung Pao* published no less than four articles condemning Cardinal Zen and other Christian churches for their support of the democracy movement.

Beijing's assaults on the ninety-year-old Cardinal Zen are nothing new. In 2019, I attended a private gathering of Catholic legislators in Fatima, the Portuguese pilgrimage site, to which the cardinal and Hong Kong's "father" of the democracy movement, devout Catholic Martin Lee, were invited. China's embassy in Lisbon dispatched a delegation of about a dozen diplomats to occupy the entire first floor of the hotel opposite ours and made multiple attempts to infiltrate our gathering. That the Chinese Communist Party was so spooked by these two Hong Kong pro-democracy octogenarians visiting a religious pilgrimage site with a group of Catholic legislators said a lot about Beijing's paranoia and fear of religion.

But what is new is that pro-Beijing media are now openly talking about restrictions on religion in Hong Kong. According to *Ta Kung Pao*, Lawrence Ma, the executive director of the Hong Kong Legal Exchange Foundation, has called on the Hong Kong government to abrogate an old colonial law, the Chinese Temple Ordinance, to reapply it to all religions. In other words, to impose new administrative measures on religion.

Ma went further in an unprovoked attack, arguing that "Western" religions are incompatible with Chinese culture, claiming—falsely—that they "encourage us to forget our ancestors." What does he think of Catholic veneration of saints, then, may I ask? Has he not read the fifth commandment: "Honour your father and mother"?

Perhaps even more chilling than Ma's interventions are the remarks by former Anglican provincial secretary-general Peter Koon, recently elected to Beijing's proxy, puppet rubber-stamp legislature in Hong Kong.

Koon, who has metamorphosized from Anglican cleric into Chinese Communist Party apparatchik, placing his sickle and star alongside his soiled dog collar, backs the imposition of a revised "Chinese Temple Ordinance," attacking Christians who supported the 2019 protests as people who had "over-reliance on Western ideologies." A co-opted religious leader, what Lenin would have called a "useful idiot," Koon is perhaps—God help us—the embryo of a State-sanctioned Three-Self Patriotic Movement in Hong Kong.

Hong Kong's retired Anglican archbishop Peter Kwong was a fully signed-up supporter of Beijing's draconian National Security Law, and an enthusiastic member of the Chinese Communist Party's Chinese People's Political Consultative

Conference. His successor, Archbishop Andrew Chan, is a little less enthusiastic, thankfully, and has chosen instead to stay largely silent.

Hong Kong's new Catholic bishop, Stephen Chow, may offer one very small, fragile flicker of hope. He was not Beijing's choice, although nor is he identified with the pro-democracy movement in the way that Cardinal Zen and Auxiliary Bishop Joseph Ha are. But in his public pronouncements since his appointment—at his initial press conference,[39] at consecration, and in one of his first media interviews[40]—Bishop Stephen Chow has shown that even if he is having to navigate his course carefully, he holds firm to principles of human dignity and freedom of conscience.

Nevertheless, as Hong Kong's freedoms overall are dismantled, we will witness the strangulation of religious freedom. We must watch for the potential subtle absorption of Hong Kong's religious institutions into the Beijing-controlled, United Front Work Department-directed operations: the Three-Self Patriotic Movement, the Catholic Patriotic Association, and the campaign of "Sinicization" of religion which Xi Jinping has unleashed.

In 1997, Congressman Chris Smith concluded, having met Chinese Communist Party leaders in Beijing, that "these people care about only one thing—control, control, control. They don't care about religious freedom at all."[41] He was right, and Xi Jinping has intensified that goal of absolute control on a whole new scale. But Christians in China like Wang Yi are clear that they won't give up without a fight. And Christianity in China has survived despite severe persecution throughout its history. As the former director of the Chinese Overseas Christian Mission, Mary Wang—whose family escaped from Qingdao in the 1950s and whom I had the privilege of knowing—put it in her book *The Chinese Church That Will Not Die*, "The Chinese church will not die, but it is sorely wounded, limping on sticks in the shadows . . . The Chinese church will not die while there remain those who will not let go of Jesus Christ."[42]

CHAPTER 5

TIBET

BLOODSHED IN THE
LAND OF SNOWS

In the Ristorante Camponeschi, in Rome's Piazza Farnese—a restaurant which claims to have been frequented by world leaders such as Al Gore, Shimon Peres, and Mikhail Gorbachev, and Hollywood stars like Sylvester Stallone and Liza Minnelli—I sat next to the "Sikyong"—or prime minister—of the Central Tibetan Administration, Tibet's government-in-exile. It was November 2021 and my first overseas visit in almost two years, having been under lockdown in London and unable to travel abroad due to the COVID-19 pandemic. My last foreign visit before the pandemic began was to Vilnius, Lithuania, in December 2019, where I had stood in the city's Tibet Square and reflected on the seven decades of Chinese occupation and repression of Tibet. I had also attended a screening of a film about Tibet, *Sweet Requiem*, in Vilnius, which had planted deep seeds of concern for Tibet in my mind. So it seemed particularly apposite that when I started travelling again two years later, one of the first people I met was the Sikyong.

Penpa Tsering was elected to his five-year term as Tibet's secular political leader in May 2021, replacing the first Sikyong, Lobsang Sangay, whom I had been privileged to meet when he visited the Houses of Parliament in London, hosted by Tim Loughton, a member of Parliament and chair of the All-Party Parliamentary Group on Tibet. The Speaker of the House of Commons at the time, John Bercow, attended the meeting and was presented by the Sikyong with a *khata*, the traditional Tibetan white ceremonial scarf. Talking with Penpa Tsering in what is often described as the best restaurant in Rome, alongside Parliamentarians from around the world at a gathering of the Inter-Parliamentary Alliance on China (IPAC) on the eve of the G20 summit, I was struck by the humility, dignity, and quiet determination of the Tibetan leader. We talked informally over a five-course traditional Italian dinner about the current situation in Tibet, the Chinese regime's increasing aggression beyond its borders, and what the world should do to confront Beijing. After over seven decades of struggle, he—and all Tibetans—know more than anyone else that when you resist the Chinese Communist Party, you have to be prepared to be in it for the long haul.

The Sikyong's role was only established in 2011, when the Dalai Lama announced his decision to relinquish his political leadership and become solely a spiritual leader. Until then, Tibet's exiled political administration, known in Tibetan as the "Kashag," was run by the holder of the office of "Kalon Tripa," subordinate to the Dalai Lama. The first direct elections for this office were held in 2001, and ever since then the Tibetan community in exile in Dharamsala, in India's northern state of Himachal Pradesh, as well as the Tibetan diaspora around the world, have organized democratic elections for their leaders. The term "Sikyong," according to *Tibetan Review*, means "political leader," and had previously been used by regents who ruled Tibet during the Dalai Lama's minority. According to the former foreign minister of the Tibetan government-in-exile Kalon Dickyi Choyang, the term "Sikyong" dates back to the time of the seventh Dalai Lama, from 1708 to 1757, and that using this title "ensures historical continuity and legitimacy of the traditional leadership from the fifth Dalai Lama."[1]

The evening following my conversation with the Sikyong, a group of Tibetan women living in Italy came to present me with my first-ever *khata*. I bowed my head as they placed it on my shoulders, and as I did so a feeling of deep and profound respect for the Tibetans filled my heart. Throughout my years of working on human rights in China, I had, of course, always been concerned about Tibet, protested alongside Tibetans, spoken at seminars organized by Tibetan human rights groups, and collaborated with groups such as Free Tibet. But whereas I had travelled widely throughout Mainland China and lived in Hong Kong, I had never visited Tibet, and, it is fair to say, I had not been as active in in-depth advocacy for Tibet as I had been for Hong Kong, the Uyghurs, persecuted Christians, Falun Gong practitioners, and human rights defenders in China. Yet

I was becoming acutely and increasingly conscious of the need to ensure that as all the other human rights concerns in China—especially the Uyghurs and Hong Kong—receive more attention, and rightly so, around the world, we must not allow Tibet to be forgotten.

Ever since 40,000 People's Liberation Army (PLA) troops crossed the Yangtze and marched into Tibet in October 1950, Tibet has been under brutal repression and occupation. The previous year, just after Mao Zedong and the Chinese Communist Party seized power in China, they declared their intent with a radio broadcast which, according to Sam van Schaik in *Tibet: A History*, "stated that Tibet was an indivisible part of China, and anyone who failed to recognize this would 'crack his skull against the mailed fist of the PLA.'"[2] In January 1950, van Schaik notes, Mao told Joseph Stalin in Moscow of his plan to conquer Tibet, and Stalin pledged his support. The Tibetan government was already aware of the danger and had appealed to the international community for help. The British, who had invaded and occupied Tibet from 1903 to 1904, washed their hands of it. "The Tibetans' first hope centred on their old allies, the British," writes van Schaik. "But after withdrawing from India, the British wanted no further entanglement with Tibet; they merely suggested that Britain's old interests in Tibet were now a matter for the newly independent Indian government. For their part, the Indians were keen to forge a close relationship with China. When overtures to the Americans were also rebuffed, the Tibetans realized that they were to face China alone."[3]

Tibet had an army, and was determined to fight the invaders, but they were totally outmanned and outgunned. A Tibetan government official, Ngapo Ngawang Jigme, in van Schaik's words, "told anyone who cared to listen that Tibet had no hope of fighting off the Chinese. He was by nature a diplomat rather than a general, but his assessment of Tibet's chances was realistic."[4] Tibet was not, argues van Schaik, "a nation of pacifists," but without significant international support, it was impossible to resist.

Mao was motivated not only by communist ideology, according to van Schaik, but by national pride. "China had suffered one humiliation after another during the previous century, at the hands of the British, the Japanese and other foreign powers . . . If China was to stand up for itself again, it was vital to begin by reasserting control over Tibet."[5]

Faced with military invasion, the Tibetans agreed to negotiate, and Ngapo was sent to Beijing to begin talks. "His instructions from Lhasa stated that he must make a claim for Tibet's independence and argue that historically the relationship between Tibet and China had been that of priest and patron," writes van Schaik. However, "if it came to a deadlock, Ngapo was authorized to accept Tibet as a part of China, as long as Tibet could keep its internal independence and no Chinese soldiers were stationed in Tibet."[6]

Even this compromise, however, was unacceptable to Beijing. China asserted its historical claim to Tibet and was in no mood to concede otherwise. In the end, an agreement was reached with two enormous concessions by the Tibetans. The first was that Tibetans would "return to the big family of the Motherland—the People's Republic of China," and the second stated that "the local government of Tibet shall actively assist the People's Liberation Army to enter Tibet and consolidate the national defence."[7] In return, the Chinese gave assurances that there would be no change to the Dalai Lama's authority, religious freedom would be protected, any reforms would be gradual, and there was no mention of the role of the Communist Party in governing Tibet.

The Seventeen-Point Agreement was announced in a radio broadcast from Beijing which, according to van Schaik, "was the first the Tibetan government heard of the agreement."[8] Ngapo had not kept Lhasa informed, and many were "shocked at how much had been given away."[9] The Dalai Lama and Tibet's National Assembly were left with little choice, and a month later, the Dalai Lama sent a telegram to Mao accepting the agreement. In the following months, Chinese troops arrived in Lhasa, "parading through the streets carrying portraits of Mao" and, van Schaik claims, "by the end of the year there were eight thousand Chinese soldiers in Lhasa, doubling the city's population."[10]

For the first decade of occupation, the Chinese worked with the Tibetan leaders, and in 1954, the Dalai Lama himself visited Beijing to meet with Mao. Writing in his autobiography, *Freedom in Exile*, he recalls that he had "at least a dozen meetings with Mao" and thought that they had reached "a workable compromise."[11] However, he recounts his shock when, despite having built something of a rapport together, Mao turned to him in their final meeting and said, "Religion is poison. Firstly, it reduces the population, because monks and nuns must stay celibate, and secondly it neglects material progress." The Dalai Lama recalls, "I felt a violent burning sensation all over my face and I was suddenly very afraid. 'So', I thought, 'you are the destroyer of the *Dharma* after all' . . . Fear and amazement gave way to confusion. How could he have misjudged me so? How could he have thought that I was not religious to the core of my being?"[12]

Resistance to the occupation grew, tensions became more violent, and the Chinese became more repressive. Describing one of many atrocities inflicted on Tibet, the aerial bombing of the monastery at Lithang in Kham in 1956, the Dalai Lama writes, "When I heard of it, I cried. I could not believe that human beings were capable of such cruelty to each other. This bombardment was followed by the merciless torture and execution of women and children whose fathers and husbands had joined the resistance movement and, incredibly, by the disgusting abuse of monks and nuns. After arrest, these simple, religious people were forced—in public—to break their vows of celibacy with one another and even to kill people."[13]

In 1959, the Dalai Lama finally fled Tibet, beginning the rest of his life in exile in McLeod Ganj, a suburb of Dharamsala, the old British hill station in India. As he writes, for almost a decade he had stayed in Tibet and worked hard to establish peace with China, even though it had "sent an army to invade my country," but "the task proved impossible." With great reluctance, he "came to the unhappy conclusion that I could serve my people better from outside."[14]

In comments His Holiness graciously delivered to me for this book, the Dalai Lama reflected on the significance of his over seven decades in exile. "Since I became a refugee, I have thought of myself as a citizen of the world," he told me. "I made this clear in the 1970s when Mark Tully, the long-time BBC correspondent in Delhi, asked me why I wanted to travel abroad. Since I came into exile, I have enjoyed the freedom to travel the world, mainly at the invitation of educational institutions and organizations committed to peace." His Holiness explained that he considers "being mindful of the oneness of humanity and cultivating a sense of universal responsibility to be more important than allegiance to a particular nation state or community of people." As a Tibetan, the Dalai Lama feels "a strong responsibility to protect Tibetan culture, which, with its focus on compassion and doing no harm, has a huge potential to contribute to peace and understanding in the world."

His Holiness emphasized to me that "we are not seeking separation from the People's Republic of China." Instead, he advocates what he calls "a Middle-Way Approach," whereby Tibet remains within China's sovereignty but enjoys a high degree of autonomy and self-rule. "I firmly believe that this would be of mutual benefit to Tibetans as well as to the Chinese," he told me. "With China's assistance, we Tibetans will be able to develop Tibet, while at the same time keeping alive our own unique Buddhist culture, as well as preserving Tibet's delicate environment. If China were to resolve the Tibet issue peacefully, taking mutual interests into account, it would strengthen its own unity and stability. Meanwhile, as increasing numbers of Chinese, Buddhists, and scholars are taking an interest in Tibet's rich Buddhist culture, this is something we can offer to them."

In life, said His Holiness, "we naturally face difficulties." But we should not allow ourselves to become "demoralized" or "discouraged," Instead, he argued, "we can always use our intelligence and look at whatever complication besets us from a wider perspective. We have this marvellous human brain and we should use it with determination." His lifelong commitment, he added, is to "raise awareness that the most important source of happiness lies within us and that warmheartedness is that source of happiness."

In their *Tibet Brief 20/20*, two international law experts, Michael van Walt van Praag and Mike Boltjes are unequivocal in their conclusion that China's presence in Tibet is "unlawful." Despite the historical interactions between Tibet and China over the centuries—from 1912 until the invasion in 1950—they argue, "Tibet was an independent state *de facto* and *de jure*."[15] Furthermore, "contrary to what the People's Republic of China (PRC) claims and to what many people take for granted, Tibet was historically *never* a part of China . . . Tibet is an occupied country and the PRC does not possess sovereignty over it. This calls for an immediate course correction to bring government policies in compliance with international law."[16]

Not only is Tibet occupied, it is brutally repressed. As van Walt van Praag and Boltjes note, "the PRC not only illegally occupies Tibet, it also denies the Tibetan people their lawful exercise of self-determination. This denial, the PRC's active opposition to any expressions of it, and its modifications of administrative boundaries of what are now the Tibetan autonomous region, prefectures and counties, all constitute violations of fundamental norms of international law."[17]

In 1959, the International Commission of Jurists published a report which concluded that China had illegally invaded and occupied Tibet, and that there was a *prima facie* case of genocide.[18] The Dalai Lama recounts that "it was not until I read the report published in 1959 by the International Commission of Jurists that I fully accepted what I had heard: crucifixion, vivisection, disembowelling, and dismemberment of victims was commonplace. So, too, were beheading, burning, beating to death, and burying alive, not to mention dragging people behind galloping horses until they died or hanging them upside down and throwing them bound hand and foot into icy water. And, in order to prevent them shouting out

'Long live the Dalai Lama,' on the way to execution, they tore out their tongues with meat hooks."[19]

When considering the situation in Tibet today, it is important to clarify what area we are referring to. There is the Tibetan Autonomous Region, which van Schaik terms "political Tibet," but there is a much wider geographical area which he describes as "ethnographic Tibet"—territory which was, at various times in history, part of Tibet and includes Tibetan populations, language, and culture. This latter area includes parts of the Chinese provinces of Qinghai, Sichuan, Gansu, and Yunnan, as well as the Himalayan kingdoms of Bhutan, Nepal, Sikkim, and Ladakh. Tibetans themselves speak of central Tibet, which corresponds to the Tibetan Autonomous Region, and "Greater Tibet," taking into account these wider territories.[20]

Today, Tibet is one of the most repressed corners of the world. Reporters Without Borders ranks it 176 out of 180 in its Press Freedom Index, and Freedom House lists Tibet as one of the worst in the world, with the lowest score for civil and political rights. "There are more foreign journalists in North Korea than Tibet," Tibet Post International told the U.K. Conservative Party Human Rights Commission's 2020 inquiry.[21] "Every aspect of Tibetan life is under siege, and Tibetans have even fewer civil and political rights than Chinese people also ruled by the Communist Party. The regime enforces its control over every aspect through the threat and use of arbitrary punishments, at times including severe violence. Any act deemed to threaten its rule . . . becomes a criminal offence."

In the past decade under Xi Jinping, repression has intensified further. Free Tibet and Tibet Watch claimed in 2020 that the regime "has introduced massive changes to Tibet in the past five years, from forcibly relocating Tibetans from their pastures or religious communities to tightening security to clamping down on religion, Tibetan culture, and the use of Tibetan language."[22]

Plenty of evidence has been documented to underline these claims. In late August or early September 2019, Choegyal Wanpo, a forty-six-year-old Tibetan monk from Tengdro monastery in Tingri county in the Tibetan Autonomous Region, accidentally left his mobile phone in a café in Lhasa. According to Human Rights Watch, the café owner gave the phone to the police, who discovered messages between the monk and Tibetans in exile in Nepal and proof that he had sent a donation to help Tibetans recover from the 2015 earthquake in Nepal. Human Rights Watch reports that "Lhasa police immediately detained Choegyal Wangpo, repeatedly beat him severely, and interrogated him."[23] This then led to a police raid on his home village of Dranak and the Tengdro monastery, in which several monks and villagers were severely beaten and at least twenty detained and held without trial for several months.

Since 2006, the Chinese regime has implemented a large-scale "rehousing" programme, forcibly relocating nomadic herders in the eastern part of the Tibetan plateau, mostly in Qinghai Province. Official figures suggest that as many as two million people—more than two-thirds of the entire population of the Tibetan Autonomous Region—were either relocated or rebuilt their houses between 2006 and 2012. According to Human Rights Watch, 20 percent of those rehoused between 2006 and 2010—about 280,000 people—had to be relocated, "some nearby and others at a great distance."[24]

A central part of the policy, Human Rights Watch explains, is that "many of those rehoused or relocated have been sedentarized, moved off the land and into permanent structures," something that "upsets many Tibetans because of its impact on Tibetan culture." Between 2005 and 2012, "large numbers of people relocated or rehoused did not do so voluntarily and . . . were never consulted or offered alternatives." Many Tibetans believe that the programme was designed "to facilitate the Chinese government's control of Tibetans, who already face sharp curbs on political, religious, and cultural expression." In 2011, the regime announced plans to send over 20,000 Party and government cadres "to be stationed in Tibetan villages, to 'live, eat, and work' with the local population."

Other alarming trends include curtailing the use of Tibetan language in schools throughout the region. According to another Human Rights Watch report, Chinese is being introduced as the medium for teaching in primary schools and even kindergartens.[25] There is a widespread concern about "the increasing loss of fluency in Tibetan among the younger generation." The number of non-Tibetan-speaking teachers in Tibetan schools tripled between 1988 and 2005, and, according to a 2017 Chinese study, 30 percent of teachers in one Lhasa county did not know Tibetan. And, in January 2016, a Tibetan campaigner on language rights, Tashi Wangchuk, was arrested and charged with "jeopardizing state security" after telling the *New York Times* that there was no longer any provision for Tibetan to be taught as a language in one prefecture in Qinghai. He was sentenced to five years in jail, for "incitement to split the country."[26]

Three United Nations human rights expert committees have repeatedly expressed concern at China's handling of mother-tongue instruction. In 2018, the UN Committee on the Elimination of All Forms of Racial Discrimination expressed concern that "Tibetan language teaching in schools in the Tibetan Autonomous Region [TAR] has not been placed on an equal footing in law, policy and practice with Chinese, and that it has been significantly restricted." China also stands accused of breaching the Convention on the Rights of the Child.[27]

As if restricting access to education in their mother tongue was not bad enough, a vast system of boarding schools in Tibet have been used to indoctrinate Tibetan children in the regime's propaganda and its process of "Sinicization." According to Tibet Action Institute, at least 800,000 Tibetan children between the ages of six and eighteen—which amounts to 78 percent of Tibetan students—live in "colonial boarding schools." Parents are compelled to send their children to these schools due to a lack of alternatives, and "students are at risk of losing their mother tongue and connection to their cultural identity" because classes are taught in Chinese, they live apart from their families and communities, and they are "subjected to a highly politicized curriculum intended to make them identify as Chinese."[28] The schools are, the report claims, "a cornerstone of an assimilationist agenda advanced by Chinese President Xi Jinping himself, intended to pre-empt threats to Chinese Communist Party control by eliminating ethnic differences." The impact of the schools on Tibetan children and families, and "the implications for whole generations of Tibetans and the long-term survival of Tibetan identity are grave."

The extent of surveillance is another way in which the long arm of Beijing has extended deep into Tibet. As the Tibetan Centre for Human Rights and Democracy puts it, "the changes in Tibet over the last decade represent a systematized social control mechanism that ignores human rights . . . Online surveillance, CCTV cameras, bugged homes, and checkpoints provide simple instruments of observation and monitoring to expand the influence of the state."[29] The report goes on to say specifically that "since 2008, when Tibetans held widespread protests calling for freedom and return of the Dalai Lama, Chinese authorities have tightened control to ensure that such an event will never happen again."

Professor Dibyesh Anand, head of the School of Social Sciences at the University of Westminster and an expert on Tibet, agrees, saying that heavy surveillance is designed to prevent protest, as there are "cameras observing every house."[30]

The International Campaign for Tibet published a report in 2021 which added to the picture of the surveillance state, arguing that "monks and nuns live in a suffocating environment under constant surveillance and control measures."[31]

Under Xi Jinping, "the repression of the monastic community has escalated even further." Since the "securitization" policies of the notorious Chen Quanguo, who served as Party Secretary in Tibet from 2011 to 2016, a period that coincided with Xi Jinping's first five years in power, the "focus on ideological control and transformation to support the Chinese state" has intensified.[32] Xi Jinping's "drive to 'Sinicize' . . . all religions in China . . . is not an empty threat."

Tenzin Choekyi, a researcher at Tibet Watch, agrees. "Chen Quanguo systematized repression, with Party cadres stationed at every street corner, in every police station, in every remote village. There are informants everywhere, creating a suffocating atmosphere," she told me.

Tsering Dawa, a former Tibetan bank employee from Lhasa who escaped Tibet in 2020 and made his way to India, is in no doubt that "repression has increased" since Xi Jinping came to power. Chen Quanguo oversaw a particularly severe crackdown, the techniques of which he then applied in his new role as Party Secretary in Xinjiang from 2016 to 2021. He had a history, too, of overseeing the persecution of Falun Gong when he was Deputy Party Secretary in Hebei Province from 2009 to 2011. "Chen Quanguo increased surveillance throughout Tibet, putting checkpoints and security cameras everywhere, and carrying out DNA tests and facial identification. My mother worked in a government hospital at that time, and I remember they took blood samples of everyone and used eye scanners, to gather data for facial recognition technology," Tsering Dawa recalled. "Many people were jailed for three years just for attending *Kalachakra* prayers by His Holiness the Dalai Lama."

Ultimately, Tsering Dawa argues, "the Chinese regime's key policy aim is to turn Tibetans into Chinese, and Uyghurs into Chinese. So, in order to really understand the Chinese Communist Party's repression everywhere, it is really important to understand its policies in Tibet and Xinjiang. There is a lack of attention towards Tibet at the moment, but as someone who was inside Tibet, what I learned was that any policy implemented in Tibet is subsequently implemented in Xinjiang and now Hong Kong. So if we do not know the situation in Tibet, we do not know the Chinese Communist Party."

Wangden Kyab, who now works as research manager with Tibet Watch in Dharamsala, was born in Amdo, in eastern Tibet, and escaped to India in 1998. He came from a family that was deeply entrenched in the resistance to the Chinese occupation. "For three generations—my great-grandfather, grandfather, and father—my family has engaged in fighting and protest against the Chinese invasion. They were imprisoned, tortured, dragged to struggle sessions, and went through unimaginable hard times in labour camps and faced a fatal end," he told me. Sometimes, Wangden would walk with his grandfather grazing sheep, yaks, and other livestock, in the mountains and along the rivers, and his grandfather would tell him stories about the Chinese invasion. "He would talk about how he and others were imprisoned, what life was like in prison, the struggle sessions, the hardships of labour camps, how he and my great-grandfather fought the Chinese People's Liberation Army (PLA). He told me about the killings they witnessed. These stories became engraved in me and inspired me to follow their footpath of resisting the occupation. Growing up in Tibet, whenever I was naughty as a child, my elders in the village would always tell me and other youngsters that we had to go through tragedy to understand how to be good. They would recall the events of 1958 and 1959, China's invasion and early years of occupation and protest, so many wars, fights, famines, and they would try to scare us with these memories. Others among the young generation who were born under the Chinese occupation sometimes could not think differently, could not distinguish between right and wrong, because they had never seen the outside world, they had never experienced any other society."

Wangden recalls one occasion when a monk from a nearby monastery returned to Tibet from India, and brought with him a Tibetan national flag, which is banned by the Chinese regime in Tibet. "That Tibetan flag was hanging inside the room of a monk, and I saw it and was amazed. To me, it was something unique, and so I asked if I could copy it. I loved drawing, and so I drew a number of Tibetan flags and showed them to my friends. Soon many households had a Tibetan flag in their home."

Such an act could have been very dangerous, but Wangden's village was in a very remote part of Tibet, and government officials seldom visited and would not pay much attention. "People hung the flag in their homes and the government did not know, so there were not many problems until I fled. However, one day, someone wrote on the wall of the township primary school—one or two kilometres from my village—slogans such as 'Independence for Tibet' and 'China out of Tibet.' The government did find these, and this was really serious. They tried to investigate who had done it. They came to my village; they searched the villages, the monasteries and questioned the monks and everybody they suspected."

A couple of years after that incident, Wangden decided to escape to India. "I learned that His Holiness the Dalai Lama was in India, that there were fellow Tibetans living there with him, and there were Tibetan soldiers led by His Holiness, fighting back against the Chinese regime, trying to free Tibet," he recalls. "That made me feel a strong eagerness to join the movement, and so I decided to leave Tibet." His family tried to persuade him not to, especially because he was the eldest son and Tibetan tradition says that the eldest stays home to look after the parents, family, and household. But Wangden was determined. "I did not know where India was, I did not know anyone in India, but I knew I had to go. As my family would never agree, I tried to flee secretly, but they caught me time and again. I said, 'Fine, you can keep me as long as you want, but one day I will go. Whether it is after five, ten, fifteen, or twenty years, I would go to India one day.' Eventually, they let me go."

The journey was treacherous. From Amdo to Nepal, Wangden walked for one month, across the Himalayas. "As I travelled, I wondered why, at such a young age, I had such a strong commitment to flee and join the movement. I knew that there were only two options—that I would reach India, or die on the way—but I was determined," he told me. "Other Tibetans who have fled Tibet have similar stories to share. There are so many risks along the way. Many people are shot at by Chinese soldiers at the border, and many people are arrested and brought back to China. Many people die in the Himalayas, crossing the Snow Mountains, dying of hunger and starvation. Many get frostbite, and face danger on the glaciers. This is not just my story; it is the story of every Tibetan who has escaped from Tibet across the Himalayan mountains."

Tsering Dawa, as mentioned earlier, escaped in 2020 and is the most recent Tibetan escapee I have had the privilege of interviewing. "I arrived in exile on February 24, 2020, the first day of the Tibetan New Year," he told me from Dharamsala in an online call. "I left because there is no freedom; there are no human rights inside Tibet. I wanted to work for Tibetan freedom, to amplify the voice of Tibetan people."

Five years earlier, Tsering Dawa had been arrested because, after applying for a passport, he commented on social media—Weibo and WeChat—about the fact that Chinese can get their own passports, but Tibetans cannot. "I travelled from Lhasa to Shigatse, but the authorities thought I was escaping, and so I was arrested at Shigatse and detained for eleven months," he told me. "First I was held in a prison in Shigatse in front of the Tashi Lhumpo monastery, for three days, and then in another prison. During that period, they tied my hands and legs and beat me. They hit me with a file box and a plastic container." Dawa showed me his scars on his head, which remain to this day. "After eleven months, they could not find any proof of any political activities. They tried to link me to political work, accusing me of having contacts in Dharamsala, but I simply said that the only thing I had done was comment on the fact that I don't have a right to a passport. So finally they released me."

After taking a break for a year to recover from his prison ordeal, Tsering Dawa got a job with the *Xizang Jinchuan*, a government office directly run from Beijing, responsible for overseeing industry, agriculture, nomadic communities, education, and economic activity in Tibet. "As I worked in that office, I received information about the situation in Xinjiang, and I also found that Tibetans were facing a similar situation to the Uyghurs. So I decided to expose this information, and I sent it all to Dharamsala. The information included details of the concentration camps in Xinjiang, as well as the forced relocation of Tibetan farmers and nomads, and other human rights violations," he recalled. "That put me at risk. The authorities were searching for who was sending information outside. For that reason, I decided to escape."

Instead of travelling across the mountains to Nepal as most Tibetan escapees have done, Tsering Dawa took a different, though no less dangerous, route. His mother, who travelled with him, was in her late sixties at the time and so the arduous mountain journey was too challenging for her. So instead, they secured Chinese passports, and managed to fly from Lhasa to Chongqing, and then on to Kunming, and from there to Thailand, Nepal, and then India. "At Kunming airport, my mother and I were stopped by security, because we were the only Tibetans there. The flight had to wait fifteen minutes because of us. It was a very scary moment. Even in Thailand, we were scared, because of Thailand's close relations with China."

When Nyima Lhamo was just thirteen years old, her uncle, Tenzin Delek Rinpoche, was arrested at his monastery in Nyagchuka county, in Kardze Tibetan Autonomous Prefecture in Sichuan Province, on April 7, 2002. A highly revered and respected Tibetan Buddhist monk—a *lama*—admired for his humanitarian and community work, building orphanages, schools, and homes for the elderly, Tenzin Delek Rinpoche was falsely accused of being involved in bomb blasts in Chengdu, Sichuan Province. On December 2 that year, he was sentenced to death, suspended for two years, on charges of "terrorism and subversion." On January 26, 2003, his assistant and distant relative, Lobsang Dondrup, was executed.

Tenzin Delek Rinpoche spent the subsequent thirteen years in prison, enduring torture and mistreatment. His family were denied regular monthly visits which, under Chinese law, they had a right to, and he was denied medical parole when his health condition became critical. "We know that the police beat him a lot, took his clothing, threw him on the floor, pushed him under hot water. They taunted him, saying if you are a *lama*, show us your magical powers. He always said that he had committed no crime. He had been arrested because he loved Tibet and His Holiness the Dalai Lama."

On July 12, 2015, he died in prison. The authorities claimed he had suffered a cardiac arrest, but according to the monks who washed his body and changed his clothes before his cremation, his fingernails, toenails, and lips were black and his head had a hollow at the back. According to Tibet Watch, the monks and his family believe that "Tenzin Delek Rinpoche had been poisoned and killed,"[33] although it has not been possible to conclusively verify that claim.

In 2016, having already herself been arrested and detained the previous year soon after her uncle's death, Nyima Lhamo decided to flee to India. "Due to the work he had been doing in Tibet, my uncle was a very popular figure among Tibetans," she told me from her new home in exile. "The fact that the Chinese government accused him of crimes he did not commit, the fact that he was put in prison and died in prison, was one of the main reasons I escaped Tibet, in order to tell his story, and the stories of other Tibetans in Tibet. The Chinese government killed Tenzin Delek Rinpoche, my uncle, and I felt that as a young person I could travel, I could escape, and then tell our story."

During her uncle's years in prison, Nyima Lhamo's mother and aunt actively campaigned for justice for him. "They collected signatures for a petition, they talked to tourists, they reached out to the police requesting permission to visit him," she told me. "They travelled everywhere, including to Beijing, to seek justice. They were not given one opportunity to meet Tenzin Delek Rinpoche, and their petitions were ignored by the authorities."

While her mother was away appealing for justice, Nyima Lhamo ran the household, but in 2009 or 2010, as she turned twenty, she became involved in the campaign, too. "I went with my mother and aunt to Chengdu, to appeal to the head of the prison. We had heard that my uncle had written a 300-page book about his life while in prison, and we wanted to ask the police to give it to us. The head of the prison recognized us when he saw us, told us 'Tenzin Delek Rinpoche is not here,' and started to walk away, but I almost grabbed him and pleaded with him, saying, 'Please, you have the book. I am sure you have read the book. You know he is innocent. You should give us the book.' My cousin and I knelt down in front of him to plead with him. The prison chief replied, 'I can't. If I give you the book, I will be in prison. They will fire me and put me in prison.'"

Hearing this, Nyima Lhamo realized how significant her uncle's case was. "If a prison chief, one of the most powerful men in Chengdu, could be arrested and put in prison just for giving away a book, then anything could happen," she recalled. "I realized this was not a regular, normal case."

The family kept appealing, but with no success. The police even refused to return property and money belonging to Tenzin Delek Rinpoche which they had seized at the time of his arrest. "The Chinese police told us, when my family asked for it, that the money would go to the relatives of those who died in the explosion in Chengdu, as compensation. Then they told us it would go to the lawyers. They always lied. I realized there would never be any justice."

From prison, the few words Tenzin Delek Rinpoche was able to express inspired and influenced his young niece. "He said, 'go to the highest court in the land, plead my case, because I am innocent.' That made me really want to do something," recalls Nyima Lhamo. "When he died, I had a really urgent desire to seek revenge, to kill Chinese leaders. But I then remembered my uncle's words: 'Even though they beat me, I did not hit them,' and I realized that would not benefit anyone, and so instead of seeking revenge, I needed to tell his story to the world. I thought that if I do not leave Tibet, I will regret it when I am older."

The day after Tenzin Delek Rinpoche's death, 300 people gathered in Lithang and protests broke out. Nine people were permitted to travel to Chengdu to see his body, and Nyima Lhamo decided to go with them. By July 15, according to Tibet Watch, "Orthok, Golok, Nyachuka and a lot of other places were already in turmoil." At the police station in Chengdu, Nyima Lhamo and her mother accused the authorities of killing Tenzin Delek Rinpoche, and Nyima decided to commit suicide. She told Tibet Watch, "Outside, there was a wooden structure, so I went outside and took off my scarf. I tried to hang myself with it. My mother was also beating her head against the wall to get them to listen to our pleas. It was only when the police saw that I was serious about hanging and killing myself that they paid attention to us . . . They called us back into the station, and since I could not walk on my own at that point, they lifted me up and took me inside."[34]

The police showed Nyima Lhamo's mother and aunt medical prescriptions and other medical documents to "prove" the cause of death, and asked them to sign a statement confirming their acceptance of this, but they refused. Instead,

Nyima and her mother submitted a five-point appeal letter, demanding an investigation into the death, release of the death certificate, return of the body, clarification of inconsistencies in the information provided by the authorities, and a request that cremation should take place only after the cause of death had been determined. Two hours later, the authorities ordered the monks to ensure the cremation was carried out the next day.

On July 17, Nyima and her mother were arrested and detained, and held in prison for more than a week. They were warned that their petitions and campaigning for Tenzin Delek Rinpoche, and their allegations that he had been murdered, were criminal acts which could be punished by life imprisonment. They were finally released, on the condition that they would not share any information about Tenzin Delek Rinpoche or his death, and would not make any accusations against the Chinese authorities.

They were kept under heavy surveillance and their movements restricted. "They had security cameras outside our house, and the police came to visit us often, asking what we were doing," Nyima recalls. A few times, she slipped out of their home despite the surveillance, and travelled to Chengdu. The authorities would ask her mother where she was. "My mother told them, 'You have cameras, why did you not see?'"

Nyima began to plan her escape. With the help of Tibetans in exile, she received funds, information, contacts, and advice for how to flee. Then, one day, she told neighbours she was going to the forest to collect caterpillar fungus, one of the major income sources for rural Tibetans. Due to its medicinal properties, it has high market value. "After a few days, I escaped at night. The CCTV cameras did not catch me. I travelled for almost half a month, by car, motorcycle, and on foot, across the mountains," she said. "At times I was so hungry, as I had only enough food to eat once a day. At times it was very steep, and scary, because I suffer from altitude sickness. I was afraid, but just for a short time."

On July 24, 2016, a little more than a year after her uncle died in prison, Nyima arrived in Dharamsala, where she had the opportunity to meet the Dalai Lama, an experience which felt, for her, "bittersweet." "I was happy I could visit him, but I was so sad that he cannot go back to Tibet," she recalled. "He told me, 'Don't be sad.' He was very respectful of Tenzin Delek Rinpoche, he asked about my uncle's students, and we discussed my plan to speak out. He asked whether I want to go back to Tibet, and I said I can't. He said if I was not planning to return to Tibet, then I should tell the story to the world."

There are tragically countless other similarly horrific stories to tell. *Tibet Post International* reported that between May 2016 and May 2020, over 1,133 Tibetans had been "arrested, arbitrarily detained, imprisoned, tortured to death in custody."[35]

In 2016, an eighteen-year-old monk, Tenpa, was arrested by ten police officers within five minutes of starting a solo protest in Ngaba, carrying the Tibetan flag and a picture of the Dalai Lama. On September 20, 2019, six Tibetans were arrested for refusing to participate in official events to mark the seventieth anniversary of the establishment of the People's Republic of China. On November 18, 2019, a fifteen-year-old monk called Nyimey was arrested for allegedly writing articles in support of four monks who had been detained eleven days earlier for distributing pro-independence leaflets.[36]

According to Tenzin Choekyi of Tibet Watch, in early 2021, two Tibetans were killed "in a very brutal way." One was a nineteen-year-old Tibetan monk called Tenzin Nyima, who was arrested, released, and rearrested on suspicion of sharing the news of his arrest to Tibetans in exile. "He was beaten in such a way that he was comatose at the end, and he passed away," Tenzin Choekyi told me.[37] The other, she said, was Kunchok Jinpa, a Tibetan who had studied in India, but returned to Tibet and worked as a tour guide in Lhasa. He shared information with exiles about protests against the mining industry in his hometown in 2010 and 2013 and was arrested and sentenced to twenty-one years in jail. He died of the injuries sustained in prison.[38]

The Dalai Lama, of course, has become the most recognized symbol of Tibet throughout the world. As his biographer Alexander Norman puts it, the Dalai Lama "sells out sports stadiums from Sydney to São Paolo, from Oslo to Johannesburg." He has received the Nobel Peace Prize, holds numerous other awards, honorary degrees, and the freedom of several cities, as well as twenty million Twitter followers.[39] He has met presidents, prime ministers, politicians, and religious leaders around the world and is much loved and respected by millions both for his non-violent, courageous struggle for justice and for his spiritual teaching.

But the position he holds in the hearts of Tibetans goes even deeper. As Tsering Dawa put it, "when Christian people take an oath, a pledge, or a promise, you swear in the name of God. For Tibetans, when we make a promise, we swear in the name of His Holiness the Dalai Lama. It is in our DNA. That's the relationship we have with His Holiness."

Wangden Kyab agrees. "His Holiness the Dalai Lama and the Panchen Lama are, Tibetans say, the sun and moon. Their images and the reverence we have for these two high lamas are deeply rooted in every Tibetan."

Inside Tibet, expressing that reverence for the Dalai Lama is extremely dangerous, but people continue to do so. "Inside Tibet, we continue to hold His Holiness in very deep respect. People love and respect him more than their parents," argues Nyima Lhamo. "The Chinese regime will not allow us to put His Holiness' picture up at home, but that does not mean we forget His Holiness. He is in the minds and hearts of all Tibetans."

Consiglio Di Nino, an Italian-born former Canadian senator who has championed the Tibetan cause for more than thirty years, can attest to that. In 1988, his wife decided to go to Kolkata (Calcutta), to work with Mother Teresa, now St. Teresa of Calcutta. Senator Di Nino, passionate about hiking and trekking, decided to visit her and take a side trip to the Himalayas, though remaining on the Indian side. He loved it so much that, two years later, he joined another trek through the Himalayas, to Mount Everest Base Camp, which took him through Tibet.

As Senator Di Nino recalls, "What we saw was the enslavement of a people. And the further we went into Tibet, the worse it became." But he had travelled equipped with about a dozen pictures of the Dalai Lama, which he kept in a camera case around his belt. "I was told that if the Chinese authorities caught me, I would probably never leave Tibet again." Despite the risks, however, those Tibetans who had a few words of English would quietly express pleas for help to the foreign tourists, and one day, while Senator Di Nino and his trekking tour group were visiting the Jokhang Temple—the most sacred of all in Tibet and the "spiritual heart" of Lhasa—someone put a piece of paper in his hand. "There was a young man, in his early twenties, cowering beside me," Senator Di Nino told me. "An American lady in the group picked up the piece of paper and said, 'It's a cry for help.'"

At that point, Senator Di Nino remembered the contraband pictures in his camera bag. "I took out a Dalai Lama picture, and walked towards this young man holding the picture on my chest. When I got close to him, I opened up my hands and put the Dalai Lama picture between my hands so that nobody could see it," he recalled. "This young man was still kneeling down. I walked over to him and smiled. His face just lit up. I thought a ray of light had come through the sky. He put the picture inside his clothes, and left. That is a picture that I will die holding in my mind. At that point, I made a commitment to do whatever I could to support Tibet, for this one young courageous man. He could have been shot and killed if he had been found with that picture."

Senator Di Nino, who chaired Parliamentary Friends of Tibet in the Canadian Parliament, went on to meet the Dalai Lama many times. "I can't say we became friends, but I would say we became spiritual brothers," he says. In 1990, Canada's prime minister at the time, Brian Mulroney, appointed Di Nino to the Canadian Senate, and soon after his appointment, the senator learned that the Dalai Lama was due to visit Montréal. "Nobody in government had ever met him before that point, so I went to Canada's foreign minister at the time, Barbara McDougall, and said, 'Barbara, you and I are going to get on a plane tomorrow, fly to Montréal, and officially welcome the Dalai Lama to Canada.' She said, 'That's a good idea.' So I booked the flights, and we went. We greeted the Dalai Lama, he gave us Tibetan scarves, and Barbara asked me, 'How did you get this approved?' I said, 'The rest of government will find out tomorrow morning when they read it in the newspapers.' I talked to the prime minister the next day, and we laughed like hell. He only found out then that his foreign minister met the Dalai Lama and he did not even know about it. The Tibetans would say, that's the power of *karma*."

In 2012, the Dalai Lama asked Senator Di Nino to host a World Parliamentarians' Convention on Tibet, in Canada. "When the Dalai Lama and I met at the opening reception, he came up to me and put his nose against mine, saying, 'Friends rub noses.' I had a beard at the time, and he yanked it and asked 'What's this?' I told him it keeps me warm," Senator Di Nino recalls.

"He is a very humble individual who has a wisdom about life which is incomparable to all the other experiences I have had," reflects Senator Di Nino. "He is very generous with his time, he does not talk at you, he talks with you, he has a dialogue, and he is deeply considerate. He has something so special; it is difficult for a human being to describe. When you are with him, there is an aura of calmness, peace, an awareness that he is a very holy man. The only other person with whom I have felt a similar aura was Pope Saint John Paul II."

British member of Parliament and former government minister Tim Loughton has similar reflections. Loughton first became involved in Tibet as a schoolboy, when he joined a protest outside the Chinese embassy, "waving Tibetan flags." Family friends in Sussex had adopted a Tibetan boy, and that drew him in to the cause. "I joined the Tibet Society, and then when I was elected to Parliament, I joined the All-Party Parliamentary Group for Tibet, and then became its chair."

Loughton has visited Dharamsala twice, hosted the Dalai Lama on his visit to the British Parliament in 2009, and met him again on his 2012 visit to London. "He is the most delightful figure. He speaks English well, with a strong accent, and every other sentence, he giggles. He is a great giggler—he chuckles at everything," Loughton reflects. "He is also the most impossible person to chaperone. When he came in 2009, David Cameron, as Leader of the Opposition, met him. I had to meet him at David Cameron's office, and then escort him to Westminster Hall to address members of Parliament there. It is a five-minute walk, but it took us at least three-quarters of an hour, because he wanted to say hello to everybody, and everybody wanted to say hello to him—from the cleaners, the police officers, everybody kept stopping and taking selfies, and, of course, he gave time to everybody. And he is so funny—everybody absolutely loved him."

When the Dalai Lama visited London in 2012, however, David Cameron was in government and Loughton was himself a minister. Although when he was in opposition Cameron had criticized Gordon Brown for not receiving the Dalai Lama in Downing Street, meeting him instead at the Archbishop of Canterbury's residence at Lambeth Palace, as prime minister, Cameron received him at St. Paul's Cathedral with his deputy prime minister, Nick Clegg.

The Speaker of the House of Commons at the time, John Bercow, hosted a lunch for the Dalai Lama in Speaker's House, but Loughton—and another minister, the Liberal Democrat Norman Baker, a long-time Tibet supporter—were instructed by the government not to attend. "We had a call from 10 Downing Street, but Norman and I said, 'Sod that,'" recalls Loughton. "But then the Foreign Office Minister Jeremy Browne spoke to Norman in person, and we were basically told that if we went to the lunch, we would be sacked as ministers. We were prepared to tough it out, but, in fact, the previous evening, we had been at an event in the Royal Albert Hall in the front row, where we had had a special audience with His Holiness, so we decided we may as well not go to the lunch. But it was so clumsily handled."

John Bercow himself told me he had no intention of giving in to any pressure not to host the Dalai Lama. He recalled that he received complaints from the Chinese embassy, to which he responded, he said, as follows: "Forgive me, but I am operating as a Parliamentarian. You are not dealing government to government. I am not a government; I am the Speaker of the British House of

Commons. And I have simply invited the Dalai Lama to a working lunch with members of the All-Party Parliamentary Group. I am grateful for your views, but I fully intend to go ahead with the event."

The former Speaker added that the Chinese complaint showed a fundamental misunderstanding of democracy and the British constitution. "There was a suggestion that they might complain to the British government, but I reminded them that the Speaker is independent of government, and this particular Speaker was particularly independent of government."

Bercow's recollection of the event itself is in keeping with that of every other person who has met His Holiness. "The Dalai Lama was extremely personable. He made some general remarks; he underlined the importance of the rights of his fellow Tibetans. Did he make a long political speech? No, he didn't," recalls Bercow. "My overriding impression of the Dalai Lama was what a kindly, godly, decent man he was. Fundamentally serious, but with a twinkle. And a great sense of humour and quite a notable giggle, which was rather endearing. And you know, he was not seeking conflict; he was simply seeking autonomy. If the Chinese Communist Party regime were wetting their pants and spewing their noodles over an invitation to Speaker's House with twenty people, then I wish I had invited him to speak in Westminster Hall, which would really have caused a row."

The Chinese regime has a habit of threatening foreign politicians who host or meet the Dalai Lama. According to Loughton, even Scotland's First Minister, Alex Salmond, declined to meet the Tibetan spiritual leader in the face of Chinese pressure. "They ring up and say, 'We won't be dealing with this company or that; we won't give money for that investment, if you go ahead,'" said Loughton. "On top of that, they pay protesters to try to wreck the Dalai Lama's speeches. They are just so manic about closing him down, that it becomes a bigger story about the Chinese regime trying to censor the Dalai Lama rather than just letting him go and speak."

Another British Parliamentarian, Lord Alton, hosted the Dalai Lama in his home city of Liverpool in 2004. Lord Alton, first inspired to take an interest in Tibet by the great Liberal Parliamentarian Eric Lubbock—who became Lord Avebury, a Buddhist, and a human rights champion—was, by this point, running a lecture series named after the great Liverpool member of Parliament and anti-slavery campaigner William Roscoe, who, along with William Wilberforce, led the campaign against the slave trade in the late eighteenth century. Lord Alton, who held an academic chair at Liverpool John Moores University, cites Roscoe as one of his "heroes," and thought it "seemed very natural" to invite the Dalai Lama to deliver one of the lectures in his memory.

Upon hearing that the Tibetan spiritual leader would be visiting Liverpool, the Chinese ambassador to the United Kingdom telephoned the vice chancellor of Liverpool John Moores University and the Lord Mayor of Liverpool. "They threatened the vice chancellor that if this went ahead, there would be no more Chinese students coming to Liverpool, and they told the Lord Mayor that if the council proceeded with the civic reception for the Dalai Lama, the twinning arrangement between Liverpool and Shanghai would be broken," recalls Lord Alton. "I was telephoned by the vice chancellor and the Lord Mayor, who asked how they should respond. I said that when a Chinese gunboat arrived in the River Mersey, they should start to get worried, but until then, if we capitulated to these bellicose threats of a bully, then the very things we as a university and a city stood for would be diminished and we would suffer a serious reputational loss."

Indeed, Liverpool stood firm, and the Dalai Lama was received by the dean of Liverpool Cathedral, to deliver a lecture hosted by the Anglican bishop of Liverpool; the Catholic archbishop; and by Hindu, Muslim, and Jewish religious leaders. Three thousand people filled the Cathedral, with vast overflows outside.

"The Dalai Lama is a deeply spiritual and good man," Lord Alton said. "I was very struck by the way he handled Liverpool during that visit. He did not try to proselytize—instead, he told people to take their own beliefs more seriously and try to live them out. He understood the sectarian history of Liverpool and the spiritual impulses of the people he was talking to, and he won hearts and minds."

His Holiness the Dalai Lama affirmed his commitment to promoting "inter-religious harmony" in an interview with me for this book. "Since all our religious traditions profess to bring about inner peace, we have to make an effort to create harmony between us," he told me. "I am a great admirer of the thought of ancient India, *Ahimsa*, which means 'non-violence' or 'do no harm.' *Ahimsa* is not just a matter of being non-violent in our actions, but also of being compassionate in our hearts. So, in India, secularism means cultivating respect for the convictions of all those of religious faith, as well as those who have none."

Western "secularism" is considered by some to mean having no respect for any religion, the Dalai Lama added, but "since all religious traditions convey a message of love, tolerance, and self-discipline, they all have the potential to serve humanity and so are worthy of respect." Religious adherents "have a responsibility to foster interreligious harmony." When he lived in Tibet, he recalled, he "considered Buddhism was best because it was what I was familiar with," but once he reached India, his view changed. "When I came into contact with Christians like Thomas Merton and Mother Teresa, as well as wonderful Hindu, Jewish, and Muslim friends, I developed a real appreciation and respect for other traditions," he said.

During the Dalai Lama's visit to Liverpool, a small film festival on Tibet was held, and Lord Alton addressed one of the opening events. "What touched me more than anything else," he recalls, "was that as I left having made my speech, I encountered two young Chinese students. I asked if they were going to see the film, but they told me they did not have tickets. I happened to have two tickets in my pocket, so I offered them to them, but I asked why they wanted to go. They said, 'because we would never be allowed to see them at home, and we would like to understand more about this issue.' That was a very powerful statement to me about the importance of academic freedom, intellectual curiosity, and the fundamental yearning all of us as human beings have: to enjoy the liberties we have been given."

As a consequence, the Chinese regime—having expressed their fury to Lord Alton—invited him to visit Tibet. On the understanding that they would be self-funding, Lord Alton organized a cross-party delegation—including the former Liberal Party leader Lord Steel, Conservative member of Parliament James Gray, and a Labour MP, Derek Wyatt—to visit Tibet and China.

"We raised individual human rights cases, we put forward proposals about the status of Lhasa, and with the full authority of the Dalai Lama, we were able to quote him as saying that he no longer believed that the way forward was for a separate state," recalls Lord Alton. "Lord Steel was able to provide insights about the Scottish model of devolution, having been the first Speaker of the first Scottish Parliament."

But as with Di Nino, Lord Alton encountered the emotions not far beneath the surface. "Privately, many people in Tibet showed us pictures of the Dalai Lama, even though they were banned and illegal," Lord Alton told me in a conversation in Waterstones bookstore off Trafalgar Square in London one January morning in 2022. "If you have to be frightened of people having a picture of a religious leader, or lighting a candle in a vigil, then it says a lot about you and your ideology—and the fear that the Chinese Communist Party regime has of religion."

Another Western politician who has met the Dalai Lama is former U.S.

ambassador-at-large for international religious freedom Sam Brownback, who travelled to Dharamsala in 2019. "I went there to specifically state the U.S. government position that we do not support the Chinese Communist Party's assertion that they get to pick the next Dalai Lama," Ambassador Brownback told me. "I wanted to go there as a government official and say we oppose this, this is ridiculous. This is not the way that the Dalai Lama has ever been chosen, in the history of Tibetan Buddhism. We are not going to stand for it. So I went there and delivered a speech, and met with the Dalai Lama." It was their second meeting, as Brownback had previously met the Tibetan leader when he was a United States senator and the Dalai Lama visited Washington, D.C. "I have always been impressed with his leadership and the Tibetans' willingness to continue to fight for their faith, through incredible hardship and lack of support from the outside world. The outside world will speak about it, but they do not act. They won't sanction China for what the regime is doing in Tibet. They will say Tibet should be free, but they won't do anything to make it happen."

During his visit to Dharamsala, Brownback was told by another Lama that their prediction is that when the Dalai Lama dies, the regime in Beijing will simply appoint the eleventh Panchen Lama as the new Dalai Lama. The Chinese regime kidnapped Gedhun Choekyi Nyima, aged just six years old at the time, on May 17, 1995, three days after he was recognized as Panchen Lama. He has been held hostage ever since. "They have raised him, enculturated him, and trained him, and so it would not be surprising if they simply wheel him out and say, 'This is the No. 2. This is the reincarnation. This is the new Dalai Lama.' Well, we need to draw the sting out of that, ahead of time. The Dalai Lama told me that they have put a succession system in place. He also told me that he believes he will outlive the Chinese Communist Party. And the Sikyong told me something that I think is really true. He said, 'either the world will change China, or China will change the world.' Either the world is going to stand up to China and change how it is operating, or China's way of operating now will become the global system. It is that stark a choice. The world has got to stand up; otherwise, the Chinese authoritarian mercantilist model will become the dominant model in the world."

Senator Di Nino believes that whoever China tries to appoint as Dalai Lama will simply not be accepted. "The system that the Tibetans have will continue. They will put in place a search team. The Tibetans in the free world will choose a Dalai Lama. China will put in some flunky and claim it is the Dalai Lama, but the world will never recognize him, and nor will Tibetans."

Tim Loughton agrees. "The Dalai Lama speaks about the question of his successor quite openly, and points out that one of his predecessors was from Mongolia, so there is a precedent of Dalai Lamas being found outside the modern borders of Tibet or China," he notes. "The Dalai Lama has made preparations for a group of learned monks to form a search party to find his reincarnation. Of course, they always identify an infant. So there will be a regent until the Dalai Lama is old enough to take over properly. No doubt the Chinese will go out and locate someone themselves; they will get some 'useful idiots' who claim to be learned Tibetan monks to lead the party, and will come up with their own Dalai Lama. Then you will have two competing Dalai Lamas, but only one will be recognized by the rest of the world."

The irony, Loughton adds, is that an atheist communist regime that hates religion would be going through a process of recognizing reincarnation. "So the Chinese are in a slightly difficult position. They could say this is all hocus pocus and we are not going along with it, and therefore there is no more Dalai Lama, but that is unlikely."

On his visits to Dharamsala, Loughton has heard first-hand accounts of the human rights situation in Tibet. "On my first visit, I recall meeting a woman whose husband, a filmmaker, had disappeared. He had been making a covert film about Tibet and had gone undercover in Tibet and been arrested by the Chinese authorities and never seen again. She was about thirty years old, had several children, was quite well educated, but was relying on selling bread in the street to make a living," he recalls. "She broke down in tears when she told us what had happened. She had no idea if she would ever see her husband again, and was reduced to selling bread in the street. I was so moved that I bought all of her bread and gave her $100, which hopefully kept her going for a while."

Everybody in Dharamsala, Loughton reflects, has a similar story. "I met other people whose relatives had just disappeared, quite a few refugees who had recently escaped, and some nuns who had escaped and showed us their torture scars. Some horrendous things had been done to them. Some of them broke down in tears, telling us through translators what had happened," he recalls.

And yet the courage, dignity, and dynamism of the Tibetans are inspiring. "We met the Tibetan Parliament in exile, visited the museum of Tibetan repression, went to see some of the schools and educational projects, and the thing that struck me was that in almost every house, there was a Tibetan on a computer communicating with somebody inside Tibet, trying to counter the Chinese regime's propaganda," Loughton recalls. "Even monks are completely tooled up and on the Internet. They are smarter than you might imagine."

Given how moderate, non-violent, and much-loved around the world the Dalai Lama is, the Chinese Communist Party regime's sheer hatred of him—as well as paranoia about foreign governments or organizations meeting him—is difficult to comprehend. Lord Alton describes it as "hatred of difference," given that the regime in Beijing is "a monochrome system that reveres only one thing—their own ideology and Party—and they see religion as an opposing force, because it gives people freedom to think about things they cannot control." In contrast to the Dalai Lama, he says, the Chinese regime "is not capable of winning hearts, and it is only capable of controlling minds, so that is why they see him as such a danger to their hegemony."

Loughton believes the regime's hostility to the Dalai Lama is "a huge miscalculation" because "everybody loves the Dalai Lama." The Tibetan people, he adds, "do not have the power to subvert the Chinese Constitution, they just want to be able to live peacefully in Tibet, talking Tibetan language, studying Tibetan culture and religion, and all of that is guaranteed to them under the Chinese Constitution and yet is patently not being observed. All the Dalai Lama asks for is the implementation of the Chinese Constitution." The regime's hatred is based, he believes, on "its paranoid need for sameness and conformity. They want to turn the huge area of Tibet into the same as the rest of China. So they have flooded Lhasa and the whole of Tibet with Han Chinese, so that the indigenous population is hugely outnumbered by the influx. They see all monasteries and cultural institutions as a threat to their way of thinking." From a propaganda perspective, it would, he suggests, "have been really clever to embrace the Dalai Lama and say, 'Yes, of course, have your schools, speak your language.' And the rest of the world would probably stop calling out human rights violations in Tibet."

Tenzin Choekyi has lived all her life in exile, growing up in India and now based in Europe. She emphasizes the challenges facing the Tibetan exile community around the world, and the importance of not forgetting their suffering, or perceiving it as separate from the repression in Tibet. "Being a Tibetan means that you are thinking of different places at the same time," she told me. "Those inside Tibet are thinking of the world outside Tibet, and those outside Tibet in exile are thinking of those inside Tibet. This is how it is to not have freedom in one's own land. It affects our daily lives."

In 2008, when protests erupted in Tibet, Tenzin Choekyi was in her final year of school in India, about to sit the All India Secondary School Examination. "It is a very competitive and stressful time for students, but it was even more difficult for us Tibetans, as we were really caught up in the turmoil in Tibet," she recalls. "One classmate stood up and proposed we march from Dharamsala to New Delhi in solidarity with Tibet—right when we were preparing for exams. We started each day with a minute's silence to mourn those who passed away. You could not really focus on your future as a student, or your career. I remember asking myself what is the purpose of education, as exiled Tibetans. The purpose is one day to get freedom and go back to Tibet."

Tibetan exiles, Tenzin Choekyi said, "live in perpetual hope of returning to Tibet, and yet, at the same time, our lives are just going on and it is really sad. In India, we are stateless people, foreigners, and yet if we want to return to our own country, we have to apply for a visa—which is often denied. Communication between exiles and their relatives still in Tibet is almost impossible now, because the Chinese regime's surveillance technology makes it too dangerous. "Many Tibetans are scared to talk to their families, and they would not share one word about what is happening," Tenzin Choekyi adds.

Escaping Tibet is becoming more and more difficult, due to the militarization of the borders. According to a survey done by the Central Tibetan Administration in 2021, following Sikyong Penpa Tsering's election, only seven Tibetans were able to reach India as of September 2021.[40] "That is a sharp fall from the hundreds and thousands who escaped in the 1990s," Tenzin Choekyi notes. It is made worse by changes in Nepal, which is now "very much under China's control." The escape route across the Himalayas and through Nepal is now much more dangerous. In elections for the Tibetan government-in-exile, the Nepalese authorities confiscated Tibetan exiles' ballot boxes. "Nepal is like the next Tibet, Tibetans often say."

The regime in Beijing has gone to extensive efforts to infiltrate, threaten, undermine, and divide the Tibetan community in exile. As Tenzin Dorjee notes in an article for the Jamestown Foundation's China Brief in September 2021, "Beijing has historically viewed the Tibetan diaspora—with its resilient government in exile and highly effective transnational advocacy movement—as a threat to China's international reputation and its foreign policy objectives" and has therefore been "expanding its overseas influence operations targeting the Tibetan diaspora, refining its strategies, and innovating new tactics to counter the Tibet movement."[41] While Dharamsala and Kathmandu "have been menaced for decades," writes Tenzin Dorjee, "this problem has now spread to Western outposts of the Tibetan diaspora."

Outside of the Indian subcontinent, the largest Tibetan diaspora community is, according to Tenzin Dorjee, in New York City, making it "a prime target for the United Front Work Department (UFWD), the agency of the Chinese government responsible for managing or pre-empting potential sources of opposition to the Chinese Communist Party's rule." The first objective for the Chinese regime is to sow division, and another is to "depoliticize the Tibetan diaspora."

One powerful tool at the regime's disposal is access to family. "All exiles dream of the home they left behind," writes Tenzin Dorjee. "For exiles who have elderly parents back home, this yearning can turn into desperation in the event of parental sickness or other emergencies. In the exiles' desire to visit their ancestral home and reconnect with their families, Beijing sees a strategic vulnerability." Careful vetting of visa applications, interrogation of Tibetans applying for a visa, and a requirement to provide details of all relatives in Tibet are some of the measures the regime now deploys. "Each piece of information surrendered to the consulate is a data point that Beijing uses to map the Tibetan diaspora, linking the individual exile to their more vulnerable family members back home. This transnational relationship mapping is designed to seed a hypothetical sense of guilt in the conscience of the exile; it is meant to instil in the targeted individual the advance feeling that her political participation in exile might endanger her family in Tibet. The ultimate goal . . . is the political deactivation of the exile."

Tibet matters. It matters as an issue of right and wrong, freedom and justice, truth and lies. But even if, for you, those values do not count, it matters for another reason, another epic challenge of our time: climate change.

Tim Loughton expressed how impressed he is with the thinking on climate change among the Tibetans in Dharamsala. "They have some really interesting academic experts, whose research on what is happening on the Tibetan plateau is crucial," he told me. "The Tibetan Plateau, which they refer to as the Third Pole, is the largest site of glaciers and permanent ice outside the North and South Pole. At its current rate, most of it will have melted by 2050. The Tibetan Plateau is directly and indirectly responsible for providing water to 30 percent of the world's population."

Having read at least one such paper, published by the University of Aberdeen and the Scottish Centre for Himalayan Research, I agree. As the authors of this report point out, Tibet is at the centre of the Third Pole Region, "a high-altitude massif at the heart of Asia comprising the Tibetan Plateau and its surrounding mountain ranges," and in this region—almost the size of Europe with an average altitude of 4,000 metres above sea level—"the Plateau's glaciers, snow, and permanently frozen ground (permafrost)—its *cryosphere*—contain within it the largest mass of frozen freshwater outside the polar regions."[42]

This region depends, the report argues, "on snowfall and freezing winters, storing frozen freshwater at high altitude," and contains the "headwaters" of ten major rivers: the Yellow, Yangtse, Mekong, Salween, Irrawaddy, Brahmaputra, Ganges, Sutlej, Indus, and Tarim. "In total, 1.9 billion people live within the watersheds of these rivers and depend upon them directly for freshwater supplies, and some 4.1 billion people are fed by agriculture and industry dependent upon these supplies—more than half the world's present population," this report claims.

"There is clear evidence that temperatures across the Third Pole Region (TPR) are increasing at a rate between two and four times the global average, a process that has been underway for more than half a century," the study notes, leading to a situation whereby "glaciers are reducing in size, permafrost is melting, snowfall is turning to rain: the overall pattern is for the Tibetan Plateau in particular to become progressively warmer and wetter." Unless there are significant changes, this will result, over the next fifty years, in "increased flooding south of the Himalayas; escalating disruption of human infrastructure in permafrost areas; the desertification of high-altitude river headlands and grasslands in eastern Tibet; and the loss of freshwater supplies to mountain communities and urban centres downstream of the TPR, particularly those in India, Pakistan, and Xinjiang that depend on glacial meltwaters." It would also lead to "a destabilization of year-round freshwater resources to inland regions around the TPR."

Tenzin Choekyi was among a group of Tibetans who participated in the COP 26 Climate Change Conference in Glasgow in 2021. "Nobody knows about the extent of the climate crisis in Tibet," she explained. "There is so much focus on island nations, but the elevation of Tibet, the icy expanse of Tibet, is just as critical as the North and South Poles. The snow is melting in Tibet, glaciers are collapsing, frozen ground that has remained frozen for thousands of years is slowly melting."

Mass forced relocations, according to Tenzin Choekyi, are also "devastating" to Tibet's environment, because they eradicate Tibetans' farming and nomadic communities and their sustainable way of life. "What the government does not seem to know is that these nomads are the foundation of the Tibetan way of life," she explained. "When it is really cold weather, they graze their livestock in the lower altitude regions, and in the summer, they go further up. The pastures are seasonal. The nomads know how to respect the land; they know the limits of the livestock. They have such a rich knowledge of animal husbandry. When you have thousands of nomads removed, that affects the eco-system of Tibet and Mainland China." In addition, she adds, "the government is diverging the rivers in Tibet to supply the parched north of China. But these water diversion schemes are disastrous. The sources of these rivers are drying up."

Tibet's environmental crisis is interlinked with its struggle for freedom, argues Tenzin Choekyi. "If Tibet was an independent country, we would have our own table to talk about our experience facing the climate crisis, determine our own policy direction," she said. "But because Tibet is colonized by China and remains under occupation, inside these big conferences such as COP, in discussions that affect the whole world, when we do speak about it, people are shocked. The Third Pole is melting; it will affect two billion people, but there is no Tibetan representation in climate change talks."

Tibet remains more closed than ever. As Loughton noted, "it is very difficult to get information out now, because there are far fewer refugees able to get out and far fewer visits by outsiders. It has been several years, for example, since a British ambassador has visited Tibet. They are just not letting outside people in, and if they are, they are very, very heavily marshalled."

What is known, however, is that the Chinese regime is attempting, simultaneously, the destruction of Tibetan identity and culture and what Loughton calls its "Disneyfication," with the construction of hotels on monastery sites and "fake Tibetan cultural sites," aimed at the domestic Chinese tourist market. "It is complete desecration," he said. The Dalai Lama has expressed concern that, due to a mass immigration programme, "the population of [Han] Chinese in Tibet now comfortably exceeds that of Tibetans. My countrymen and women are today in grave danger of becoming nothing more than a tourist attraction in their own country."[43]

As Senator Di Nino concluded, it is vital that we "should not forget the Tibetan cause." And we should ask the Chinese regime, as he does, "What are you hiding?" If, as Beijing claims, life in Tibet has improved, "then allow free and open access."

One of the signs of how desperate the situation has become is the practice of self-immolation. As Professor Anand said, self-immolations continue "because other gatherings are not allowed."[44] Human Rights Watch reports that between

2009 and 2020, 155 Tibetans have self-immolated. As Wangden Kyab told me, "it is not easy to sacrifice one's life. They are not drunk when they do this. It is a sign of their desperation and commitment. They feel they are burning themselves for their forefathers and future generations. Even when their whole body is on fire, they are shouting 'Free Tibet.'"

Today's Tibet, Wangden Kyab said, "is a prison" in which "your movements are monitored, your thoughts corrected, and your rights confiscated, snatched, crushed." However, like almost all the Tibetans I spoke to, he holds on to hope. "They cannot kill all the Tibetans. So, as long as there is a single Tibetan on this earth, their spirit will remain for generations. One day, we can have our own country."

Nyima Lhamo expressed a similar belief. "Our hope is driven by the fact that the truth always prevails, truth is on our side," she told me. "That is why Tibetans are hopeful, because truth always wins."

For her and most Tibetans, their two desires are to meet the Dalai Lama, and to see Tibet free. "We want to be able to live our own lives, to live in freedom, to live with our heads held high," she said.

Lobsang Tseten, a young Tibetan who was translating for Nyima Lhamo in our interview, added an additional aspiration. Born and raised in exile, he said he had "no bigger desire than to be a citizen of a free Tibet, to walk on the streets of Tibet, and—as a football fan—to watch the Tibetan national football team play in the World Cup." Admitting it was "a far-fetched dream," nevertheless, he said, "I want to sit in a stadium and cheer the Tibetan football team. For us, freedom comes in these small forms. I also want to take part in a nation-building process, to elect Tibetan leaders in Tibet."

According to the Dalai Lama, "the truth remains that, since the Chinese invasion, over a million Tibetans have died as a direct result of Peking's [Beijing's] policies."[45] Despite that, he argues that Mao's comment that "political power comes from the barrel of a gun" is "only partly right." The barrel of a gun, His Holiness believes, "can be effective only for a short time. In the end, people's love for truth, justice, freedom, and democracy will triumph. No matter what governments do, the human spirit will always prevail."[46] I hope he is right, and that Nyima Lhamo, Tsering Dawa, Wangden Kyab, Lobsang Tseten, Tenzin Choekyi, and all the other Tibetans who have shared their sufferings with me see freedom, and that His Holiness the Dalai Lama returns to Tibet, one day.

CHAPTER 6

UYGHUR GENOCIDE

CALL IT BY NAME

"Son, they are taking me." Those were the last words Kuzzat Altay heard from his father, in a WeChat message in 2018. His father, a sixty-seven-year-old Uyghur in Xinjiang (or "East Turkistan" as the Uyghurs prefer to call it), is believed to be among the estimated one million—perhaps as many as three million—people forced into "extra-legal internment camps," sometimes referred to as re-education camps or, by the Chinese authorities, "concentrated educational transformation centres," in China's northwest region, known as the Xinjiang Uyghur Autonomous Region (XUAR), in the most severe crackdown on human rights since the Cultural Revolution.[1]

"I don't know if he is still alive," Kuzzat added. "None of my relatives now are outside the concentration camps."

In the Uyghur cultural centre Kuzzat sponsors in the U.S. state of Virginia, he asked a gathering of 300 Uyghurs which of them have family members in the camps. Every single hand went up. "The main centres in our cities—our equivalent of New York's Times Square or London's Trafalgar Square—are empty," he explained. "People don't even have the freedom to breathe."

Similar stories have been recounted to me by almost every Uyghur I have met. Rahima Mahmut, a Uyghur singer and activist based in London, has not been able to speak to her family since January 2017. "When I could not get hold of anyone, I became very worried," she told me over lunch in a Uyghur restaurant in north London. "One day, I rang my eldest brother non-stop until he finally picked up the phone. I asked him why no one was answering. He replied, 'They did the right thing. We are fine. Please leave us in God's hands, and we will leave you in God's hands, too.' Since then, I have not spoken to any of my family. I don't have any information about them. I have really bad repeated nightmares, imagining that my sister and brothers have been taken away. This is quite common for most Uyghurs in exile."

Nury Turkel was born in a re-education camp at the height of the Cultural Revolution. Now he is an American citizen, a lawyer, and the chair of the United States Commission on International Religious Freedom, nominated to the body by the Speaker of the House of Representatives, Nancy Pelosi. "My mother was sent to a re-education camp, my father was sent to a forced labour camp, and I was brought into this world in those conditions by my wonderful parents who were punished simply because of who they were—their educational background and family ties," he told me. "Fifty years later, I have to tell these stories again. I had thought this was over; I thought that we would no longer have to talk of collective punishment, but today it is happening again." And what is most painful to him is the world's inaction. "I never thought the world would look the other way, in the face of this industrial-scale repression and genocide. I never thought that I would have to use my own story to make the case for why people should not be indifferent. Silence is tacit approval. I never thought that the civilized world, the business community, some in academia, and some politicians would be so entangled in Chinese economic interests that they would fail to do the right thing. Is this the 'humanity' we teach?"

The Uyghurs are a Turkic people, numbering in total around 13.5 million and inhabiting the historical Silk Road trading route that links Asia and Europe, across the Taklamakan Desert within the Tarim Basin, a vast area in Central Asia. They have been a predominantly Muslim people since the seventeenth century, and were introduced to Islam in the tenth century. Islam spread from the west to the east of the region, from Kashgar to Turpan, over several hundred years. James Millward states that "Xinjiang was Islamicized by the seventeenth century," although "the process had begun earlier, its onset signalled by the tenth-century conversion of Satuq Bughra Khan."[2]

Uyghur culture has always remained distinct from that of the Han Chinese. Uyghurs have their own language, religion, traditional music, literature, poetry, and cuisine, which have much more in common with Central Asian and other Turkic cultures than with Han culture. Indeed, as Sean Roberts notes in his book

The War on the Uyghurs: China's Campaign Against Xinjiang's Muslims, the region the Uyghurs inhabit "only really started becoming a constituent part of a larger China when the Qing Dynasty conquered it in the 1750s, and only became integrated into a larger Chinese territorial polity in the late nineteenth century when the Qing made it a province of its domain."[3] It was named "Xinjiang—which in Chinese means "new frontier"—by the imperial invaders, and for that reason Uyghurs themselves reject the term.

With the exception of a period of some thirteen years when a warlord from Khoqand, Yaqub Beg, wrested control of the region from the Chinese empire in 1865, Xinjiang had been under various forms of Chinese rule since Emperor Qianlong annexed it. However, after the fall of the Qing Dynasty and the formation of the Republic of China in 1912, Uyghurs staged several uprisings against Chinese rule. Between 1933 and 1934, the First East Turkistan Republic was formed,[4] but its independence was short-lived and Chinese warlord Sheng Shicai ruled the region from 1934 to 1943. Sheng Shicai's brutal reign fuelled discontent among the Uyghurs and other Turkic peoples in the region, leading to the Ili Rebellion in 1944, which resulted in the establishment of a second East Turkistan Republic, backed by the Soviet Union, that lasted from November 12, 1944, until December 22, 1949.

Uyghurs' modern experience of independence ended when Mao Zedong and the People's Liberation Army invaded and incorporated the region into the People's Republic of China. Eight Uyghur leaders, including the leader of the Second East Turkistan Republic, Ehmetjan Qasim, died in a mysterious plane crash on their way to negotiate a settlement with the new Chinese Communist Party rulers. To this day, Uyghurs suspect foul play.

Like everyone in China, Uyghurs suffered from the catastrophic famine caused by Mao's agricultural reform campaign known as the Great Leap Forward, and the repression and chaos of the decade of the Cultural Revolution from 1966 to 1976. Mosques were destroyed or vandalized, and Uyghurs were subjected to religious and racial persecution. Those who owned private property or businesses had their property taken by the Party and were sent to the countryside.

Rahima Mahmut, who grew up in Ghulja, recalls the experience. "My father had a business selling fruit, and making leather boots. I am one of eleven siblings in my family, and we had an eight-bedroom house in Ghulja city. But after the communists came, all private businesses were closed. Even people selling fruit were forced to leave the city and go to the countryside," she told me.

The family moved to her grandfather's house in a remote mountainous village called Noghaytu, but even there, they were afraid. "My grandfather was quite well off; he had a really big, beautiful house. But he feared the regime would take away his house because he owned more land than the government allowed," Rahima recalled. "He gave us half his orchard, and my father built a house for us. But life was not easy. My father came from a religious background, and he never stopped practising religion, and praying. Every time we prayed, my father always told us not to tell anyone; otherwise, the police would take us away."

After the chaos and destruction of the Cultural Revolution, Deng Xiaoping—who succeeded Mao—launched his "Reform and Opening-Up" policy, inviting foreign investment, encouraging a market economy, and modernizing the country. Declaring famously that "to get rich is glorious," the Party under Deng adopted a somewhat more relaxed approach to social freedoms, religious practice, and cultural traditions. "The mosques reopened, and I could see the joy on people's faces, being able to gather as a community at the mosque again," recalled Rahima.

Dolkun Isa, president of the World Uyghur Congress, agrees. "The 1980s until 1990, those ten years were a golden time for the Uyghurs if you compare it to now," he told me in an online call from his home in Germany. "There were signs of some sort of freedom of expression and assembly. That time we set up students' clubs, such as the students' cultural and science union, and held gatherings and demonstrations. I was not killed; no one was killed."

Born in Aksu, Dolkun enrolled in Xinjiang University in Ürümchi, the region's capital, to study physics in 1984. The following year, demonstrations broke out in Ürümchi against nuclear testing in the region, the one-child policy, and forced population transfer to the region, and for democracy.

Since the 1960s, the Chinese government had been conducting nuclear tests at the Lop Nor Nuclear Test Base, which it had established in the eastern fringe of the Tarim Basin, between the Taklamakan and Kumtag Deserts, although it called a moratorium on nuclear testing in 1996. Japanese Professor Jun Takada has documented forty-six nuclear tests over approximately thirty years, causing up to 190,000 deaths in the surrounding areas.[5] Later, in 1998, another Uyghur friend of mine, a surgeon called Enver Tohti, helped a documentary film crew from Britain's Channel 4 News "Dispatches" series research and produce a powerful film about the public health effects of China's nuclear tests in Xinjiang. *Death on the Silk Road* claimed that the nuclear bombs China was testing were 300 times more powerful than the bomb dropped on Hiroshima, and had caused a dramatic increase in cancer patients in the region and deformities in children. "Cancer is everywhere in Xinjiang," one doctor said. Indeed, deaths from cancer doubled from 1993 to 2000. And, of the cancers that were increasing most rapidly, it was malignant lymphoma, lung cancer, and leukaemia that predominated—the three cancers most closely associated with nuclear radiation.[6]

Dolkun, who took part in the Ürümchi protests in December 1985, recalls that the university and the authorities were quite lenient in response. "No student leaders were punished. After graduation, a few student leaders were sent to rural areas, but that was all. That December 1985 pro-democracy movement had a strong impact on me and played a huge role in influencing my future activism," he said.

"In addition, I realized that under the Chinese Constitution as it is written, we have a lot of rights," he added. "We had to go to political study classes in university, once a week, where we learned about the Constitution, about the autonomy law, about Chinese central government policy. I learned that everyone has the right to assembly, to demonstrate, and, under the autonomy law, we have linguistic rights and that Uyghur is an official language. But in reality, these rights are not implemented. Naively, I thought maybe the problem is implementation, combined with the fact that so many Uyghurs and Kazakhs are illiterate, so they are not knowledgeable about their rights and do not know how to demand them. There was an urgent need to educate our people."

So Dolkun decided to mobilize Uyghur students to volunteer to educate the illiterate people and to teach them about the Constitution and autonomy laws. He established a Students Cultural Science Union in 1987, which held seminars every week and sent thousands of students to rural areas during the summer and winter holidays to give classes throughout the region. But although the university authorities approved of the initiative, the local Chinese Communist Party put up "a lot of barriers," recalled Dolkun. "It was then that I understood that the Chinese Constitution, the autonomy laws, and other laws are just for show. It is all fake. If you actually try to exercise your rights according to the Constitution and the law, it is not possible."

So on June 15, 1988—a year before the Tiananmen Square pro-democracy protests and massacre—Dolkun and his fellow students organized a big protest on campus, with 8,000 participants.

"That same day, I and my colleagues were invited to meet with high-level

Chinese Communist Party officials, including the region's Party Secretary, education minister, finance minister, the president of Xinjiang University, and other Party officials," he recalled.

"For more than five hours, we had a debate about all sorts of issues—discrimination in daily life, discrimination in education, language rights, and many other issues—but we could not get a compromise," he said. "After five hours, I returned to the university, and we started the demonstration."

The Party's patience with Dolkun had run out, and at midnight, he was taken to the university authorities and placed under house arrest for four months. After the demonstration, the Chinese government set up a large investigation working group, stopped classes for three days, interrogated every student, and coerced them into writing confession letters about their involvement. Then Dolkun and one other student leader, Waris Ababekri (who would later die following his release from one of the detention camps in November 2019), were expelled from the university, without graduating.

A year later, nationwide pro-democracy protests erupted, culminating in the massacre on June 4, 1989 in Tiananmen Square. One of the main student leaders in Beijing was a Uyghur, Wu'erkaixi, who became the second most wanted student among the government's targets for arrest. On May 18 at 11 a.m., together with Wang Dan and other student leaders, he publicly met with Premier Li Peng and other Chinese Communist Party leaders in the Great Hall of the People, in front of television cameras.

"When Li Peng and other top Party leaders accepted our invitation to meet representatives of the student movement, we felt that perhaps we were winning, perhaps he was going to ask us what we want and propose some compromises and solutions," Wu'erkaixi recalled. "That was the basic logic of the whole movement, that we would apply enough pressure on the government that they would be forced to sit down and accept our demands, or at least meet somewhere in the middle."

But when he arrived, Li Peng's attitude only enraged the students further. "He gave us a long monologue, lecturing us. He claimed he had arrived twenty minutes late for the meeting because we students had caused so much chaos in Beijing that his motorcade was blocked. It was a non-apology," Wu'erkaixi said. "I interrupted him and said, 'I am sorry, Premier Li Peng, I have to interrupt you. You may think that you have been late for only five minutes. May I point out you have actually been late for a month, not five minutes. I am referring to the meeting we wanted for April 17 at Zhongnanhai. And then on April 22 and in front of the Great Hall of the People, we had implored you to come out and talk with us. We had called out aloud to you: 'Li Peng, come out.' We demanded a dialogue. Now, you are finally seeing us on May 18. So we are saying you have actually been late for one month.'" I discussed it with Wang Dan who was sitting next to me, and we agreed that this was not at all what we had hoped to come from the meeting. It was a signal of something else—a sign that this government could not change, that the Communist Party could not change its mentality. They were still playing by the old rule book, and the hard-liners were poised to crack down. Li Peng then announced martial law.

Other Uyghurs, including Rahima Mahmut, took part in the protests, too. A student of petrochemical engineering at Dalian University of Technology at the time, Rahima joined protests in Dalian and then, together with 2,000 other students from Dalian, took a twenty-one-hour train journey to Beijing to join the demonstrations in Tiananmen Square.

"In late May, however, we heard there would be a military crackdown, and so we tried to persuade students to leave the Square," Rahima recalled. "Obviously, the students did not want to go until they had achieved their demands. So we left on June 2, because we did not want to be trapped in Beijing. On June 4, back in Dalian, we were summoned to the university central hall and instructed to watch the television. I watched in disbelief as the State media reported that students were killing soldiers. It was an unbelievable lie. There was nothing about the army shooting the students. From that point on, I never believed any news in China."

It should not be forgotten that one of the key Chinese Communist Party leaders who persuaded Deng Xiaoping to crush the protests by military force was Wang Zhen, who had been head of the military government in Xinjiang from 1950 to 1952, and had earned a reputation for brutality towards Uyghurs. Known as the "Butcher of Xinjiang," Wang once described Uyghurs as a "trouble-making minority" and advised Mao that they be wiped out.[7] He was also head of the Xinjiang Production and Construction Corps, a body sanctioned by the United States in 2020 for its role in the current repression of the Uyghurs. Known in Chinese as the *Bingtuan*—which means "military unit"—this organization, which consists mostly of former People's Liberation Army (PLA) soldiers and their families, governs much of Xinjiang and functions as a "state within a state," enjoying commercial relations with over one hundred countries around the world. [8] According to the *Tiananmen Papers*, Wang told other Party leaders two days before the massacre, "We should announce in advance to those people occupying the Square that we're coming in. They can listen or not as they choose, but then we move in. If it causes deaths, that's their own fault. We can't be soft or merciful toward anti-Party, anti-socialist elements. Military orders have to be inviolable; otherwise, we have no way to enforce discipline."[9]

Dalian University of Technology, however, was more lenient, according to Rahima. "The university decided to protect most of the students. They only handed over the key organizers of the protests. I was just a participant, and so I was not given any serious punishment. A lot of students received warnings that they may not be able to find a job after graduation. They carried in their file a warning that they were suspicious. But I did not have any stains on my file, and I got a job in a petrochemical company."

However, soon after beginning her working life, Rahima discovered "deeply rooted discrimination" against Uyghurs. Despite graduating top in her class, from one of the country's top ten universities, she could not secure a job in the region's capital, Ürümchi. "The mentality among many [Han] Chinese is that they are superior, clever, more hard-working, and that Uyghurs are lazy and should not be given opportunity," she said. "But on the contrary, Uyghurs are hard-working and quite intelligent people."

Working in a petrochemical plant in Xinjiang, Rahima was shocked to find that while 10 percent of the 3,500-strong workforce were Uyghurs. The other 90 percent were Han, the majority from the *Bingtuan*.

"They built their own little villages, living completely separate lives from the Uyghurs. They did not know anything about the Uyghurs; they just regarded us as backward," she recalled. "They were not like the Han Chinese who had come and settled among the Uyghurs in the past. We did not have problems with our Chinese neighbours before. They learned about the Uyghurs, and we did not consider each other different. But the *Bingtuan* workers, they were different." Eventually, Rahima resigned, and took up a job teaching in a vocational training school.

Enver Tohti, a Uyghur surgeon born in Kumul (known in Chinese as Hami), in eastern Xinjiang, recalls being invited to the home of a Han Chinese school classmate and neighbour for Chinese Lunar New Year in 1970. At the time, meat was a luxury. "When they invited me and offered me pork, they treated me as a VIP. But they did not understand that we do not eat pork. When I told them, my friend got upset because he was waiting for the chance to eat meat. He asked me,

'Why don't you eat meat?' and I told him we do eat meat, but not this meat. They asked why and I said I do not know why. But then his father said, 'Pigs are the Uyghurs' ancestors; therefore, they do not eat pork,'" Enver recalled. "This belief exists quite widely in Chinese society. That woke me up, because I had thought that, like the Han Chinese, I was a *long de chuan ren*—a descendant of the dragon. From that time on, when I look at Han Chinese, my view is tainted, because they don't accept me, and I felt inferior."

On another occasion, while working as a surgeon in a hospital, Enver encountered another aspect of the racism towards Uyghurs—a more subtle, backhanded expression of superiority. "In our department, there were eight surgeons, and I was the only Uyghur. One day, a nurse came into the office where we were all sitting, and asked a question. I gave the answer. The nurse replied, 'Oh, I never knew you, a sheep brain eater, were so clever.' This is their way. They will call somebody who is stupid *zhu naozi* or 'pig's brain.' But she called me a 'sheep brain eater,' referring to the fact that I don't eat pork, and therefore drawing attention to the fact that I am a 'minority,' as well as suggesting that she thought I was stupid, to make me feel down. I replied, 'Pig's brain and sheep's brain, which one is cleverer? Pig's brain is the lowest; sheep's brain is much higher' and she was speechless."

Chinese human rights lawyer Teng Biao confirms that racism towards the Uyghurs is now widespread in Chinese society. It increased sharply after the Chinese Communist Party adopted the rhetoric of the "Global War on Terror" in 2001, and deepened further after regional authorities launched the "People's War on Terror" in Xinjiang from 2014. "The Han chauvinism, a kind of racism, is rampant among Han Chinese people," he said. "Many of them, even many liberal, pro-democracy intellectuals and activists, have that racist tendency. They are discriminating against Muslims."

There is some evidence that in the early 1990s, China's new president, Jiang Zemin, recognized the concerns about discrimination against ethnic minorities and attempted to introduce more inclusive policies in order to keep the minorities loyal. In January 1992, concerned about rising separatism that would shortly lead to the breakup of Yugoslavia, and following the breakup of the Soviet Union in 1991, Jiang gave a major speech at the First National Conference on Ethnic Affairs, in which he promised preferential policies, including economic opportunities and other incentives, for minorities,[10] while making it clear that the government would not accept any separatist movements.[11] From the Uyghur perspective, this was too little, too late. The Chinese State continued to hold a monopoly on resources, including in Xinjiang, and it continued to use incentives to attract Han Chinese migrants to Xinjiang, organized by the *Bingtuan*.[12]

Dolkun Isa moved to Beijing after being expelled from university, and enrolled in an English-language course at Beijing Foreign Languages University. In 1992, he opened a Uyghur restaurant in Beijing and made many foreign friends. "Actually, the Chinese government claimed that it was an international exchange centre," he said, "because in one street in Beijing there were ten or fifteen Uyghur restaurants, and so many foreign students used to come to the restaurant because they loved Uyghur food. Most of them had no idea who were the Uyghurs. They said, 'Your food is different; your faces are different.' They did not know our country was occupied."

But Dolkun's movements were still being monitored by the authorities. Eventually, he received a message from a friend in Ürümchi warning him to leave China. "Very quickly, I managed to get a foreign passport. In China, if you pay money, you can do almost anything," he said. In 1994, he fled to Turkey, leaving his pregnant wife behind in Beijing. "After six months, my first child was born. I was in Turkey, my wife was in Beijing, and communication was very difficult. Telephone calls were very expensive."

In Turkey, Dolkun got together with other Uyghur students and established the East Turkistan Students Youth Organization. In 1996, he was granted political asylum in Germany and established the World Uyghur Youth Congress. Eight years later, he co-founded the World Uyghur Congress, as an umbrella organization for the Uyghur exile community.

On February 5, 1997, Uyghurs in Rahima Mahmut's home city of Ghulja (known in Chinese as Yining), on the China-Kazakhstan border, protested peacefully in the streets, demanding the release of Uyghur religious scholars and protesting about the treatment of Uyghur women arrested by the Chinese police the previous day.[13] They were met by bloodshed in what is now remembered as the Ghulja massacre.[14]

Sean Roberts writes that "although accounts of the event are contradictory, it appears to have begun with a protest by Uyghurs against limits on religious observation, and it spiralled out of control after security forces clashed with protesters, leading to multiple casualties."[15]

Gardner Bovingdon states in his book, *The Uyghurs: Strangers in Their Own Land*, that while Chinese authorities denied any casualties, "non-Chinese sources reported up to 130 killed that day and up to 500 arrested."[16] More than 200

Uyghurs were sentenced to death and over ninety were given life sentences in jail, Amnesty International reported.[17] Later reports, Bovingdon notes, "indicated that the protesters had been hosed down with cold water and then held outdoors in sub-zero temperatures for hours, with the result that many developed frostbite and had to have their feet or hands amputated."[18]

In 1996, a new government regulation—"Document No.7"—set out the regime's strategy for curtailing Uyghur religious activities and "separatism," including curbs on the construction of new mosques in the region and the closure of religious schools and Quranic study gatherings. It called for enhanced surveillance of Uyghurs. The Ghulja protests occurred "despite, or perhaps in part due to, the extensive control measures called for by 'Document No. 7,'" notes Roberts.[19]

Rahima, who was in Ghulja at the time, says the protest happened "after so many Uyghur young scholars, who had influence in society, disappeared. Police had raided mosques and private religious gatherings and taken away worshippers, and their families did not know what had happened to them. Uyghurs were already feeling it was difficult to breathe freely. Discrimination and oppression was everywhere, and getting worse year by year. Uyghurs saw more and more Han Chinese being brought in every single day, starting businesses, while Uyghurs were pushed into a corner, their businesses taken away. These were the root causes of the protests."

Although she was not at the scene of the protests, Rahima heard gunshots. "The regime deployed the military, and the crackdown took place that night. It continued for two weeks. There were door-to-door searches."

Contrary to the figures quoted by Bovingdon, Rahima believes "the number of arrests were 4,000 to 5,000, mainly young men." Dr. Joanne Smith Finley, an academic at Newcastle University in the United Kingdom, heard from local people in Ghulja in 2002 that an estimated one in ten men disappeared after the 1997 crackdown.[20] Among those arrested were religious scholars, including the brother-in-law of Rahima's ex-husband, who was sentenced to twelve years in prison. Rahima confirms the reports of frostbite. "A lot of people died because of the cold. Ghulja is a small town, and there were not enough prisons for so many arrestees, so a lot of people were locked up in places with no heating facilities. Many people got frostbite, which then resulted in infection and deaths."

One person who witnessed the aftermath of what some Uyghurs refer to as the Ghulja massacre was Rebiya Kadeer, a Uyghur businesswoman and member of China's National People's Congress at the time.[21] Later arrested herself and jailed for five years, she subsequently went into exile and served as president of the World Uyghur Congress. After the Ghulja massacre, she concluded that the Uyghurs had no future within China.

Unrest grew over subsequent years, as a result of what Smith Finley describes as "the dehumanization of the Uyghurs" by the authorities' use of the "Global War on Terror" as the framework for their narrative.[22] Uyghurs came to be seen as "potential terrorists" or "potential terrorist sympathizers."

In the aftermath of the 9/11 attacks in the United States in 2001, China manipulated the situation to provide a pretext for escalating its repression of the Uyghurs, framing the crackdown as an anti-terror operation.[23] Allegations that Uyghurs belonging to the East Turkistan Islamic Movement (ETIM) had been trained in Afghanistan began to circulate. ETIM leader Abdullah Mansour declared China an "enemy of all Muslims," and Uyghurs in Afghanistan called for *jihad* ("holy war") against China. The U.S. State Department was persuaded by China to list several Uyghur organizations, including the ETIM and the Uyghur Liberation Organization, as terrorist groups.[24] China revamped the previous "Shanghai Five" group into the Shanghai Co-operation Organization, as an economic, political, but also security alliance with Central Asian states as well as India, Pakistan, and Russia, and used it to put pressure on Central Asian nations, especially Kazakhstan, to suppress and monitor Uyghur groups in their jurisdictions.

On July 5, 2009, riots broke out in Ürümchi. The spark was an argument in a factory in Guangdong between Uyghur migrant workers and Han Chinese in which at least two Uyghurs were killed. According to Rahima, "Chinese people posted videos of how they beat Uyghur factory workers to death in Guangdong Province. That triggered Xinjiang University students to protest. That was heartbreaking, because after what had happened in Ghulja, they must have known how brutal the crackdown would be."

As a sign of their desperation, Uyghur protesters in Ürümchi turned violent, destroying businesses and shops, and injuring or killing scores of Han Chinese after the authorities adopted a heavy-handed approach and took away the protest organizers.[25] "Uyghurs took the matter into their own hands, attacking Chinese people. Relations between Uyghurs and Han Chinese completely broke down," Rahima recalled. She suspects that the decision to post videos of the beatings in Guangdong may have been a deliberate strategy to spark Uyghur anger. "The

Chinese Communist Party may have deliberately triggered the riots, as a strategy to, in their words, 'bring the snake out of the cage,'" she said.

If the Ghulja massacre was a turning point for the Uyghurs, and the Ürümchi riots of 2009 marked the complete breakdown of relations between Uyghurs and Han Chinese,[26] far worse was to come.

Two incidents over subsequent years helped China perpetuate the notion that their campaign against the Uyghurs was a counterterrorism campaign. On October 29, 2013, Roberts notes, "an SUV with a black flag bearing the *Shahadah* waving outside one of its back windows drove recklessly towards the Forbidden City in Beijing's Tiananmen Square, struck numerous people, and caught fire near the palace that has long symbolized Chinese power." The driver and passengers were Uyghurs.[27]

The following year, a knife attack carried out by four Uyghurs dressed in black left thirty-one Han Chinese dead in Kunming train station.

Less than two months after the Kunming attack, Xi Jinping made his first visit as general secretary of the Chinese Communist Party to the Uyghur region in late April 2014. As he was ending his visit, it was reported that a Uyghur had detonated an explosion at Ürümchi train station.

Dolkun Isa is adamant that the vast majority of Uyghurs reject violence, terrorism, and extremism, as does the World Uyghur Congress. Those who have engaged in acts of violence are doing so, he believes, because "people have no way to defend themselves, no right to express feelings peacefully."

Rahima Mahmut agrees. "From childhood, I know my people are mostly kind, generous, and peaceful," she said. "I cannot relate my people with terrorism. I denounce any form of violence. None of these attacks have been independently verified, and those who perpetrated them were from a very tiny minority. At the same time, of course, the attacks were disturbing, because they can derail what is a right and just cause." Indeed, the peaceful nature of the Uyghur movement is striking. "Despite all the suffering, in which some of our smartest and brightest have been killed, with one crackdown after another, 99 percent of Uyghurs are still very peaceful. If there is hatred, we need to ask, who instilled this hatred? The answer is the Chinese regime, which has pushed people to the brink," observes Rahima.

In response to these incidents, the Chinese authorities launched a "Strike Hard Campaign against Violent Terrorism" and designated "Uyghur Separatism" as one of the "Three Evils of Separatism" and an act of terrorism. But it was the securitization since 2009, in which nearly 90,000 new police officers have been recruited in Xinjiang and the public security budget increased by 500 percent, that had provoked some Uyghurs into violence.[28] As Smith Finley argues, "the State's securitization of religion was counterproductive: heightening societal insecurity and promoting interethnic conflict between Uyghur and Han communities."[29]

The scale of the crackdown from 2014 onwards—supposedly in the name of countering terrorism—was shocking. Instead of pursuing, in a targeted way, those who had carried out violent acts, every single Uyghur became a target, including those who promoted dialogue, peace, and reconciliation.

On January 15, 2014, for example, the authorities arrested Ilham Tohti, a respected Uyghur economist at the National Minzu University of China in Beijing, after raiding his home.[30] In September that year, Tohti was sentenced to life in prison for the alleged crime of "separatism." A fluent Mandarin speaker, Tohti worked hard to improve relations between Uyghurs and Han Chinese. Although he had set up a website, called Uighurbiz, which promoted discussion of Uyghur issues,[31] in contrast to many Uyghurs who reject the idea of incorporation within a Chinese state, Tohti was the most prominent advocate of peaceful relations between Uyghurs and Han, and advocated for Uyghur autonomy on democratic principles within the Chinese State. In 2022, the first compilation of his writings was published in English, titled *We Uyghurs Have No Say: An Imprisoned Writer Speaks*.[32]

"The reason they targeted Ilham Tohti," Rahima believes, "is because everything he said was the truth. He was not asking for independence, he tried to build bridges with the Han Chinese, and he did not directly attack the Party. He advocated respect for the Chinese Constitution. He analyzed the issues, urged the government to tackle the root cause of the tensions, and pointed out that the root cause was the marginalization of the Uyghurs. He did not advocate anything illegal; he just pointed out, in a very mild tone, the mistakes the government was making. But they targeted him because of his popularity. He was like Nelson Mandela. They had to find a way to silence him, to stop others following in his footsteps. In Chinese, they call it 'killing the chicken to scare the monkey.'"

With the arrest of Ilham Tohti, the authorities sent the message that no Uyghur was safe. They developed an extraordinary surveillance state in Xinjiang, using a combination of expanded traditional police and intelligence presence, neighbourhood reporting, and modern technology. Dr. Yang Jianli, founder and president of Citizen Power Initiatives for China, writes in a paper titled "Virtual Gulag: China Is Perfecting its Surveillance State in Xinjiang and the Rest of the PRC," that in addition to the "human layer of the surveillance system," there is the "invisible layer of the digital surveillance system." Security cameras are on every street corner, surveillance apps are deployed to watch "every household," and three particular platforms—Skynet, Safe-city, and Sharp-eyes— use televisions, cellphones, and other devices to form "an advanced and integrated surveillance system." To summarize, Dr. Yang said, "today, unmanned drones patrol over Xinjiang cities, satellites track cars and trucks on the roads, cameras with artificial intelligence on lamp posts read pedestrian faces, irises, and analyze their emotions and gaits."[33]

When Smith Finley last visited the region in 2018, she was told by Uyghur friends that "there are eyes and ears everywhere. You must take care at all times about what you're saying, to whom, and where you say it. Police trucks parked at the roadside contain surveillance equipment, allowing police to listen in on public conversations up to a distance of fifteen metres."[34]

On top of this, the authorities have established a system known as "Becoming Family," where Chinese Communist Party cadres move in—uninvited—to Uyghur homes, often those where the husband has been taken away to a detention camp. According to Human Rights Watch, about 110,000 officials have been deployed for this purpose since 2016.[35] As Geoffrey Cain puts it in his book *The Perfect Police State: An Undercover Odyssey into China's Terrifying Surveillance Dystopia of the Future*, "you might wake up every morning next to a stranger appointed by the government to replace your partner whom the police 'disappeared.' Every morning before work, this minder will teach your family the state virtues of loyalty, ideological purity, and harmonious relations with the Communist Party. He'll check on your progress by asking you questions, ensuring you haven't been 'infected' with what the government calls the 'viruses of the mind' and the 'three evils': terrorism, separatism, and extremism."[36]

Although intensification of repression and surveillance was clearly ordered by Xi Jinping, the architecture was implemented by Chen Quanguo, appointed Party Secretary for Xinjiang in 2016. Chen had implemented a similar crackdown in Tibet when he served as Party Secretary there from 2011 to 2016. In Xinjiang, within months of his appointment, he had ramped up security, with regular checkpoints, mobile phone checks, and artificial intelligence. Chen established so-called "convenience police stations" across all cities and villages, granting police the authority to inspect and monitor local residents' online activities and digital devices. Radio Free Asia reported that "little more than a year into Chen Quanguo's tenure as Communist Party chief in the Xinjiang Uyghur Autonomous Region (XUAR), critics came to believe he was building an 'open-air prison' in the vast region of mountains and deserts."[37]

In what became known as the "Karakax List," a leaked document from Karakax (spelled Qaraqash in Uyghur) county in Khotän Prefecture, subdistrict officials compiled extensive details of individuals' behaviours and data, including blood type and height, and even their use of electricity and gas stations. Uyghurs must swipe their identity cards when they enter their apartment buildings or streets and are required to carry their identity cards wherever they go. Every move is recorded, and if they talk to foreigners, they are immediately questioned.

According to anthropologist Dr. Adrian Zenz, the Karakax List, which spans over 137 pages and includes the personal details of over 3,000 Uyghurs, "presents the strongest evidence to date that Beijing is actively persecuting and punishing normal practices of traditional religious beliefs, in direct violation of its own constitution."[38] It outlines reasons for the internment of 311 people specifically and, Dr. Zenz argues, "based on the principles of presumed guilt (rather than innocence) and assigning guilt through association, the State has developed a highly fine-tuned yet also very labour-intensive governance system whereby entire family circles are held hostage to their behavioural performance." He concludes: "More than any other government document pertaining to Beijing's extra-legal campaign of mass internment, the Karakax List lays bare the ideological and administrative micromechanics of a system of targeted cultural genocide that arguably rivals any similar attempt in the history of humanity. Driven by a deeply religio-phobic world view, Beijing has embarked on a project that, ideologically, isn't far from a medieval witch hunt, yet is being executed with administrative perfectionism and iron discipline."

Since 2017, over one million Uyghurs, Kazakhs, and other people from Muslim minority communities have been incarcerated in hundreds of camps across Xinjiang. Some sources put the number of detainees as high as two or three million.[39]

The Chinese Communist Party has long used Xinjiang as an equivalent of Siberia for political dissidents, and labour camps—or *laogai*—have always existed in Communist China.[40] It was the activist Harry Wu Hongda, whom I had the privilege of meeting several times, who documented these camps extensively.

Well-thumbed, signed copies of his books *Bitter Winds: My Years in China's Gulag* and *Troublemaker: One Man's Crusade against China's Cruelty*, sit on my bookshelf. But since 2017, the regime has built hundreds of new extra-legal detention camps across Xinjiang.

Extraordinarily, one of the people who first brought the existence of these camps to light was a young Chinese student in Canada called Shawn Zhang, who unearthed evidence by searching satellite images on Google. "I started this research in 2018," Zhang told me. "At that time, there was very little news about Xinjiang, but some news about the concentration camps was coming out of China on social media and some foreign media, and it was really shocking. As a Chinese from Mainland China, I was skeptical at first because it was so different from my experience of life in China. It was beyond my imagination, because we only heard of concentration camps in history books. I thought there must be some exaggeration. So I just wanted to verify it personally."

Zhang began to search Google, using some key words. "Through this research, I found some very detailed information, including Chinese government procurement notices for construction of 're-education' camps, and the locations of these camps. So I followed Google Maps and found some major construction sites. I could see from Google Satellite some astonishing security features, such as razor-wire fences and watch towers, just like a prison. The procurement notices referred to 're-education' schools, but I became convinced that they were concentration camps."[41]

Zhang published the information he gathered on his Twitter and Medium blog, explaining how he found the evidence, his process for verification, and other details. "At first, I did not publish so many examples, less than twenty. But as I continued to search, I found more and more. It was really surprising that there were so many concentration camps. In the end, it was about 200 or 300."

Journalists, researchers, and human rights groups began to take notice of Zhang's research. "Before my research, I don't think many people had found the satellite images. Even some journalists who had visited Xinjiang did not have satellite images. So when I published the satellite images, it seems the world found a new way to investigate Xinjiang," said Zhang.[42]

Of course, his research has not come without consequences. "For the first several months, nothing happened. But after 2019, the Chinese government began to really pay attention to me," Zhang told me. "They visited my parents, they called my parents to the police station, and they harassed most of my relatives."

Zhang believes Han Chinese need to understand the Uyghurs' suffering and unite together. "We Han Chinese people cannot get our freedom at all, either. So we must fight together with others for all our rights," he said. "The Chinese government wants total control of all its peoples. Many well-informed Chinese people know that the Chinese government is doing horrible things in Xinjiang. They read international news; they know that the Chinese government is not treating Uyghur people well, but they never thought that the Chinese government would commit genocide. But I also know many people who do not believe the news about the concentration camps, or the accusation of genocide, because they rely heavily on Chinese-language media, they depend on WeChat—which is heavily controlled by the Chinese government—and so it is really difficult for them to find other sources of information. In addition, many people do not know Xinjiang, do not know Uyghur people, and, unfortunately, in the past ten years, Uyghur people have disappeared from the general daily life of the Chinese population."

In addition to Zhang's courageous research, there have been several incredibly brave Chinese people who have travelled to Xinjiang to document the situation. The publication *Bitter Winter* has published several videos filmed inside the concentration camps, including one near Ghulja. "In the video, you can see very clearly inside the camp prison-style facilities, with iron gates and a centralized surveillance system," said Zhang.

In November 2021, a young Han Chinese with the pseudonym Guanguan released a twenty-minute documentary on YouTube, filmed covertly on a visit to Xinjiang.[43] "I visited Xinjiang once in 2019, on a bike trip, but the purpose of my visit this time is completely different," said Guanguan in the video. "I read a story on *BuzzFeed News*, in which the reporters identified the locations of many detention centres in Xinjiang through cross-comparing satellite imagery."[44] So he followed the Mapbox Satellite map created by the news outlet, along with satellite images from China's Baidu Maps service, to film eighteen detention facilities across eight cities in Xinjiang. "Due to the Chinese government's regulations, it is now very difficult for foreign journalists to gain access to Xinjiang to conduct interviews. I was thinking, while foreign journalists can't go to Xinjiang, I can still go there," he said in the video.

Some international media have been able to gain access to the region, and there have been powerful documentaries and reports on BBC, Reuters, and other outlets. In 2021, Associated Press was granted extraordinary access to Ürümchi

No. 3 Detention Centre in Dabancheng during a State-guided tour of the region. "The detention centre is the largest in the country and possibly the world, with a complex that sprawls over 220 acres—making it twice as large as Vatican City. A sign at the front identified it as a '*kanshousuo*,' a pretrial detention facility," AP reported. "Chinese officials declined to say how many inmates were there, saying the number varied. But the AP estimated the centre could hold roughly 10,000 people and many more, if crowded, based on satellite imagery and the cells and benches seen during the tour."[45] When taken alongside the other many varieties of detention centres, prisons, and camps in the region, this illustrates what anthropologist Darren Byler describes as China's move "from police state to mass incarceration state," in which "hundreds of thousands of people have disappeared from the population."[46] In his book *In the Camps: Life in China's High-Tech Penal Colony*, Byler argues that at least 1.5 million Uyghurs, Kazakhs, and Hui are in a system of "re-education camps," making it "the largest internment of a religious minority since World War II." He details what he calls an "archipelago of over three hundred camps and other newly built or expanded extrajudicial detention facilities."[47]

Testimonies that have emerged in recent years of the conditions and treatment endured in the prison camps are truly harrowing. Torture, forced labour, and rape are widespread and commonplace. In a powerful testimony at a hearing of the United States Congressional-Executive Commission on China on November 28, 2018, Mihrigul Tursun described her experience:

"I clearly remember the torture I experienced in the tiger chair the second time I was incarcerated. I was taken to a special room with an electrical [sic] chair. It was the interrogation room that had one light and one chair. There were belts and whips hanging on the wall. I was placed in a high chair that clicked to lock my arms and legs in place and tightened when they press a button. My head was shaved beforehand for the maximum impact. The authorities put a helmet-like thing on my head. Each time I was electrocuted, my whole body would shake violently and I could feel the pain in my veins. I thought I would rather die than go through this torture and begged them to kill me."[48]

Male Chinese guards select girls at night and gang-rape them repeatedly. Exiled Uyghur scholar Abduweli Ayup reported that his niece Mihray Erkin, a young teacher living in Japan where she had been volunteering to teach Uyghur refugees, had been called back to Kashgar, where she had been repeatedly raped, humiliated, and eventually killed by Chinese police officers.[49] There are also reports of Kazakh women being forced to undress Uyghur women to be raped by Han men. Gulzira Auelkhan, who spent eighteen months in a camp, claims that she would strip Uyghur women naked and leave them alone with Han men.[50] There have also been cases of male rape. Ayup himself told how he had been gang-raped by police officers in his cell.[51]

As well as being a tireless advocate for her people, Rahima Mahmut often works as a translator for international media organizations, including the BBC. She has interpreted for numerous documentaries and research projects about the Uyghurs and translated many testimonies of torture. "The most shocking story was from a lady in Turkey," she recalls. "Our interview lasted eleven and a half hours. This lady, originally from Ghulja, spoke about her ordeal. Her father was arrested in 1997, after the Ghulja massacre and later died in custody. Her two brothers were also arrested and later executed. Then she was arrested because she was secretly teaching children about religion," Rahima recalled. "She was arrested along with these children, who were forced to watch the torture. They dragged the children in naked, and when a child screamed, they beat the child to death. During her four years in prison, this woman was subjected to various forms of torture daily. They forced her to squat for hours, standing in a 'motorcycle' position. They pulled all her nails out. They forced her to watch gang rape for a year before she was subjected to it herself. She was in prison for four years."

A former Chinese soldier and police officer who fled to Germany after becoming disillusioned with the Chinese government, and is known only as "Jiang," went public in October 2021 and confirmed the torture and abuse of Uyghurs, and the transportation of Uyghurs from other parts of China on packed prison trains, in which they are blindfolded, hooded, handcuffed together, forbidden from going to the toilet, denied food, and only allowed bottle caps to drink water—"to moisten their lips."[52] He also confirmed the use of forced labour, admitting that "prisons and re-education centres both contained factories."[53] Uyghurs are made to do things "which can make money, but nobody wants to do," he said.[54]

Uyghurs are not used for forced labour only in Xinjiang's prison camps. A report by the Australian Strategic Policy Institute (ASPI) in March 2020, titled "Uyghurs for Sale," strongly suggests the use of Uyghur slave labour in the supply chains of at least eighty-two well-known global brands, including Apple, BMW, Gap, Huawei, Nike, Samsung, Sony, and Volkswagen.[55]

"It is the policy of the central government," two of the report's authors—

Vicky Xiuzhong Xu and Nathan Ruser—argue, resulting in "tens of thousands of people pushed out of their homes every year and sent to eastern provinces to work in the supply chains of international brands."[56]

ASPI's report estimates that "more than 80,000 Uyghurs were transferred out of Xinjiang to work in factories across China between 2017 and 2019, and some of them were sent directly from detention camps." [57]At least twenty-seven factories in nine provinces have been identified as using Uyghur labour. Some of those factories, such as the Taekwong Shoes Company in Qingdao, Shandong Province, are "equipped with watchtowers, razor wire, and inward-facing barbed-wire fences." Public Security Bureau and United Work Front Department agents are stationed inside factories "to report daily on the 'thoughts' of the Uyghur workers."[58]

Research by the Uyghur Human Rights Project, the Center for Strategic and International Studies, and Dr. Adrian Zenz confirms the use of Uyghur forced labour, which the Uyghur Human Rights Project describes as "a central part . . . of the crackdown" in Xinjiang.[59]

China is the largest global producer of cotton, and 84 percent of this cotton comes from Xinjiang. In 2020, a coalition of 180 human rights organizations highlighted the fact that as a consequence, many of the world's biggest fashion brands and retailers are complicit in the human rights violations perpetrated against the Uyghurs.[60]

In addition to the internment, incarceration, and torture of upwards of a million[61] and the enslavement of hundreds of thousands, the Chinese government has also separated Uyghur children from their families, and forced them into boarding schools, orphanages, or "child welfare guidance centres" where they are forced to shout patriotic slogans, learn Mandarin, and answer questions regarding their parents' religious beliefs. One media outlet has reported that, based on a 2017 document from the government, at least 500,000 children have been separated from their parents.[62] There are reports of dreadful conditions and poor food. Further reports allege that many of the children suffer deep trauma, depression, and psychological damage.[63]

Uyghurs are subjected to serious religious persecution. Mosques and shrines have been destroyed,[64] and normal religious activities such as praying, fasting, reading the Quran, or abstaining from pork or alcohol can land you in a camp. The same is true for men with lengthy beards, or women wearing the *hijab*. According to Christian Solidarity Worldwide, "thousands of mosques" have been destroyed, and "even small-scale, peaceful everyday religious activities and expressions of religious identity are viewed as suspicious by the authorities."[65] Uyghurs have, in some instances, "been forced to eat pork or drink alcohol," CSW reports.

The World Uyghur Congress and the Uyghur Human Rights Project confirm that religious activities have been particularly targeted. Even halal food is restricted, children are banned from participating in religious activities, and participation in the Hajj—the pilgrimage to Mecca—is permitted only if it is State-organized.[66]

On a visit to Xinjiang in 2018, Smith Finley documented examples of religious freedom violations. Mosques were empty, she writes, and "each mosque complex heavily securitized with high metal fences covered in coiled razor wire, padlocked gates, PRC flags, and entry permitted only via securitized data gates (facial recognition) which no one seemed to want to use."[67] One Uyghur told her, "We want to go in the mosque . . . but if we do, they will take us to prison." In Kashgar, Smith Finley said, "mosques were completely out of service, and many were desecrated . . . All were covered in propaganda on the outside walls about 'de-extremification' . . . Tellingly, 'Love the Party, Love the Country' banners had now replaced the earlier 'Love the Country, Love Religion' . . . banners."[68]

Although the majority of Uyghurs are Muslims, there exists a small community of Uyghur Christians, and they are no better off. Alimjan Yimit, a Uyghur Christian house church leader, was arrested in Kashgar in 2008, and the following year, he was sentenced to fifteen years in prison. Enver Tohti—himself a Uyghur convert to Christianity—told me, "Nowadays, Uyghurs do not like the term 'Uyghur Muslims,' because there are also Uyghur Christians, and they are persecuted by the Chinese Communist Party, too—as Uyghurs and as Christians."

Zenz has revealed evidence of a campaign of forced sterilization and forced abortion. In a report published in 2020,[69] he details how at least 80 percent of Uyghur women of child-bearing age in the four Uyghur-dominated prefectures are targeted for forced sterilization. A courageous Uyghur doctor told ITV that she had personally conducted at least 500 to 600 operations on Uyghur women, including forced contraception, the insertion of intrauterine devices (IUD); forced abortion, even in the last two weeks of pregnancy; forced sterilization; and forced removal of wombs. On at least one occasion, she said, a baby was still moving when it was discarded into the rubbish.[70] Others have reported killing babies by lethal injection if they survive late abortion.[71]

There is also evidence that Uyghurs have been targeted for forced organ harvesting. The practice of State-sanctioned organ harvesting—the forcible removal of human organs from Chinese prisoners—has been going on for some time, and will be examined further in the next chapter. But there is a belief that the practice first began in Xinjiang in the 1990s.

Ethan Gutmann devotes the opening chapter of his book *The Slaughter* to the subject, which he calls "The Xinjiang Procedure."[72] There is evidence that the authorities have been providing Uyghurs with free "health checks" and carrying out DNA tests, procedures that could well be designed to assess the quality of organs.[73] There are also reports of organ transplant "tourist" "fast lanes" in the Ürümchi and Kashgar airports,[74] and of "Halal organs" taken from Uyghur Muslims for Saudi tourists in Tianjin hospitals.[75]

Even outside China, Uyghurs are not safe. The Chinese Communist Party spies on and harasses Uyghurs around the world, particularly in countries in the region such as Kazakhstan and Turkey, but also in Europe and North America.[76] Some Uyghurs have been forcibly repatriated to China.

Dolkun Isa has faced constant threats from the Chinese authorities since he began his activism in exile. In 1997, China issued an international warrant for his arrest, and, as a consequence, Interpol issued a "Red Notice"—which was only revoked in 2018.

"China is constantly saying that I am a terrorist," says Dolkun. "The Chinese government constantly threaten me. They demanded that Germany extradite me to China. They published my pictures on State media in China."

Today, Dolkun is recognized internationally as a respected activist. The World Uyghur Congress, and Dolkun personally, have received several prestigious human rights awards, including, in 2019, the World Democracy Award, presented at the United States Congress by the Speaker of the House of Representatives Nancy Pelosi.

But for several years after the Interpol Red Notice, Dolkun faced constant challenges, particularly for international travel. On one occasion, he went to the United States Consulate in Frankfurt, to apply for a visa to visit Washington, D.C., for a conference. "I was detained there, and handed over to German police, who took me to a police station," he recalls. "They asked me, 'Did you kill someone?'"

In 2006, Dolkun was stopped at Washington's Dulles International Airport and sent back to Germany, and in 2009, he was detained in South Korea, where he was due to attend an international conference. "I was nearly deported to China that time," he recalls. "The South Korean government was ready to co-operate with China. There were even Chinese police waiting for me in Seoul. In the end, due to very strong pressure from Amnesty International, German media, the German government, and the United States, I was sent back to Germany."

In 2013, while attending a session of the United Nations Human Rights Council in Geneva, Dolkun was approached by UN security, at China's request, and asked to leave the UN building. And, in 2016, as he planned to visit Dharamsala, his Indian visa was revoked, again because China intervened.

Perhaps the most heartbreaking and difficult form of intimidation the Chinese government uses against Dolkun, and other Uyghur activists abroad, is threats to their relatives back home.

"My brother, sister, parents all live in East Turkistan (Xinjiang)," says Dolkun. "The Chinese government strongly pressures them. Their homes are monitored twenty-four hours a day. It is not possible for my family to receive visitors, because the Chinese police is monitoring all the time. The telephone is monitored, and my family is not allowed to use Internet. I had my last telephone conversation with my parents in 2017. One year later, I learned that my mother died in one of the concentration camps. Then my father passed away in 2020. My elder brother, a mathematics professor, was jailed for seventeen years. In 2021, my younger brother was sentenced to life imprisonment. This is the price my family has paid."

Rushan Abbas, an activist who founded the U.S.-based Campaign for Uyghurs in 2017, has faced a similar tragedy. On September 11, 2018, her sister, Dr. Gulshan Abbas, was taken by Chinese police, six days after Rushan had spoken about the Uyghurs' plight on a panel discussion at the Hudson Institute in Washington, D.C. She was subsequently sentenced to twenty years in prison. Rushan told me, "I carry my sister's picture everywhere. I have no idea where my sister is being held. My first priority is to get proof of life for her and to see her released."

Rayhan Asat, a Uyghur human rights campaigner and lawyer, is in the same situation. Since 2020, she has been leading an international campaign to seek the release of her brother, Ekpar Asat, a Uyghur entrepreneur and philanthropist who founded a social media app for Uyghurs, featuring history, literature, music, entertainment, and news. Previously respected by the Chinese government as a star in the technology sector and as a peace builder, in 2016, he disappeared after returning to China from a three-week leadership programme organized by the US State Department. He is believed to be held in one of the camps, and is

ABOVE LEFT: *Tank Man, Tiananmen Square.*

ABOVE RIGHT: *A banner in a jungle hut in Myanmar—a question we must all answer.*

LEFT: *Riot police and Special Tactical Squad officers make mass arrests in Wong Tai Sin following scuffles during a mass rally on the seventieth anniversary of the People's Republic of China on October 1, 2019.*

CREDIT: James Wendlinger

BELOW: *Hong Kong protests.*

CREDIT: lsb.co

"If you have not been to the Great Wall," said Chairman Mao, "you are not a real man." The author not only visited the wall several times but also slept on it.

RIGHT: *Qingdao No. 9 Middle School, with its wonderful motto displayed on the main building.*

BELOW LEFT: *The Hope Hotel in Qingdao, where the author lived for six months.*

BELOW RIGHT: *The author teaching English in Qingdao, aged eighteen.*

Morning exercises in the schoolyard at No. 29 Middle School.

The beach in Qingdao.

Qingdao's German-built Catholic cathedral.

A market street in Yangshuo.

The amazing He Liyi and his fascinating book Mr. China's Son. *The author had the privilege of meeting him in the café he ran in Dali.*

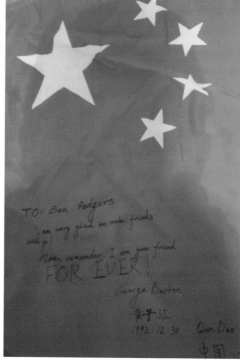

A gift to the author from a Chinese friend. It illustrates that he is not anti-China—he is just opposed to the Chinese Communist Party regime.

Tiananmen Square, which the author often walked through at night, sensing the souls of those massacred there in 1989.

Victoria Harbour in Hong Kong— a place the author visited most days during the five years he lived in the city.

Hong Kong iMail
Wednesday, October 31, 2001 — OPINION — A11

Chinese checkers

Despite having come a long way, Beijing still needs to make the move towards democracy, accountability and legitimacy

BENEDICT ROGERS
— ○ —
COMMENTARY

One of the author's many columns in the Hong Kong iMail, advocating for democracy in China. In the early years after the handover, it was possible to publish such articles freely.

One of the author's many articles criticizing Hong Kong government officials. The worst that happened was that Regina Ip complained to the paper's editor—who laughed.

RIGHT: *A typical night in Hong Kong in 2019.*

CREDIT: lsb.co

BELOW: *Armed only with umbrellas, protesters faced extreme police brutality.*

CREDIT: lsb.co

TOP LEFT: *The siege of Hong Kong Polytechnic University, November 2019.*

CREDIT: lsb.co

TOP RIGHT: *As the police became more brutal and the authorities more intransigent, some protesters turned to more radical action.*

CREDIT: lsb.co

LEFT: *In 2019, thousands filled the streets peacefully day after day for months.*

CREDIT: lsb.co

The final edition of Apple Daily, *forcibly shut down in 2021.*

This is another audacious blow to Hong Kong's autonomy. I am shocked and saddened that the Chinese government is warning foreigners about who they can meet in Hong Kong and then openly admitting complicity in barring Benedict Rogers from entry to the city. Beijing claims that this is an 'internal matter,' but Hong Kong's autonomy and freedoms are guaranteed by international treaty, so are a global concern—particularly as China seeks to actively erode pro-democracy voices in the city. This incident is a breach of the Basic Law and it must send a chill through all corporations and countries that have an interest in maintaining Hong Kong's freedoms. There must be a concerted effort to push back with the leaders in Beijing and the government in Hong Kong. We all have a stake in ensuring Hong Kong remains an open city, with the rule of law and guaranteed rights currently unavailable in Mainland China.

**CONGRESSMAN CHRIS SMITH
COCHAIR, CONGRESSIONAL-
EXECUTIVE COMMISSION ON CHINA**

Congressman Chris Smith's statement on the author's denial of entry to Hong Kong.

Pastor Allen Yuan and his wife.

The author with Bishop Ding Guangxun in Nanjing in 1997.

Chinese Communist Party propaganda is projected onto the Potala Palace, the residence of the exiled Dalai Lama, in June 2021.

TOP LEFT: *Monks from Rongwo Monastery in Rebgong march towards local government headquarters as part of the 2008 Tibetan Uprising.*

TOP RIGHT: *The destruction of crosses.*
CREDIT: Bitter Winter

BOTTOM LEFT: *Chinese officials meet Tibetans as part of a drive to make them display portraits of CCP leaders in their homes. These shrines would usually be reserved for images of the Dalai Lama.*

TOP LEFT: *A surveillance camera disguised as a prayer wheel, filming in Lhasa's Barkhor area.*
CREDIT: High Peaks Pure Earth

TOP RIGHT: *Dolkun Isa, president of the World Uyghur Congress.*

MIDDLE: *A heavy Chinese military presence outside Kumbum Monastery during a Tibetan prayer festival in 2015. One worshipper was reported as saying, "I was so afraid that I forgot to pray."*
CREDIT: VOA News

BOTTOM: *Former Canadian senator Consiglio Di Nino with the Dalai Lama.*

TOP: *Rushan Abbas and her sister, Gulshan, sentenced to twenty years in prison.*

RIGHT: *Rahima Mahmut speaking at the alternative Olympic torch relay organized by Never Again Right Now.*
CREDIT: Kit Lee

BOTTOM LEFT: *The Uyghur Tribunal, chaired by Sir Geoffrey Nice, KC, concluded that China is committing genocide.*

BOTTOM RIGHT: *Anastasia Lin with John Bercow, then Speaker of the UK House of Commons.*

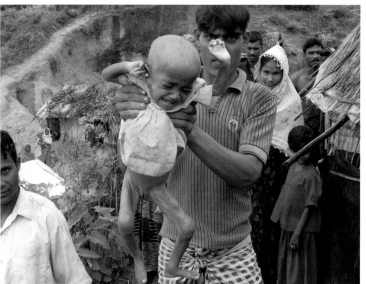

TOP LEFT: *Myanmar children's drawing of atrocities.*

TOP RIGHT: *The author with with Aung San Su Kyi, Myanmar's democra leader.*

LEFT: *Rohingya refugee survivors of genocide.*

A burned-out village after an attack by the military regime in Myanmar.

In Pyongyang, North Korea, with Lord Alton and Baroness Cox.

Looking out over Kim Il Sung Square in Pyongyang.

The author with Nathan Law.

The author speaking at a protest for Hong Kong in Trafalgar Square, London.

The author with Finn Lau and Simon Cheng at a protest in Parliament Square.

CREDIT: Howard Cheng

TOP LEFT: *The author with Congressm[an] Chris Smith.*

TOP RIGHT: *The author delivering a petition to 10 Downing Street.*

LEFT: *Speaking at a protest outside Downing Street on June 4, 2022.*
CREDIT: Howard Cheng

The launch of Hong Kong Watch, in Speaker's House, December 10, 2017.

A demonstration in Hong Kong's Legislative Council after the author's deportation in October 2017.

香港警務處
香港灣仔軍器廠街一號
警察總部

HONG KONG POLICE FORCE
Police Headquarters,
No. 1 Arsenal Street,
Wanchai, Hong Kong

OUR REF: (10) in LM(1/2022) NSD/S/135/42/2930
YOUR REF:
TELEPHONE:
FAX:

10 March 2022

Benedict Rogers

████████████████████████

Dear Mr. Rogers,

        This is a notice under section 7(2) of Schedule 4 to the Implementation Rules for Article 43 of the Law of the People's Republic of China on Safeguarding National Security in the Hong Kong Special Administrative Region ("Rules") to require you to remove an electronic message on an electronic platform.

        Section 6 of Schedule 4 to the Rules provides that the Commissioner of Police may, with the approval of the Secretary for Security, authorize a designated officer to exercise one or more of the powers specified in section 7 of Schedule 4 to the Rules if the Commissioner has reasonable ground for suspecting that –

    (a)   a person has published an electronic message on an electronic platform; and

    (b)   the publication is likely to constitute an offence endangering national security or is likely to cause the occurrence of an offence endangering national security.

        Section 7(2) of Schedule 4 to the Rules provides that the designated officer may require the person who has published the electronic message on the electronic platform to remove the message from the platform before the deadline specified by the designated officer.

        There is reasonable ground for suspecting that you, as the Co-founder and Chief Executive of "Hong Kong Watch", have published an electronic message, which is a website at https://www.hongkongwatch.org/ ("the Message") and the publication of the Message is likely to constitute an offence endangering national security or is likely to cause the occurrence of an offence endangering national security (please refer to the screen captures of some examples of the contents of the Message in Annex), namely, "Collusion with a Foreign Country or with External Elements to Endanger National Security",[1] contrary to Article 29 of the Law of the People's Republic of China on Safeguarding National Security in the Hong Kong Special Administrative Region.

        Pursuant to the authorization of the Commissioner of Police with the approval of the Secretary for Security under section 6 of Schedule 4 to the Rules, **I, as the designated officer appointed by the Secretary for Security under section 13 of Schedule 4 to the Rules, hereby require you to remove the Message within 72 hours from the time of sending of this notice.**

        Please note that under section 10(1) of Schedule 4 to the Rules, a person who fails to comply with the above requirement commits an offence and is liable on conviction on indictment to a fine of HK$100,000 and to imprisonment for 1 year.

        You are reminded to keep confidential any information pertaining to the case and not to make any disclosure that may prejudice investigation or other law enforcement action by the Hong Kong Police Force.   You are hereby reminded that there is a continuing obligation to ensure that the Message is removed.

        If you have any queries, please contact the undersigned at (852) 3660 0761 or nsd-ict@police.gov.hk

Yours faithfully,

(Annette CHENG)
for   Commissioner of Police

A letter to the author from the Hong Kong police.

Tibet Square in Vilnius, Lithuania.

ABOVE: *The author with the Chinese artist Ai Weiwei.*

BELOW: *The message in an anonymous letter, postmarked in Hong Kong, that was delivered to the author's neighbours in a suburb of London.*

Anti-extradition protesters are seen on Hennessy Road, Hong Kong, on June 9, 20 Hundreds of thousands of Hong Kongers turned to the streets to protest the extraditi bill amendments.

CREDIT: James Wendlinger

(Watch him)

reported to have been in solitary confinement since 2019. In 2020, he was sentenced to fifteen years in prison in a secret trial, charged with "inciting ethnic hatred and ethnic discrimination."[77]

Why is the Chinese Communist Party doing this? Why risk provoking an international outcry by such intense and shocking persecution of the Uyghurs? Why did Xi Jinping not learn from his own father, Xi Zhongxun, a senior Communist Party official in the Maoist era who adopted the opposite approach to the Uyghurs from his son? In 1949, Xi Zhongxun ran the newly installed Chinese Communist Party's Northwest Bureau, which included responsibility for Xinjiang. According to Joseph Torigian, in an article in *The Diplomat*, Xi Zhongxun believed that dealing with the country's ethnic groups "needed a soft touch" and argued that "co-opting Muslim leaders into the PRC's state apparatus could help persuade sceptics to give up violence."[78] He was reportedly furious with the two top leaders in Xinjiang in 1952, Wang Zhen and Deng Liqun, for their handling of the situation, and was critical of mass arrests. "What is the logic for treating minority women wearing the veil and wearing a dress or men growing a beard as feudal things?" he apparently once asked. And, in 1981, he made a telephone call to the new Chinese Communist Party Secretary in the region, Wang Enmao, to instruct him to use peaceful means to resolve protests in Kashgar. "Zhongxun explicitly forbade the local authorities from worsening the situation by conducting a mass persecution," writes Torigian.

Enver Tohti agrees. "Uyghurs could live under Xi Zhongxun. We could even live under Hu Jintao. But not under Xi Jinping."

There are a number of factors behind Xi Jinping's assault on the Uyghurs. First, although it is without doubt the most egregious example, it sits in the context of a wider crackdown on dissent, difference, religion, and civil society throughout the country. Second, Xi appears to be fixated on security and stability. And third, there are economic considerations at stake.

Dolkun Isa believes that Xi Jinping's Belt and Road Initiative (BRI) is the major factor. This plan to connect trading routes and develop infrastructure across the globe, from China through Asia to Europe, is Xi's signature project. Scholar David Shambaugh describes it as a "$1.2 trillion mega-project that spans the globe" and "an infrastructure development initiative unparalleled in history"[79] with, China claims, 123 countries and twenty-nine international organizations participating. As Elizabeth Economy writes, it "would connect some of the lesser-developed, interior regions of China to external markets by building the necessary hard infrastructure. It also would provide a market for Chinese over-capacity . . . Finally, the BRI would add a political gloss to China's global infra-structure empire."[80] Rush Doshi argues in *The Long Game* that the BRI is at the core of China's effort to "pursue offensive economic statecraft that would allow China to build its own coercive and consensual economic capacities over others" and "gain greater financial influence."[81]

Xinjiang is at the centre of the BRI, and this is one of the major reasons behind the crackdown on Uyghurs, in Dolkun's view. "From Kashgar to Karachi, and from Ürümchi to Kazakhstan, this is the heart of the BRI," he said. "Xi Jinping believes that 'if Uyghurs exist, problems exist,' and if Uyghurs are not completely eradicated, their identity eradicated, problems exist. He doesn't want to have problems for the BRI. That's why he put millions of Uyghurs in concen-tration camps."

In addition, Dolkun argues, while the Chinese Communist Party's aim has always been the assimilation of the Uyghurs, after seventy years, they realized that they had not succeeded. Xi Jinping is determined to change that. "In 2013, Xi visited Kashgar. He thought that Uyghurs were assimilated, but when he heard Uyghur songs, saw Uyghur food, heard Uyghur language spoken, he was very shocked and surprised," Dolkun recalled. "In 2018, I heard about this from a high-level Chinese government official who was Uyghur and had defected. After Xi returned to Beijing from Kashgar and Ürümchi, he held a high-level secret meeting. He said that nothing has changed for the Uyghurs in seventy years. He was angry, and he issued a new directive about the *Zhonghua Minzu*—the fifty-six Chinese 'nationalities.' 'Uyghurs belong to the Chinese,' he said. He turned very openly, very quickly, from assimilationist policy to a genocidal policy."

Perhaps another factor is the lack of international outcry. "Xi Jinping imple-mented this genocidal policy step by step, testing the response of the international community and international law, and testing the Muslim world in particular," said Dolkun. "In 2014, fasting during Ramadan was forbidden. No one said anything. Then identity cards were required for entry to mosques, and checkpoints were set up. There was no reaction from the international community. In 2016, they col-lected the passports of Uyghurs and stopped international travel. Then they stopped the Internet, social media, WhatsApp. Still, there was no reaction from the inter-national community. So Xi thought, *I am strong. Nobody is against me. I can take off my mask and implement this genocide policy. We can succeed.* This is the reason why Xi Jinping intensified the repression of the Uyghurs so aggressively."

Belatedly, the international community has started to react—but arguably, too little, too late.

In June 2020, over fifty UN Special Rapporteurs called on the United Nations to establish a mechanism to investigate the human rights situation in China.

Western democracies have led several joint letters to the Human Rights Council, with thirty-nine countries signing one in 2020 and forty-four in 2021.[82]

The UN High Commissioner for Human Rights, Michelle Bachelet, made repeated attempts to gain access to the region. In 2022, just before the Winter Olympics in Beijing, she announced that she was delaying the release of a report on Xinjiang, which would be based on the findings of the UN Human Rights Council's independent monitoring mandate, in anticipation of a visit to China. There are deep concerns that her desire for "access" may have rebounded and given Beijing a free pass. Indeed, when she did finally visit China, including Xinjiang, in May 2022, becoming the first UN High Commissioner in seventeen years to travel to the country, she was widely criticized for whitewashing the human rights crisis in her press conference at the end of the visit, and she delayed the publication of the report until the final minutes of her last day in office in August 2022. That said, the long-overdue report, finally released at midnight on August 31, was stronger than many had feared and concluded that China is committing "serious human rights violations" against the Uyghurs and other predominantly Muslim communities, which could amount to "crimes against humanity."

The United States, Canada, the United Kingdom, and the European Union have imposed targeted sanctions on a handful of individual officials and entities in Beijing and Xinjiang. Most significantly, in December 2021, President Biden signed a new law passed by the U.S. Congress that bans all imports to the United States from Xinjiang, unless it can be proven that a particular product was not made by forced labour.[83] This latest step by the United States is truly historic. "The Uyghur Forced Labour Prevention Act is a very positive move," Shawn Zhang believes. "All products in Xinjiang should be presumed as forced labour products unless they can provide evidence that they are not." However, he also warns of the challenges of implementing this ban. "It depends how well customs officials enforce the law, because it is really difficult to figure out which products are from Xinjiang and which are from other parts of China. And the Chinese government transports Uyghur forced labour out of Xinjiang to other Chinese provinces, so some products made outside Xinjiang are made by forced labour, too. That could lead to a very big loophole."

Targeted sanctions, Zhang believes, are the best way forward. "We should target companies involved in the worst human rights violations, such as Hikvision, which has provided video surveillance technology in Xinjiang," he argues. "The United States government has sanctioned Hikvision, but I don't think the sanctions are serious enough. We need to impose stricter sanctions against these top companies, in order to completely shut down their operations and send a strong warning signal to other companies. Right now, the deterrence is not strong enough."

Rushan Abbas agrees. "To stop the genocide, it is necessary to stop business as usual, stop empowering the economy, stop forced labour, stop making genocide a profitable venture," she argues. "It is not just about the Uyghurs' future, it is about saving the free world from a brutal, racist, nationalist regime. Unplug the power line to the Chinese Communist Party and stop doing business with this Mafia crime syndicate that rules China."

In retaliation for Western sanctions, China has imposed its own.

In the U.K., the former leader of the Conservative Party Sir Iain Duncan Smith MP; the then chair of the House of Commons Foreign Affairs Committee, Tom Tugendhat MP; along with three other members of Parliament; two members of the House of Lords (including Lord Alton, who has written the Foreword to this book); Dr. Joanne Smith Finley; Sir Geoffrey Nice, KC, who chaired the Uyghur Tribunal, the Conservative Party Human Rights Commission, the China Research Group, and the Uyghur Tribunal itself; and lawyers at Essex Court Chambers were all sanctioned in March 2021, in retaliation for the U.K.'s sanctions. Although not singled out by name, I am myself indirectly sanctioned, as deputy chair of the Conservative Party Human Rights Commission.

Elsewhere, Dr. Adrian Zenz was also targeted, as were five members of the European Parliament and its Subcommittee on Human Rights, four members of the United States Commission on International Religious Freedom, Canadian member of Parliament Michael Chong and the Canadian House of Commons Subcommittee on International Human Rights, along with Human Rights Watch's China Director Sophie Richardson and the U.S. Commission on International Religious Freedom, including its chair, Nury Turkel, a Uyghur.

In January 2019, I introduced Kuzzat Altay—whose story this chapter begins with—to the British lawyer Sir Geoffrey Nice, KC, who prosecuted Slobodan Milošević and chaired the independent China Tribunal into forced organ harvesting. I have had the privilege of knowing Sir Geoffrey for many years, and worked with him previously on human rights, justice, and accountability in the context of Myanmar and North Korea. Kuzzat and I—together with Bob Fu from China Aid—asked Sir Geoffrey a simple question: What could be done to hold the Chinese government to account for the atrocity crimes it was perpetrating against the Uyghurs?

Several conversations then followed over subsequent months, and I facilitated a meeting between Sir Geoffrey, Dolkun, Rahima, and Nury Turkel. Out of these discussions emerged the idea of an independent "People's Tribunal" to assess and answer one specific question: Do the actions of the Chinese regime against the Uyghurs and other Muslim-majority groups in the Xinjiang region constitute "genocide"?

In July 2020, the U.K. foreign secretary at the time, Dominic Raab, acknowledged that "gross, egregious human rights abuses are going on which are 'reminiscent of something we have not seen for a very long time.'" Six months later, he referred to "industrial-scale" violations. But he stopped short of calling it "genocide" because, he said, "one has to be careful" about the term. He is correct—"genocide" is a very specific legal term which requires a very high threshold of proof. It is not a term to be used lightly. It is the "crime of crimes," the highest level of egregious atrocity crime under international law.

Nevertheless, indicators of genocide were growing. Leaked high-level Chinese government documents spoke of showing "absolutely no mercy" to the Uyghurs, and Chinese State media had declared that the aim of the crackdown was to "break their lineage, break their roots, break their connections, and break their origins." As a *Washington Post* editorial put it in 2019, "it is hard to read that as anything other than a declaration of genocidal intent."[84]

In recent years, the suffering of the Uyghurs has moved from being an unknown or forgotten tragedy to a cause which is receiving growing attention.

In August 2020, seventy-six faith leaders from all major religions—including Rowan Williams, the former archbishop of Canterbury—called for investigation and accountability. On the sidelines of the G7 in Cornwall in 2021, the Bishop of Truro and the Coptic Archbishop Anba Angaelos hosted an event that highlighted the plight of the Uyghurs.

Most significant of all, the Jewish community is comparing the Uyghur tragedy with the Holocaust. That is remarkable, for Jews usually—and understandably—view such comparisons as profoundly sensitive, regarding the Holocaust as entirely unique in history.

So for the president of the Board of Deputies of British Jews, Marie van der Zyl, along with many Jews, to make that comparison speaks volumes. In a letter to the Chinese ambassador in London, she wrote that nobody could see the evidence and fail to note what she describes as "similarities between what is alleged to be happening in the People's Republic of China today and what happened in Nazi Germany 75 years ago: People being forcibly loaded on to trains; beards of religious men being trimmed; women being sterilised; and the grim spectre of concentration camps."

Over the course of 2021, several Parliaments around the world—including Canada, the Netherlands, the Czech Republic, Belgium, Lithuania, and the United Kingdom—passed resolutions recognizing the suffering of the Uyghurs as a genocide, and in one of his last acts on his final day in office as U.S. secretary of state, on January 19, 2021, Mike Pompeo issued a statement determining the atrocities against the Uyghurs as genocide. "I believe this genocide is ongoing, and that we are witnessing the systematic attempt to destroy Uyghurs by the Chinese party-state," Secretary Pompeo declared.[85] Within hours, his Democrat successor, Antony Blinken, told his Senate confirmation hearing that he agreed.

To some, these may look like breakthroughs. But Nury Turkel finds it frustrating. "Over 150 countries are parties to the Genocide Convention. It is disturbing that only a handful of Parliaments and governments have called out the Uyghur genocide," he said. "And we have not seen a concrete plan anywhere in the world to stop this genocide. State parties to the Genocide Convention have a responsibility to call out genocide, to stop genocide, and to hold those responsible for genocide accountable. Yet State parties have failed to do so."

Furthermore, while some scholars and politicians were increasingly recognizing the genocide, albeit too slowly, no legal body had yet done so—and because of China's veto power and influence, no formal international court would ever be likely to do so. In this context, it seemed that only an independent "People's Tribunal" would do what governments and multilateral institutions such as the United Nations refuse to do unless convenient: establish the truth. Initiated by civil society and with no enforcement mechanism, it has nothing more than moral authority and intellectual credibility drawn from having a high-level panel of experts who would assess, impartially, the evidence presented to them. But in an age when moral authority is a scarce commodity, it has considerable value. Its judgment may not lead to action—but it can remove almost all excuse for inaction.

Following in the tradition of past people's tribunals, beginning with the 1966 inquiry into America's actions in the Vietnam War co-chaired by philosophers Bertrand Russell and Jean-Paul Sartre and subsequent tribunals into atrocities in Iran, Kashmir, and the 1965 massacres in Indonesia and Burma, the Uyghur Tribunal functioned like a court jury. Over the course of just over a year, from its launch in September 2020 to the delivery of its final judgment on December 9, 2021, its seven-member panel—consisting of five professors (among them two of Britain's most distinguished medical specialists), business leaders, philanthropists, and lawyers—heard from over seventy witnesses through eight days of public hearings in London in June and September 2021, and through an online hearing in November 2021. In addition, according to counsel to the Tribunal, Hamid Sabi, over thirty researchers spent over 10,000 hours reviewing hundreds of thousands of pages of documents, including 500 fact witness statements. The database of evidence that has been compiled may, as Mr. Sabi said, be one of the most complete databases on this issue. That in itself is an achievement, as it will serve policy-makers, historians, and perhaps prosecutors in coming years well. Even if the perpetrators of the grave atrocity crimes alleged are never brought to justice, the history of the persecution of the Uyghurs will be told with greater accuracy. All of the public hearings, held in Church House in Westminster, were open to anyone who wished to attend, and were livestreamed online. All of the evidence sessions are available on the Tribunal's website to this day.[86]

Four other very important points should be made about the Uyghur Tribunal.

First, almost all of this work was done, in the words of Sir Geoffrey, "*pro bono publico.*" Apart from some of the most junior lawyers and researchers who received a modest fee because they need to earn a living, no one involved received any remuneration. They undertook this work in the public interest.

Second, the Tribunal made repeated invitations to Beijing to present its side but received no reply. As Sir Geoffrey said when he delivered the judgment, the Tribunal disregarded evidence it had reason to believe was unfounded or unfair towards Beijing, and it subjected some submissions to the scrutiny of independent experts.

Third, it drew extraordinary wrath from Beijing. Before the hearings in June, the Chinese authorities called a press conference, in which they denounced Sir Geoffrey, absurdly, as "a notorious human rights abuser and a British spy" and claimed that all witnesses were paid actors giving fake evidence. Even worse, relatives of witnesses were paraded on television, forcing them to denounce their loved ones giving evidence. In September 2021, as the Tribunal was concluding, it emerged that the new Chinese ambassador to London, Zheng Zeguang, had threatened the British government over the Tribunal—even though the government had nothing to do with it.

That leads to the fourth key point: documentary evidence published in the third, online, session of the Tribunal by Adrian Zenz, directly linking Xi Jinping and the senior leadership of the Chinese Communist Party regime to the intensification of repression of the Uyghurs. This consists of eleven documents from April 2014 to May 2018, including three speeches by Xi Jinping in April 2014 covering security, population control, and the need to punish the Uyghur population.[87] In one speech, Xi argues that the BRI requires domestic stability and security.[88] Many had previously held Chen Quanguo responsible as the "pioneer" of Xinjiang's concentration camps. But from Zenz's research, it is clear that Chen was just the implementor of instructions that came from the very top.[89]

On December 9, 2021, together with many others—Uyghurs, activists, campaigners, scholars, journalists, and Parliamentarians—I sat in Church House in Westminster and awaited the judgment from the Uyghur Tribunal. As I listened to Sir Geoffrey go through the contours of the process and the details of international law with a meticulous and methodical rigour, I thought back to that day almost three years previously when Kuzzat, Bob, Sir Geoffrey, and I explored whether such a tribunal might be possible, and all the hours of preliminary and preparatory discussion between Dolkun, Rahima, Nury, Sir Geoffrey, myself, and others. I thought about all those who had given their time voluntarily to make this process possible: the jury panel; the Counsel to the Tribunal and his team; the researchers; the administrative team; Rahima, who interpreted many hours of harrowing witness testimony; the advisors, including my friends Luke de Pulford from the Arise Foundation and Dr. Ewelina Ochab from the Coalition for Genocide Response; all those campaigners from the Stop Uyghur Genocide Campaign, Burst the Bubble, and Yet Again—whose role will be explored in a later chapter—and most of all those who had, often at grave risk, possessed the courage to testify. And I listened to Sir Geoffrey with bated breath.

There were moments as he delivered the judgment that I thought the Tribunal had found against the charge of genocide. The Tribunal disregarded comparisons others have made with the Holocaust, cast doubt on some reports submitted, and concluded that, while there have been killings of Uyghurs "in various ways," the evidence does not show that it has occurred on a scale that could threaten the destruction of the group, in whole or in part, as the Genocide Convention sets out.

Nor—surprisingly—did the Tribunal find sufficient proof that "causing serious bodily or mental harm" or "deliberately inflicting conditions of life calculated to bring about destruction" of the Uyghurs reached a level that could be described as genocide.

Even among the eleven qualifying acts deemed as crimes against humanity, the judgment concluded that neither systematic murder, extermination, nor enslavement was proved. Up to this point, the authorities in Beijing might have had their champagne corks poised to pop.

But—and this is why this judgment is so powerful and should be taken so seriously—that is not the end of the story.

On crimes against humanity, the charge sheet is clear. The crimes of deportation and forcible transfer of people; imprisonment; and severe deprivation of physical liberty, torture, rape, and sexual violence; persecution; enforced disappearances; and "inhumane acts" are all proven, according to the Tribunal, "beyond reasonable doubt."

The separate charge of torture is unarguable.

And on the charge of genocide, the Chinese regime is found guilty, on the single but irrefutable accusation of "imposing conditions intended to prevent birth." Forced sterilization, forced removal of wombs, forced abortions, and forced contraception all result, the Tribunal judges, in "significantly fewer births" among the Uyghur population. And the Tribunal pronounced itself satisfied that these measures, "intended to destroy a significant part of the Uyghurs," mean that "beyond reasonable doubt" the government in Beijing has committed biological genocide.

This conclusion, delivered with weighty legal analysis and accompanied by twists and turns and ifs and buts worthy of any top lawyer, is historic. It is the first time any quasi-judicial body, independent of any government, has offered such a judgment. In the absence of any international justice mechanism or formal court proceedings, the independent Uyghur Tribunal has presented the most credible judgment—and it must not be ignored.

The judgment summarizes harrowing evidence of horrific human rights atrocities inflicted upon Uyghurs. In a detached tone, Sir Geoffrey described accounts of hundreds of thousands of Uyghurs detained "without any, or any remotely sufficient reason," subjected to "acts of unconscionable cruelty, depravity, and inhumanity." Many, he said, were tortured; many "shackled . . . immobilized for months on end"; others "confined in containers up to the neck in cold water; and detained in cages so small that standing or lying was impossible." One young woman had been gang-raped by policemen in front of a hundred people forced to watch. "Women detainees have had their vaginas and rectums penetrated by electric shock rods and iron bars," he recounted.

The litany of horrors described in the Uyghur Tribunal's judgment is not new to anyone who has been studying the situation in China's Xinjiang region in recent years, nor is it new to governments—although the severity, intensity, and systematic nature is shocking. But it is the first time it has been presented to the world in such a comprehensive form, with the authority of such an eminent panel, chaired by one of the world's top human rights lawyers, and with the conclusion that, under international law, the regime in Beijing is committing the most egregious atrocity crimes: genocide, torture, and crimes against humanity.

The value of this judgment lies in its ability to awaken the moral conscience of the international community and mobilize a response. The Tribunal has done its job. It is up to governments around the world now to do theirs. They have a duty to stop genocide, a responsibility to protect. They must activate the arsenal of policy actions within their armoury, ranging from targeted sanctions, a ban on products made by slave labour, measures to ensure slavery is eliminated from our supply chains, the diversification of supply chains, divestment of pension funds from Chinese companies complicit with these crimes, and an exploration of all possible avenues for prosecution.

It is time now to call the atrocities inflicted upon the Uyghur people by name: genocide.

CHAPTER 7

A CRIMINAL STATE

THE PERSECUTION OF FALUN GONG AND THE STORY OF FORCED ORGAN HARVESTING

Beauty queens, pageant contestants, and movie stars are not usually in my orbit. Indeed, I was only vaguely aware of the Miss World contest and had never previously paid any attention to it. But when the news broke in November 2015 that Miss World Canada Anastasia Lin, a Chinese-born Canadian actor, had been turned away from a flight from Hong Kong to Sanya, on Hainan Island, where the Miss World finals were taking place, I took notice.

Declared *persona non grata* by the Chinese Communist Party regime, Anastasia was excluded from contesting the world pageant because of her outspoken advocacy against the persecution of Falun Gong, and the practice of forced organ harvesting. A practitioner of Falun Gong herself, she had taken the Miss World slogan—"Beauty with a purpose"—seriously and intended to use her platform in the contest to, in her own words, "advocate for those who cannot speak for themselves—those who suffer in prisons and labour camps, or whose voices have been stifled by repression and censorship."[1]

Three months later, I sat beside the swimming pool in the sunshine in a hotel in Bangkok, having just a day of "down time" after a long visit to Myanmar. Scrolling through my Facebook feed, I stumbled across a video of Anastasia speaking at a debate at the Oxford Union, a few days previously, on the motion that "This House would sacrifice trade with China in protest of human rights abuses"[2] I could easily have scrolled on as I often do, especially as I was trying to have a short break. But I felt prompted to watch it, and as I did, I was deeply impressed by her intelligence, courage, passion, eloquence, and force of argument.

I then had what at the time seemed a crazy idea. The UK Conservative Party Human Rights Commission, which I had co-founded and serve as deputy chair, was preparing to hold its first enquiry into the human rights situation in China. Anastasia, I thought, would be a perfect witness to testify at one of our hearings in Parliament. The Commission had no funds at all to be able to fly in witnesses from outside the United Kingdom, and it was highly likely that Anastasia would, in any case, be booked up with other engagements, but I thought that there was nothing to be lost by enquiring.

So, I messaged her on Facebook, asked how long she would be in the U.K., and whether she might testify to the Commission. Within minutes, she replied, informing me that she was already back in Canada but might be willing to come to London again for our enquiry. When I explained that we had no means to cover the costs, she assured me that she could work around that, if I could also set up a programme of appointments for her to make the journey more worthwhile. I proposed to set up meetings with senior Parliamentarians, including the Speaker of the House of Common, John Bercow; Lord Alton; and others, and a round of media interviews.

And so, less than a month later, Anastasia returned to London. I will never forget our first meeting together, at her hotel near Russell Square, where we arranged to discuss the programme for her visit. She told me she had a craving for scones, and so we asked the hotel waiter if they served scones in the lounge. The waiter took one look at Anastasia and said that they did not, but that he would personally go and find some. Some minutes later, he returned with scones, jam, and cream, which he had purchased outside the hotel, and refused to take payment. That never happens to me, I thought—I need to hang out with Miss World Canada more often.

The next day, on March 23, 2016, Anastasia appeared before our Commission in the Houses of Parliament. She told us of the personal threats she and her family in China had received from the Chinese regime because of her public advocacy. "My feeling of duty to speak up was tested by the threats endured by my father after I was crowned Miss World Canada," she said. "He was paid a visit by

State security agents and, under great pressure, tried to have me abandon human rights concerns. At one point, I wanted to withdraw from the whole thing rather than put my future and family in danger by speaking up for people I did not know. In the end, I felt that the only thing I could do was follow my conscience rather than submit to fear and silence."[3]

Falun Gong is a spiritual movement which describes itself as "an ancient Buddha School practice" based on the principles of "truthfulness, compassion, and forbearance." Over the past few years, I have come to know at least a dozen Falun Gong practitioners well—I have had dinner with them, visited them in their homes, talked deeply with them. Without exception, every single one of them lives up to those three principles. They are intelligent, hospitable, generous, kind, and interesting people—a far cry from the "evil cult" the regime portrays them as.

According to Anastasia, "Falun Gong is many things: a set of meditative exercises, a moral code, a way of life. If you have seen people practising it in parks, you might have noticed that its exercises and meditation forms resemble tai chi or yoga. But, more importantly, Falun Gong is a cultivation way. Cultivation refers to inner transformation—a continual process of refining one's character, letting go of selfishness and negative thoughts, and nurturing virtue. The core principles that Falun Gong teaches are truthfulness, compassion, and forbearance. Practitioners do their best to bring these principles into their lives and apply them to whatever difficult situations they may encounter. In fact, Falun Gong teaches that these principles of truth, compassion, and forbearance represent the very nature of the universe itself—an immutable moral law, and the criteria for discerning what is right from wrong."

Since 1999, this peaceful, spiritual practice—consisting principally of meditative exercises—has attracted the fury of the Chinese Communist Party, which fears any belief system or movement that inspires significant numbers of adherents. By 1998, China's National Sports Commission estimated that as many as seventy million people in China were practising Falun Gong.

"This is one major reason that Falun Gong was targeted by the Chinese Communist Party," Anastasia said. "Such a huge, independent group in society is unprecedented in Communist Party history. The regime had spent the first fifty years of its rule actively destroying all forms of civil society and religious belief—effectively atomizing individuals so that they would find no insulation from the pervasive power of the State. The Communist Party was the sole source of moral authority in the land, and when faith in Marxist-Leninism waned, the Party promoted materialism and money-worship to fill the ideological vacuum. Falun Gong practitioners were, without even realizing it, creating an immense, silent challenge to all that. It was a popular revival of the traditional beliefs in the divine, and it taught that material wealth was not the true purpose of their life. Although Falun Gong was strictly apolitical, its moral message was seen as being incompatible with the beliefs and values of the Communist Party."

The following year, Jiang Zemin, China's president, announced a directive to eradicate the practice, declaring, "Destroy their reputations, cut them off financially, and eradicate them physically."

Anastasia described the "systematic and sustained persecution" that has since ensued and told the Commission that it "permeates every level of society." It is, she believes, "the largest concerted action of China's security forces since the Maoist era" and akin to "another Cultural Revolution, except it was aimed only at one part of the population."

Without exception, she added, "everyone was forced to express their stance against Falun Gong. Party members were taken to brainwashing classes. The military was 'cleansed' of Falun Gong practitioners. Lawyers were forbidden from defending Falun Gong clients. Families were broken apart, as husbands and wives were expected to express their firm political stand if their partner persisted in the faith. Labour camps were built, and new means of brainwashing—called 'transformation'—were developed. Hundreds of thousands were detained without trial to face harrowing torture. A whole publishing industry sprung up to spread anti-Falun Gong propaganda. The State-run press inundated the public with lies about Falun Gong, meant to incite hatred towards it."

Having interviewed many Falun Gong victims of persecution herself, Anastasia explained, "When practitioners are taken into custody, the one goal of the labour camp guards was to force them to sign a statement renouncing the practice, and to accept the Communist Party's propaganda against it. Extreme measures, like torture with electric batons or sleep deprivation, are used widely. Practitioners who were released reported being told that it did not matter if they died in custody: they would just be written up as suicides. Their lives were worthless, they had ceased to officially exist, and they had no legal protections—they were non-people."[4]

One of the camps where Falun Gong practitioners are jailed is the notorious Masanjia re-education-through-labour camp, in Yuhong district near Shenyang, in Liaoning Province. According to some former detainees, Falun Gong practitioners make up between 50 and 80 percent of the camp's inmates.

In October 2010, Julie Keith, an ordinary woman living in Oregon, who worked as a manager at Goodwill Industries, bought some Halloween items at her local Kmart store, but did not open them immediately. Instead, she put the box in the loft, and brought it out only two years later, when her daughter requested a Halloween-themed fifth birthday party. As Keith unpacked the box, a piece of paper, tightly folded, fell out. "Sir," it began. "If you occasionally buy this product, please kindly resend this letter to the World Human Rights Organization. Thousands people here who are under the persecution of the Chinese Communist Party Government will thank you and remember you for ever."[5]

The letter continued: "People who work here have to work 15 hours a day without Saturday, Sunday break and any holidays. Otherwise, they will suffer torturement, beat and rude remark. Nearly no payment (10 yuan/1 month). People who work here, suffer punishment 1–3 years averagely, but without Court Sentence (unlaw punishment). Many of them are Falun Gong practitioners, who are totally innocent people only because they have different believe to CCP. They often suffer more punishment than others."[6]

Keith sent copies of the letter to Human Rights Watch, US Customs, and *The Oregonian* newspaper, and very quickly the world's media, including *The New York Times* and CNN, ran the story.

Several years earlier, one brave Falun Gong practitioner in Masanjia camp risked his life writing notes of this kind and hiding them in boxes of Halloween decorations which he and other prisoners were forced to produce. Sun Yi, a former engineer who had been arrested in 2008 and sentenced to two and a half years in prison in Masanjia, estimated that he wrote at least twenty such letters.[7] After his release in 2010, he discovered on the Internet the news reports about Keith's discovery, and realized it was his letter. Using a pseudonym, he contacted Keith to thank her, and also agreed to talk to a journalist from *The New York Times*. Canadian film director Leon Lee then made contact with Sun Yi—still in Beijing at the time—and Sun Yi agreed to co-operate on a film about his story, *Letter from Masanjia*. Knowing the enormous risks, he sent Lee footage of himself, but before long, he was arrested again as part of another crackdown on Falun Gong. However, remarkably, he was released on health grounds when his health deteriorated in custody, and, in 2016, he took the chance to flee China, travelling to Jakarta, Indonesia, where he applied for refugee status.

In 2017, I had the privilege of meeting Sun Yi in Jakarta twice. He wanted to improve his English and I tried to find a volunteer in Jakarta to give him tuition. He wanted his application for refugee status expedited by the United Nations High Commission for Refugees (UNHCR), and I tried to advocate for him to that effect. He was a deeply and profoundly impressive man: humble, quiet, gracious, gentle, but as his story illustrates, he possessed an inner core of extraordinary steely courage and strength. Upon learning of his escape to Indonesia, Keith flew out to meet him in person. "He was living without work or money, and struggling to learn the language," she wrote. "But he greeted me warmly with a bunch of flowers and was keen to show me the tiny flat he called home."[8]

Tragically, on October 1, 2017—just two months after my last meeting with him—Sun Yi died suddenly. As Keith wrote, "The official cause of death was kidney failure, but we suspect foul play. Despite everything he had been through, the man I met was a fit-looking 50-year-old who still hoped to be reunited with his wife."[9]

In August 2018, I was in Jakarta again. In my hotel room one evening—the very same hotel where I had met Sun Yi—I watched *Letter from Masanjia*, which had been released earlier that year. It is a remarkable, powerful film—and it is a tragedy that the man whose story is the focus of the film never lived to see it himself.

Former U.S. ambassador-at-large for international religious freedom Sam Brownback said that the intensity of the Chinese Communist Party's hatred of Falun Gong "has been a puzzle to me ever since I met my first Falun Gong practitioner twenty years ago." Despite being totally peaceful and simply practising their meditative exercises, there is, as Brownback said, "nothing that the Communist Party would not do to Falun Gong practitioners. For the life of me, I do not understand the depth of their hatred." It may relate to their ability to organize mass demonstrations, he added, and the knowledge that "historically, spiritual movements had dislodged royal lineages," and for those reasons, the regime is "scared of Falun Gong."

Among the range of human rights violations in China which Anastasia detailed in her testimony, one stood out as especially shocking: the allegation of forced organ harvesting from prisoners of conscience. This was an issue I had been aware of for quite some time but had never previously looked into in depth. Indeed, if I am honest, I, like many, was rather skeptical, as it sounded so extreme, so nightmarish, so outrageous as to be unreal.

On a Saturday morning in the middle of March 2016, after I had already made contact with Anastasia but before the Commission's hearing, I was busy preparing to travel to the United Nations Human Rights Council session in Geneva to advocate for religious freedom in Myanmar. I was accompanying Myanmar's Cardinal Charles Bo and a delegation of interfaith activists from the country. Somewhat out of the blue, an email from someone called Ethan Gutmann popped up in my inbox, urging me to call him immediately. Not knowing anything about Ethan, and preoccupied with preparing for Geneva, I replied explaining I was about to travel and would be in touch in due course. A reply came immediately, arguing that this was about a very important matter and demanding I call him straight away. A little irritated at his insistence, I reluctantly picked up the phone to him. Over the course of half an hour or so, he won me over—I was persuaded that what he had to tell me was urgent, grave, and credible, and merited attention, and I came to respect and appreciate deeply his dogged persistence.

In 2014, Ethan, an American China analyst and human rights researcher, had published a groundbreaking book titled *The Slaughter: Mass Killings, Organ Harvesting, and China's Secret Solution to Its Dissident Problem*, which tells in gripping, horrifying detail the practice of forced organ harvesting from prisoners of conscience.

In our telephone call, Ethan told me that he had recently teamed up with the other two world experts on this issue, former Canadian MP and Cabinet minister David Kilgour and Canadian human rights lawyer David Matas, whose report "Bloody Harvest: The Killing of Falun Gong for Their Organs" was first published online in 2006 and republished in print in 2009. The three of them, Ethan told me, were preparing to release a new publication—*Bloody Harvest/The Slaughter: An Update*—which would combine their research and provide further evidence based on data from hospitals across China of organ transplant operations. They estimated that the Chinese claims of performing 10,000 transplants a year were intentionally low—the real figure is more like a minimum of 56,000 and possibly as many as 110,000 a year, leading to an estimated total, by 2016, of 1.8 million organ transplant operations in China since 2001.

China does not have a tradition of organ donation. Indeed, in 2018, the government's official figures put the number of organ donors around 6,000, donating a total of 18,000 organs. Yet this, claim Kilgour, Matas, and Gutmann, is "easily surpassed by just a few hospitals." So the key question is, Where are all the other organs coming from?

I invited Ethan to testify to the Commission alongside Anastasia. He told the hearing that previous reports of approximately 40,000 to 65,000 organs being extracted from prisoners of conscience should now be regarded as serious underestimates. Furthermore, he claimed that Chinese hospitals were informally confirming the use of Falun Gong prisoners as their primary organ source.

"There have been persistent allegations that large numbers of Falun Gong prisoners of conscience have been killed to supply China's lucrative trade in vital organs," Anastasia told the Commission. "Uyghurs and other prisoners of conscience may have been victimized in a similar way . . . I first learned about these allegations nearly a decade ago. But it took me a long time to really confront the gravity of these crimes, to consider deeply what it means that tens of thousands— or hundreds of thousands—of innocent people have been killed for their organs."

Indeed, as Ethan told the U.S. Congressional-Executive Commission on China on September 18, 2015, the practice began in 1994 when "the first live organ harvests of death-row prisoners were performed on the execution grounds of Xinjiang." In 1997, Uyghur political prisoners were targeted for their organs to be forcibly donated to high-ranking Chinese Communist Party officials. By 2001, Chinese military hospitals were "unambiguously targeting select Falun Gong prisoners for harvesting," and, by 2003, the first Tibetans were being targeted as well. "By the end of 2005, China's transplant apparatus had increased so dramatically that a tissue-matched organ could be located within two weeks for any foreign organ-tourist with cash."[10]

The claims Ethan and Anastasia made were shocking to all of us who sat in the hearing in Parliament. And it became clear to me that they could not be ignored. There was an urgent need for the international community to act. Some action had already been taken by this point, but much more was required.

In 2010, Professor Jacob Lavee, the director of the Heart Transplantation Unit at Israel's largest medical centre, led an initiative that resulted in Israel legislating to prohibit "organ tourism" to China. "The transplants committed in China thrive on transplant tourists," he said, although local candidates for organs could also receive organs from executed prisoners and prisoners of conscience. "They are acting against every convention and against every basic principle of ethics that conducts the entire business of transplants worldwide. The basic principle is that organ donation should be done only, only on the free will of the donor or his family. And they're breaching this principle. Once that's breached, it becomes a crime against humanity." He called for the international community to work together, to "make Parliaments press politically and diplomatically through their own connection with China and through the United Nations so that the process will stop in China altogether."

In 2013, the European Parliament passed a resolution expressing its "deep concern over the persistent and credible reports of systematic, State-sanctioned organ harvesting from non-consenting prisoners of conscience" in China, "including from large numbers of Falun Gong practitioners imprisoned for their religious beliefs, as well as from members of other religious and ethnic minority groups."[11]

In 2015, the Canadian Parliament, the Italian Senate, and the Taiwanese legislature all passed legislation prohibiting organ tourism, and the Council of Europe adopted a treaty against forced organ harvesting.

In June 2016, the U.S. House of Representatives unanimously passed a resolution condemning "State-sanctioned forced organ harvesting" in China, calling on China to end the practice, demanding an end to the persecution of Falun Gong, urging the U.S. medical community to raise awareness about the issue, urging China to allow "a credible, transparent, and independent investigation into organ transplant abuses," and calling on the U.S. State Department to "conduct a more detailed analysis on State-sanctioned organ harvesting" and report annually to Congress on the implementation of measures to ban visas for Chinese or other nationals "engaged in coerced organ or bodily tissue transplantation."[12] The House of Representatives Foreign Affairs Committee held a hearing on forced organ harvesting in China on June 23, 2016. The following month, the European Parliament adopted a Written Declaration calling for an international investigation; in October 2016, an Early Day Motion was tabled in the British House of Commons calling for action; and in the same month, the issue of forced organ harvesting in China was debated on the floor of the House of Commons. Several British Parliamentarians—notably MPs Fiona Bruce and Jim Shannon, and, in the House of Lords, Lord Alton—have persistently and repeatedly pursued the topic since then, with parliamentary questions, debates, and motions.

In September 2016, one of the world's most respected voices in the field of organ transplantation ethics, Dr. Annika Tibell, chief physician at the New Karolinska Hospital Project in Sweden, called for an international inquiry. She had been the lead author of the Transplantation Society's first policy statement on China in 2006 and one of the founders of the Declaration of Istanbul Custodian Group, a major organization focused on transplantation ethics.[13]

Even the president of the Transplantation Society, Dr. Philip O'Connell, who had previously been more skeptical and more defensive of China, addressed remarks to the Chinese regime at a press conference in Hong Kong following the Society's conference: "There remains, in many sectors, a deep sense of mistrust of your transplant programs. It is important that you understand that the global community is appalled by the practices which you have adhered to in the past. Many people in the global community are not persuaded that China has changed."[14]

As Anastasia told the inquiry, "United Nations Special Rapporteurs have taken up this question and called on the Chinese government to account for the sources of organs. This has not happened. Recent reforms to the transplant system have seen prisoners reclassified as regular citizens for the purpose of organ "donation"—thereby further obscuring the truth about organ sourcing and concealing gross violations of medical ethics." She ended with these powerful words: This shocking practice "forces us to confront the question of how humans—doctors trained to heal, no less—could possibly do such great evil." And she answered her own question: "The aggressors in China were not born to be monsters who take out organs from people . . . It is the system that made them do that. It is the system that made them so cold-bloodedly able to cut people open and take out their organs and watch them die. No one is born to be so cruel."

I had not been looking for a new cause to take up, and had a full plate with other human rights challenges in China, alongside Myanmar, North Korea, Indonesia, and beyond. But after what I learned from Ethan and Anastasia, I could not stay silent. So shocked by the evidence were the entire Commission that, in September 2016, we decided to hold a follow-up hearing, for which Anastasia returned, alongside Ethan and one of the co-authors of the original groundbreaking investigation into forced organ harvesting, Canadian lawyer David Matas. We also heard from a Uyghur surgeon, Dr. Enver Tohti.

The most important point made by David and Ethan in their evidence is that previous research into forced organ harvesting in China significantly underestimated the scale of the practice. Their new research based on forensic enquiry into the public records of 712 hospitals in China carrying out liver and kidney transplants leads them to conclude that between 60,000 and 100,000 organs are transplanted each year in Chinese hospitals. One hospital alone, the Orient Organ Transplant Center at the Tianjin First Central Hospital, was performing thousands of transplants a year, according to its own bed-occupancy data. China officially claims 10,000 organ transplants a year, but the authors contend that this is "easily surpassed by just a few hospitals." The evidence points to what David Matas called, in testimony to the U.S. Congress, "mass killing of innocents."[15]

In an interview translated by Australian researcher Matthew Robertson—who himself has written widely on this subject—former prisoner Yu Xinhai provides a shocking first-hand account of what happens:

> Everyone in the prison knows about this. Usually in the prison, regardless of whether the person is deceased, if he is sent to the prison hospital, he faces the reality of having his organs removed at any moment. . . . Everyone in prison knows that there exists a list of names. People [are] taken away, and no one will return. Every year it's like this. They always take away a group of people. Not too many. Sometimes several dozen, sometimes under twenty, from every place they call a "prison ward." The harshest time was in the middle of 2006. I remember it was at midnight . . . Suddenly, we heard the noise of a vehicle starting outside. We were very curious, because the whole prison was very quiet. So I stuck my head out of the window to look, as did some other prisoners. We saw parked outside were three or four large buses, with iron bars blocking the windows. There were also a few armed police's military vehicles, as well as the prison guards' cars and some ambulances like the ones from the hospital, but they were not official. Then, in several columns the armed police and the prison guards entered into the prison ward I was in. Then, starting from the first floor, noises kept arising. When it finally reached our floor, the third floor, I heard that the guards and the police were scolding the prisoners, "Don't look. Turn your face. Lie on the bed. When your name is called, come out immediately. You are not allowed to bring anything." Then only names were called, one after another. Sometimes only one name would be called for a prison cell. When they reached my cell, they called away three prisoners. I saw that everyone's eyes were filled with fear . . . One night, a lot of prisoners were forcibly taken away and they were put into the same jail as me. A few buses parked here. The armed police were guarded outside with their cars parked here, too. And then the prison guards and the armed police entered the empty courtyard of the building I lived in; afterwards, they entered into the building and made the prisoners come out group by group. Then they led them onto the buses outside of the walls. Then

they quickly took them away. I once asked a prison doctor, because this particular doctor was very sympathetic to us Falun Gong practitioners. He was especially sympathetic towards me, because we were from the same hometown. Once he told me secretly, saying, "Don't go against the Communist Party. Don't resist them. Whatever they tell you to do, just do it. Don't go against them forcefully. If you do, then when the time comes, you won't even know how you will have died. When it happens, where your heart, liver, spleen, and lungs will be taken, you won't even know either." At that time, the doctor also told me, "Falun Gong practitioners, they all practise *qigong*. They often exercise their bodies, so their bodies are very good. So think about it, those organs are, of course, very good also. So do you think we rather pick you practitioners or those other prisoners? Those prisoners all abuse drugs or alcohol. Otherwise, they still have many unhealthy habits. It might happen that, when you take their organs, they are damaged beyond repair. You practitioners' organs are the best."[16]

Dr. Enver Tohti was a cancer surgeon in Ürümchi, Xinjiang Province. In 1995, he was instructed by two of the chief surgeons in his hospital to prepare the mobile surgery equipment and wait for them the next day at a hospital gate, with an ambulance and three other assistants. The following morning at 9 a.m., the two chief surgeons arrived in a car, and he was told to follow them. They arrived about half an hour later at Western Mountain ("Xishan"), an execution ground.

Enver described what happened next: "We had been told to wait behind a hill, and come into the field as soon as we'd hear the gunshot. So we waited. A moment later, there were gunshots. Not one, but many. We rushed into the field. An armed police officer approached us and told me where to go. He led us closer, then pointed to a corpse, saying, 'This is the one.' By then, our chief surgeon appeared from nowhere and told me to remove the liver and two kidneys. He urged me to hurry up, so we took the body into the van and removed his liver and kidneys. An operation to repair an organ is very difficult and takes a very long time to do, but this time it was totally different. It was an operation of extraction, so it was easy and quick. Then our chief surgeons put those organs in a special box, and got into the car. They told me to take my team back to the hospital, and left. I have no idea where they went. I, on the other hand, led my team back to where we came from. That was the end of that. Nobody has ever talked about what we did that day. It is something I wish hadn't happened. I wish for that man to rest in peace."

Enver knew he had no choice. "If I had said no, I knew what would happen. If you live in that society, you would not say no. Watch *Squid Game*. The first nine episodes of the first season are a description of the Chinese Communist Party. Once you join the game, you cannot say, 'I don't want to play.' Once you are working with the Communist Party, if you leave, you are a traitor."

It became clear to me that what we were being presented with was evidence of some of the gravest atrocity crimes imaginable. While the term "genocide" requires a very high burden of proof, this surely amounted to crimes against humanity. Ethan described it as "a form of genocide cloaked in modern medical scrubs," and Anastasia pointed to the fact that the dehumanization of a target population is a key ingredient of genocide. "Chinese citizens who practised Falun Gong were outside the protection of the law . . . This explains how organ harvesting could come about," she said. "With potentially millions of practitioners incarcerated in China's vast network of prison camps, they became worth more dead than alive. They are blood-typed, and when a blood match is made, they can simply be led away and killed—or simply anesthetized to have their organs removed while they're still alive."[17]

The evening before the Conservative Party Human Rights Commission's hearing on organ harvesting, the Speaker of the House of Commons, John Bercow, hosted a screening of Anastasia's latest film, in his state rooms at Speaker's House. A packed audience of Parliamentarians, non-governmental organizations, activists, academics, and journalists watched the gruelling, harrowing film, *The Bleeding Edge*, in stunned silence. I had helped arrange the event, because although the film itself is a fictional thriller, it depicts the shocking truth about forced organ harvesting in China.

Bercow, who said a few words of welcome before the film was shown, recalls it as "pretty graphic stuff." Having met Anastasia earlier that year, he had offered to host the screening. "My instinct was that if I, with the enormous privilege of being the occupant of Speaker's House and with the state rooms available to me, could bring this cause to a wider audience, and lend some parliamentary dignity to Anastasia's battle for human rights in China, I should do so," he said. "Anastasia is a remarkable person, who could have simply taken part in beauty competitions and probably made a very good living on that basis, but she had a commitment to principle which was important to her, even if—as it did—it imperilled her competition entries and acting career. Her distinctiveness [and] bravery, and the truly stomach-churning abuse of human rights that organ harvesting represented led me to offer to host a screening."

From then on, I tried to do whatever I could to awaken consciences. I wrote opinion articles in *The Diplomat, The Huffington Post, The Spectator, The Catholic Herald*, and the Asian Catholic news service UCA News. Later, in February 2019, the *Wall Street Journal* published my article headlined, "The Nightmare of Human Organ Harvesting in China." I am told that this was considered a breakthrough, as that newspaper had previously been skeptical about the allegations and reluctant to publish commentary on the subject.

In my article in the *Wall Street Journal*, I wrote this:

> Patients in China—including foreigners—are promised matching organs within days. Former Canadian politician and prosecutor David Kilgour, lawyer David Matas, American journalist Ethan Gutmann and a team of researchers have confirmed this by posing to Chinese hospitals as patients. Dr. Huang Jiefu, China's former vice minister for health and chairman of its organ-transplant committee, ordered two spare livers as *backups* for a 2005 medical operation. They were delivered the next morning. In most advanced Western countries, patients wait months or even years for transplants. . . . Where are the organs coming from? . . . China's figures don't add up. To provide healthy, matching organs within days to patients at hundreds of hospitals, using only several thousand voluntary donors a year means there must be an additional, involuntary source of organs.
>
> Death-row inmates cannot account for all of these. China executes more people than the rest of the world combined, but still only about a few thousand a year. Besides, Chinese law requires prisoners sentenced to death to be executed within seven days—not enough time to match their organs to patients and have them ready on demand, as is China's practice.[18]

I was persuaded to join the advisory board of the newly formed International Coalition to End Transplant Abuse in China (ETAC), and when I learned, in 2017, that the Vatican was hosting a conference on organ harvesting around the world and had invited Huang Jiefu—the former Chinese deputy health minister believed to be the architect of the organ harvesting policy—as the sole speaker on China's record, I went into overdrive, lobbying all my contacts in Rome and Catholic politicians around the world. We were unsuccessful in our attempt to persuade the Vatican to invite one of the experts—Ethan, David Matas, or David Kilgour, for example—to speak, or to withdraw the invitation to Huang Jiefu, but Pope Francis withdrew his agreement for an audience with conference participants, thus depriving Huang from the desired photograph and propaganda coup. The Pope, after all, was on record saying that "trade in organs is immoral and a crime against humanity."

Despite being convinced of the evidence myself, I became increasingly concerned that unlike other human rights violations in China, the claim of forced organ harvesting was met with considerable skepticism by many. In contrast with other violations, forced organ harvesting is extremely difficult to prove conclusively, because it suffers from the fact that the evidence is swept off the operating room floor, the victim does not survive, and the witnesses are also the perpetrators or accomplices and therefore unlikely to implicate themselves. As Anastasia said, "On the street, if someone assaults you or steals your purse, you can scream for help. Tied to a hospital bed in the surgical room of a labour camp, no one can hear your screams. In China, it is the State itself that is involved in organ stealing."[19] For these reasons, despite the remarkable efforts of dedicated researchers like Ethan, David Matas, David Kilgour, Matthew Robertson, Dr. Torsten Trey who leads Doctors Against Forced Organ Harvesting (DAFOH), and a few others, many policy-makers, journalists, and some human rights organizations were unconvinced.

I felt that some independent, legal analysis was required. At some point in 2017, I asked one of Britain's most prominent lawyers, Sir Geoffrey Nice KC—who had prosecuted Slobodan Milošević and later went on to chair the Uyghur Tribunal into the question of genocide in Xinjiang—if he would consider looking at the claims of forced organ harvesting in China. I had worked with Sir Geoffrey on human rights in Myanmar and on the campaign for a United Nations enquiry into crimes against humanity in North Korea, and knew him to be one of the finest legal minds in the land. I presented him with the reports and books by Ethan and the two Davids, documentary films on the topic including *Human Harvest* and *Hard to Believe*, and other information, and asked if he might provide a legal opinion as to what this evidence amounts to under international law.

We met in a restaurant in Sloane Square in London, and I handed over the documents and DVDs. Sir Geoffrey agreed to go through them, but then he looked me in the eyes and said with a smile, "Why don't we go one better? Why don't we establish an independent people's tribunal?"

I have described in the chapter on the Uyghurs what such a tribunal is, but at the time, I knew nothing about them. I asked what it would entail. Several discussions ensued, and then I introduced him to ETAC. In 2018, the China Tribunal into forced organ harvesting from prisoners of conscience in China began. The seven-member panel included one of Britain's top medical experts, Professor Martin Elliott, a specialist in cardiothoracic surgery at University College London; one of Asia's leading human rights lawyers, Andrew Khoo, who had served as chair of the Malaysian Bar Council's Human Rights Committee; U.S. lawyer Regina Paulose and Iranian lawyer Shadi Sadr; an American historian specializing in China, Professor Arthur Waldron; and British businessman Nicholas Vetch. Meeting in the Grand Connaught Rooms in Covent Garden in London, the Tribunal held evidence hearings over three days in December 2018 and two days in April 2019, all of which were open to the public and published in video and transcript form online.[20] Selected specifically on the basis that they did not have any prior expertise or position on the question at hand, the panel sat through long days hearing dozens of witnesses testify.

The format is something of a cross between a courtroom interrogation by counsel, a hybrid panel of judge and jury, and the feel of a parliamentary committee hearing. The weakness is that, unlike, say, a UN-mandated commission of enquiry or a parliamentary inquiry, there is no official ability to enforce the conclusions or recommendations. But you could say the same of a UN-mandated enquiry.

Repeatedly, the Tribunal invited evidence from the Chinese government, from the Transplantation Society, and from others who might dispute the claims of forced organ harvesting in China. They refused.

In a surprise move, the panel decided at the conclusion of the first three days of hearings to issue a draft interim judgment, in which they noted the following: "We, the tribunal members, are all certain, unanimously, and sure beyond reasonable doubt, that in China, forced organ harvesting from prisoners of conscience has been practiced for a substantial period of time, involving a very substantial number of victims. We will deal in our final judgement with our finding as to whether any international crimes have been committed by this practice. If so, by whom, and with detail as to the time periods concerned, and the number of victims, which will all be derived from further analysis of present evidence, and other material yet to be provided and to the legal advice yet to be received, but, to repeat, it is beyond doubt, that forced harvesting of organs happened on a substantial scale, and by state organised or approved organisations and individuals."

In their final judgment, in 2019, they were even more conclusive. They found that it was beyond reasonable doubt that the Chinese State has been forcibly extracting human organs from prisoners of conscience for the transplant industry. The China Tribunal concluded that this amounts to a crime against humanity and that anyone engaging with the Chinese State should do so in the knowledge that they are "interacting with a criminal state."

Ambassador Brownback believes Sir Geoffrey Nice has made a major contribution to the effort to "get this charge taken seriously." Like many, when he first heard the allegations of organ harvesting, Brownback was skeptical. "For years, there were too many people outside China who did not take the charge seriously. There were questions around the credibility of the sources. And yet, the charge kept coming up. There could have been a simple answer for the Chinese Communist Party to give, which was to just open up their books and show where all the organs were coming from, because we in the West have so much difficulty getting organ donations, with long waiting times for transplants." Now, he added, "it is becoming much more recognized that the Chinese Communist Party is forcibly harvesting organs. I believe it is happening; otherwise, the Chinese government would open up their books and show us the source of the organs. Of all the graphic, horrific things that a government could do to its own people, forced organ harvesting has to be among the most egregious. I am trying to imagine anything more horrific, other than drawing and quartering a person as they did in medieval times."

It is now up to our governments and legislators to decide how to respond to the China Tribunal's judgment, and how to hold that "criminal State" to account. It is time to act.

CHAPTER 8

BROKEN PROMISES, SHATTERED DREAMS

THE ALL-OUT ASSAULT ON HONG KONG'S FREEDOMS

In a corner of the reception of Portcullis House—one of the British Parliament's office buildings, opposite Big Ben and overlooking the River Thames—sat a young, slim, bespectacled twenty-three-year-old student from Hong Kong.

Two months previously, he had been elected as the youngest-ever legislator in Hong Kong, and two years earlier, he had been one of the leaders of Hong Kong's Umbrella Movement, as the president of the Lingnan University Students' Union.

As I came through the security doors to greet him, I immediately recognized him as he, together with Joshua Wong, had become one of the most public faces of Hong Kong's democracy movement. I had seen him on television, including on BBC's *Hard Talk*, but until that evening, November 22, 2016, we had not met.

"Nathan," I greeted him. "It is such a privilege to meet you. Congratulations on your election, and welcome to London."

He responded with his typically modest, warm smile and a word of appreciation. That was how Nathan Law and I first met. I had received a request a week or two earlier from a mutual friend in Hong Kong's democracy movement, informing me that Nathan was coming to London, and asking me to arrange some meetings for him with Parliamentarians, which I was glad to do.

Together, we had several meetings with senior members of Parliament, and, the next night—November 23, 2016—we shared the interesting experience of riding around London on a red double-decker bus with Lord Alton of Liverpool, as part of the inaugural "Red Wednesday" campaign to highlight religious persecution around the world. The Houses of Parliament, Westminster Abbey, the London Eye, and other famous landmarks around the city were illuminated in red, and the organizers of the campaign—Aid to the Church in Need—had rented this bus to help promote the cause. As a courageous campaigner himself, we thought Nathan might enjoy experiencing this creative campaigning.

After the bus ride, Lord Alton hosted us for dinner in the House of Lords. As someone who himself was first elected to Parliament in a by-election in 1979 as the youngest member, known in parliamentary parlance as the "Baby of the House," aged just twenty-eight, Lord Alton told Nathan, "Us 'Babies of the House' must stick together."

Nathan and I went on to share many experiences together, including being targets of verbal attacks by the China Global Television Network (CGTN) reporter Kong Linlin, as described in the Introduction, at the Conservative Party Conference in 2018, after Nathan had been released from prison, and many times since, especially after he went into exile in London when the National Security Law was imposed on Hong Kong in June 2020.

In August 2017, less than a year after we first met, Nathan was sentenced to eight months in prison for his role in the Umbrella Movement, having already been disqualified from the legislature in July that year for having quoted Mahatma Gandhi when he took his oath of office as a legislator.

I was in Indonesia when I heard the news of his jailing, along with the imprisonment of Joshua Wong and Alex Chow. Walking along a beach in Bali, supposedly trying to have a break, I found myself thinking, "Somebody should do something. Somebody should organize a statement by international political and public figures. Somebody should speak out." And then it dawned on me: "Maybe that 'somebody' is me."

Within twenty-four hours of their sentencing, I had drafted a statement and gathered at least twenty-five signatories, including former British foreign secretary Sir Malcolm Rifkind, former leader of the Liberal Democrats in the U.K. Paddy Ashdown, former Canadian secretary of state for Asia-Pacific David Kilgour, Canadian MP Garnett Genuis, Canadian senator Consiglio Di Nino, United States congressman Chris Smith, and politicians and diplomats from Australia and Europe.

But I deliberately ensured that the statement was not only supported by the "usual suspects" from Western democracies. The former president of the Maldives Mohamed Nasheed; the daughter of the former president of Indonesia, Alissa Wahid; Myanmar's Cardinal Charles Bo, and famous comedian Zarganar, South Korea's former ambassador for human rights Jung-Hoon Lee, Indian writer and activist John Dayal, Malaysian member of Parliament Charles Santiago and the former chair of the Malaysian Bar Council's human rights committee Andrew Khoo were among the signatories, too. They all happened to be friends of mine from my human rights work across Asia—but if you can't call on your friends in such an emergency, when can you?

The statement described the jailing of these three activists—Hong Kong's first political prisoners—as "an outrageous miscarriage of justice, a death knell for Hong Kong's rule of law and basic human rights, and a severe blow to the principles of 'One Country, Two Systems' on which Hong Kong was returned to China twenty years ago." It concluded that "Joshua Wong, Alex Chow and Nathan Law should be honoured, encouraged and supported, not jailed. Yesterday was a dark day for Hong Kong and it should be met with international condemnation."[1]

It was covered prominently in *The Guardian*, *The South China Morning Post*, *Hong Kong Free Press*, and other media, and apparently caught the authorities in Hong Kong and Beijing by surprise. Hong Kong's chief executive Carrie Lam—speaking in London a month later—said she was "extremely disturbed" by it. It would not be the only time my actions disturbed her.

During their time in prison, I wrote to Nathan, Joshua, and Alex. On one occasion, I received a letter from Joshua, whom I had the privilege of meeting in London in 2015 and had helped facilitate meetings for him in Parliament in 2017. His note read, "Thank you for your continuing prayer and support. I believe we are not alone. Global civil society stand firm on our side with political prisoners. Look forward to meet you again in London next year." Sadly, that never happened, as Joshua has faced a succession of arrests and prison sentences over recent years, and, in the short time when he was out of prison, he was unable to make it back to London. But a well-thumbed copy of his book, *Unfree Speech: The Threat to Global Democracy and Why We Must Act, Now*, sits on my bookshelf, with its prescient warning that Hong Kong is the "canary in the coal mine" and the "first line of defence" against the rise of a totalitarian superpower.[2] "Today's Hong Kong is the rest of the world's tomorrow," he warns, as he urges us to "act now, before it's too late."[3] An equally well-thumbed copy of Nathan's excellent book, *Freedom: How We Lose It and How We Fight Back*, sits alongside it, carrying a similar message.

In July 2020, as Hong Kong began locking up more activists following the imposition of the draconian National Security Law, Nathan left the city and flew to London. He did so not simply because he knew he would be arrested if he stayed, but because he and his colleagues knew that the movement needed an advocate outside Hong Kong, to keep the flame alive and the world spotlight on the city. If all prominent activists were jailed, who would be able to do that?

So as Hong Kong began to be locked up, he slipped away quietly with just one backpack and a single piece of carry-on luggage. A few days after he arrived in London, just as the United Kingdom was emerging from the first COVID-19 lockdown, we met in a café in Wimbledon Village. Nathan was the first friend I met in person since the pandemic began.

After lunch, we walked to Wimbledon Common, and passed the home of one of my political heroes, William Wilberforce.

In 1780, Wilberforce was elected as an MP at age twenty-one—two years younger than Nathan was when he was first elected—and ended up leading what amounted to perhaps the first-ever human rights campaign, against the slave trade. It took him more than forty years, but year on year he introduced legislation to abolish slavery and, with the help of grassroots activists and a nationwide campaign, he chipped away at it until he succeeded. In one speech, Wilberforce said words that stay as my motto: "We can no longer plead ignorance, we cannot evade it . . . we cannot turn aside."

I showed Nathan the writing on the blue plaque: "On this site lived William Wilberforce, Statesman and Emancipator, 1759–1833." I wondered silently whether one day there will be a blue plaque for Nathan with a similar epithet. It is a house and a plaque I cycle past quite often, and every time I do so, it gives me pause for thought, and prayer.

* * *

When I left Hong Kong in 2002, I never anticipated that one day I would have friends in the city who are political prisoners and other friends from the city who have become political refugees. I also never expected that Hong Kong, which had once been the base of my advocacy for freedom in other parts of Asia, would end up being the focus of my activism today. The city where I had once led protests for other freedom struggles—Myanmar and East Timor in particular—is today the topic of demonstrations and rallies at which I speak regularly in London, in solidarity with Hong Kongers. Where did it all change?

For me, personally, the turning point was the Umbrella Movement in 2014.

As I followed the developments, I knew that I could not be silent or inactive. Not since the mass protests of up to half a million people in 2003—a year after I left Hong Kong—against the Hong Kong government's plan to introduce an anti-subversion law in line with Article 23 of Hong Kong's Basic Law, had Hong Kong seen such large numbers of people take to the streets. The demonstrations in 2003 had succeeded in pushing then chief executive Tung Chee-hwa's government to withdraw the plan, precipitating a loss of confidence in Tung's leadership from Beijing and his eventual resignation halfway through his second term.

Perhaps it was then that the seeds were sown for a movement for universal suffrage for the election of Hong Kong's chief executive. That movement for change in Hong Kong was lubricated by sporadic campaigns on specific issues, such as the campaign known as "Scholarism," in which fifteen-year-old school students Joshua Wong, Agnes Chow, and others first came to prominence as opponents of the proposed Communist Party propaganda "moral and national education" school curriculum in 2012. But it was Beijing's decision to renege on its own promise for universal suffrage that sparked the 2014 protests.

The system in place for selecting Hong Kong's chief executive—an equivalent to a mayor of a major city or a governor of a province—is that they are "elected" by an Election Committee consisting of 1,500 members. However, the composition of the committee is heavily stacked with pro-Beijing figures, meaning, even in a supposedly contested election, there is no danger of Beijing's choice failing.

Similarly, the Legislative Council—until changes in 2021 which turned it into a blatant and outright pro-Beijing rubber-stamp puppet body—consisted of seventy seats, thirty-five of which were directly elected from geographical constituencies, while thirty-five were from "functional constituencies" representing professions, such as the business, finance, legal, accounting, industrial, technology, tourism, real estate, and other sectors. The nature of the system meant that even if the pro-democracy camp won a majority of the directly elected geographical seats, it was never able to secure a majority in the legislature because the pro-Beijing camp had the functional constituencies sewn up. So Beijing had a built-in majority, and all the pro-democracy parties could hope to do was to scrutinize, amend, or delay legislation.

Hong Kong's mini-constitution—known as the Basic Law—states in Article 45 that "the ultimate aim is the selection of the Chief Executive by universal suffrage upon nomination by a broadly representative nominating committee in accordance with democratic procedures." Article 68 makes the same promise for all seats in the Legislative Council. While admittedly vague on timing, it is clear about the ultimate aim of universal suffrage.

As early as 1993, four years before the handover, China's chief negotiator on Hong Kong, Lu Ping, told *The People's Daily*: "The [method of universal suffrage] should be reported to [China's Parliament] for the record, whereas the government's agreement is not necessary. How Hong Kong develops its democracy is completely within the sphere of autonomy of Hong Kong. The central government will not interfere." According to the last governor, Chris Patten, China's foreign ministry confirmed this the following year.[4] In 2000, the British House of Commons Foreign Affairs Committee noted that, "The Chinese government has therefore formally accepted that it is for the Hong Kong government to determine the extent and nature of democracy in Hong Kong."[5]

Except by 2014, it had become clear that Beijing acted as though it had accepted no such thing. As Mark Clifford notes in his book, *Today Hong Kong, Tomorrow The World*, "Beijing didn't simply renege on those promises. It never showed any attempt to fulfil them."[6] Since 1997, the Chinese government kept shifting the goalposts, delaying the introduction of universal suffrage several times.

In June 2014, an unofficial referendum was organized by a civil rights movement known as "Occupy Central"—or, more officially, "Occupy Central with Love and Peace"—which had been initiated by law professor Benny Tai, Reverend Chu Yiu-ming, and Chan Kin-man on March 27 the previous year. Almost 800,000 people voted in the poll, in which a number of different electoral systems were proposed. About 42 percent of those who participated voted for a proposal allowing the public, a nominating committee, and political parties to name candidates for chief executive.[7]

On August 31, Beijing gave its answer. It confirmed that the 2017 chief executive election and the 2020 Legislative Council election would be by universal suffrage—but with the candidates entirely handpicked by Beijing. As the "father" of the democracy movement, Martin Lee, noted, "Hong Kong people will have one person, one vote, but Beijing will select all the candidates—puppets. What is the difference between a rotten apple, a rotten orange and a rotten banana? We want genuine universal suffrage and not democracy with Chinese characteristics."[8]

In response to Beijing's broken promises, a protest movement—already underway—intensified. Students from more than twenty universities announced a class boycott on September 22, and five days later, police used pepper spray against protesters outside government offices. On September 28, Occupy Central began in earnest, with tens of thousands of people coming onto the streets in Hong Kong's financial district for seventy-nine days. The song "Do You Hear the People Sing?" from the musical *Les Misérables* became one of the movement's anthems. Hong Kong's Catholic Bishop Emeritus, Cardinal Joseph Zen, aged eighty-two at the time, participated in the protests and was arrested. Martin Lee described being tear-gassed. "At 76 years old, I never expected to be tear-gassed in Hong Kong, my once peaceful home," he wrote in *The New York Times*. "Like many of the other tens of thousands of calm and non-violent protesters in the Hong Kong streets . . . I was shocked when the pro-democracy crowd was met by throngs of police officers in full riot gear, carrying weapons and wantonly firing canisters of tear gas. After urging the crowd to remain calm under provocation, I got hit by a cloud of the burning fumes. The protesters persevered. They ran away when gassed, washed their faces and returned with raised hands. But the police continued to escalate the crisis. Their aggressive actions hardened the resolve of Hong Kongers, many of them too young to vote, to defend our freedoms. These include the long-promised right to elect our leader."[9]

Nathan Law joined the movement soon after being elected president of the Lingnan University Students' Union. Speaking to me in the appropriately named "Pure" café in London's Waterloo train station, just next to the "Victory Arch" memorial to railwaymen who died in World War I and World War II, he recalled that "this was really the first time that Hong Kong people had been involved in civil disobedience actions on a massive scale." For more than two and a half months, protesters camped out in tents in the protest sites. Many were university and school students who interspersed their demonstrations with diligently doing their homework and studies in their protest tents. "Seeing those roads, which were usually major runways of Hong Kong, so full of people, and at night seeing people putting up their phone flashlights in unity, the scene was magical. It was really powerful—it showed the power of the people," Nathan reflected.

Another of the movement's student leaders was Alex Chow, at the time secretary-general of the Hong Kong Federation of Students. I came to know Alex subsequently when he was a postgraduate student at the London School of Economics, and then a doctoral candidate at the University of California at Berkeley. Speaking to me in an online call in late 2021, Alex told me, "I became one of the leaders of the movement simply by accident. When I was still an undergraduate student at the University of Hong Kong, I was just an ordinary student trying to complete my degree and enjoy my student life. I was passionate about literature, I loved writing, and I wanted to use writing to raise awareness about various social issues. So I joined the student magazine on campus, and through that, I was exposed to a larger political debate. Around that time, the debate around electoral reform began."

Through increasing engagement with civil society and pro-democracy parties, Alex received training in activism and began to think about a wide range of social and political issues, including housing and land reform, infrastructure, media freedom, academic freedom, and human rights. "Gradually, I rose up in the movement," he said. But further back, in 2011, Alex recalls an incident when some students in Hong Kong University were arrested for protesting against Chinese leader Li Keqiang, who later became premier. That had already marked him. "An invisible hand was manoeuvring politics in Hong Kong, and so even an ordinary student like me could feel the heat and was aware that something is going wrong."

Occupy Central—which transformed into what became known as the Umbrella Movement—was a remarkable alliance of young radical students, middle-aged mainstream academics, and the old guard of the pro-democracy movement. There were tensions between the different generations and differing strategies, but as Nathan Law emphasizes, "we have far more in common than our differences. In a situation like this, we have to be united." He highlights his admiration for the experience and international advocacy of leaders such as Martin Lee, and Benny Tai's "tireless campaigning for civil disobedience." Even if there are differences, he adds, he always wanted to be a "bridge," to bring people together. "As long as they are really democrats, people who fight for democracy, I am willing to work with them," he notes.

For Alex Chow, one of his memories of the 2014 movement was when the students were taken seriously. "It was important to let the public know that students could be a part of the movement, and that they are the future leaders of the city, they should be consulted and involved in shaping the debate about the future of Hong Kong," he recalled.

Alex was first arrested during one of the earliest protests, on July 1, 2014—the seventeenth anniversary of the handover of Hong Kong to China. He described the scene: "You had students and people from all walks of life taking part. It was illegal, unauthorized, and so, from the government's point of view, unlawful. So, we got arrested. But what was important to me was that it was one of the very first times I had been involved in taking direct action, confronting the Hong Kong government and the Beijing regime, daring to seek change, signifying that we will not give up, we will not succumb to any kind of pressure, and we have our ideas about how political reform should proceed. People used their bodies to occupy the street; they knew they would have to bear some cost, but they felt that it was a risk they had to take."

Another highlight, Alex recalled, was when the Hong Kong government eventually agreed to talks with protest leaders. Initially scheduled for October 10, Hong Kong's chief secretary at the time, Carrie Lam, called off the talks the day before. Eventually, a meeting took place on October 21, though it turned out to be fruitless. Alex believes the fact that the meeting happened at all was significant because "it is quite rare for government officials to speak to protesters directly in a live televised context." For Carrie Lam and the then chief executive CY Leung, it was a "concession" because "they could feel the heat and the pressure imposed by the citizens." However, the fact that the talks led nowhere resulted in "more desperation," said Alex, leading people to "think or act more radically." That, he believes, led to more severe confrontation with the police, which led to more serious clashes in years to come.

Occupy Central transformed into what became known as the Umbrella Movement because protesters began to carry yellow umbrellas. According to Alex, the colour yellow was chosen early on, and people distributed yellow ribbons. "The colour yellow became the symbol at the very beginning of the movement, and then umbrellas came in when the police starting firing tear gas. People used umbrellas to protect themselves, to use as a shield against tear gas and pepper spray. Then artists began to recreate scenes or create artwork celebrating the courage of the protesters, and then the 'Yellow Man' statue, created by a young artist, was erected in the protest site in Admiralty. That is how it became the yellow Umbrella Movement." It was, he believes, "a catalyst, an incubator for ideas and emotions for the future."

The profiles of Alex, Nathan, and Joshua, though already very high, gained even more prominence through their leadership of the occupation of "Civic

Square," a fenced-off area just outside the Hong Kong government's main buildings, in September 2014. "That was important, because it showed that students were making a real contribution in preparing for a larger movement to come, which was the Umbrella Movement in late September," Alex told me. "The student boycott served as a segue from the Occupy Movement into the Umbrella Movement. The occupation of Civic Square was a last straw for the Hong Kong government. It was sending a message that Hong Kongers—ordinary citizens— had had enough. We will stand up and say no."

Nathan lost count of how many times he was arrested—probably four or five times in total, he thinks, and three times in 2014. For his leadership of the occupation of Civic Square, he was sentenced in 2016 to eighty hours of community service. "I worked in a library for blind people, I helped them with cleaning, and I participated in some painting work for different charities," he recalled. "But even though I completed all my community service, the government appealed and I was sentenced to jail."

Nathan's time in jail, together with Joshua's and Alex's, is mentioned at the beginning of this chapter. Nathan's recollections of the experience are raw. "It was quite destabilizing initially, to be so out of place, away from home, away from your partner and family. The first few days were the toughest," he told me. "There is a lot of mental preparation, but essentially you are thrown into an unknown place where there is no way to seek help, no support group, no prior knowledge." Now, in 2022, he adds, so many activists and protesters have done jail time that people have some idea of "how life looks as a political prisoner," but back then, as among the first political prisoners, it was a much more uncertain picture. "I did not know whether the Chinese regime would hire gangsters to harass me. And indeed, in the first few days in jail, we were all over the news, and everybody was watching. As a result, they were very curious. When I was in my cell, or in the canteen, people would peek in. It was like I was an animal in a zoo. I did not feel very secure."

After a few days, Nathan was transferred to another prison in the New Territories, which was better. Sentenced to eight months, he knew that in Hong Kong—at least at that time—sentences would be cut by a third, so he assumed he had five months. "I knew I was there for a few months. I was living in a twenty-man cell, and we shared two toilets. We shared everything," he recalls. "Our daily routine was work, rest, work, lunch, work, exercise, then back to the cell. We were treated like a number, not a human."

Nathan says he was not physically tortured, but psychologically, he felt dehumanized. "They always called me by my number; I felt like a number. It was as if they wanted to erase your connection with the world, to erase your critical thinking," he told me. "It is called a correctional service, but there is no element of correction. They do not teach you anything." He spent his time making clothing for other prisoners. "I was the lowest ranked worker, so I cleaned the floor, cleaned the toilets, ironed the clothes, sewed on buttons."

Besides work, prisoners in Hong Kong—perhaps in contrast to those in Mainland China—are, at least until now, able to receive a wide range of reading material. Nathan continued his undergraduate programme in jail, wrote essays in prison, and read widely. He read Michel Foucault's *Discipline and Punish*, about life in an eighteenth century French jail, as well as works by Francis Fukuyama, Mahatma Gandhi, and Martin Luther King. "I also read comics, which circulated in prison—but they were illegal, because in prison, you cannot share anything with others," he notes. "You could be locked in solitary confinement for sharing a hair clip. Ridiculous."

Unlike Nathan, Alex Chow did not serve a community service sentence because, by 2016, he had plans to move to London, to study for a master's degree at the London School of Economics. Taking this into account, the judge sentenced him to a suspended sentence of three weeks in prison instead, which he could serve on his return to Hong Kong. The following year, having completed his studies in London, Alex returned to his home city, only to find that the government appealed against the sentence, and he was hit with a seven-month prison term instead.

"At that time, not many people serve long jail sentences for their participation in a political movement. It was not like the 2019 movement. Back in 2017, young activists and protesters being sentenced and jailed was a really serious development which broke many people's hearts," Alex recalled. "I was really sad. Before I went to court, I cried for several days. The night before the trial, and even at lunchtime just before we came to the courtroom, I cried, because I was so regretful for my parents. I was split in two. One part of me knew that what I did was the right thing to do, but another part of me was heartbroken because of the pain the sentence caused my parents, my partner, and my companions."

In prison, parental visits were permitted, but the visitor and the prisoner were divided by a glass screen. Alex recalls one visit in September 2017 from his mother. "She came alone. When she came in, I was allowed to walk to my seat, but we were separated by a glass screen. My mother walked towards me, and before she was even seated, she cried. I was very, very sad, from the bottom of my heart, just because I felt so sorry that she had to go through all this hardship, seeing her son in a prison uniform. She feared I might be mistreated or punished, and she could not do anything to help me. I felt very angry. Why have I let my mother suffer like this? I did not do anything wrong—we simply want a better future, a better political system, accountability for Hong Kong officials, policies to take care of the well-being of people in Hong Kong."

Alex recalls that in his experience, in 2017, the prison staff generally treated him well. "Many of them were pro-democracy leaning, and they were very friendly to activists. Even those who were more pro-establishment were still friendly, at least in my case," he told me. "So I started observing what I could do in prison, and I began some mini-advocacy work for other prisoners. Many of the inmates had a lot of grievances. They complained about the food, about why they are ordered to squat, about poor access to information, why they could not read the newspapers in the morning, and some legal questions. For them, it was a way to maintain their dignity and sanity, to feel like they are still being treated as humans. So I started making requests on their behalf. I asked if we could receive the newspapers in the morning, if the practice of squatting could be abolished—or at least if we could be told the meaning of the orders to squat—and I asked if the blankets could be washed. Some requests were granted—we received the newspapers earlier, and the practice of squatting was abolished. I do not know whether that remains the case today, but at the time, these little achievements felt that we could still do something—even in prison."

Being in jail alongside real criminals—people imprisoned for drug dealing, theft, petty crime, and violent crime—gave Alex insight into the margins of society. "I was raised by a middle-class family, but in prison, I met people from different social classes, people who were underdogs. I realized that even though Hong Kong was a materially very prosperous city, it really lacks a policy or even a mentality to serve people on the margins. It was always about how to serve the people who have power, and if you don't have power, you will be forgotten," he said. "When I left prison, I really started thinking how we could reform and rebuild the city to make it more humane. Hong Kong could be a city that served everyone, regardless of age, sexuality, family background, income. That was my goal when I left prison, drawing on the insights I developed in prison. Being in prison was a transitional moment for me, from being an ordinary student who rose up to a leadership role in the movement, to having some reflection in prison about Hong Kong's story."

The Umbrella Movement ended on December 15, 2014, after seventy-nine days, when bailiffs and police came in to clear the protest sites. But Hong Kong's fight for freedom—and Beijing's crackdown—continued to intensify.

One other key development in 2014 that laid the foundations for the dismantling of Hong Kong's freedoms and autonomy over subsequent years was Xi Jinping's White Paper on the judiciary. Published in June—at the same time as Hong Kong citizens participated in an unofficial referendum on democracy—the paper, titled *The Practice of One Country, Two Systems*, declared that Hong Kong judges are mere "administrators"[10] subject to a "basic political requirement" to love the country.[11] It was a forerunner of the 2021 requirement for civil servants and politicians to take an oath of allegiance to Beijing, and it marked the juncture where, as Martin Lee wrote, Hong Kong begun to be run directly "by Communist Party cadres" who created a situation where "the rule of law is under attack."[12] A senior retired Hong Kong judge, Judge Kemal Bokhary, concluded a speech in April 2016 that his warning in 2012 of a "storm of unprecedented ferocity" facing the judiciary had now come about, noting that his "fears have been realized, much as I wish they were not." There were, he confirmed, "very serious problems now . . . grave challenges" which would mean that "the things which were second nature to you and I may recede to the back row where judicial independence is eroded."[13]

Between October and December 2015, one of the incidents which illustrates Beijing's encroachment on Hong Kong most shockingly was the abduction, one by one, of the five Causeway Bay booksellers. Causeway Bay Books, founded by Lam Wing-kee in 1994, published and sold controversial, sensitive, scandalous, and sometimes salacious Chinese-language books about Chinese politics and the lives of China's political leaders. It became popular among Mainland Chinese tourists for this reason. By late 2015, it appeared that the patience of the men in Beijing had worn thin.

Lui Bo, the bookstore's manager, was the first to disappear, reportedly from his wife's home in Shenzhen in mid-October. Gui Minhai, a Swedish national, author of many books and a shareholder in the bookstore's parent company, Mighty Current, was abducted on October 17 from his holiday home in Pattaya, Thailand—a foreign national kidnapped from a third country. Lam Wing-kee disappeared a week later, followed by Cheung Chi-ping and Lee Bo, a British citizen. British Foreign

Secretary Philip Hammond at the time expressed particular concern about Lee Bo, reported that he had been "involuntarily removed to the Mainland without any due process under Hong Kong SAR law," and asserted that the incident "constitutes a serious breach of the Sino-British Joint Declaration and undermines the principle of 'one country, two systems.'"[14]

In 2019, at the height of the protests against the proposed extradition law in Hong Kong, I met Lam Wing-kee in a crowded coffee shop in Taipei. He had moved to Taiwan earlier that year, fearing for his safety if the extradition law passed.

On October 24, 2015, Lam was arrested as he crossed the border into the Mainland Chinese border city of Shenzhen. There then followed an eight-month nightmare, in which he was first imprisoned in Ningbo, and then moved to Shaoguan, a small mountain town in Guangdong Province where he was assigned to work in a library—better off than in prison, but still not free, and completely cut off from the outside world. "I was not physically tortured, but mentally, I was threatened and subjected to brainwashing," he told me.

When he was first arrested, Lam was forced to sign two statements: surrendering his right to inform his family of his whereabouts, and his right to a lawyer. Over the eight months he was held in China, he was forced to write confessions over twenty times. Several times he was filmed, with an interrogator behind him whom he could not see, and these were then broadcast on national television—one of many forced televised confessions that have become a feature of Xi Jinping's regime. "If I didn't write what they wanted me to write, they would write it for me," he said. "If my confession was not satisfactory, they would tell me what to write."

When he asked what crimes he had committed, Lam's interrogators told him simply, "If we say you have committed a crime, you have committed a crime." So much for the rule of law. "I never went to court. I never saw a judge," he told me. He was accused of being a counter-revolutionary, damaging the Chinese Communist Party and attempting to split the nation.

Lam was finally brought back to Hong Kong in June 2016, not for the purposes of releasing him but in order to obtain his computer which contained the details of some of the bookstore's customers. Lam described to me in detail that episode, including the fact that he was accompanied by Mainland Chinese officials who provided him with a cellphone with a tracking device. Whenever he wished to leave his hotel, he had to inform his "minders"—and he was warned never to turn off the cellphone.

After a series of meetings with colleagues to obtain the computer, and a false start in which he was given the wrong computer, he finally made his way, as instructed, back to the border where he was expected to hand over the computer with clients' details, and return to his restricted life as a librarian under the regime's control in the mountains of Guangdong. He was offered the chance, in the future, to work again in what had been his own bookstore but was now under Beijing's ownership, and to do so as a spy for the Chinese regime. "I did not want to be controlled by the Chinese Communist Party, or to lose my freedom," he said. "They wanted to turn the bookstore and publishing company from one that believed in freedom of expression into one that would be a speech-monitoring centre. I couldn't do that."

On the way, and after stopping for three cigarettes, Lam had a rethink. "I was afraid that if I gave my computer, the regime will kidnap, arrest, or prosecute all my customers. I couldn't do that. I thought, if I go public, and tell Hong Kongers the truth, I might save some people," he said. "But I faced a dilemma. I might endanger my colleagues. But they can't speak out, because they all have relatives in China. I realized I was the only one who could reveal the truth."

And so, at the very last minute, on his way to the border, Lam switched off the cellphone, aborted the journey, borrowed another phone, called a prominent pro-democracy lawyer, and went public.

From 2016 to 2019, although back in Hong Kong and supposedly "free," Lam was followed regularly. The Hong Kong government, he says, "pretended to communicate with Beijing" about his case, but in reality did nothing to help.

And while the booksellers were missing, their company was mysteriously bought out by, according to Lam, "people sent by Beijing."

I first met Angela Gui, the daughter of Gui Minhai, in 2016, just when she was beginning her global advocacy in pursuit of justice for her father. An impressively intelligent, articulate postgraduate student at the University of Cambridge, she had not sought to be an activist—but was compelled to speak out for her father after he was abducted.

When Angela first heard of her father's disappearance, she told me that it had not come as "a complete surprise" because she was aware of his passion for human rights and democracy and his dissident publishing, and because the realization of what had happened came "over the course of two or three weeks." Initially, she noticed her father was not responding to her messages. "But, at first,

I did not think much of it, because I thought that he had just got wrapped up in a work project—because that is the way his publishing house worked, with tight deadlines," she told me. She had been making plans to visit her father in Thailand, perhaps over her university Christmas vacation. "We discussed the idea, over Skype, and then he said, 'Oh, I have to go. But let's talk again in a week or so?' I said okay. So when I did not hear from him, at first I was a bit annoyed, as I needed to plan and book tickets. But after a week and a half, I started worrying. But I thought perhaps he had had an accident."

Then one morning, Angela woke up and opened her emails to find a message from Lee Bo, her father's colleague, informing her that they also had not heard from him. "He said they had not heard from my father for over twenty days, and he was concerned that he might have been taken by Chinese government agents for political reasons," she recalled. "I called Lee Bo, and he shared what he knew, and we tried to find out more together. I started to contact my dad's friends. In the process of doing that, I realized the magnitude of what was happening."

Angela tried to file a missing person report with the Thai police, and to seek the intervention of the Swedish authorities. "I was told I needed to go to Thailand to pursue the case, but I was advised not to do so because it might not be safe," she told me. "After further investigation, it appears there was no record of my father ever leaving Thailand. And yet he ended up in incommunicado detention and then prison in China. It does not seem like he travelled by any usual means. One of the poems he wrote from prison details a boat journey along the Mekong River, which suggests he may have been taken from Thailand through Cambodia to China."

The next thing Angela knew, in January 2016, her father appeared on Chinese State television, giving a "confession" to a drunk driving traffic accident that occurred in 2003. "He said he had chosen to return to China voluntarily, to confess to this crime. I do not even know if the traffic accident actually happened, but it was clear to me that it had nothing to do with why he was actually there, and most people understood that. He was not speaking freely," she recalled.

Since then, Gui Minhai has been held in Ningbo—initially under house arrest, and then in prison. In 2020, he was sentenced to ten years in jail, charged with "illegally providing intelligence overseas"—a far cry from a traffic accident. Between his abduction in 2015 and his sentencing in 2020, Angela had occasional stilted, closely monitored telephone conversations with him, but otherwise, little news. In 2018, there had appeared to be a breakthrough, where Swedish diplomats had negotiated his safe passage from Ningbo to Beijing to meet the ambassador and for a medical examination. He had, Angela believes, already been issued with a new Swedish passport, but, at the last minute, Chinese agents grabbed him from the train under the very eyes of the Swedish diplomat accompanying him, and put him back behind bars.

Angela is disappointed by the "largely inadequate" response of the Swedish government. "Sweden has not used all the knowledge available to it and all the tools available to make an actual attempt to secure my father's freedom," she said. "When he first disappeared, they issued a press release, but seemed to downplay his Swedish citizenship, saying he had not lived in Sweden for many years, as if to imply he was less worthy of consular assistance. When I tried to meet the Swedish Embassy in London, they did not register the magnitude of what was happening and told me it was outside their remit. This sort of tardiness with which they reacted has been a constant feature of the Swedish response. Still today, Sweden is failing to meaningfully hold China to account for the disappearance of my dad. The ten-year prison sentence was not inevitable. Sweden, and the European Union, could have acted to bring him home before his sentence, and because they failed to do so, he is now serving a ten-year sentence."

Why were they targeted, and why is Gui Minhai the only one of them still not released? According to Lam, it all relates to a document which Gui allegedly has in his possession, regarding a love affair which Xi Jinping reportedly had while he was vice governor of Fujian in 1999. "No one knows if the document is real, but Xi Jinping clearly cares about it a lot," said Lam.

On the night of February 8, 2016, another outbreak of unrest occurred in Hong Kong. This time, it was not directly about universal suffrage or democracy, but ostensibly a protest at the police crackdown on unlicensed street hawkers in Mong Kok during the Lunar New Year celebrations. Dubbed the "Fishball Revolution," in honour of the popular snack sold on street stalls, the clashes between protesters and police were fuelled by mounting political grievances and a significant deterioration in relations between the public and the police. The indiscriminate use of tear gas and pepper spray, as well as the beating of protesters, by the police in 2014 had dramatically changed how Hong Kongers viewed the once-respected force.

Edward Leung, a student activist who co-founded the pro-independence group Hong Kong Indigenous in 2015, and his colleague Ray Wong were among the leaders of the Fishball Revolution and were both arrested. Edward—whom I had the privilege of meeting several times in 2017—was sentenced in 2018 to six years in prison for rioting and assaulting a police officer. Ray, also accused of inciting a riot and participating in an illegal assembly, escaped Hong Kong and sought asylum in Germany in 2017, becoming the world's first Hong Konger political refugee, long before hundreds of thousands followed from 2020 onwards.

Now a student at the University of Göttingen, fluent in German, and studying philosophers such as Immanuel Kant—in German—Ray continues his activism in exile. In an online interview from his home in Göttingen in October 2021, Ray recalled the events of 2016 and 2017. "I was arrested and charged under an outdated colonial law, the Public Order Ordinance, which has been criticized by the United Nations for being incompatible with Hong Kong's international human rights treaty obligations. I got bailed with a huge amount of bail money, but at that time, I had no plan to leave Hong Kong. I was ready for prison. I thought I might be imprisoned for between six and ten years, and I was ready for that," he told me. "However, in discussions with my colleagues in Hong Kong Indigenous, we agreed that it might not be wise if we were all jailed. Someone should go abroad, to tell our story and raise awareness. I thought Edward Leung was the right candidate to do that, because his English was much better than mine at the time. So I thought he should go and I would stay in Hong Kong and serve the sentence."

The situation changed very rapidly, however. Edward Leung contested a Legislative Council by-election on February 28, 2016, in the New Territories East constituency, and during the campaign, he coined the slogan "Liberate Hong Kong, Revolution of Our Times," which became prevalent during the 2019 protests. He won more than 66,000 votes—15 percent of the vote—and prepared to contest the 2016 Legislative Council elections later that year. However, the Hong Kong authorities were clearly alarmed by his popularity, and required all candidates for the elections to provide a written declaration of their political stance ahead of the campaign. Edward signed a declaration renouncing his previous support for Hong Kong independence, but despite this, he was barred from contesting.

"The whole localist movement reached a point where we were very seriously oppressed and did not have any room to do our advocacy work," recalls Ray. "My personal security was threatened, and my mother was threatened by Chinese agents. Our family members were followed regularly."

In August 2017, Edward—who had been studying at Harvard for the year—returned to Hong Kong. "He told me he had decided to stay in Hong Kong. It was the moment I started to reconsider my road," Ray told me. "I really struggled with the decision. On the one hand, once I fled my city, I could no longer go back, could not see my friends, could not hike, could not go to my favourite places on earth. But on the other hand, I knew it was my responsibility to continue the movement. For around two weeks, I was in depression. I could not eat and could not sleep."

After two weeks, however, Ray made up his mind to leave. "I applied for my passport from the courts. I did not have time to say goodbye to friends. I did not tell anyone except my mother," he explained. "I still remember my last day in Hong Kong. I went on a hike with friends, and it was a wonderful day. But it was unforgettable because I was having such a nice time, and yet they did not know that within a few hours, I would leave the city."

Ray chose Germany because, at the time, the only two other countries he thought were possible options—the United Kingdom and Canada—had strong relations with China. "It was 2017, when the U.K. had the so-called 'Golden Era' of Sino-British relations. I was worried that I might be deported back to Hong Kong. In comparison with the U.K., at that time, Germany seemed the right place for me to seek asylum."

On arrival in Germany, he faced three main challenges.

"The first was how to integrate, while preserving my Hong Kong identity," he recalled. "Before I disclosed publicly that I had fled to Germany, no one knew I was in Germany, except for a few German and international friends. I did not have any Hong Kong friends in Germany. In such an environment, it is very easy to distance yourself from Hong Kong affairs."

The second major challenge, Ray describes, was "survivor guilt." Almost every day, he said, he witnessed "fellow Hong Kongers standing trial, getting arrested, going to prison—while I was breathing free air, living not a bad life in comparison to theirs." Whenever he started to enjoy life, he explained, "there is another force in my mind telling me 'You are not supposed to feel happy; you do not deserve to feel happy. It is your responsibility; they are serving their sentence for you.'" For three years, he struggled with this, but eventually realized that "the longer you deprive yourself of happiness, the worse your mental condition will get, and it would not help you to fulfil your responsibilities and do your work properly." People in prison, he added, "do not want us to suffer. This is a long-term fight, and maintaining our own health is essential for our future development."

Ray never set out to be a political activist. His plan was to become a freelance designer, earn some money, and then go backpacking. "That was my plan, before the Umbrella Revolution changed my whole life. I realized I had to do something for the place I love and for the democracy movement," he told me.

Two years after playing a leading role in the Umbrella Movement, Nathan Law stood as a candidate for the Hong Kong Island constituency in the 2016 elections for the Legislative Council. In April that year, together with Joshua Wong and Agnes Chow, he had co-founded a new political party, named Demosisto, to campaign for democracy and for a referendum on Hong Kong's future when the "one country, two systems" model expired in 2047. "We felt we were not represented at all by any of the existing political parties, and we wanted to inject the energy of youth into the political process and build on the spirit of the Umbrella Movement," Nathan told me.

On September 4, 2016, he won his seat with a large margin, the second-highest vote among all candidates for Hong Kong Island's six seats, at the age of twenty-three, becoming the youngest-ever legislator in Hong Kong's history. "Being elected was definitely exciting. But it was also stressful, because when you win with that many votes, people have a lot of expectations of you," he recalled. "The challenge was how to live up to the expectations of others and make people believe that their vote was well placed. That was how I felt when I stepped into the chamber of the legislature for the first time—that I was beginning a very difficult mission."

Just over a month after his election, on October 12, Nathan took his oath of office as a legislator. He took the oath entirely properly, but after the oath, he pledged to serve the people, "not the regime that brutally oppresses the people," and he quoted Mahatma Gandhi's words: "You can chain me, you can torture me, you can even destroy this body, but you will never imprison my mind." Nathan had sought legal advice in advance and had been told that there were plenty of precedents for incoming legislators adding some remarks before or after the oath-taking, and that it was in order. "We had a tradition for many years of making such statements at the oath-taking, but then the Chinese Communist Party changed the rules of the game," he told me.

On November 7, the National People's Congress Standing Committee reinterpreted Article 104 of Hong Kong's Basic Law, standardizing the procedures for oath-taking. Although Nathan's oath had been validated by the legislative council clerk, Hong Kong's chief executive CY Leung initiated an unprecedented legal challenge against Nathan and five other pro-democracy legislators, resulting in their disqualification by a court. After serving as an elected legislator for nine months, on July 14, 2017, Nathan was forced to relinquish his seat. It was a blatant attempt by Beijing to rid the legislature of members who opposed the regime. Almost a month later, Nathan was in jail, as described earlier. Within the space of a year, he had gone from being the youngest elected legislator in Hong Kong's history to being one of Hong Kong's first political prisoners.

From then on, Hong Kong's freedoms were increasingly chipped away. More candidates for elections were disqualified, as "political screening" was introduced. In September 2018, the Hong Kong government ceded to Mainland Chinese jurisdiction parts of the West Kowloon high-speed railway terminal, resulting in Hong Kong residents being arrested in the station and taken across the border. One victim of this was Simon Cheng, a local employee of the British consulate-general in Hong Kong.

On August 8, 2019, Simon was detained by the Chinese State Security Bureau at the West Kowloon high-speed railway terminus in Hong Kong, as he returned to Hong Kong at the end of a business visit to Mainland China. He was detained for fifteen days in Mainland China and endured shocking torture. I met him soon after he arrived in London later that year, and he gave evidence to the Conservative Party Human Rights Commission's hearing in 2020. He told the commission, "I had heard rumours that Hong Kongers would be targeted at border checkpoints for examinations of cellphone for evidence of attendance or support of the protests. I arranged with my girlfriend and friends that I would keep reporting my whereabouts and safety. I was stopped while I was passing through the border from [the] Mainland within Hong Kong West Kowloon High-speed Railway Station, after I took the high-speed train from Shenzhen Futian Railway Station. The uniformed police wore tiny cameras on their shoulders and started to film me . . . The uniformed police claimed they stopped me because of the order instructed by senior officials . . . They asked for the passcode to access my iPhone. I refused because it is a work phone which contains sensitive work information and private conversations . . . From this police station, I was sent to Shenzhen by high-speed train and handed over to plain clothes police officers. I later learned they are from the State Security Bureau (the political/secret police)."[15]

Simon has described the torture he endured in some detail in various media interviews and parliamentary hearings, and in conversation with me. He told the Conservative Party Human Rights Commission: "During the interrogation, I was in a cell sitting on a steel 'tiger chair.' I had been buckled up on the chair and could not move . . . I was hung (handcuffed and shackled) on a steep X-cross doing a spread-eagled pose for hours after hours . . . It was extremely painful . . . They beat me . . . using something like sharpened batons . . . I was blindfolded and hooded."[16]

That undermining of the "firewall" between Mainland Chinese and Hong Kong law, and between a legal system in China based on "rule by law" versus what had been Hong Kong's much-respected "rule of law" system, escalated even further with Chief Executive Carrie Lam's catastrophic proposal to impose an extradition law that would allow for suspects to be extradited from Hong Kong to the Mainland. In January 2017, a Chinese businessman, Xiao Jianhua, had been abducted from the Four Seasons Hotel in Hong Kong, and, as noted earlier, there were the disappearances of the Causeway Bay booksellers in 2015. Now, under Lam's bill, people could be legally sent across the border for trial.

Dennis Kwok, an experienced lawyer and a pro-democracy legislator representing the legal sector's functional constituency in the Legislative Council, recalls telling John Lee, secretary for security at the time and now Hong Kong's chief executive, that the proposed extradition bill was "the worst idea I have ever heard." He warned the government that if they insisted on pushing this through, there would be a massive public outcry. He was absolutely correct—and the outcry came from a wide cross-section of society, uniting the legal, business, and other professional sectors with the more traditional pro-democracy camp and the general public.

"The American Chamber of Commerce and other chambers of commerce spoke out, the international community opposed it, and in May, the European Union issued a *démarche*. They had never done that before," Kwok recalls. "On the other hand, sadly, too many people in Hong Kong had decided to sit on the fence or leave politics to somebody else over the many decades since the 1980s. This had enabled Beijing to gradually weaken Hong Kong beyond the point of no return."

Mass demonstrations began in June 2019, with a million people taking to the streets, entirely peacefully, on June 9. "I was at the Hong Kong Jockey Club swimming one day in early June, and I met someone who said, 'See you on June 9.' I thought, 'This is the Jockey Club, not normally a haven for demonstrators,'" said Kwok.

A week later, on June 16, two million marched. "The Hong Kong government and Beijing had a choice at that point," Kwok noted. "They could have withdrawn the bill and things could have been salvaged. But the lesson is that authoritarian regimes cannot back down in the face of the people's power. Hong Kong people had a voice, but that voice was ignored. A crackdown became inevitable."

Andrew Heyn, British consul-general in Hong Kong at the time, agrees. "You could sense the degree of anger against the Hong Kong government. It was mishandled at so many levels. But the scale of the protests caught us all by surprise."

Right from the start—although the protest movement began entirely peacefully—the police response was shocking, with the completely disproportionate use of force: deploying tear gas, pepper spray, rubber bullets, and batons indiscriminately.

Joey Siu was a student in 2019 and served as vice president of the City University of Hong Kong's student union. She had become involved in the anti-extradition bill campaign several months before the mass movement broke out in June, organizing workshops, seminars, and discussion groups against the bill. Then, on June 9, she joined the protests.

"I never decided to become an activist, but I really felt that this was the time for me to fulfill my responsibilities as a Hong Konger, to do whatever I could to protect the city from harm, and our values from being encroached on by the Chinese Communist Party regime," she told me in a call from Washington, D.C., where she is now based.

The experiences of 2019, Joey says, are "still very traumatizing to me" because previous rallies and demonstrations had been totally peaceful, and police brutality was rare. But that all changed in 2019. "I remember very clearly the night of June 9, after the demonstrations outside the Legislative Council in Admiralty had ended and people were leaving and going home. But some protesters had decided to try to enter the Legislative Council," she recalled. "Very quickly, a lot of police arrived and started dispersing the crowd, using batons and pepper spray. They started to beat people up."

Joey tried to get to the MTR (Hong Kong's subway) station, but before she could do so, she was attacked by the police. "I had no weapons. I was not aggressive in any sense, but I was beaten by a police officer with a baton. He beat me and told me that I was not allowed to leave. That was my first experience of police brutality, and it was very traumatizing."

Despite that experience, Joey continued to participate in and help organize protests over the following six months. "Being at the scene of these protests was very terrifying for me, especially after August and September 2019 when the police went insane, firing tear gas, rubber bullets, and pepper spray everywhere," she recounted. "Every time, it would start as a peaceful protest, and then very soon, the police would arrive and become very aggressive. Then very suddenly, you would hear the sounds of firing of tear gas and rubber bullets. You would hear people starting to panic, and then people would start to run. I witnessed my friends being attacked, beaten up, and arrested by the police, almost every single day throughout the second half of 2019. Friends were denied legal representation and were treated inhumanely."

A few times Joey herself was "on the edge of being arrested" but managed to avoid arrest. Some of the most dangerous moments came during the sieges of universities in November 2019, particularly the Chinese University of Hong Kong, from November 11 to 15, and then the horrific Polytechnic University siege for almost two weeks, from November 17 to 29.

"During the sieges, police were also stationed around my university, so protesters came and set up roadblocks to try to prevent the police from entering our campus," she recalled. "Then, after the sieges ended, pro-Beijing supporters stormed into our campus, with lots of different weapons and flags, very aggressively saying they were fulfilling their responsibility as patriotic citizens to tidy up the mess created by 'cockroaches.' As a student union leader, I had to go and talk to them, so I went out, dressed in very ordinary clothes, to say that they do not have permission to enter the campus or to take our belongings. I told them we will tidy up ourselves, but they refused to leave, and then they called the police to arrest me. When the police came, I told them these pro-Beijing people had stormed our campus and the police should be asking them to leave, but instead, they stopped and searched me, and warned me that if I created a scene, I would be arrested. They took my identification number and warned that if anything happened, I would be called to the police station for investigation."

Hong Kong's police force used to be known as "Asia's finest." When I lived in Hong Kong, although I had very little reason to interact with the police, I never felt afraid to do so. I regarded them in the same way as the British police force—not perfect, but by and large good men and women trying to protect law and order and keep us all safe from crime. However, by 2019, the Hong Kong Police Force had very clearly lost its way and turned into something that almost resembled a criminal mafia. In addition to the physical violence they meted out indiscriminately, they also resorted to shocking dehumanizing verbal abuse of protesters, calling them "cockroaches."

Joey Siu believes the police had undergone training and "brainwashing" aimed at making them believe that "blindly following orders from higher-level officials, blindly following orders from the government, was the right thing to do." The number of Mainland Chinese immigrants to Hong Kong had risen significantly in recent years, and Joey believes there were more Mainland Chinese in Hong Kong's police force. "We often heard policemen speaking in very pure Mandarin on the frontlines, giving instructions and orders," she recalled.

Joey also believes that, under the surface, the Hong Kong Police Force was always more corrupt than we realized. "It is just that in the years before 2019, their corruption and lack of order was not so visible," she said. "They were still trying to restrain themselves and maintain their public image. But in 2019, Beijing felt threatened by the protests, and the police force, with Beijing's support, felt they did not need to worry about restraint, knowing that they would not suffer any investigation, any consequences for beating people up." And indeed, they were right. While over 10,000 protesters were arrested, not a single police officer was ever brought to justice; demands for an independent inquiry into police brutality were rejected and the police acted with impunity.

Ted Hui, a legislative councillor from the Democrat Party, was the target of police violence on several occasions. The fact that the police would attack an elected legislator tells you something about how out of control they had become. "I was tear-gassed and pepper-sprayed from head to toe countless times," he recalled. "On one occasion, I was in Causeway Bay, and the moment the police saw me in the street, they started mocking me and shouting abuse, swearing at me very angrily. I tried to stay calm. I was holding a microphone, so I said to the police, 'These young people are gathering in a peaceful assembly. It is inappropriate and improper to use force; they are just young kids.' I tried to negotiate with the commander, but, of course, they would not listen. Then, quite suddenly, one of the police officers approached me, took off my goggles, and sprayed me right in the eyes, not once but two or three times. If an elected legislator can be treated like that, in front of the cameras, imagine how much violence they used to ordinary people, especially when the cameras and journalists are not there."

Journalists were also targets for the police. One former *South China Morning Post* photojournalist, a foreign national, told me of several occasions when he was tear-gassed at close range, deliberately targeted as a journalist. In a café in Kingston one evening in February 2022, he recalled an incident in Lockhart Road in Causeway Bay. "We saw the police punching a guy and pushing him into a van. I took pictures of the guy being punched, and the riot police turned around and sprayed a gel at me, which went over every part of my body," he said. "My camera was dripping with this gel. And then it started to burn. My whole body was burning."[17] On another occasion, this same photojournalist was sitting by the side of the road in Happy Valley, taking a short break after following the police who were chasing a group of protesters. "We were sitting on the ground, and we had taken off our gear, our masks and helmets and other protective gear. The police came and sprayed tear gas directly at us. The hatred that the police showed against the media was shocking."

Matthew Leung, a reporter for *Ming Pao* at the time, recalled that he was shot at least four times with pepper balls. "The first time was in Yuen Long, about a week after the July 21 mob attack. I was going up an escalator trying to get a top shot, heard a pop, and found my safety goggles were sprayed with powder. If I had not been wearing goggles, I would have been shot in the eye," he said. "Then, after the first day of protests at Polytechnic University, over thirty journalists were held inside the cordon, including ones who I considered important. After most of them were released at 5 a.m., we were starting to leave, and two police officers who appeared mentally out of control yelled at us to leave. I yelled back, 'We are leaving,' and got hit."[18]

One of the most serious assaults on a journalist occurred on September 28, 2019, when an Indonesian reporter, Veby Mega Indah, was on a footbridge in Wan Chai reporting on the protests. Despite wearing a high-visibility jacket labelled "PRESS," and protective goggles and helmet, the police waved their weapons towards her and other media workers and someone shouted "journalists, journalists." She was hit in her right eye by a projectile fired by the police and left partially blinded.[19]

Medical workers and first-aiders providing help to people on the frontlines of the protests also became targets, as did human rights monitors. Darren Mann, an experienced British surgeon who had worked in Hong Kong for more than twenty years, was one of the first people to draw international attention to the violations healthcare workers faced. On November 21, 2019, he published an article in the leading medical journal *The Lancet*, claiming that the Hong Kong police had fallen "far below accepted international norms for the handling of volunteer emergency medical providers."[20] He had been among the healthcare workers at Polytechnic University on November 17, and had witnessed many of his colleagues—doctors, nurses, first-aiders—being arrested. "The arrest of these personnel is almost unheard of in civilised countries and is incompatible with the compact of humanitarianism," he wrote. "Furthermore, the chilling effect can only serve to deter would-be volunteers from offering their services in the much-needed medical care of injured people in this ongoing uncivil war."

The Lancet is not normally among my regular reading material, but Darren's article arrived in my email inbox the day after it had been published, on a listserv of Hong Kong articles, and as I scrolled through my emails, it caught my eye. I debated whether or not to contact Darren. On the one hand, what he was reporting struck me as incredibly serious; on the other hand, he is probably inundated with enquiries, questions, and offers of help. Should I bother him? In the end, I decided there was nothing to lose by getting in touch and seeing whether my advocacy experience and international political and media contacts could be of any help.

Within a day or so Darren replied, and we arranged to speak. It turned out that, at the time, I was the only foreign activist to reach out, and we then collaborated on a plan to bring him to Geneva to talk to the United Nations and the International Committee of the Red Cross (ICRC), to Brussels to brief the European Union, and to London to address the All-Party Parliamentary Group on Hong Kong. Darren claimed that not only were healthcare workers arrested, but the police were commandeering ambulances and storming into hospitals in full riot gear, demanding access to patient records and even entry to operating rooms. Later, in evidence to the Conservative Party Human Rights Commission, Darren summed up his observations:

"There have been widely publicized and shocking instances in which large numbers of humanitarian healthcare workers have been arrested, handcuffed with zip-cords, and arrayed as so many terrorists—most in the vicinity of violent confrontations, but in selected instances whilst in the course of performing their duties. Professional medical sector workers are able to prove their identification and qualifications—and yet they have been arrested by police, accused of taking part in a riot, detained for twenty-four hours, and released on police bail pending possible charges."[21]

Darren's claims were investigated by four United Nations Special Procedures—the Special Rapporteurs on the right to physical and mental health, freedom of peaceful assembly and association, the right to privacy and the Working Group on Arbitrary Detention, who issued a letter in February 2020 to the Chinese government, detailing evidence of the harassment, intimidation, and arrest of healthcare workers in Hong Kong and highlighting "the misuse of healthcare transport, facilities, and confidential information."[22] Hospitals are allegedly "often patrolled by police units in full riot gear, bearing shields, batons, and firearms loaded with beanbag rounds and rubber bullets," and police have "hindered healthcare staff at public hospitals when they perform legitimate health duties, insisting on being present when doctors privately consult patients, including in delivery rooms, and attempting to enter operating rooms when persons suspected to have participated in protests are due for surgery."

Their report followed an intervention the previous month by two other UN Special Rapporteurs, who highlighted "the allegedly inappropriate use of chemical agents," including "hazardous substances such as tear gas, pepper spray, pepper balls, and irritating chemical constituents dispersed from water cannons."[23] Such chemical agents, they alleged, were used "in closed spaces, in close vicinity of schools, kindergartens, and institutions housing sensitive segments of the population." According to some estimates, 88 percent of Hong Kong's population may have been affected by the use of tear gas, they reported, and that such indiscriminate and disproportionate use of tear gas is in violation of international norms and Hong Kong's own standards.

Human rights observers were another target for the police. On November 17, 2019, for example, two members of a Hong Kong-based group called Rights Exposure were monitoring the protests at Polytechnic University and were arrested on "suspicion of participating in a riot," despite explaining their role to the police. According to their submission to the Conservative Party Human Rights Commission, "the two were clearly identifiable as human rights observers, including by bilingual high-visibility vests and work ID cards."[24] They were restrained with plastic hand ties and taken to Hung Hom police station, where they were questioned and subjected to "a torrent of verbal abuse," including "racial slurs" and "sexual slurs." They were held for between fifteen and twenty-six hours, and denied adequate food, a place to sleep, or blankets. "Legal representatives for the two observers were delayed for several hours by the police from timely meeting with their clients," they claimed, "and one observer, a U.S. national, was not provided with timely access to her consulate despite repeated requests."

The two Rights Exposure observers also witnessed what they believe amounts to ill-treatment by the police of other detainees, including overhearing a struggle behind a curtained area. "The curtains were moved, allowing one of the observers to then witness a man being held by his collar and pushed into a corner . . . and pushed against a metal shutter," they reported. "The howls of pain indicated to the two observers that the man was experiencing sustained and considerable pain (rather than short bursts of pain from blows) . . . This may have been from pain caused by twisting, pressure, or invasion. The nature of the sound made them conclude that it was highly likely the individual was being subjected to what could constitute ill-treatment at the hands of the police."[25]

Two of the worst incidents of violence in 2019, aside from the university sieges, were the mob attack at Yuen Long station on July 21, and the police attack at Prince Edward station on August 31. At Yuen Long, a town in the New Territories, a mob of armed gangsters—suspected to be Triads—dressed in white, indiscriminately attacked people in the streets with steel rods and rattan canes, before attacking people in the MTR station. Footage shows shocking scenes of unprovoked, indiscriminate, and severe violence against ordinary members of the public, resulting in at least forty-five people injured. Despite over 24,000 calls to the emergency hotline, the police arrived thirty-nine minutes after the attacks and one minute after the mob had left, and made no arrests that night, although a few of the suspected Triads were arrested in subsequent days.

The government was equally slow to respond, with Carrie Lam holding a press conference ten hours after the incident. Radio Television Hong Kong (RTHK) reporter Nabela Qoser challenged Lam and Police Commissioner Stephen Lo about their delayed response, contrasting it with their 4 a.m. press conference on the night protesters stormed the Legislative Council. When Lam refused to respond to her questions about collaboration between the police and Triads, Qoser urged her to "answer like a human being." She also asked whether government officials could sleep well at night in light of the attack, and why they did not arrest any of the mob that night. Her line of questioning was praised in the media as the work of "a reporter with conscience," but it led to her sacking from RTHK.

Another RTHK journalist, Choy Yuk-ling—known as "Bao Choy"—produced an investigative documentary about the Yuen Long attack, which was broadcast a year on from the incident, in July 2020. Titled *7.21: Who Owns the Truth?*, it drew on CCTV footage to identify vehicles parked near suspected gangsters and, through searching publicly available vehicle registration records, it identified the owners, and therefore suspects, linked to the attack. Four months after the programme had aired, Bao Choy was arrested and charged with making false statements under the Road Traffic Ordinance and was suspended from RTHK. In April 2021, she was fined HK$6,000 (approximately US$770) but avoided a prison sentence. Reporters Without Borders condemned her arrest and fine, citing it as an example of the "decline in press freedom" in Hong Kong.

While Yuen Long was an incident of mob violence perhaps facilitated by police collusion, the incident at Prince Edward MTR station a month later was a horrific example of police brutality. Jim Wong, a filmmaker who had joined the protest movement, was one of its primary victims.

I first met Jim within days of his arrival in London, after he had fled Hong Kong in July 2020. We met in Wimbledon, and as we walked to a pub called the Hand in Hand, across Wimbledon Common, we bumped into Britain's minister of state for foreign affairs, who has responsibility for human rights, Lord Ahmad. I know Tariq Ahmad quite well, both through my wider human rights work and because, as a follower of the Ahmadiyya Muslim tradition, we share a passion for defending freedom of religion or belief in particular. Tariq and his wife, out for a summer evening's walk, greeted me, and I introduced them to Jim. The minister spent several minutes hearing a little bit of Jim's story and welcomed him to the U.K. I had to explain to Jim afterwards that bumping into government ministers out for a walk on Wimbledon Common was not an everyday occurrence.

At the end of our dinner together, Jim asked to take a photograph. I checked with him whether he wanted it to remain private, or to share on social media, and he put a specific request to me.

"Please, would you post it on social media, and I will tell you what to say alongside it," he said. He explained that he was known as "Hon Bo Sun," that many people thought he might be dead or disappeared, and he wanted me to let people know he was alive and safe. So, later that evening, I tweeted as requested: "#HongKongers: I just want to tell you—'Hon Bo Sun' from 831 太子站事件 [Prince Edward station incident] is not dead. He is alive and well. And it was a privilege to spend the evening with him today."

Jim had been in Prince Edward station on the night of August 31, 2019, on his way home from a protest in Causeway Bay at which, he said, the police used water cannon vehicles and fired live ammunition for the first time. Since June 12, he had joined protests almost every day and resigned from his job at the broadcasters TVB. "There were a lot of undercover agents in Victoria Park," he recalled, "so some of us moved on to Tsim Sha Tsui and Mong Kok. But I saw a lot of police there, too, so I went to Prince Edward station. Some passengers got upset with us, knowing we were protesters, and a fight broke out. Pro-Beijing thugs attacked us with sticks, hammers, and box cutters, and then after ten minutes, the police came into the station and arrested protesters. When I saw the police running into the station, I instantly ran to the opposite platform, but the police grabbed me, beat me with a stick, pushed me to the ground, and arrested me."

Jim's arrest was caught on camera. "I was beaten very badly and I could not breathe. Another protester tried to rescue me, but they were not able to. I was pressed on the ground, and thought I was going to die," he recalled. "The police mocked me, saying, 'Let's see how far you can run. Do you think you are achieving democracy?' I requested to go to hospital because of my injuries, and I was taken to hospital, where I met my lawyer, and then I was transferred to a police station, and from there to San Uk Ling Holding Centre, which is notorious for holding a lot of protesters and beating them badly."

After forty-eight hours, Jim was released because there was no evidence found against him, but a month later, he was called back to the police station. "I walked into the police station and they arrested me immediately. They charged me with nine offences, but then released me on bail," he explained. Almost a year later, on June 23, 2020, Jim was called back to the police station early in the morning and arrested again. "This time, they told me I was charged with eight offences: two charges of rioting, two charges of criminal damage, one charge of illegal assembly, robbery, common assault, and assault causing damage. But they released me on bail again, because they had no evidence against me."

The charges were absurd. In reality, according to Jim, all he had done was use a fire extinguisher to alert people to leave the station, due to the fighting with pro-Beijing mobs. "A woman tried to film me on her phone, and then, when I tried to leave, she tried to grab me by my shoulder. The common assault charge against me was for this—they claimed I harmed the woman's finger. It was ridiculous."

Aged twenty-nine, Jim faced the possibility of at least five years in jail. "My trial was scheduled for the next month, July 2020. I thought to myself, 'This is the time to decide. Do you want to be a human being or a slave?' I decided to go into exile," he said. "My lawyer and I were worried I might be detained before the trial, but my lawyer helped secure bail. I booked a return ticket and tried to dress like an exchange student. At that time, there were not too many checks at the airport, so I was able to leave. In early July 2020, I arrived in the U.K. and claimed asylum in September. A year later, on September 29, 2021, my refugee status was confirmed."

The Prince Edward attack was a truly appalling act of police violence. Footage available on the Internet clearly shows police officers beating and tear-gassing ordinary passengers on the metro train, creating an atmosphere of absolute terror. Together with the Yuen Long mob attack, its anniversary is commemorated each year by Hong Kongers in mourning.

In addition to the documented acts of police violence, there are many incidents that have never been explained. "A lot of people reported bodies floating in the harbour, dressed in black," notes Jim. On November 8, 2019, a university student, Chow Tsz-lok, plunged to his death from the third storey of a car park very close to Jim's home. Although the cause was unclear and no conclusive evidence has been found, Jim believes Chow was pushed.

On October 1, a police officer used live ammunition for the first time, shooting an eighteen-year-old high school student in Tsuen Wan at point-blank range. On November 11, police opened fire again, wounding at least one protester in Sai Wan Ho. That same day, another police officer drove his motorcycle directly into a group of protesters.

It is important to acknowledge that a small minority of protesters also resorted to violence, making and throwing Molotov cocktails, firing slingshots, throwing bricks at the police, and carrying out vandalism and arson. On July 1, 2019, the twenty-second anniversary of the handover of Hong Kong to China, hundreds of frontline protesters managed to storm the Legislative Council, smashing in the glass doors and then occupying the chamber. They sprayed anti-government and pro-democracy slogans on the walls and defaced the Hong Kong emblem. But even in this extreme action, they had a purpose and they had discipline. Their purpose was to halt the passage of the extradition bill, and they were clear that their vandalism was targeted. As Stephen Vines notes in his excellent book *Defying the Dragon: Hong Kong and the World's Largest Dictatorship*, "signs were put up telling the protesters not to damage books of historic value and a drinks fridge bore a hastily attached notice telling them not to take anything without paying: 'We are not thieves, we don't steal,'" it said."[26]

Even if some protesters used tactics which I could never condone, it was not difficult to understand how they had reached that point. They faced a police force that had started the violence, tear-gassing, pepper-spraying, and beating peaceful protesters, and a government that simply refused to listen. Among the slogans protesters spray-painted in the Legislative Council was one which read: "It was you who taught me peaceful marches did not work," and another that said, "There are no rioters, only tyrannical rule." Heartbreaking, but tragically true. They had reached a point of desperation, and all non-violent means of action were becoming more and more closed off to them. One should also not discount the possibility that there may have been *agents provocateurs* in some cases, who may have infiltrated parts of the movement.

If Carrie Lam had listened to the lawyers, the chambers of commerce, and the international community and withdrawn the extradition bill in March, April, or May 2019, things could have turned out very differently for Hong Kong. If she had listened to the over one million Hong Kongers who marched peacefully in June, the movement may have dispersed. But instead, she refused to budge until it was too late.

"Of course, things could have been handled very differently," Andrew Heyn told me. "If Carrie Lam were to look back, she would know she messed it up. The problem was that it took so long to get from her attitude of 'I am right and I am going to push this through regardless' to 'I am a little bit sorry' to 'I've messed it up' that tensions escalated so severely."

Only on July 9, just over a week after the storming of the legislature, did she announce that the bill was "dead," and even then, it was another three months before it was finally withdrawn officially. By the autumn, the anti-extradition bill movement had become a pro-democracy movement, with "Five Demands, Not One Less"—an investigation into police brutality, amnesty for arrested demonstrators, admission that protesters should not be labelled "rioters," and the introduction of full universal suffrage for direct elections for the chief executive and the Legislative Council, in addition to the withdrawal of the bill.

By October 23, the movement had achieved one of its five demands, but the government was unwilling to make any compromise in relation to the other four. That intransigence further radicalized some protesters, and the slogan "Liberate Hong Kong, Revolution of Our Times" took hold. The early days of peaceful protests in June, where people sang the Christian chorus "Sing Hallelujah to the Lord," or even the defiant anthem of the movement, "Glory to Hong Kong," seemed in the distant past by the end of 2019.

The slogan *Laam Caau*—"If We Burn, You Burn With Us"—was coined by activist Finn Lau, a chartered surveyor in exile who branched out into advocacy. Finn told me that when he saw a few thousand people protesting outside the Chinese Embassy on June 9, he thought, "Is that the best you can do?" He wanted to "harness" the brains of tens of thousands of Hong Kongers around the world, and so he launched the campaign "Fight for Freedom Stand With Hong Kong." Using the Hong Kong channel LiHKG, his posts went viral and his message caught fire. He crowdfunded millions of dollars in order to run a global newspaper advertising campaign and mobilize rallies around the world.

Christmas Eve and New Year's Eve were marked by yet more police brutality.

Catherine Li, an activist living in London, returned to Hong Kong in December 2019 and took part in almost every protest while she was there. Often, she volunteered as a "scout," to alert protesters when the police were coming.

On Christmas Eve, a human chain of protesters formed at 11 p.m. in Tsim Sha Tsui, blocking Nathan Road. "As a scout, I had to try to hold off the police so that frontliners could leave," Catherine told me over a meal in a Korean restaurant in New Malden. "That night, water cannon trucks came, and the police were beating people. I was in a place where there was nowhere to escape. I witnessed beatings, and tear gas fired at super-close distance. I celebrated Christmas Eve with people I did not know. We greeted each other with 'Merry Christmas' surrounded by spent tear gas cannisters."

It was the same for New Year's. "On New Year's Eve, I walked from Tsim Sha Tsui to Mongkok, surrounded by a lot of pepper spray," Catherine said. "On January 1, we marched from Victoria Park to Chater Gardens, and were stuck for two and a half hours. We started forming human chains to pass materials to protesters in Wan Chai from Causeway Bay. Protesters formed an umbrella wall in defence against the water cannon trucks. When I eventually left, I passed a broken umbrella on the ground—a poignant symbol."

On another occasion, Catherine joined a rally in Edinburgh Place, just outside City Hall, to raise awareness for the Uyghurs—a sign of the growing solidarity between different groups facing the Chinese regime's persecution. It was, she recalls, "super peaceful—until the police came." Tear gas, pepper spray, and rubber bullets were unleashed.

Responsibility for the carnage in Hong Kong lies squarely on the shoulders of Carrie Lam and her government, especially when they ignored the opportunity offered to them by the results of the district council elections held on November 24, 2019.

Despite the chaos of the daily protests and police brutality, the district council elections went ahead—even as the siege of Polytechnic University continued. On Election Day itself, Hong Kong people proved once again their preference for democracy. Given the chance, Hong Kongers prefer to express themselves peacefully, at the ballot box. Three million people—approximately 71 percent of those eligible to vote—turned out on November 24. And they voted overwhelmingly for the pro-democracy camp, which won an absolute majority in all but one of the eighteen district councils, and a total of 388 seats out of all 479 seats, tripling their number. The pro-Beijing camp lost ninety-six seats, its biggest defeat in history, and only retained control of one district council using its *ex officio* seats. This unprecedented turnout proved that, while they may not have condoned some of the protesters' more extreme actions, the majority of Hong Kongers shared their desperation and supported their broad objectives of justice and democracy.

Finn Lau believes the results of these elections were an indication that "Hong Kongers were trying to show they wanted democracy." Lord Alton, who led an international election observation mission—set up by the campaign group Stand With Hong Kong—to monitor the elections, found it "an exhilarating experience" witnessing "a surge of democracy in a place we were told people were only interested in money." The election, he believes, was a "referendum" on Beijing's rule—although, he added, "my heart was heavy as I knew Beijing would not tolerate the idea of a robust democracy in Hong Kong for very long."

Lee Ka Wai, a former journalist who won a surprise victory in Tuen Mun district council against a candidate of the pro-Beijing New People's Party—founded by former secretary for security Regina Ip—thought he had no chance and had planned to help another candidate campaign. "But no one in Fusun constituency wanted to stand, because no one wanted to fight a student of Regina Ip. So I thought, 'What if I took the chance?' I resigned from my job and ran for election, realizing that I might not have a chance to go back into journalism, my dream job, but asking the question, 'If not now, when. If not me, who?'" he told me as we met in a restaurant on London's South Bank. "When I won, Regina Ip came to the constituency, to apologize to her supporters for losing. She got humiliated. She responded angrily, claiming we were rioters. But we were not; we were people who chose democracy. And yet still the government did not listen to us."

The district council elections gave Carrie Lam a potential opportunity to break the deadlock. She could have acknowledged the results, recognized the popular desire for democracy, and used it as an opportunity for dialogue. She could have engaged the democratically elected district councillors as interlocutors who had a mandate as legitimate representatives of the people. Instead, she found ways to create jobs for the defeated pro-Beijing councillors and ignore the elected representatives. As Lee Ka Wai told me, "We had hoped to change Hong Kong into a better place. But we soon discovered we could not do anything in the system. It made no difference. The government started to restrict the district councils. We could not pass a budget. Our powers were restrained. Government officials would not even meet us." Lord Alton believes "Carrie Lam wasted this extraordinary opportunity, and it is a tragedy for Hong Kong."

Two years on from their election, district councillors were required—along with all public officials in Hong Kong—to take a new oath of loyalty to Beijing. The oath was not just an ordinary oath of loyalty to the country, but implicitly a clear pledge of allegiance to the Chinese Communist Party. Dozens of district councillors quit rather than swear such an oath, and dozens more were disqualified for not taking the oath "sincerely." Lee Ka Wai did not even bother to resign but went into exile in the United Kingdom in March 2021. "By January that year," he told me, "a lot of my friends had been locked behind bars. I thought I could face charges, face political persecution, because of what I have said or who I have supported. I was sure I would be caught soon, so I decided to leave." He estimates that by early 2022, there were almost one hundred district councillors in exile, the vast majority in the U.K.

By early 2020, the protest movement was slowing down—in part, due to exhaustion, fear, and trauma, but also due to a new virus that emerged from Wuhan, COVID-19, which spread across the world in a devastating pandemic. Coronavirus restrictions were introduced in Hong Kong, as they were in many parts of the world, shutting down public gatherings—potentially, legitimately, in public health terms, but providing the authorities with a convenient tool to silence dissent.

And then came the most devastating blow of all, an intervention from Beijing that would destroy Hong Kong's freedoms, autonomy, rule of law, and all the promises made under the "one country, two systems" principle completely: the National Security Law. This legislation is among the most dangerous, draconian, repressive laws in the world, and the manner in which it was introduced signalled Beijing's intent. Instead of the Hong Kong government pushing through a bill in the Legislative Council, which at least would have preserved a veneer of Hong Kong's autonomy and the principle of "Hong Kong people running Hong Kong," and potentially allowed for some degree of scrutiny, debate, and transparency, the legislation was fast-tracked through Beijing's National People's Congress, with a high degree of secrecy and no transparency. On May 20, 2020, the National People's Congress voted by 2,878 votes to one to authorize its Standing Committee to promulgate a National Security Law for Hong Kong. It is said that even Carrie Lam did not know the details and content of the law until it was revealed on June 30, and took immediate effect from July 1.

The National Security Law details four particular crimes: secession, subversion, terrorism, and "collusion with foreign political forces." While many countries have national security legislation, and all countries wish to prevent terrorism, there is the question of how such crimes are defined. In Beijing's law imposed on Hong Kong, the definition of these crimes is left extremely vague and broad. "Collusion" with a foreign entity could be something as simple as talking to a foreign journalist, advocating to a foreign politician, or communicating with a foreign activist. The law also applies, according to Article 38, extraterritorially—in other words, it does not matter whether or not you are in Hong Kong when you commit the crime, or indeed whether or not you are a Hong Kong resident. Anyone, anywhere in the world could be deemed to be violating Hong Kong's National Security Law—as I discovered two years later when, in March 2022, the organization I co-founded and lead, Hong Kong Watch, became the first foreign-registered, foreign-run non-governmental organization to be threatened under this law, and I personally became the first foreign activist to be targeted by the Hong Kong Police Force and National Security Bureau, for being a serious threat to China's national security.

The impact of the law has been calamitous for civil society, political opposition, independent media, academic freedom, and just basic freedom of expression. Over fifty civil society groups have been disbanded, including trade unions, political parties, human rights groups, protest organizers, and independent media outlets. And more than 150 people—principally, pro-democracy activists, politicians, and journalists—have been arrested under the National Security Law since it was imposed on Hong Kong.

In the biggest single mass arrest, on January 6, 2021, fifty-three pro-democracy activists and politicians, including several former legislators, were rounded up, accused of "inciting subversion of State power" for holding a primary election in the summer of 2020 to choose their candidates for the Legislative Council elections scheduled for September that year. Subsequently, forty-seven of them were charged and have been imprisoned for more than a year without trial. The pro-democracy camp had already been pushed out of the Legislative Council on November 11, 2020, and the elections had been postponed for a year under the excuse of COVID-19.

Dennis Kwok was among the legislators initially targeted for disqualification. He began to hear rumours three days earlier and was "mentally fully prepared." A founding member of the Civic Party, you could not ask for a more moderate, reasonable, mainstream democrat than Kwok, who served as the deputy chair of the House Committee. His use of filibustering was what particularly annoyed Beijing.

"Under the unfair electoral system, even though the pro-democracy camp always had majority support among Hong Kong people, we were the minority inside the legislature. We had nothing else but to make use of every rule and procedure within the Legislative Council to push back on draconian legislation that seriously contravened human rights and the rule of law in Hong Kong—including Article 23, the National Security Law, and the controversial national anthem law, which criminalizes anyone who shows 'disrespect' when the anthem is played. That is all we were doing," he told me. "In a sense, we forced the Chinese Communist Party to reveal its true face, and to show that it cannot be trusted to honour its word or keep its treaty promises."

Three other legislators—Alvin Yeung, Kwok Ka-ki, and Kenneth Leung—were disqualified alongside Kwok, and the remaining fifteen pro-democracy legislators resigned *en masse* in protest. "I walked out and told the press that if fighting for democracy, the rule of law, and human rights leads to disqualification, then I count it an honour." The removal of the entire pro-democracy camp from the legislature removed any last vestiges of credibility for the body, and, a year later, under a new electoral system which effectively bars pro-democracy candidates from even contesting seats, Beijing installed an entirely puppet, rubber-stamp body in Hong Kong that is completely dominated by loyalists. The days of any scrutiny, accountability, debate, or transparency are now long gone.

Kwok believes, with hindsight, that moderate democrats like himself were "way too naive." Hong Kong people, he notes, "are not stupid," but they were "too pragmatic" and "too ready to abide by Beijing's edicts." There was always a high degree of skepticism as to whether Beijing would keep its promises, but "we were too afraid of angering Beijing."

Ted Hui was among the pro-democracy legislators who resigned. "There had been disqualifications before, but this was the first time Beijing disqualified elected members through decree, with no procedures at all," Hui told me. "We all realized that it would therefore be meaningless to remain in the Legislative Council after our colleagues had been disqualified—and we knew that if we did not obey Beijing, every one of us would be disqualified. So we made the decision to resign together."

Hui was also facing criminal charges for his participation in protests and his own acts of protest in the Legislative Council chamber. "They were not National Security Law charges, but they did mean I could be locked up for five years or even a decade. I had three cases and nine charges against me," he explained. Due to his continued status as a serving district councillor, even though no longer a Legislative Council member, Hui was able to persuade the courts to allow him to hold on to his passport, as he might need it for official duties. That gave him an escape route, and on December 1, 2020, he arrived in Denmark, ostensibly to hold meetings with Danish Parliamentarians on environmental issues. Once safely out of Hong Kong, he announced he would not be returning.

The Hong Kong and Beijing authorities were furious. HSBC froze Hui's bank accounts and the accounts of his family, at the behest of the regime, and Beijing threatened the Danish politicians and activists who had helped him. Surprisingly, however, for six hours someone in HSBC unfroze Hui's accounts—enough time for him and his family to move their funds overseas. The accounts were then refrozen and remain so to this day. "I am looking for ways to start legal proceedings, to get my remaining money back," Hui told me.

Hui came to the United Kingdom from Denmark, and I had the privilege of meeting him a week or two after he arrived, just before Christmas, in a café on London's South Bank. However, after three months in London, he and his family relocated to Australia, where he has relatives. Just before he left for Australia, we went for a walk in beautiful Richmond Park, where we observed the deer and talked about the fight for freedom around the world, and he presented me with some of his own beautiful calligraphy as a parting gift.

Despite the pain of leaving Hong Kong, he was in no doubt how fortunate he was to get out, especially when so many of his former colleagues and friends were arrested. "I had participated in the primary election in July 2020, and won one of the highest votes, so I would definitely have been arrested if I had not left Hong Kong," he told me. "We had thought that there was nothing wrong, even though Beijing's Liaison Office warned us that we might be violating the National Security Law. We thought, it is only a primary election. Now, all my colleagues are in jail, and are refused bail. I did not expect that the regime would go that far. I think that is why so many former candidates and participants in the primaries did not go into exile—the crackdown came so suddenly and so early, and they all got caught. It is heartbreaking. They are lifelong friends, my closest comrades."

Hui was not the only Hong Konger to leave Hong Kong in dramatic fashion. In August 2020, twelve Hong Kong activists facing charges under the National Security Law attempted to escape by sea on a rickety speedboat, with the aim of reaching Taiwan. They included Andy Li, a young pro-democracy activist who had facilitated the international election observation mission for the district council elections. Others had made the same dangerous voyage successfully, but the twelve were not so fortunate. They were intercepted in Chinese waters by the Chinese police, arrested, charged with illegal border crossing, and detained in a Chinese prison near Shenzhen. Two minors in the group were released after four months, Li and seven others were held for seven months, and two others were sentenced to two and three years, respectively, in prison in China. Those who were returned to Hong Kong were immediately rearrested in the city, to face various charges for involvement in the 2019 protests and breaches of the National Security Law.

What has happened in Hong Kong since the National Security Law was imposed on Hong Kong is like a living paraphrase of Pastor Martin Niemoller's famous quotation in Nazi Germany:

First they came for the socialists, and I did not speak out—because I was not a socialist.

Then they came for the trade unionists, and I did not speak out—because I was not a trade unionist.

Then they came for the Jews, and I did not speak out—because I was not a Jew.

Then they came for me—and there was no one left to speak out for me.

In Hong Kong, first they came for the protesters, then the pro-democracy legislators, then the civil society groups and trade unionists, academic freedom, and then the independent media. Religious freedom is highly likely to be the next target, and there are already signs that it is under increasing pressure—a point to which we will return shortly. But first, let us turn to the dismantling of press freedom.

Over recent years, media freedom in Hong Kong has been almost completely dismantled. Since the imposition of the National Security Law, almost all independent media outlets have been forced to close. At the time of writing, at least twenty media workers have been arrested and twelve are in jail awaiting trial. The public service broadcaster RTHK has lost all editorial independence and moved from being Hong Kong's highly respected and much-loved equivalent of the BBC to being a propaganda outlet for Beijing. At least twelve of its flagship programmes have been axed and much of its archive and Twitter history deleted, and key journalists either have been sacked or have resigned. A new director of broadcasting, Patrick Li, was brought in, in 2021 who was a career civil servant with no media experience whatsoever, and, according to the veteran broadcaster Stephen Vines, who lived in Hong Kong for thirty-five years, Li ruled by diktat. "We would simply be told that 'the director has decided this,' with no consultation," Vines told me as we talked in a café near his new home in St. Alban's. "We were told, every proposal for a theme, a story, a programme had to be approved by the management. There were so many redlines, but they were never spelt out . . . Programmes were becoming CCTV-style propaganda."[27]

One of the most dramatic turning points in the crackdown on press freedom was the forced closure of Hong Kong's largest pro-democracy, Chinese-language, mass circulation daily newspaper, *Apple Daily*, on June 23, 2021. Until that point, *Apple Daily*—founded in 1995 by the remarkable entrepreneur and pro-democracy campaigner Jimmy Lai—had courageously held out, despite intense pressure. For years, the newspaper had been in Beijing's sights, loathed by the regime for its independent stance. It had survived financial pressure from advertising boycotts generated by Beijing; harassment, intimidation, and violence from pro-Beijing thugs; and a police raid on the newsroom in August 2020, when one hundred police officers arrested Lai at his home, paraded him through the newsroom in handcuffs, and arrested five other senior executives. But Lai was released within forty-eight hours, and the newspaper vowed to keep publishing. Indeed, its public support soared, with people queuing in the early hours of the morning to buy copies, and its share price rising over 1,000 percent.

When the death of *Apple Daily* finally came, as 550 police officers raided the newsroom on June 17, 2021, arresting top company executives and the editor-in-chief, Ryan Law, among others, it was personally heartbreaking for me. Almost exactly a year before, despite the introduction of the National Security Law, *Apple Daily* invited me to contribute a weekly opinion column for the English-language edition of the newspaper. I was delighted to accept, although I did ask them if they were really sure. They were; they knew the risks, and they wanted to push the envelope. They told me I could write on any topic I wanted, as long as it had a relevance to Hong Kong or the region, and there was no word count. It is the only publication I have ever written for that literally never edited, censored, or limited me. For a year, every Wednesday night, I would write my weekly column and send it off, and every Friday, it would be published. Until June 16, 2021.

That night, I wrote my piece as usual and sent it to my editor. The next morning, I woke up, switched on my phone and laptop, and saw the news of the police raid. Immediately, I contacted my editor, to check if they were safe. The reply came: "I am fine, working from home, and it is business as usual." I had received a very similar response when the previous police raid of the newspaper occurred in August 2020.

But on the Friday, my article did not appear, so I enquired gently and discreetly with my editor what the plan was. The previous August, I had asked if they wanted me to discontinue, and they adamantly insisted on my continuing to write for them. This time, they replied suggesting that, for a couple of weeks, we might need to take a break, and that I could find another platform for that week's article. I completely understood. Less than a week later, the newspaper and all its platforms—including its website and archive—closed.

Despite the extraordinary courage and determination of its staff, and despite having HK$400 million in the bank and 600,000 paid subscribers, enough to enable it to continue to print for at least another eighteen months, the decision by the Hong Kong authorities to freeze *Apple Daily*'s bank accounts meant that it was simply unable to pay salaries, rent, and other bills. As Mark Clifford, a director of the parent company, Next Digital, and former editor of the *South China Morning Post*, told me, "We were frozen out of business." At least seven former *Apple Daily* employees are in jail. Jimmy Lai, aged seventy-four, is in prison serving multiple sentences and awaiting trial for several more charges, and is likely to spend the remainder of his life in jail. I closely followed the scenes of *Apple Daily* staff, and hundreds of members of the public gathered outside the newspaper's offices on its last night, June 23, and watched them flashing cellphone lights to one another in solidarity. I received a copy of the final edition, published on June 24, 2021, in which it is a privilege to be featured. That last edition of the newspaper sits on my bookcase, a reminder that even though it may have been killed, its spirit lives on.

Almost exactly six months later, the last remaining major pro-democracy media outlet, *Stand News*, was raided by 200 Hong Kong police officers. Its assets were frozen and seven people were arrested, including acting chief editor Patrick Lam, and two of its former board members—who had already resigned earlier in the year—prominent lawyer Margaret Ng and popular singer Denise Ho, who hold British and Canadian citizenship, respectively.

Stand News announced it would close immediately, and soon after its announcement, on January 3, 2022, *Citizen News* also decided to close. Hong Kong has gone from being one of Asia's most vibrant media hubs, where I began my career as a young journalist fresh out of university, to being a place of censorship, self-censorship, and almost zero press freedom. The Foreign Correspondents' Club of Hong Kong—where I used to be a member, and a place where I often used to hang out—has made multiple statements describing the assault on press freedom, as have Reporters Without Borders, Article 19, the Committee to Protect Journalists, and the International Federation of Journalists, among others, but to no avail. In its 2022 Press Freedom Index, Reporters Without Borders rank Hong Kong 148 out of 180 in the world, a fall from 80 in 2021 and 18 in 2002, the year I left the city.[28]

The crackdown on press freedom in Hong Kong is multi-faceted—at times brutal, violent, dangerous; at times subtle, complicated, restrictive. It ranges from police raids on newsrooms and police spraying tear gas at journalists, to restrictions on access to public records and the weaponization of visas for foreign correspondents. But it also ventures into truly bizarre territory. When I was researching a report for Hong Kong Watch, titled *In the Firing Line: The Crackdown on Media Freedom in Hong Kong*, Chris Wong, a former TVB news presenter, told me over dinner in my home about his experiences of censorship. Just one example made me wonder if I was mishearing or hallucinating. In November 2019, when pro-democracy district councillor Andrew Chiu was attacked in Tai Koo Shing, and his ear was bitten off—an incident very clearly documented with photographs and film footage—Chris was presented with a script for the evening news that presented a rather different version of events. He told me: "The script that the editor provided said that Mr. Chiu's ear fell off naturally, somehow. Nobody did anything. It was not a bite, and the ear just fell to the floor. The editors did not want to cover violence by pro-Beijing 'blue' supporters."[29]

As I served Chris and his wife a dish called Chicken Mandalay, which I had cooked for them—and been filmed cooking for their YouTube channel—I was unsure whether to laugh at the absurdity, cry at the audacity, or feel sick at the barbarity of it. I probably felt all three emotions.

With media freedom almost dead, the wider world of the arts and entertainment is also affected. According to Catherine Li, "even hinting at political leanings could result in a warning or arrest." Pro-democracy singers such as Anthony Wong and Denise Ho have been arrested; performances, film screenings, and exhibitions have been shut down and books have been withdrawn. "The arts sector is now very risky," Catherine—a passionate young actor, singer, and model—told me. "Arts and music are what saved me, and we can use the 'soft' power of the arts to continue the fight, and conserve our culture, but increasingly within Hong Kong, performers have to be super-low profile about their political views unless, and until, they leave."

And religion is clearly next. The alarm bells have been ringing for the past two years, as outlined in the chapter on the persecution of Christians. The arrest of ninety-year-old Cardinal Zen in May 2022 shook the Catholic Church in Hong Kong. Now, it looks as though the storm is about to break.

Of course, an independent judiciary is the other pillar of a free society that has been defenestrated in Hong Kong. Dennis Kwok believes "there is no independent judiciary anymore." Judges, like all public servants, are now required to swear an oath of allegiance to Beijing. "They can remove judges summarily for oath-breaking. They have weaponized the oath-making system. The *People's Daily* determines trial verdicts. It is ludicrous to say that the judiciary is still independent," he told me in a call from his new home in Boston. "Judges have a loaded gun pointed at their head. The writing is on the wall. If they are fired, they have to pay back millions of dollars in salary, and lose their pension. They would face total financial and career ruin. Even if there are still some brave individuals, the whole system is undermined."

In January 2015, a group of lawyers came together, in the aftermath of the Umbrella Movement, to form the Progressive Lawyers Group, to support the democracy movement. Similar professional, "progressive" groups for teachers, doctors, accountants, and insurance professionals were also formed. As one former member of the now disbanded group told me, "We formed it because the established organizations—the Bar Association and the Law Society—were considered unable to represent the legal profession's views on democracy and human rights." With the exception of outspoken human rights defenders Philip Dykes, who served as chair of the Bar Association from 2018 to 2021, and Paul Harris, who held the post for a year from 2021 to 2022, both the Bar Association and the Law Society were, according to one Hong Kong lawyer, "the preserve of conservative, pro-establishment lawyers." In March 2022, Harris was called in for questioning by the Hong Kong Police Force on suspicion of violating the National Security Law, and left Hong Kong for the U.K. that night.

The Progressive Lawyers Group published annual reports and regular analysis and provided commentary to the media, and campaigned against repressive laws such as the co-location arrangement at the West Kowloon rail terminus, the copyright law, the extradition law, and, of course, the National Security Law. They also provided lawyers to represent protesters who were arrested during the 2019 movement. According to one lawyer who represented many demonstrators, "we were always so worried about arriving at the police station on time when our clients were arrested, because if we were not there, the police would often extract a confession statement which they could use as evidence." The police would warn parents not to believe their lawyers, he said, or would keep the door open when the lawyer and client are talking, so they could overhear. "We were not allowed to take photographs in the police station. That was to prevent us taking photos of injuries," he recalls. In some exceptional cases, however, some police officers and even prosecutors made it clear that they were supportive of the movement. "Sometimes they did so implicitly, by making your job as a lawyer easier, and occasionally, they were explicit. So you cannot always assume everyone is against you. You can get a sense in your first interactions how they are going to conduct the case."

One of their former members told me that today, Hong Kong is a "police state" and also a "dual state" in terms of its legal system. "Day-to-day law is still intact, but there is now a superior law—the National Security Law—which overrides that. Hong Kong now has bifurcated rule of law, whereby—for now—commercial and normal criminal law is still in place, but for sensitive political cases, suddenly, there is a whole new set of rules, decided by the government. In the past, there was normally a presumption of innocence, and bail was applied, but today, in political cases, it is very difficult to get bail." Hong Kong's legal profession, he believes, will become more and more similar to that in Mainland China's. "There will remain some very committed, courageous lawyers ready to challenge the system. But for most people, the choice is shut up or get out." That is why the decision by the then British foreign secretary Liz Truss, Deputy Prime Minister and Justice Secretary Dominic Raab, and President of the Supreme Court Lord Reed to withdraw Britain's serving judges sitting as "non-permanent" judges in Hong Kong's Court of Final Appeal in March 2022 was absolutely right, because—as Liz Truss said—their continued presence is "no longer tenable" and could result in "legitimizing oppression."[30] The decision by Canadian and Australian judges to stay on, along with retired British judges, is disappointing.

In 2015, a dystopian film about Hong Kong's future was released, titled *Ten Years*. It predicted much of what has transpired in Hong Kong but expected it would be within a decade of the film. It became reality in half that time.

So what is the future? Chung Ching Kwong says she does not have hope, because "it was never hope that motivated me—if it was hope, I would have quit a while ago." What keeps her, and other activists, going is more a sense, she says, that "what I am doing is right." In the Umbrella Movement in 2014, she adds, there was a saying among activists: "We don't persist because we see hope; we only see hope because we persist."

Ted Hui is realistic that "Hong Kong will not return to how it was, not in the near future, not in a decade, because all the institutions have collapsed." But in the long term, he adds, we should not be pessimistic. "It has been amazing how many people have been woken up by the movement. They feel like they have been sleeping for decades, without knowing they were under persecution, but now they know, and they will never sleep again. Everyone in Hong Kong now knows how tear gas tastes, how it smells, and it is a smell they will never forget, or forgive. I am very confident that even though they have little space to fight back now, the seeds for freedom and democracy are deep in their hearts. Hong Kongers are only waiting for an opportunity to rise again one day."

Both Nathan Law and Alex Chow used the same expression to discuss Hong Kong's short-term future: "grim." But Nathan believes that as "the dominance of China starts to decrease" and the world becomes "more aware," Beijing will face an increasing "legitimacy crisis" which could lead to change. In the meantime, the increasing number of Hong Kongers in the diaspora face a dual challenge: to maintain their identity and culture in exile, and to use the freedoms they have in exile to continue the struggle. For Alex, Hong Kong's struggle is part of a global fight for democracy. "The fight for Hong Kong has to be a fight for the world."

In contrast, Finn Lau is "quite optimistic." Before the movement in 2019, he told me, many Hong Kongers "seem to forget our culture and our history. They tended to go to Shenzhen for weekends. They spoke Mandarin." Now, Hong Kongers are "waking up," he said. "They have a determination to fight the Chinese Communist Party regime."

As Catherine Li encapsulated it, "Hong Kongers have shown remarkable flexibility and adaptability, symbolized by our slogan 'Be Water.' That fluidity and flexibility will lead to success," she argues.

In her diary, Catherine—who throughout the protests and until late 2021 remained anonymous—recounts her experiences of a split profile, that probably spoke for many. She writes in March 2020:

Dear Diary,

I am unable to connect with different parts of myself. To be more specific, I am unable to embrace the two separate identities that I own. I am obliged to write about my feelings as of today, as I fear if I do not note it down somewhere, they will just become the sentiments that exist merely inside my head.

I am currently known by two names. One begins with the letter C and one begins with J. The former (C) is my real given name and is included on my ID, and I have always been happy with this name ever since I was born. I love the name all my life. It shapes parts of my identity and character. All my social media handles are associated with the name C. I have never thought that I would change it or get a new name, until last summer. The aforementioned latter name (J), now my alter ego, emerged as a result of the pro-democracy movement in my hometown, Hong Kong.

The movement started because the Hong Kong government was trying to push forward an extradition bill, which could result in any suspects being sent to mainland China for trial. Promised in an international treaty Sino-British Joint Declaration signed by both the UK and China back in 1984, citizens of Hong Kong should be able to enjoy a high degree of autonomy and freedom after the handover in 1997, and this situation should remain unchanged for fifty years. The movement eventually evolved to become a pro-democracy movement as Hongkongers began to realize that the government never listened to public opinions and were determined to fight for universal suffrage. The excessive police brutality revealed, and the arrest of thousands of protesters also fuelled the anger of Hongkongers to keep the movement going for more than eight months up to date.

If you dare trying to say something against the Chinese government, the government might as well hunt you down, ask you to shut up in certain unpleasant ways. That is why I needed a new name. I don't want people to know that I am part of the movement. It is really pathetic to think in this way because a Hongkonger is supposed to enjoy freedom of speech, at least until 2047. I was educated that everyone should enjoy fundamental human rights and freedoms. This motivated me to take part in the movement, yet in a different identity, to protect myself.

This new name changed my life. I felt that I am split into two distinct characters every day when I am sometimes C and sometimes J. When I call myself C, I feel that I am just the girl that I am used to be my whole life, who lives up to family's expectations, and always stays far away from politics because it used to be none of her business. I did not care much back then in the Umbrella Revolution, partly because I thought politics was not relevant to me, and I was not mature enough to understand what was going on, and my parents had been brainwashing me about how I should focus on earning more money instead. When I call myself J, I volunteer with a bunch of Hongkongers, who are equally concerned for the movement as I do, on international campaigns to help Hong Kong. I was sent to lobby the policy-makers in the Parliament and my teammates trusted me on organizing rallies for Hong Kong. I never thought I was capable of doing so much. I do not know my teammates by their real names, but I have met them more frequently than my family and friends. Consequently, I became very attached to the name J. It is a bit ridiculous to say, but in a sense, J is a bit more *me*. Simultaneously, in front of my family, I am C, the innocent girl who stays away from politics. They know nothing about J or what I am fighting for secretly.

I am really torn at times—who am I? Why do I have to invent a new identity when I am fighting for something that is supposed to be ours? When can I tell everyone that even though I enjoyed being J, I *still* want to do what J does in the name of C?

I guess the struggle will stay until the day we win.

And until then,

I would just be,

Sincerely,

J.

Almost all pro-democracy activists in Hong Kong are now either in prison, on trial, or in exile. I have lost almost all contact with friends in Hong Kong, because either they are in jail or they are keeping their heads down and I do not want to endanger them. Jimmy Lai may spend the rest of his life in prison, Joshua Wong will be behind bars for many years, and Martin Lee and Margaret Ng have effectively been forced into silence by the suspended sentences imposed on them.

The uncontested selection of John Lee as Hong Kong's new chief executive in 2022 symbolizes—and perhaps completes—Hong Kong's transition from "Asia's World City" to "Asia's Police State." Lee has, in his career, known nothing other than policing. A cop for thirty-five years before joining government, the positions he has held in the administration were as former chief executive CY Leung's under-secretary for security and Carrie Lam's secretary for security.

Lee presided over police brutality in the Umbrella Movement in 2014 and the 2019 protests, enthusiastically backed the extradition bill, and championed Beijing's National Security Law with zeal. Until his promotion as chief secretary—the No. 2 to Lam—in June 2021, his only experience of government was of locking people up, spraying them with tear gas and pepper spray, condoning beatings and torture, covering up rape, and permitting indiscriminate police brutality with impunity. No experience of finance, the economy, healthcare policy, education, housing, infrastructure, transport, welfare, constitutional affairs, or international relations. He is a thug, not a leader. And that is exactly why Beijing picked him.

The mere fact that he was chosen unopposed, without even a charade of a contest, is itself emblematic of the totalitarian curtain that has fallen on Hong Kong. Now, not even Xi Jinping is pretending.

To see this happen to the city where I began my career as a journalist and activist, once one of the freest and most open cities in Asia, is heartbreaking. And to see it happen with impunity is infuriating.

One day, I believe I will return to a free Hong Kong. Much more importantly, one day, Nathan Law, Alex Chow, Joey Siu, Dennis Kwok, Ted Hui, Ray Wong, Chung Ching Kwong, Jim Wong, Finn Lau, Catherine Li, Roy Chan, Lee Ka Wai, and all the other Hong Kongers whose stories are included in this chapter will be able to return home. I just do not know when that will be. And it can only be when the city—and all of China—is free.

CHAPTER 9

THE THREATS TO TAIWAN

WHY THE FREE WORLD SHOULD DEFEND THE ISLAND

In March 2019, I landed in Taipei, my first visit to the island in over twenty years. My only previous visit had been a weekend break to see friends when I was living in Hong Kong. Walking through Taipei's Taoyuan International Airport, seeing signs and hearing announcements in Mandarin Chinese, a sense of joy emerged in my heart and mind. It felt so good to be back in a culturally and linguistically Chinese environment where I felt welcome and not threatened, and a Chinese-speaking culture that was free and democratic, and where human rights were not just protected but celebrated. It was almost eighteen months since I had been denied entry to Hong Kong, but in Taiwan, I could meet freely with government ministers and officials, Parliamentarians, activists, and journalists.

I was there to attend a conference on religious freedom, organized and hosted by the Taiwan Foundation for Democracy and initiated by the United States Ambassador-at-Large for International Religious Freedom, Sam Brownback, as part of an effort to stimulate the emergence of "roundtables" for religious actors and civil society to meet in different parts of the world to address serious violations of the fundamental human right—set out in Article 18 of the Universal Declaration of Human Rights—for freedom of religion or belief.

Signifying Taiwan's desire to play a leading role as a defender of human rights and democracy, Taiwanese president Tsai Ing-wen was the opening keynote speaker and Deputy Foreign Minister Hsu Szu-chien also addressed the conference and hosted a reception in the Ministry of Foreign Affairs for participants. President Tsai delivered a powerful speech extolling the virtues of human rights and freedom.[1] She said religious freedom, in particular, means that "the state does not try to control religious organizations. It also means that government creates an environment of tolerance and acceptance, and a respect for minorities and diversity." That, she added, was what brought those of us who cherish freedom together. "We are not separated by our different beliefs, but bound together by this shared tolerance, and acceptance of one another's differences," she argued. "So we can work together—believers and non-believers alike—to meet the challenges of the twenty-first century . . . Freedom of religion has become central to our democratic way of life."

President Tsai's speech put down a marker. "Anyone can contribute a chapter to the story of Taiwan," she said. Yet how about across the straits? "In countries where human rights and democratic values are suppressed," she added, without naming them, "governments engage in discrimination and violence against people who simply want to follow their faith. In those countries, religious organizations are being persecuted, religious statues and icons are being destroyed, religious leaders are forced into exile, and people are held in re-education camps and forced to break their religious taboos. Taiwan knows how it feels when someone tries to take away your rights, wipe away your identity, and challenge your way of life. So, we choose to stand with those who were oppressed and whose religious rights were taken away by authoritarian regimes."

In a further significant step, President Tsai had a private meeting with Ambassador Brownback—who, only a few days before, had delivered a powerful speech in Hong Kong (already referred to in an earlier chapter), in which he accused China's dictatorship of being "at war with faith." It is, he added, "a war they will not win." What, after all, he asked, does the Chinese Communist Party have to fear? "Why can't it trust its people with a Bible? Why can't Uyghur children be named Mohammad? Why can't the Tibetans choose and venerate their own religious leaders like they have for more than a thousand years?" Following their meeting, President Tsai announced she would appoint a Special Ambassador for International Religious Freedom, Dr. Pusin Tali, and donate $1 million over five years to an international religious freedom fund.[2]

After the conference, I had meetings with a variety of officials, about Hong Kong and about human rights in China. The Foreign Ministry invited me to give a presentation to a gathering of officials and experts on human rights in China, and we had a two-hour discussion. Radio Taiwan International and Formosa TV interviewed me, and I was told that the radio interview would be broadcast on ten different frequencies across Mainland China to millions of listeners. I was asked by Radio Taiwan International about the difference between Mainland China and Taiwan, and I replied quite simply: while China is experiencing its worst crackdown on religion since the Cultural Revolution and Taiwan is hosting a conference on religious freedom and appointing a special ambassador for the issue, it is a difference between night and day. The interviewer asked if China is "night" and Taiwan is "day," what is Hong Kong? "Dusk," I replied. With hindsight that was perhaps a shade too optimistic.

One of the people I was privileged to meet in Taipei on that visit was Li Ching-yu, the young, gracious, courageous wife of Li Ming-che, a Taiwanese activist in jail in China. I had met her previously when she visited London the year before, to raise awareness of her husband's plight, and just a month before my visit to Taiwan, she had sat in the gallery for President Donald Trump's State of the Union Address, as the guest of Congressman Chris Smith.

"Even in prison, my husband is a human rights activist, and he wants the world to speak out, not only for his freedom but for all prisoners of conscience in China," she said, fixing me with a steely, dignified, determined look as we met in a Taipei restaurant. "The last time I saw him, he told me, 'Go everywhere and tell everyone.'"

Li Ming-che was arrested in March 2017 entering Mainland China from Macau. Ten days after he disappeared, China revealed that he was detained on suspicion of "endangering national security." For 177 days, his wife received no news, until his trial on September 11, 2017. Allegedly, he confessed to having "disseminated articles and essays that maliciously attacked and defamed the Chinese government" and had "incited the subversion of State power." It is believed that his televised confession, like so many in China, was obtained under duress. In November 2017, he was sentenced to five years in jail, for "subverting State power." In April 2022, he was released.[3]

China accused Li of writings penned within its jurisdiction, even though he is Taiwanese operating from Taiwan. Li, who supported civil society in China, is believed to be the first foreign activist imprisoned under China's new foreign non-governmental organization (NGO) law. Even though Beijing regards his activities from Taiwan as within China's jurisdiction, the regime stripped him of rights which Chinese prisoners enjoy, because he is a "foreigner"—in violation of China's own regulations.

Held in Chishan Prison, in Hunan, Li was subjected to forced labour, denied warm clothes, and existed on prison rations. According to his wife, he lost "an incredible amount of weight." In breach of prison regulations, which mandate no more than eight hours of labour over five days, plus a day of education and a day of rest each week, Li was forced to work more than ten hours a day without a day of rest. "There is not a hair's breadth of difference between re-education through labour in prison and working at a sweatshop," Mrs. Li said.

Li's wife tried to send books, published legally in China. They included Jeremy Black's *The Holocaust: History and Memory*, Albert Camus' *Reflexions sur la Guillotine*, and Primo Levi's works. Li was ordered to sign papers sending the books back. "Every book that I have sent was published in simplified Chinese and reviewed and approved by China," she said. "The books of literature and history that he enjoys discuss historical developments and philosophy dating back hundreds of years. Yet these 'legally published' books were restricted by Chishan Prison."

For more than two years, from 2020 to 2022, Mrs. Li had no contact with her husband, and her applications for permission to visit were refused more than sixteen times. Her letters took many months to reach him, and she did not receive any from him. He was not permitted to make telephone calls. The last time she saw him was in December 2018. In January 2019, she was informed that because she had made a public statement that "disrupted the prison's standard operations for upholding the law and impeded the reformation of the criminal Li," her visits were suspended.

Li, his wife insisted, was "a prisoner of conscience suffering in prison only because he showed concern for the families of victims of political oppression, and only because he upheld the universal value of freedom . . . As a political prisoner, not only his body, but his mind and soul are locked up in jail."

Human rights abuses in China, Mrs. Li said, "are not only to Chinese citizens . . . When they start persecuting Taiwanese citizens like my husband, the persecution of human rights by the Chinese Communist Party has already extended beyond China's borders. So the whole world should be concerned about China."

When I wrote an article about Li's plight in the *Wall Street Journal*,[4] with his wife's agreement, the Taiwanese government expressed its appreciation. Myra Lu, of the Taipei Economic and Cultural Office in New York, wrote in a letter to the *Wall Street Journal*:

We appreciate Benedict Rogers's "Beijing's Chilling Imprisonment of a Taiwanese Critic" (op-ed, April 1) which once again throws the limelight on Li Ming-che's case. His is a sad state of affairs. His rights have obviously been violated from the very beginning with a sham trial that presented no evidence except for his "confession." Having been falsely imprisoned, he is now being denied visits from his wife on grounds that only the authoritarian regime in Beijing can fathom. Beijing's intentions are clear: to intimidate the Taiwanese people.

The absurdity of it all is that Mr. Li's democratic leanings are construed as "a subversion of state power"—a state, by the way, that has no jurisdiction over Taiwan or its people. We are told that his democratic thoughts are being "corrected" by watching Chinese state television during the prolonged detention before his trial, which pretty much sounds like brainwashing. This behavior on the part of China couldn't be in starker contrast to the values to which the international community subscribes.

Mr. Li, a Taiwanese citizen who is jailed for thought crimes by China's authoritarian regime, holds up a mirror to the rest of the world. Anyone in his situation would be powerless to rise against it. But if the global community would consider human-rights issues as more than a mere afterthought to economic and trade issues, there may yet be a glimmer of hope for people like Mr. Li.[5]

Less than three months after that visit to Taiwan, I was invited back for another conference on religious freedom—again addressed by President Tsai. Speaking to the Taiwan International Religious Freedom Forum in Hsinchu city in northern Taiwan, eighty-four kilometres southwest of Taipei, in late May 2019, Taiwan's president said, "Taiwan's religious freedom sets the standard in the Indo-Pacific," and she offered Taiwan's support to those who are persecuted for their beliefs around the world. But she also reminded us that Taiwan has not always been free. "Taiwan walked a dark path on the road to religious freedom," she said. "The freedom we enjoy today is built on the blood, sweat, and tears of our predecessors. So we in Taiwan know better than anyone how precious freedom is."[6]

The vice president at the time, the respected epidemiologist Chen Chien-jen, also attended the forum, and addressed a press conference at the end where declarations were released on the persecution of Uyghurs and forced organ harvesting.

Vice President Chen said that what had been presented during the forum had "forced us all out of our comfort zone" and had "pushed us to take action against religious persecution so that religious freedom can take root and grow in all parts of the world."[7] Vice President Chen, a practising Catholic, referred to the social doctrine of the Catholic Church, emphasizing that "we must seek and serve the least of our brothers and sisters with love and virtue." He reminded us that Pope Francis has urged Catholics to "stand up from behind their walls and not be afraid of getting their hands dirty." The Pope, he added, "asks us all to love, to forgive, and to be open-minded."

The declaration to end forced organ harvesting in China, agreed unanimously by participants, was presented to the forum by Kenneth Starr, the former U.S. solicitor-general famous for his work as independent counsel investigating President Bill Clinton's conduct over the Monica Lewinsky affair. The declaration expressed deep concern about "the substantial, credible, and growing body of unrefuted evidence that the Communist Party of China has authorized and sanctioned—and continues to carry out—a systematic program of 'organ harvesting' with a horrific and cruel loss of human life." It called on the public to adhere to a pledge not to "receive or accept, directly or indirectly, any organ transplant from China."

A similar declaration on the persecution of the Uyghurs was also drafted and released, calling on corporations to "end all sales and collaboration with programs of surveillance, racial profiling, religious persecution, and mass detention in the Uyghur region" and urging governments to impose export restrictions and sanctions on such transfers or co-operation. It also called on pension funds and charitable foundations to divest their holdings from any company connected to the repression of the Uyghurs, and urged scholars to speak out against the persecution and suspend co-operation with China's Ministry of Education as long as Uyghur academics and students continue to be detained. It urged the World Health Organization, the Transplantation Society, the Pontifical Academy of Social Sciences, and the worldwide medical profession to suspend co-operation with China's transplantation system until China verifiably ends forced organ harvesting. The declaration also called on governments to provide humanitarian relief and refugee resettlement for Uyghurs and urged the International Committee of the Red Cross to seek access to all detention facilities holding Uyghurs, and all State facilities holding Uyghur children.[8]

In a further act of boldness, earlier in the conference, a letter from the Dalai

Lama was read out by his representative, in which he said, "Religious freedom is a basic human right. Human rights are something we all share, because all of us want to be happy and we are all entitled to be happy," the letter read. "I am happy to observe that in a robust democracy like Taiwan, the law protects and defends human rights. Everyone on this earth has the freedom to practise or not practise religion as they see fit."[9] President Tsai expressed appreciation for His Holiness' message.

Radio Taiwan International announced it would launch a new channel dedicated to broadcasting on religious freedom issues—"Voice of International Religious Freedom"—and a group was established to lead an initiative to provide healthcare to victims of persecution. The Taiwan International Religious Freedom Roundtable was also announced. It was clear that President Tsai's government is keen to build on the work begun under President Chen Shui-bian, who established the Taiwan Foundation for Democracy in 2003.

Just a week before the religious freedom forum, President Tsai met with prominent Tiananmen Square activists Wang Dan, Wang Juntao, Zhou Fengsuo, Fang Zheng, and Wu Renhua in the presidential office, to mark the thirtieth anniversary of the 1989 Tiananmen Square massacre.[10] She is the first president of Taiwan to do so. A few days after the conference, I went to Taipei's appropriately named Liberty Square to a commemoration of the massacre on June 4. A giant inflatable "Tank Man" image dominated the square in front of the National Chiang Kai-shek Memorial Hall, and a moving candlelit vigil and rally in the evening heard from Mainland Chinese and Hong Kong dissidents.

Through these events and the meetings I had with Taiwanese politicians, officials, journalists, and activists—including the leader of Taiwan's 2014 "Sunflower Movement," Lin Fei-fan, and with Hong Kong activists either visiting Taipei or who had moved into exile there, like Lam Wing-kee, the bookseller abducted into China in 2015 who has now opened a bookstore in Taiwan—it became abundantly clear to me how valuable and important Taiwan is as a democracy, and how vital it is that the free world do more to stand in solidarity with the island and prepare to defend it in the face of increasing aggression from Beijing.

Taiwan, after all, has made a truly remarkable transition from authoritarian dictatorship to one of the region's most vibrant democracies. After Chiang Kai-shek and the Kuomintang (KMT) retreated to Taiwan following their defeat by Mao Zedong and the Chinese Communist Party in 1949, he put the island under martial law, a situation which endured for thirty-eight years. After his death in 1975, he was succeeded by his son, Chiang Ching-kuo, who—despite previously being in charge of internal security and presiding over a ruthless purge known as the "White Terror" in which perhaps as many as 140,000 people were jailed and between 3,000 and 4,000 executed for direct or perceived opposition to the KMT regime—recognized, in the words of scholar Brendan Taylor, "that continued KMT rule hinged upon the party's ability to reflect the will of the Taiwanese people."[11] The island had developed into a prosperous economy and a well-educated society. "While Chiang was certainly not as committed to democracy as the founding father of the KMT, Sun Yat-sen . . . he did recognise that greater liberalisation was necessary to stave off a major political crisis," writes Taylor.[12] In 1986, two years before his death, Chiang Ching-kuo decided not to crack down on the establishment of an opposition party—the Democratic Progressive Party (DPP)—and after his death, his deputy, Taiwan-born academic Lee Teng-hui, assumed the leadership of the KMT and continued a process of political liberalization. On March 23, 1996, Lee became Taiwan's first democratically elected president. Since then, according to a 2021 report by Richard Bush for the Brookings Institute, "there have been three presidential transfers of power, an indicator of democratic consolidation."[13] The party system, Bush notes, is "institutionalized," with "two large, distinctive parties"—the KMT and DPP—and various smaller parties. "Elections are free, fair, and highly competitive. In presidential races, turnout usually exceeds 70%."[14]

Lin Fei-fan, whom I first met when he was studying at the London School of Economics and with whom I reconnected on my visits to Taiwan, contributed much to strengthening and protecting Taiwan's freedoms. In 2012, as a precursor to the Sunflower Movement, he led a movement to safeguard press freedom in Taiwan. "We called it the anti-media monopoly movement, because, at that time, there was a Taiwanese food company with significant investment in China, which started to buy up quite a lot of media groups in Taiwan from 2008 onwards," Lin recalled. The company, Want Want Holdings, one of the largest food manufacturers in Asia, bought several Taiwanese media outlets, including the *China Times* newspaper; the terrestrial television station China Television Company and its digital channels; cable television CTI TV; and, in 2011, Taiwan's second-largest cable television provider, China Network Systems.[15] Want Want Group's chairman, Tsai Eng-meng, gained a reputation for interfering in the editorial lines of the media groups under his control, and took a pro-China position.

"People worried that this kind of company, with a lot of investment from

China, could build a media monopoly in Taiwan, which they started to do, step by step," recalled Lin. "This would affect our people and how they receive news, and it would result in a lot of fake news and manipulation, especially during elections. So a movement grew—including students, activists, scholars, and others—to campaign to prevent the takeover and merger of media companies. In the end, we successfully stopped this merging of the media, and the government stopped giving television networks owned by Want Want licences, so they can only broadcast online, not on television. But even now, a lot of people worry about China buying Taiwanese media to infiltrate, influence, and undermine freedom of speech and press freedom in Taiwan."

Concern over Mainland Chinese stakes in Taiwanese media groups was the precursor to a wider concern over Cross-Strait business deals which gave rise to the protests known as the Sunflower Movement in 2014. Lin, one of the main leaders of that movement, explained its origins: "It was a convergence of several movements that had arisen since about 2006, including the environment movement, protests about housing and land issues and against neo-liberalism, but also it was becoming clear that China's influence was becoming a major concern. From 2008 onwards, the president at the time, Ma Ying-jeou, from the KMT, pursued a policy of signing more cross-straits deals, and engaging in more dialogue with the Chinese Communist Party regime. Many people worried about whether Taiwan would put itself in the orbit of China, and whether our freedoms would be undermined as a result."

In 2013, according to Lin, public opinion against too many deals with China reached a peak. "Previously, people may have thought that cross-straits peace and better relations would bring economic benefits, but after five years, by 2013, people actually felt that more and more business was going to China, more and more investment from China was coming into Taiwan, but Taiwan was not receiving much in return," he said. "You could see more and more young talent absorbed by Chinese markets, and people were beginning to think after graduation that their only option was to go to China to look for a job. The gap between rich and poor was increasing, and economic livelihoods were not improving."

Popular discontent was triggered by what was perceived to be a flouting of parliamentary due process by the KMT government in pushing a major trade deal with China through the legislature. The Cross-Strait Services Trade Agreement (CSSTA) was negotiated and signed "behind closed doors," according to Ian Rowen, a professor at Nanyang Technological University in Singapore, in Shanghai on July 21, 2013, and would "open eighty sectors of China's economy to Taiwanese investment and sixty-four sectors of Taiwan's economy to Chinese investment, including hotels, tourism, printing, and medical services."[16] It followed the Economic Cooperation Framework Agreement (ECFA), which Rowen describes as "a broad agreement for increased economic integration between Taiwan and China, signed in 2009." Even though the Taiwanese government's own Chung Hua Institute for Economic Research estimated the CSSTA would only bring a 0.025 to 0.034 percent increase in Taiwan's annual GDP, President Ma presented both the CSSTA and ECFA as "major boons for Taiwan's economy."[17]

Taiwan's service industry, Rowen notes, accounts for approximately 70 percent of its GDP. Opponents of the CSSTA expressed particular concern for the impact of increased Chinese "penetration" into Taiwan's economy on "small and medium-sized businesses, media culture, and freedom of expression." Supporters of Taiwan's sovereignty and democracy also argued that the trade deal had "ominous implications" for national security and self-determination. "Others suggested that a president who had polled months earlier at an astonishingly low 9 percent approval rating had no mandate to push for such legislation," Rowen recounts.[18]

On March 17, 2014, the KMT tried to fast-track the bill to enact the CSSTA, which, according to Rowen, "reneged on a June 2013 agreement with the opposition party, the Democratic Progressive Party (DPP), for an item-by-item review" of the deal.[19] Instead of allowing the promised review and debate, KMT legislator Chang Ching-chung, the convener of the committee, "unilaterally declared that the review period had already ended and that the bill would be submitted to a plenary session" to be held on March 21.[20] According to Lin Fei-fan, this provoked "an actual battle, actual fights, in the legislative chamber" and resulted in KMT leaders having to "go into the toilets and use a mini microphone to announce the passage of the bill." This procedural "scandal" was, Lin added, "a terrible joke for Taiwan's democracy," which sparked him and others to mount a "civil disobedience action."

On March 18, protesters from across Taiwan's civil society, including students and NGOs, under the umbrella of a coalition known as the Defend Taiwan Democracy Platform, gathered for a press conference and rally in front of the legislature. Later that evening, around 9 p.m., a group of students climbed over the walls of the legislature and stormed the building. "Unexpectedly," writes Ming-sho Ho, "their hastily planned action evolved into a twenty-four-day confrontation. The so-called Sunflower Movement, named after the floral gift sent to protesters as a symbol of hope, won widespread public sympathy in Taiwan. Thousands of supporters camped on the streets surrounding the legislature, which made it difficult for the government to evict the intruders. Yet the government refused to accept the demands from the protesters to postpone the free trade agreement."[21]

Lin believes the legislature's failure to uphold procedure and represent the will of the people justified the protesters' radical action. "We believed that the people have the right to say no to this bill, and their voice should be represented by the legislature," he told me. "But the legislature failed to meet this expectation, and that is why the students occupied the legislature for twenty-four days."

At the beginning, Lin recalled, "it was just a small group of students, about one hundred." But on the second day, "it became tens of thousands, and by the end of March, we held rallies in front of the presidential office with half a million people in the movement. Television stations were reporting it live, twenty-four hours a day."

Former Tiananmen Square protest leaders Wang Dan and Wu'erkaixi, recognizing what Rowen calls "the broad geopolitical implications of a protest against ostensible KMT collusion with China,"[22] entered the legislature briefly on March 19 to support the students, as did some Hong Kong and even Mainland Chinese students studying locally.

The occupying protesters demanded a review of the CSSTA, a legislative mechanism for the review of cross-strait agreements, and a public audience with President Ma. The president sent Premier Jiang Yi-huah as his representative for a televised public meeting with Lin Fei-fan on the street in front of the legislature, but—as Rowen notes—"during a tense ten-minute stand-off, after Jiang affirmed that he was unauthorized to accede to protester demands, Lin thanked Jiang for his visit and sent him away."[23]

With little sign of compromise from the government, the mood became even more radical, and on March 23, a group of students stormed the Executive Yuan, Taiwan's cabinet building. The police responded with speed and violence, leaving over 150 activists injured and many hospitalized.[24]

Lin and his colleague Chen Wei-ting announced a major rally planned for Sunday, March 30, and it turned out, according to Rowen, to be "the largest non-partisan, pro-democracy rally in Taiwan's history."[25] Organizers claimed at least 350,000 protesters gathered in the streets in front of the presidential office.

Similar solidarity protests were organized around the world, with live feeds with the protesters inside and outside the legislature.

President Ma eventually offered to meet the protest leaders privately in his office, an offer that Lin and Chen rejected, insisting it should be public and televised. Finally, however, on April 6, the Speaker of the legislature, Wang Jin-pyng, alongside DPP legislative leader Ker Chien-ming, visited the legislature and spoke with the students occupying it. They promised—to the KMT's shock and fury—that the CSSTA would not be passed without review and without the passage of a cross-strait regulatory supervision mechanism. Although this proposal did not meet all the students' demands, it was enough for the leaders of the movement to decide to end the occupation and leave the legislature four days later, on April 10. "Before leaving . . . in a carefully choreographed march strewn with real-life sunflowers, students cleaned up the space and invited assessors to estimate costs for property repairs," writes Rowen.[26]

After ending the occupation of the legislature, Lin and others turned themselves in to the judiciary. "We went to the prosecutors to declare that we are willing to take all the responsibility," he told me. "So we were prosecuted. But after two rounds of trials, the judges found us not guilty. In the first trial, they concluded that it was an act of civil disobedience. This was the first time in Taiwan's judicial system that the judiciary ever adopted this kind of principle—the civil disobedience principle—so that was significant. In the second trial, they concluded that it was freedom of speech, so not guilty again. Some students who got into fights with the police were prosecuted for violence, but the Occupy Movement as a whole was identified as not guilty, and as upholding freedom of speech and civil disobedience."

What was the lasting achievement of this movement? "The most important legacy is the willingness of young Taiwanese to participate in politics," Lin believes. "In the past, Taiwanese always said that the younger generation does not care about politics or about Taiwan's future. But now, you can see the trend, that the youth are willing to participate in politics, not only by voting, but by organizing, forming NGOs [and] student movements, and joining political parties. Also, the 2014 election changed the whole landscape of Taiwanese politics. A lot of cities held by the KMT were won by the DPP, and also some smaller parties gained seats."

Ming-sho Ho agrees. "The Sunflower Movement set off a political tidal wave," he writes. "A late 2014 poll indicated that more than half of Taiwanese respondents (53.3 percent) supported the movement . . . The Sunflower Movement helped encourage public scrutiny of closer economic integration with China, hamstring the trade proposal, and stymie subsequent efforts to liberalize trade with Beijing."[27] Participants, he notes, "have driven new forms of protest and activism, played meaningful roles in both new and existing parties, and encouraged the government to reassess key policy issues." Taiwan "provides a model of how activists can sometimes transition from extra-institutional protests to conventional forms of political participation."

At least ten Sunflower Movement activists were directly involved in Tsai Ing-wen's presidential campaign in 2016, and in the new legislature, about a dozen were employed as aides to DPP legislators. "After the inauguration of the DPP presidency," writes Ming-sho Ho, "former student activists also found their way to jobs in the Executive Yuan, the Presidential Office, and the National Security Council, arguably the pinnacle of the state apparatus."[28]

As Rowen notes, none of the protesters "expected that the occupation, later known as 318 or Sunflower Movement, would last twenty-four days, spawn the biggest pro-democracy protest rally in the island's history, reframe popular discourse about Taiwan's political and social trajectory, precipitate the midterm electoral defeat of the ruling party, and prefigure unprecedented protest in nearby Hong Kong."[29]

The fact that the Sunflower Movement and Hong Kong's Umbrella Movement, examined in the previous chapter, came in close succession was not a coincidence. "It was a mutual exchange process," Lin recalled. "In 2012, when we had the anti-media monopoly movement in Taiwan, there was the anti-national education movement in Hong Kong. I met Joshua Wong and a lot of civil society groups from Hong Kong, and over the years, we sent Taiwanese activists to Hong Kong and they sent delegations to Taiwan; we had workshops together, to learn skills and share experiences. We supported each other's movements."

And of course, the crackdown in Hong Kong has made a significant impact on attitudes in Taiwan. "When the Umbrella Movement happened in Hong Kong in 2014, it was the first time we saw big-scale police violence," Lin recounted. "The police in Hong Kong fired tear gas and were pretty brutal in their attacks on people. At the time, there was a slogan repeated by many: 'Today's Hong Kong will be tomorrow's Taiwan.' But, actually, many Hong Kong friends did not like it, and preferred to say, 'Today's Taiwan, today's Hong Kong,' because we are all on the frontline of the fight for freedom and against the expansion of China's authoritarianism." The police brutality against the 2019 protests in Hong Kong was even more severe, and was followed by the introduction of the draconian National Security Law in the city, dismantling Hong Kong's remaining freedoms.

"Hong Kong's experience tells us two things in Taiwan," Lin Fei-fan said. "The first is that China's threats are clear. And its promises cannot be trusted, because it breaks its commitments; it broke the Sino-British Joint Declaration. The second is that the Chinese regime is a threat to us all. They have squeezed out civil society space in Hong Kong, and they will try to do the same to Taiwan, by using investment in Taiwanese media and other forms of economic coercion and disinformation. So we need to strengthen our civil society, our media, and other institutions to safeguard Taiwan's freedoms."

Kolas Yotaka, spokesperson for the president of Taiwan, whom I spoke to in early February 2022, told me, "The most important lesson Hong Kongers gave the Taiwanese is that 'one country, two systems' is an illusion. And that the Chinese Communist Party regime will never keep their word. So the whole world has to be alert."

Vincent Chao, a former Taiwanese diplomat who served in Taipei's representative office in Washington, D.C., and previously as chief of staff to Taiwan's foreign minister, agreed. "Hong Kong has been a wake-up call. It has really been an eye-opening experience for Taiwan," he said. "There has always been a segment of the Taiwanese population that was naturally suspicious of the Chinese regime, and another part of the population that viewed the regime as benign, but I think now any illusion that the CCP can be benign has been shattered."

Amidst the multitude of threats Taiwan faces from the regime in Beijing, countering disinformation from China is particularly important. "Civil society and politicians are discussing a lot about how to fight the disinformation campaign," Lin Fei-fan said. "We have built quite a lot of tools for fact-checking on the Internet, but we need to do more, and faster, and to learn how to use new technologies. In the past, we worried that YouTube or Facebook could become monopolies for the Chinese regime or be influenced by the regime, but recently, we are more concerned about platforms used by the younger generation, such as TikTok. And we also worry that the Chinese will infiltrate civil society through different apps and social media. In every mayoral election, general election, and presidential election, we have seen attempts at manipulation from China."

Dr. Ketty Chen, vice president of the Taiwan Foundation for Democracy, agrees. "In the midst of the struggle between authoritarian uprising and democratic backsliding, Taiwan stands at the forefront of China's influence operation," she told me. "The most utilized method of influence operation is the use of information manipulation. China's influence operation against Taiwan can be categorized as serving four purposes: to corrode democratic institutions, national and local elections, and public trust in the democratic system; to undermine Taiwanese people's confidence, so that their will to resist is weakened and their feeling of abandonment and isolation magnified—for the Taiwanese people to feel that becoming part of China is inevitable; to polarize division and promote hatred; and to co-opt politicians, retired military officers, civil servants, and the business community."

Taiwan, says Chen, has dedicated "many resources to counter China's political influence campaign," including appointing Audrey Tang, a former hacker herself, as Taiwan's first digital minister. "Part of her portfolio is dedicated to combating disinformation and improving media literacy," according to Chen. "The government of Taiwan also reached out to social media companies such as LINE, Facebook, Google, and Yahoo for collaboration to fight against information manipulation."

The Taiwan FactCheck Center, MyGoPen, Cofacts, and others are all examples of civil society initiatives countering disinformation and validating facts, Chen points out, along with Open Culture Foundation and Fake News Cleaner. "Taiwan's civil society organizations have come together to strategize and develop methods to combat information manipulation," Chen told me.

Puma Shen, an assistant professor in National Taipei University's Graduate School of Criminology, is one of Taiwan's experts in information warfare. In an interview with the *Liberty Times*, he said that "information warfare has as its goal victory without military resistance. It is a component of hybrid and unrestricted warfare. The 'United Front' strategy paves the way for expansion or promoting unification with China at a time of peace."[30] China's main goal "is the annexation of Taiwan, which would be much cheaper than armed conflict," and it is using a variety of information warfare in pursuit of that goal tools, he says. "Recently, many Facebook pages in Taiwan have been acquired. It looks like there is a demand for acquiring fan pages. It could also be that overseas Taiwanese businesspeople are paying public relations and marketing companies to acquire the pages to sell to China . . . Facebook can prompt people to vote by changing its algorithms; for example, by showing positive news stories for a week."

Taiwan's temple system, and the ranks of village and borough wardens, and political groups or parties, as well as think tanks and the media, are other channels. "China has matured its information warfare," he added. "Since the 1990s, it has been discussing information warfare. The Chinese People's Liberation Army (PLA) has stolen Taiwanese data, including household registrations, driver's licences, and information on neighbourhoods and boroughs." Some of this, Shen explained, is for China's United Front Work Department "to get a grasp on the lifestyle preferences of Taiwanese and engage in political marketing."

In another interview, Shen noted that there are two ways in which China disseminates fake news in Taiwan. "One is 'online.' The other is 'offline,'" he told *New Bloom*.[31] "Online, it's through Facebook, or through content farms that fake news spreads. Content farms are often based in Malaysia, with some in Taiwan. When they operate content farms, they are usually operating fan pages at the same time . . . Regarding the offline element of fake news, this is more difficult to tackle. First, there are 'rumours.' Rumours depend on village or borough chiefs who are often in communication with China. Or heads of temples. While holding events, they'll use this as an occasion to spread rumours. This spreads by word of mouth. These rumours will circulate in Taiwanese society, leading to some fears, or leading people to have a good impression of China. This is becoming more advanced now. They'll put text online, using LINE groups to spread this. In the first few months, we can see half of fake news in Line groups originates from China." LINE, the online messaging app, is the most significant channel besides Facebook in Taiwan, Dr. Shen says. "Disinformation continues to spread on Line . . . But much disinformation on Line comes from Weibo or Weixin."

In addition to disinformation, infiltration, influence, and manipulation efforts by the Chinese Communist Party regime, Taiwan is subjected to an intense campaign of economic coercion and diplomatic isolation from Beijing. It ranges from retaliation against multinational corporations that inadvertently recognize Taiwan, to pressure on sports stars and organizations that hint at any sympathy for Taiwan, to blocking Taiwan's participation in multilateral organizations.

In recent years, China has pressured forty-four commercial airlines, as well as the International Air Transport Association (IATA), not to refer to Taiwan as a country. Many, including Air Canada, United Airlines, Delta Airlines, American Airlines, and British Airways, complied. Only the United States and Australian governments spoke out against this form of blackmail.

In January 2018, China shut down the Marriott Hotel chain's website for a week, forcing the corporation to apologize for listing Taiwan as a separate country. The Royal Bank of Canada was one among several international companies to edit its public information, to show Taiwan as a part of China. The clothing store chain Gap apologized for selling T-shirts decorated with a map of China that did not show Taiwan, and Japanese retailer Muji was fined US$31,000 for selling products labelled "Made in Taiwan." Audi and Zara have also caved in to pressure from Beijing.

American wrestler and actor John Cena apologized for calling Taiwan a country, ludicrously issuing a toe-curlingly contrite statement. "I made a mistake, I must say right now. It's so so so so so so important, I love and respect Chinese people," Cena said to his 600,000 fans on his Chinese Weibo account. "I'm very sorry for my mistakes. Sorry. Sorry. I'm really sorry. You have to understand that I love and respect China and Chinese people."[32]

In 2021, Taiwan won gold and silver medals for badminton at the Olympic Games in Tokyo, but the International Olympic Committee (IOC) insisted on referring to the island as "Chinese Taipei" and refused to use the Taiwanese flag or anthem.

In multilateral organizations, China has successfully sidelined Taiwan. From 2009 until 2016, Taiwan—which has a quality public health system, had observer status at the World Health Assembly, for example—has been pushed out by Beijing. Perhaps the most egregious example of China's efforts to marginalize Taiwan was the apparent pressure on the World Health Organization (WHO) not to engage Taipei in regard to the COVID-19 pandemic.

In March 2020, as the COVID-19 pandemic was beginning to spread across the globe, a reporter from Hong Kong's public service broadcaster Radio Television Hong Kong (RTHK), Yvonne Tong, interviewed a WHO advisor, Dr. Bruce Aylward. When Tong asked Aylward a question about Taiwan, and whether the WHO would consider Taiwan's membership, astonishingly, he pretended not to hear her and suggested she move to the next question. When she repeated her question on Taiwan, he then hung up on her. RTHK called him back and Tong asked him how Taiwan has done containing the virus. His response, before ending the interview, was, "Well, we've already talked about China, and when you look across all the different areas of China, they've actually all done quite a good job. So with that, I'd like to thank you very much for inviting us to participate."[33]

At least 210 complaints were made to Hong Kong's Communications Authority, with pro-regime voices accusing Tong of advocating Taiwan independence. Secretary for Commerce and Economic Development Edward Yau claimed RTHK's show had violated the "one China" principle. In June 2021, the Communications Authority dismissed the complaints as unsubstantiated, although Tong, an award-winning journalist, had already resigned from RTHK after enduring a sustained campaign of criticism and online abuse from the pro-Beijing camp.

China has also put pressure on Taiwan by seeking the extradition of Taiwanese citizens from countries with extradition agreements with China. Safeguard Defenders has documented that over 600 Taiwanese nationals between 2016 and 2019 were extradited to China from around the world, from countries as diverse as Cambodia, Malaysia, Vietnam, Indonesia, the Philippines, Kenya, and Spain. Between 2017 and 2019, Spain extradited around 300 Taiwanese nationals accused of involvement in telecommunications fraud in China. This practice violates past agreements between China and Taiwan and is a tool used to undermine Taiwan's sovereignty.[34]

In recent years, the number of countries which recognize Taiwan diplomatically has dwindled. Panama, the Dominican Republic, and Burkina Faso cut ties with Taipei, and—as described in an earlier chapter—Beijing is wooing the Vatican, although, so far, that has not resulted in a change of diplomatic recognition. Only fifteen countries today maintain official diplomatic relations with Taiwan as a sovereign country: Guatemala, Honduras, Haiti, Paraguay, Nicaragua, Eswatini, Tuvalu, Nauru, Saint Vincent and the Grenadines, Saint Kitts and Nevis, Saint Lucia, Marshall Islands, Palau, and the Vatican City.

There are, however, signs of a fight-back from Taiwan, and a change of heart on the part of some in the international community. In 2018, in an interview with the *Financial Times*, the Secretary-General of Taiwan's National Security Council David Lee called on Taiwanese citizens to boycott those international airlines that have chosen to bow to pressure from China and recategorize Taiwan on their websites. He criticized the regime in Beijing for their "excessive aggressiveness," and said Taiwan would consider legal action against the airlines. "It is a signal that we are fighting back, that we won't just sit idle here," he said.[35]

And in a speech marking the fifteenth anniversary of the founding of the Taiwan Foundation for Democracy, President Tsai Ing-wen called on global democracies to stand together in the face of Chinese repression.[36] She detailed the pressure Taiwan faces from China, and told Agence France-Presse in an interview that it was in the interests of all democracies to unite. "This is not just Taiwan's challenge, it is a challenge for the region and the world as a whole, because today it's Taiwan, but tomorrow it may be any other country that will have to face the expansion of China's influence," she said. "Their democracy, freedom, and freedom to do business will one day be affected by China."[37]

Since 2020, a growing number of politicians from across the free world have started to recognize this and show increased solidarity with Taiwan. Arguably, it started with the Czechs, when, in September 2020, a ninety-member parliamentary delegation visited Taiwan, led by the president of the Czech Senate Milos Vystrcil, who stood before the Taiwanese legislature and, in an echo of president John F. Kennedy's famous speech at the Berlin Wall, said, "I am Taiwanese." He added: "Kennedy said freedom is indivisible, and when one man is enslaved, all are not free."[38]

Predictably, the Czech delegation's visit was met with fury and threats from Beijing, but instead of the usual kowtowing and apology, European leaders stood firm in their support for the delegation. The Czech foreign minister summoned the Chinese ambassador to protest at the threats, and at a press conference alongside China's Foreign Minister Wang Yi in Berlin, Germany's Foreign Minister Heiko Maas said he had spoken by telephone with his Czech counterpart and stood in solidarity with them. In response to Wang Yi's warning that the Czechs would pay "a heavy price" for their action, Maas said, "We as Europeans act in close co-operation—we offer our international partners respect, and we expect the same from them. Threats don't fit in here."

Even before the visit took place, sixty-eight European Parliamentarians signed a statement of support for the visit, condemning Beijing's threats, and the chair and vice chair of the European Parliament's Delegation for Relations with the People's Republic of China, Reinhard Bütikofer and Maria Spyrak, wrote to the Chinese ambassador to the EU, reiterating that "EU Member States and Parliamentarians in particular have every right to develop economic, cultural and other relations with Taiwan free of PRC interference." They expressed "regret" for what they called "the increasingly bellicose attitude which your government is displaying."[39]

In November 2021, a European Parliament delegation visited Taiwan for the first time officially, almost immediately after Taiwan's Foreign Minister Joseph Wu had made a rare visit to Europe. Wu travelled to the Czech Republic and Slovakia, addressed a conference of the Inter-Parliamentary Alliance on China (IPAC)—which I attended—on the eve of the G20 summit in Rome, and visited Brussels to meet European Union leaders. Former vice president Chen Chien-jien visited Poland and Lithuania a month later.

In the same month that the European Parliament was escalating its engagement with Taiwan, two delegations from the United States Congress travelled to the island, and in January 2022, the British House of Commons Foreign Affairs Committee announced it was planning a visit, too. It was subsequently delayed due to COVID-19, but it will be the first such visit since 2006. In February 2022, the House of Commons debated U.K. relations with Taiwan, adopting a motion noting the importance of the relationship and calling on the British government "to continue to work towards the strengthening of the UK-Taiwan trade relationship and deepening of security cooperation" and to "support Taiwan's recognition in the international community."[40] In March 2022, former U.S. secretary of state Mike Pompeo visited Taiwan and called for diplomatic recognition of the island as "a free and sovereign country."[41] And in early August 2022, the Speaker of the U.S. House of Representatives, Nancy Pelosi, became the highest-ranking U.S. official to visit Taiwan, provoking a dramatic escalation in Chinese military manoeuvres around the island.

While European and American legislators were visiting Taiwan in November 2021, one European country took a decision which may, on the surface, seem a small detail, but in reality was a gesture of solidarity which provoked significant consequences. Lithuania announced it would allow the Taiwanese government to open a representative office in the country's capital, Vilnius, under the name "Taiwan," becoming the first European country to do so.

Other European countries host representative offices—de facto embassies—for the island, but using the name "Taipei," a compromise that satisfies Beijing insistence on recognition of China's sovereignty and a "one China" policy. Lithuania's decision to buck this trend infuriated Beijing, provoking the regime to impose a trade boycott on the Baltic state. "The Chinese obviously fear that if they do not make a sufficient example of Lithuania now, we may see other countries follow suit," Vincent Chao told me. "But their failure to meaningfully damage the united support from across Europe shows that their strategy is failing. They always pick off the weakest targets one at a time, and make examples of them, but they have never had a scenario where other countries rally behind the weakest one to prevent China inflicting sufficient damage to them. I think this is going to open up a lot of opportunities for Taiwan."

Taiwan, in gratitude to, and solidarity with, Lithuania, immediately increased its imports of Lithuanian goods, including buying 24,000 bottles of Lithuanian rum.[42] According to Kolas Yotaka, the initial batch of 12,000 bottles of rum went on sale at 9:30 a.m. on the first day of the Lunar New Year, and sold out "within five minutes." Taiwanese taxi drivers refused to charge Lithuanian passengers, she added. "Taiwanese people really appreciate Lithuania's support. We feel we are not alone. Of course, we know you cannot run a country only by selling rum, and we know Lithuania is facing severe economic threats, so we would like to co-operate more with them, by contributing technology, digital industries, artificial intelligence, 5G, [and] medical products, and in the fields of agriculture and green energy. We would love to co-operate with our allies, because as long as our allies are strong economically, we can help each other in terms of security."

Xi Jinping, unlike his predecessors, made clear in his first year in power that the question of Taiwan "cannot be passed on from generation to generation"— Beijing and Taipei must "reach a final solution."[43] In set-piece speeches in 2017 and 2018, he intensified the rhetoric, and, at the beginning of 2019, Xi Jinping said that Taiwan "must and will be" reunited with Mainland China and that the island's de facto independence could not continue forever.[44] Many see Taiwan as a legacy issue for Xi, to put himself alongside Mao Zedong and Deng Xiaoping as one of the three greatest Communist Party leaders. If Mao founded the People's Republic of China and Deng opened up its economy, Xi may wish the reunification of Taiwan with the Mainland to be his legacy. It features as a centrepiece in his "China dream" vision.

Ian Easton, senior director at the Project 2049 Institute and author of *The Chinese Invasion Threat*, believes the threats from Beijing are "very, very severe and growing over time" and describes the threat to Taiwan as "existential in nature." This, he adds, has always been the case with successive Chinese Communist Party leaders, who have been focused on "undermining Taiwan's democracy and preparing for a future potential war of annihilation, an all-out invasion." But the dangers have intensified significantly under Xi Jinping. "After China's military reforms and reorganization were announced in 2016, it became very clear that Xi Jinping does intend to annex or conquer Taiwan, at some point in the future," he believes. "For the people of Taiwan and for Taiwan's democracy, this is going to be a life-and-death struggle."

In recent years, China has dramatically increased its military intimidation efforts, regularly flying fighter planes into Taiwan's air defence zone. Over the course of four days in October 2021, a record 150 aircraft flew incursions into Taiwan's air defence zone, including thirty-four J-16 fighters and twelve nuclear-capable H-6 bombers. This was followed by the second-largest incursion on January 23, 2022, when thirty-nine warplanes flew into the zone in one day.[45] Following the U.S. withdrawal from Afghanistan in August 2021, Chinese State media published several articles taunting Taiwan. "After the fall of the Kabul regime, the Taiwan authorities must be trembling," tweeted Hu Xijin, the editor of China's State-controlled *Global Times*.

Twelve days after Vladimir Putin's invasion of Ukraine, China announced its biggest increase in military spending since 2019, raising the defence budget by 7.19 percent, to $229.5 billion in 2022, making it the second biggest global spender on arms. According to a report in the *Daily Telegraph*, because a Chinese soldier is paid much less than an American soldier, "the money can go further." In addition, unlike the United States and other Western powers, the article argues, "China does not have the global presence that America has, instead concentrating forces and equipment within its borders—making its local presence far more intense." In total, the People's Liberation Army (PLA) has more than one million ground force personnel, 6,300 tanks, and 7,000 artillery pieces, while the navy has more than seventy submarines, including six ballistic submarines fitted with long-range missiles, and more than 130 destroyers, frigates, and corvette ships. Its air force has 1,600 fighters, 450 bombers, and 400 transport aircraft. Taiwan, in contrast, has just 88,000 troops, 800 tanks, 1,100 artillery pieces, twenty-six ships, two submarines, only 400 fighter aircraft, no bombers, and just thirty transporters.[46] China, of course, also has a large nuclear arsenal.

"We are used to the threats," Kolas Yotaka told me. "I don't think they will stop flying planes into the Air Defence Identification Zone (ADIZ) or the surrounding seas. This will never end. They will never stop. It is bad, and it is going to intensify. Of course, we hope that it will not, as we are a country that loves peace. The last thing Taiwanese people want is a war, and we are trying our best to avoid a war."

The only factor preventing war at the moment, Vincent Chao believes, is Beijing's calculation of "risk and cost"—although, as the PLA's modernization campaign continues, "over time, the risk and cost will continue to go down." However, he adds, the Chinese Communist Party's tolerance of risk is low, because failure in a military campaign "would mean the end of the CCP as a political model." It is therefore essential that Taiwan and its allies "continue to ensure that the costs remain insurmountable for the CCP."

Easton, however, is concerned that Taiwan is unprepared to deal with any escalation. "One of Taiwan's greatest weaknesses," he told me, "is that it faces a nuclear-armed enemy, and Taiwan does not have nuclear weapons. It is also outside the American nuclear umbrella, so there is no extended deterrence that Taiwan can benefit from the way Japan, South Korea, and the Philippines do. So that puts Taiwan in a very dangerous position. Taiwan does not have the ability to deter a Chinese attack. All they can hope to do is make it a very painful and risky operation for the Chinese military."

Easton also worries about "complacency," both in Taipei and in Washington, D.C. Putin's invasion of Ukraine may have changed that to some extent, but he believes that "even for top-ranking generals in the Pentagon or in Taiwan's Ministry of National Defence, nobody actually believes China will do something so seemingly irrational and insane and extreme. That inability to take the Chinese Communist Party at its word and to look at the things that they are doing to prepare—the training, the military reforms, the spending, which are all underway—leaves Taiwan in a very dangerous position. Top policy-makers tend to deny it or wish it away. There is no way a country as small and as diplomatically isolated as Taiwan could, by themselves, deter or defeat an attack. They would need help from the United States and the international community. But that help has not been forthcoming, despite all the warning signs that are there. There has been some rhetorical support, some arms sales, but there is so much that needs to be done."

Chao believes Taiwan is taking two specific measures to prepare. "Firstly, there is a programme of military reform underway in Taiwan, developing a more robust asymmetric capability, inclusive of more Harpoon missiles; more survivable, dispersible, nimble, cost-effective capabilities; sea mines; small littoral coastal warships," he said. "Secondly, we are looking at defence policy in depth, recognizing that we no longer have air superiority or naval superiority. We do not have air or naval security. If conflict broke out, it would only be a matter of time before they would be on our beaches. So our beaches cannot be our last measure of defence. Therefore, we need a better reserves system, a better way of mobilizing, training, and equipping reserves."

Easton argues that even more needs to be done in Taiwan. "They should be having a serious debate about returning to conscription. They should have more intensified training. Right now, they have four months of mandatory military training, cut from ten months previously. In the past, they had two years of military service, but that ended, and their military has shrunk to a very small size.

There is a lot of hard work to be done if war is going to be prevented."

The international community, particularly the United States, also needs to step up. "When the Chinese Communist Party senses weakness from democracies, when it has the impression that the forces of authoritarianism are on the march, then it is only natural for a revanchist, expansionist leadership, and for a dictator as ambitious as Xi Jinping, to see that as an opportunity," believes Easton. The West's withdrawal from Afghanistan, the failure to stop the genocide of the Uyghurs, the failure to address atrocities in Tibet or the dismantling of Hong Kong's freedoms and autonomy, the failure to prevent the invasion of Ukraine, and the failure, so far, to respond to the increasing aggression by Beijing towards Taiwan all contribute, he argues, to Xi Jinping's "much greater appetite for aggression." Perhaps the fact that the West did respond to the invasion of Ukraine with unexpected speed, unity, and strength, the robustness of the sanctions imposed on Russia, and the fact that the invasion did not go according to Putin's plan, may give leaders in Beijing pause for thought. But, just as likely, it could merely make them delay rather than abandon any plans, and learn lessons from Ukraine which they would hope to avoid repeating in Taiwan. Time will tell.

In order to "deter a Chinese attack on Taiwan and ratchet down the tensions," Easton has a long list of steps the United States and its allies should be doing. "In the run-up to an invasion, you do not generally go from zero to one hundred miles an hour in one go. It is a gradual uptick. So for deterrence to fail, there are [a] hundred things that need to go wrong. That means, there is a lot we can do," he explained.

As a first step, Easton believes the president of the United States should start talking regularly with the president of Taiwan. The incursions of the ADIZ would be justification enough for President Biden to "immediately get on the phone" to President Tsai. The two leaders, he adds, "should also be able to tweet to each other and acknowledge each other as leaders of countries." That does not necessarily mean full diplomatic recognition or normalization of relations, he adds, but "we should be developing a pathway to that longer-term goal."

A second step, he suggests, is for people in senior positions in the U.S. government and military to visit Taiwan regularly. "It is deeply irresponsible that people who are responsible for giving the president advice and options in the event of an emergency are currently not allowed to visit Taiwan. It is a dereliction of duty," argues Easton. "It means that our top commanders do not know their counterparts, do not know the battle space, do not know what it looks like. They do not know anything about Taiwan other than what they can read. That is unacceptable. There is no other potential flashpoint on the planet where we would want our generals and admirals to be so blind that they do not even visit and see with their own eyes what the potential battle space looks like. So we should have all our senior officials rotating through Taiwan now—if necessary in secret and sometimes openly—in order to signal deterrence."

A third step, in Easton's view, is to start having "very large-scale, very serious bilateral military exercises with the Taiwanese military, so that army, navy, air force, and marines are all training with their Taiwanese counterparts and simulating what they would do in the event of a supreme emergency." There should be "joint drills," and the U.S. should deploy Special Operations Forces to Taiwan. "The Green Berets should go to Taiwan, learn the culture, learn the language, learn the history, develop relationships of trust," he adds.

Fourthly, the U.S. and her allies should, according to Easton, be preparing to pre-position supplies in Taiwan. "We need to make sure there are plenty of supplies—ammunition, fuel, spare parts, equipment, food—pre-positioned in Taiwan. We do it in South Korea. We do it in Israel. We do it in Guam. But at the moment, none of this is being done in Taiwan," he said. "If we are serious about deterrence, we should be doing all these things."

Chao believes it is vital that "the idea that the U.S. would intervene if Taiwan is attacked should be baked into Chinese military scenarios." In other words, the U.S. should end its current position of "strategic ambiguity." If Japan and Australia, as the two regional powers, were also to strengthen their promised support for Taiwan, that would, in his view, go a long way towards "introducing new uncertainty and new cost and risk" for Beijing to consider.

Easton agrees. "Today, Japan does almost nothing to support Taiwan's defence and security, and Australia does even less, other than rhetorical support, which only started recently. To my knowledge, there is no public interaction between Japan's government or military and Taiwan. Their diplomats in Taipei focus on economic issues," he notes. "They should translate some of the very good rhetoric into action, and that would entail sending delegations to Taiwan to discuss defence and security issues, and do more intelligence sharing."

Chao is more positive about the prospects of support from Japan and Australia. "Australia and Japan have done a stellar job in recent months," he told me. "Japan has come out with unprecedented statements that the peace and security of the Taiwan Strait is directly connected with the peace and security of Japan. Australia has said that if the U.S. intervenes, they cannot imagine a scenario where Australia would not. That helps create cost and uncertainty at the outset for the Chinese regime to consider."

The North Atlantic Treaty Organization (NATO) cannot ignore Taiwan either, Easton argues. "If China attacks Taiwan, the U.S. and China are almost certainly going to be at war with each other, and that means that if NATO wants to continue to exist, it is going to have to support the U.S. There is no way NATO can stay out of it. Nobody wants to talk about it, but the U.S. would certainly expect all our allies to support us." Of course, that could involve non-military support—through economic sanctions, intelligence, cyber intelligence, satellites—and diplomatic and political support, but it could also mean, as Easton suggests, "naval, air force, and special forces backup."

Yet the dangers of a war with China are immense, so why would it be in the free world's best interests to invest so much in defending Taiwan, an island of twenty-three million people versus the world's second-largest economy of 1.4 billion people? Why does Taiwan matter?

Chao argues that Taiwan matters for two key reasons: its strategic geopolitical importance, and the values argument. "Taiwan holds a central position in the 'first island chain' and is deeply interconnected with two major U.S. allies, Japan and the Philippines. If you lose Taiwan, it is only a matter of time before you lose Japan and the Philippines. And the Koreans will be long gone if Taiwan falls," he believes. "It would shatter morale in Japan, and Japanese confidence in the United States, if Taiwan fell and the U.S. did not act. In the Philippines, it would shatter confidence in U.S. ability to project power in East Asia. That is the geopolitical aspect. But there is also the democracy aspect. Both Taiwan and Ukraine are indicative of the struggle between democracy versus authoritarianism. If Ukraine and Taiwan both fall, the forces of authoritarianism will be seen to be overpowering the forces of democracy, and that will endanger fragile democracies throughout the world."

Kolas Yotaka concurs. "Taiwan matters because we believe in democracy, freedom, human rights, and the rule of law," she told me. "We speak the same language as countries around the world that share those values."

Gray Sergeant, a Democracy and Human Rights Fellow at the Taiwan Foundation for Democracy, believes Taiwan is an issue that creates "common cause" between realists and idealists, liberals and conservatives, hawks and doves.

"What people emphasize depends on their outlook—realists would focus on Taiwan's geopolitical importance: where it is and what it does, its situation in the first island chain; the implications for Japan, South Korea, and the Pacific if it was invaded; and its economic significance; while idealists would emphasize the values argument; Taiwan being a liberal democracy; the importance of self-determination, self-governance, sovereignty; and the international rules-based order. But it matters for all these reasons."

Easton believes there are "dozens of reasons" why we should care about Taiwan. "The most important is that Taiwan is a liberal democracy and, politically speaking, a miracle. It is one of the great success stories of the last thirty years," he argues. "It is a democratic country, and it has one of the highest human development index ratings on the planet. Just read the reports by Reporters Without Borders, Freedom House, Human Rights Watch—all of their annual reports indicate that Taiwan has one of the best governments on the planet, bar none. It is up there with Canada and the Scandinavian nations in terms of good governance. It is truly a bastion of human rights, and it is the kind of government you would want for anybody. And so it matters that you would never want to see a government like that destroyed by an authoritarian power."

Taiwan matters, too, for the international rules-based order. "You do not want to live in a world where might makes right, where fascist and communist governments are on the march, where dictatorships feel able to conquer their neighbours. That world—with a jungle rule in which the powerful can do what they want, and the weak suffer most—is a nightmarish world," said Easton. "That is why, after World War II, we built the United Nations system, and it is why we have worked so hard to maintain that system and why it is so important to stand up for vulnerable democracies. We do not want the wheel of civilization turned backwards. Taiwan matters for the entire liberal world order. If we lose Taiwan, we lose that liberal world order, and we will all suffer for it."

Of course, Taiwan also matters economically. Taiwan is the United States' tenth largest trading partner in the world, and the United Kingdom's eighth-largest Asia-Pacific trading partner. It is the eighth largest economy in Asia, and the eighteenth largest in the world. It is, as Easton notes, an "engine of the world economy" and "the nerve centre of the world," especially as the world's largest producer of semiconductors, which form the microchips that power most electronic devices, from smartphones to computers. "If that capacity fell into the hands of the Chinese regime, that threatens our freedoms at home," Easton said. "If we were to lose Taiwan, it would devastate our economy. The entire world would go into an almost instant depression. And if Taiwan's technology sector—especially microchips—fell into the hands of the Chinese Communist Party, then we are in grave, grave danger. If Taiwan falls, it poses an existential threat to us all."

Taiwan is also of significant importance for the free world's intelligence services. "We have a very close relationship with Taiwan in terms of intelligence sharing. We have a lot of early warning radars and listening posts. Taiwan occupies a very strategic location that enables us to monitor what the PLA is doing. So, if Taiwan were to fall, it would devastate our military and security situation, and make it very difficult to defend Japan, South Korea, and the Philippines," Easton believes. "Even U.S. territories such as Northern Marianas and Guam could be very vulnerable to follow-on attacks. So Taiwan is just so incredibly important on so many levels, but, unfortunately, many of our leading thinkers are deeply ignorant about it because they do not go there."

What do Taiwanese people want? Kolas Yotaka told me very clearly: "We want to be treated equally, as a country. The international community can help us by respecting the Taiwanese people and our government, because respecting the Taiwanese people is not a crime. We deserve to be treated equally at the United Nations organizations, or in Olympic competitions, just like other independent countries. The status of Taiwan cannot be defined by China. We want self-determination. Our twenty-three million Taiwanese people who have elected Taiwan's leaders are showing, in doing so, our self-determination. No authoritarian government has any place to comment on this."

Over the past decade or more, a sense of Taiwanese identity has grown considerably. Ho Ming-sho notes that, in 2008, when Ma Ying-jeou was elected, a leading survey from National Chengchi University indicated that 48.4 percent of respondents in Taiwan identified as Taiwanese, 43.1 percent identified as both Chinese and Taiwanese, and 4 percent identified as predominantly Chinese. By 2014, the gap had grown significantly, with 60.6 percent identifying as Taiwanese and 32.5 percent as both Chinese and Taiwanese. "The identity shift among young Taiwanese has been particularly noticeable," Ho writes.[47]

In 2021, according to a public opinion survey, more than 80 percent of the public expressed support for President Tsai's emphasis on strengthening Taiwan's democracy and self-defence, and almost 90 percent oppose the Chinese Communist Party's proposal of "one country, two systems" for Taiwan.[48] According to Brendan Taylor, other recent polling suggests that 100 percent of those under the age of twenty-nine see themselves as "exclusively Taiwanese," and 70.3 percent of those under the age of forty "would be willing to fight for Taiwan should Beijing attempt forceful reunification."[49]

For these reasons, as Easton argues, the international community should do much more to ensure access for Taiwan in multilateral organizations and to strengthen ties with Taipei. "As long as we treat Taiwan as a diplomatic pariah, as long as we isolate Taiwan, then that favours the Chinese Communist Party, puts Taiwan in a very vulnerable position, and puts us in a very vulnerable position in a time of crisis, too," he said.

Wu'rkaixi, one of the student leaders of the Tiananmen Square protests in Beijing in 1989, and now a Taiwanese citizen, concurs. "Taiwan has been under Communist threat for a long time, and one element that makes this threat real is the world's willingness to allow the Chinese threat to be realized. The so-called 'one China' policy that much of the world has adopted has put Taiwan in a position where it has become illegitimate," he argued. "That is how ridiculous it is today: that a regime that opens fire on peaceful demonstrators, that has no democracy, represses freedom of assembly, expression, information, is the regime that is recognized as legitimate; while a free, vivid, and exemplary democracy, with free elections, free flow of information, freedom of assembly, and where the military is under a civilian-elected government and neutral from the political process, is the one the world calls illegitimate. It is ridiculous." If China threatened to invade India or Japan or any other country, he added, "the world would not tolerate it—and Beijing would not dare, because the consequences would be clear."

Kolas Yotaka agrees. "It would make a huge difference if other countries can be a little less scared of China and a little more supportive of Taiwan. Taiwan's democracy and security do not depend on Taiwan alone. They rely on other countries, too. If we do not work together, it is not only Taiwan that will face security issues. So we need to expand regional and international co-operation. Taiwan's future is other countries' futures, too. We are connected. We have to walk together."

But in addition to doing more to support Taiwan—diplomatically, politically, economically, and militarily—the international community should also realize how much we can learn from Taiwan. The contrast between Taiwan's handling of COVID-19 and the behaviour of the regime in Beijing at the start of the pandemic is just one illustration, and had we heeded Taiwan's early warnings rather than believed Beijing's lies, the course of the pandemic may well have turned out differently. As Gray Sergeant writes, "following the outbreak of Covid-19, the

Taiwanese government, having contained the virus, used its privileged position to provide advice and donate personal protective equipment and medical supplies to those countries hit hardest by the pandemic . . . If Taiwan had more of a voice on the international stage, it could have contributed even more to prevent the spread of the virus. Taiwan managed to contain the spread of the virus, without excessive curbs on civil liberties, by responding to the warning signs early with health screenings for incoming flights from Wuhan at the end of December 2019. Subsequently, Taiwan successfully implemented measures such as contact-tracing and quarantining. Had the rest of the world followed suit, things might have been different. Yet the real problem is not that Taiwan was not listened to but the fact that it was denied the opportunity to meaningfully participate in the WHO."[50]

Kolas Yotaka believes Taiwan's example illustrates the importance of its transparency. "What a mistake the WHO made in trusting China too much," she said. "COVID-19 was a disease that had never happened before, so no one knew how to deal with it at the start, but one of the reasons the virus spread in China was because the government hid what was happening. In contrast, right from the beginning, as spokesperson for the Cabinet, I realized that in order to reduce people's anxiety, we had to be transparent with information. So we held press conferences every day, with doctors and officials, and we worked with the television channels on regular broadcasts and videos, providing information on how to protect against the virus."

The lessons should be clear. As Ketty Chen told me, "Speak up against authoritarian intimidation of Taiwan, and dispel authoritarian information manipulation and rhetoric against Taiwan's democracy." As she argues, "democracies need to come together to support each other, as authoritarian regimes would never be satisfied with taking over just one democracy."

For every free and democratic country in the world, Taiwan is a friend and an inspiration. It is an impressively reliable, innovative, entrepreneurial partner in the fields of trade, investment, technology, climate change, public health, among others, and an ally in the promotion of democracy, human rights, and the rule of law around the world. It is both morally right, and in our own self-interest, that we do everything possible to stand with Taiwan.

CHAPTER 10

IN CHINA'S BACKYARD

BEIJING'S COMPLICITY WITH MYANMAR'S CRIMES AGAINST HUMANITY

We waited until nightfall in a small hotel in Yingjiang, in Yunnan Province, just over one hundred kilometres from the Myanmar (Burma) border. The previous day, I had flown from Beijing to Kunming, the capital of Yunnan Province, in southwest China, and stayed overnight at the Jinjiang Hotel before flying to the small town of Mangshi, near Ruili. After a four-hour drive on winding roads with hairpin bends, through the lush green mountains from Mangshi to Yingjiang, we decamped at the hotel, to have lunch, rest, and wait until it was dark. Crossing the border from China to Myanmar was safer to do at night, my guides advised.

When we set off again, we drove another three hours or so, and then stopped somewhere near Nabangzhen. Then we walked, in the dark, for about ten minutes, where we were met by motorbikes and a pickup truck. Placing our luggage in the back of the truck, we hopped onto the backs of the motorbikes and sped through the jungle. After another ten minutes, we arrived in Laiza, headquarters of the rebel Kachin Independence Organisation (KIO) and its armed resistance wing, the Kachin Independence Army (KIA). We were in Kachin State, Myanmar.

That was in 2006, my first visit to the Kachin. I had been working on Myanmar since 2000 and had travelled many times to visit the ethnic groups such as the Karen, Karenni, and Shan, who were refugees on the Thailand-Myanmar border, and several times to the Chin people on the India-Myanmar border, but this was my first time in northern Myanmar, crossing the border from China.

At the time, Myanmar's military, known as the Tatmadaw, which had ruled the country as a dictatorship since General Ne Win took power in a coup in 1962, had a ceasefire with the KIA. But, in reality, the ceasefire did not mean peace. It meant an absence of active fighting, but no end to the military's human rights violations.

The ceasefire had been agreed in 1994, and for several years, KIO leaders had been cautious about inviting international human rights groups, NGOs, or journalists to their territory, or engaging in international advocacy, for fear that it might destabilize the ceasefire.

But, by 2006, they were starting to feel frustrated, and invited me to meet the leadership, as well as Kachin civil society and church pastors. They wanted me to conduct workshops to train young Kachin activists in human rights documentation, reporting, and advocacy. "We have been crying for a long time for someone like you to help us. We felt we had been forgotten. We felt alone," one Kachin pastor told me.

That visit was the first of several I made to the China-Myanmar border between 2006 and 2012. Each time, I crossed the border with Kachin guides, not with a passport or visa, but across a river and a dirt track, usually at night. Each time we crossed back into China, a decoy vehicle would go ahead of us, in order to alert us as to whether or not there were Chinese checkpoints along the road. On all of my visits, I was fortunate—I made it in and out safely, and was never once stopped, questioned, or arrested.

I did have some close calls, however. In Laiza, the Kachin kept me fairly well hidden, not permitting me to go out of the hotel by myself, and only allowing me out in a four-wheel drive Land Cruiser with darkened windows, so that I could not be seen by passersby. I was virtually smuggled in and out of the hotel via a back door.

On one visit, half an hour after entering the hotel to meet a man who had come especially from Myitkyina, the Kachin State capital, to see me, I received a message from my Kachin hosts. "We have just received news that the Myanmar Army's Northern Region commander and the Kachin State commander are passing through town. They will have lunch in this hotel. Do not under any circumstances leave the room you are now in until we let you know," they said. Suddenly, I was sitting two floors above two of the most senior officers in Myanmar's military regime. I remained hidden in the room, but when I glanced cautiously out of the window, I saw that the courtyard was swarming with soldiers, their guns glistening in the midday sun. Under the terms of the ceasefire, the KIO/KIA maintained control of Laiza, but the Tatmadaw could come and go when they wished.

That ceasefire, however, lasted until June 2011 when, after seventeen years, the Tatmadaw broke the agreement and launched a major offensive against the Kachin. At least 60,000 Kachin civilians were displaced from their villages in that initial campaign, causing them to flee to temporary camps around the KIO strongholds of Laiza and Maijayang and across the border to China. Over subsequent years, hundreds of thousands have been displaced, as villages have been burned, women raped, churches destroyed, pastors tortured and murdered, and ordinary civilians beaten, jailed, or used for forced labour.

About six months after the ceasefire broke, I travelled to the region again, to visit the displaced peoples. It was now an active war zone, and the conditions were dire—overcrowded camps set up in old warehouses, in factories, and in the jungle were full of people sleeping on thin mats on cold concrete floors, with minimal rations. Aid from the international community was almost non-existent—a few agencies provided some support, and the United Nations had brought one small convoy of trucks with basic supplies for no more than 800 families, but the people were primarily dependent on their own Kachin community for help. An impressive group of young Kachin activists established an umbrella organization to co-ordinate humanitarian efforts.

Attempts were made by the two sides to hold talks. Indeed, while I was in Laiza in January 2012, KIO leaders met with the Tatmadaw in the Chinese town of Ruili, about 200 kilometres—or a five-hour drive—further south along the China-Myanmar border. I followed the talks closely through my Kachin hosts, and it was clear that the KIO were taking a firm position. After learning the lessons of the previous fragile seventeen-year ceasefire, they were not going to be bought off this time with promises of economic development. They wanted a political process resulting in a political solution that would give them the autonomy within a federal democracy for which they had strived for over fifty years. "We are committed to a federal Myanmar," one senior KIO leader told me.

That goal of federalism is one shared by all of Myanmar's major ethnic groups, all of which have been fighting a defensive armed struggle against the Tatmadaw for much of the past seven decades. Myanmar is the world's longest-running civil war.

For the past three decades or more, Myanmar has also faced a painful struggle for democracy. Born as a democracy when it claimed independence from British colonial rule on January 4, 1948, it was also born into tragedy. Its founding father, General Aung San, was assassinated the year before, depriving the country of perhaps the one person who might have been capable of uniting it. U Nu served as prime minister for the first decade of fragile, parliamentary democracy, before apparently voluntarily handing power over to a military caretaker government led by General Ne Win in 1958, ostensibly to "restore order." Fresh elections were held in 1960 and won overwhelmingly by U Nu, but after only two years in office, he was overthrown in Ne Win's coup, which ushered in decades of military rule.

Every time the people of Myanmar have been given a say in a free and fair ballot on whether they wish to be ruled by soldiers or democrats, they have spoken clearly in support of democrats. They did so in 1960, in 1990, in 2015, and in 2020. Only once—in 2015—were their wishes respected. On the three other occasions, the military disliked the electoral outcome and so seized power yet again, overturning the ballot with their bullets. And the only time the military has ever "won" an election was in 2010, when they effectively barred the democratic opposition from contesting, rigged the ballots, and put up their own candidates who had merely shed their military uniforms for business suits, *taikpon eingyis* and *longyis* (the traditional Myanmar dress).

Nevertheless, in August 2011, there were signs that perhaps at long last Myanmar was beginning to change. The former general Thein Sein, who had become president after the 2010 rigged elections, invited Myanmar's democracy leader, Aung San Suu Kyi—daughter of Aung San—to talks. It was the first time the two had met since he had become president and she had been released from her last period of house arrest in November 2010. Aung San Suu Kyi had led the democracy movement since the protests in 1988 and had won an overwhelming mandate in the 1990 elections, but she had never been allowed to form a government. Instead, she spent fifteen of the subsequent twenty-one years under house arrest.

That meeting between Thein Sein and Aung San Suu Kyi appeared to herald the dawn of a new era. Political prisoners were released, space for civil society and independent media opened up, ceasefires were signed with many of the ethnic groups, a peace process began, and democratic, multi-party elections were held. In 2012, Aung San Suu Kyi was elected to Parliament in a by-election, and her party, the National League for Democracy (NLD), won forty-three out of the forty-four seats they contested. She engaged with the military, sought to make compromises, and, in 2015, won the General Election and formed Myanmar's first civilian-led, democratically elected government in more than fifty years.

Of course, the decade of fragile democratization—or at least some degree of liberalization and opening—was far from perfect. Indeed, as the country appeared to open up on some levels, the dark clouds of religious nationalism gathered and the embers of ethnic and religious hatred and intolerance were stoked by the military. The genocide of the predominantly Muslim Rohingyas, the rise of wider anti-Muslim discrimination and violence in other parts of Myanmar, and continued conflict in northern Myanmar's Kachin and Shan States showed that there was still a very long way to go before Myanmar could truly be free.

Furthermore, while it was the military that carried out the attacks and fuelled racial hatred within society, it happened on Aung San Suu Kyi's watch. Not only did she fail to stop it or condemn it, she also appeared to defend it, tarnishing her reputation on the world stage in the process. When she travelled to The Hague to defend the military against genocide charges at the International Court of Justice (ICJ), her transformation from saint to pariah in the eyes of many was complete.

I travelled to Myanmar many times during those years, giving workshops throughout the country for civil society activists, religious leaders, ethnic groups, and political campaigners. I saw both the potential for a country that was opening to the world, and the dangers of extremist religious nationalism and identity politics stalking the land. I met Aung San Suu Kyi on several occasions, and while I eventually reached a point where I could not defend or condone her complicity with the military's atrocities, I also recognized that her situation was far more complex than many people realized.

Yet, given how far she had gone to compromise with the military, the coup on February 1, 2021, caught me completely by surprise. In the elections in November 2020, Aung San Suu Kyi and the NLD won another overwhelming majority, and looked set for a second term. While barred from the presidency under the constitution drafted by the military, Aung San Suu Kyi had been the de facto head of government since 2015, serving in the newly created role of "State counsellor," with a president handpicked by her. It was no secret that, in the 2020 elections, the outgoing commander-in-chief of the military, Senior General Min Aung Hlaing, wanted to be president and had deluded himself into believing that the people would elect him. When it became clear that he could not fulfill his ambition through the ballot box, he resorted to seizing power by the bullet and the gun barrel in a coup that dialled the clock back for Myanmar by more than a decade, undid years of reform, and plunged the country into yet more conflict and repression. Aung San Suu Kyi and her NLD colleagues were arrested and jailed, civil society and independent media were shut down, and the military escalated attacks in the ethnic areas and turned their guns on peaceful protesters in the cities. At the time of writing, over 13,000 people have been arrested and almost 2,000 killed since the coup, the United States has recognized the atrocities against the Rohingyas as genocide, and the United Nations accuses the military of war crimes and crimes against humanity.

So where is China in all this? What is the nature of the relationship between the regime in Beijing, the regime in Naypyidaw, and the other stakeholders in Myanmar? How should China's Myanmar policy be judged?

Ultimately, the Chinese Communist Party regime in Beijing is motivated only by one factor: its own interests. Questions of morality, ethics, or humanitarian concern do not arise in the minds of the men in Beijing. China's border with Myanmar stretches 2,200 kilometres from just beyond the Diphu Pass near India in the north; past the Nanmi Pass and Hkakabo Razi, the highest mountain in Southeast Asia; across the Hengduan and Gaoligong mountains; to the Mekong River near Laos in the south. Beijing's primary concern is the stability of that border, and the security of its economic and geopolitical interests in Myanmar.

Angshuman Choudhury, a senior research associate at the Centre for Policy Research in New Delhi, India, believes there is one word to describe China's relationship with Myanmar: "multi-dimensional." The regime in Beijing has generally adopted what it would regard as a pragmatic approach, working with whoever is in power in Myanmar. "What China aims to do is maintain its foothold and leverage with various actors. It is a functional, utilitarian relationship," said Choudhury.

Jason Tower, director of the United States Institute for Peace's Myanmar programme, agrees. "China's relationship with Myanmar is about China trying to advance its three key interests, rather than it wanting to maintain allegiance with any particular stakeholder," he told me in a call from Bangkok. "It seeks to protect its immediate economic interests, ensure control and stability of the borderlands, and prevent Western actors from gaining influence in its highly strategic periphery."

In addition, Tower believes China also "uses Myanmar as one of many cases to leverage in order to try to weaken global democracy and human rights norms.

So, frankly, whether you are looking at the Yunnan provincial government or the Beijing level, they do not really care who is in power in Myanmar—apart from preferring that those with whom they have created special business relationships hold influence. They could not care less whether it is the NLD or the military. It is more a question of which actors will be easier to instrumentalize and influence for Beijing's objectives."

That is why, when Aung San Suu Kyi was in government, Beijing went to some lengths to develop a relationship with her even though, as the leader of the democracy movement, she would not normally be a natural bedfellow for Xi Jinping. She chose China as the destination for her first state visit after taking office, visited Beijing five times, and met Xi Jinping five times, and, especially after the Rohingya crisis in 2017, she "started pivoting towards China" in the face of Western criticism. "She found that China was willing to support her administration at the international level," explains Choudhury.

In January 2020, Xi Jinping visited Myanmar for the first time. It was the first State visit by a Chinese president to the country in twenty years, and one in which China and Myanmar signed thirty-three bilateral agreements that would draw the country even closer into Beijing's orbit. The multi-billion dollar deals, part of Xi's Belt and Road Initiative (BRI), include rail and deep-sea port projects along an economic corridor that links southwest China to the Indian Ocean. A $20 billion high-speed rail line from Yunnan to Myanmar's coast and a new expressway are in the works. They also agreed on the establishment of a new special economic zone on the Chinese border.

Myanmar's ethnic armed organizations have also pursued a complex relationship with Beijing. "All the key actors—the ethnic groups, the People's Defence Force (PDF) movement, other political parties, as well as the NLD, the exiled National Unity Government (NUG), and the Tatmadaw—are all thinking about the influence that China has on the trajectory of the conflict," Tower told me. "Some of them are more strategic than others in terms of thinking through how best to leverage the China angle. Others, such as the KIA, have their own communities—the Kachin or Jinghpaw—on the other side of the border, whom they connect with and will leverage to pursue their own interests with regard to the Chinese. So everyone is highly sensitive to anything China does. They all want information, and they all want to know where China is headed." In summary, it is "a love-hate relationship," according to Tower, because "they all see where China is trying to gain advantage over them, they see where China's moves are blocking their efforts, but they also see that without having some level of support from China, their own prospects are quite dim."

China's lack of allegiance to any one side became clear in its response to Min Aung Hlaing's seizure of power in a coup, overthrowing Aung San Suu Kyi's democratically elected government. Beijing was quick to switch allegiance. "Initially, Chinese State media described the coup as a Cabinet reshuffle, and tried to underplay the takeover," Choudhury notes. "They tried to pass it off as some sort of normal administrative change, not a regime change. In so doing, China was trying to signal to the international audience, and the Myanmar audience, that things will not change as far as China's relationship with Myanmar goes."

On March 16, 2021, just six weeks after the coup, the China Global Television Network (CGTN) ran an article on its website headlined "Enough with the interference in Myanmar already!" As Myanmar expert Bertil Lintner noted, "beyond the poorly worded banner, the write-up consisted of an unusually vitriolic attack by a Chinese state-operated news agency on the West's reaction to the Feb. 1 coup in Myanmar . . . The article went on to claim that voices from the West are encouraging unrest in Myanmar and if it continues, the country risks 'falling into civil war,' as if there wasn't already a decades-long civil war there. 'Egging' the demonstrators on 'with empty words of support is irresponsible,' CGTN concluded."[1]

In contrast, China claims to adhere to a policy of "non-interference" in the "internal affairs of other countries." "That, to anyone familiar with Myanmar's recent history, is pure balderdash," writes Lintner.[2] "No country has interfered in Myanmar politics and internal conflicts as much as China has." Since the early 1950s when 143 cadres from the Communist Party of Burma (CPB) trekked to China to request support for their rebellion against the government in Yangon, to the sanctuary provided to Myanmar Communists in Chengdu where they received political training, as well as refuge given to Kachin leaders, who were not communists, China has long been deeply engaged in Myanmar. After Ne Win's coup in 1962, China gave the CPB all-out support, allowing it to print propaganda materials in Beijing, and, after anti-Chinese riots in Yangon in 1967, China's support for rebel groups increased.

Since the 1980s, however, China has backed whoever was in power—mostly the generals—becoming the Tatmadaw's main supplier of arms and the regime's primary economic lifeline. Indeed, Lintner argues that "Myanmar's dependence on China became so overwhelming that the ruling military felt it had to open up to the West in order to counter what internal, classified documents seen by this writer described as a 'threat to the country's sovereignty and independence.'"[3]

That opening up, from 2011 until the Rohingya genocide of 2016 and 2017, opened a brief window in which Myanmar "went from being an international pariah to becoming the darling of the West." The Rohingya genocide, and then the 2021 coup, closed all that, and Myanmar returned to its pariah status. "China, not surprisingly, took full advantage of the situation, shielded the Myanmar military at the UN Security Council and stepped up its public relations campaigns inside the country," notes Lintner. "Myanmar may be the clearest—and most aggressive—example of Chinese interference in another country's 'internal affairs' . . . China's silence on the increasingly thuggish behaviour of the Myanmar military and police is viewed as complicity in human rights abuses."

On April 3, 2021, China's foreign minister, Wang Yi, issued a statement which, although it called for preventing further bloodshed, blocked United Nations Security Council involvement in Myanmar and, ironically, called on the international community to stop "foreign powers from exploiting chaos in Myanmar to advance their selfish interests."[4]

China's high-level participation in the Tatmadaw's Armed Forces Day celebration on March 27, 2021—less than two months after the coup—"sent a strong signal" of its "willingness to continue protecting the Tatmadaw," writes Tower, and an essay published by the Chinese think tank Taihe Institute illustrates Beijing's position: "The [Civil Disobedience Movement] is fully backed by Western NGOs . . . meanwhile the Committee Representing Pyidaungsu Hluttaw (CRPH) has popular support . . . but it is extremely weak compared to the military, it is an illegal association, and its leaders are wanted for sedition."[5]

Indeed, in April 2022—well over a year after the coup and following a year of brutal repression and conflict in Myanmar—China's foreign minister, Wang Yi, told the military regime's foreign minister, Wunna Maung Lwin, that China would back Myanmar's regime "no matter how the situation changes."[6] He said China "has always placed Myanmar in an important position in its neighbourly diplomacy" and wants to "deepen exchanges and co-operation."

That said, when it became apparent that Beijing's rapid rush to embrace the generals did not go down well with the people of Myanmar, and was fuelling anti-China sentiments in the country, the Chinese changed tack a little. Protests were held outside the Chinese Embassy in Yangon, there were calls for a boycott of Chinese goods, and then dozens of Chinese textile factories around Yangon were attacked and set ablaze, causing losses of around $37 million.[7]

Fuelled by suspicions that China was actually behind the coup—for which there is no evidence—and strong anger at China's readiness to accept the coup—which was more obvious—the fury at China was in danger of boiling over. As Tower writes, "China's non-interference policy has recognized the party with the gun, but the gun is the only tool that the Tatmadaw now has available to hold power and maintain rank and file discipline. By viewing Myanmar as a battleground for keeping Western values and influence out of its periphery, China is gradually losing any possible support from the Myanmar public and from the armed groups, including those dependent on China."[8]

According to Tower, Beijing "definitely knew" one year before the coup that Min Aung Hlaing might be plotting something. "In my many exchanges with Chinese scholars, before and after the coup, it was clear that they were in no doubt about his ambitions to be president, and as early as January 2020, Chinese academics were talking about how the United States would respond if he took power," Tower recalls. "I always told them that it was an impossibility that he could achieve that goal within the Myanmar political system. So it was clear that Min Aung Hlaing and the Tatmadaw were signalling their intentions. When he met Chinese Foreign Minister Wang Yi in Naypyidaw about a month before the coup, he clearly aired his so-called grievances to Wang Yi."

However, it is unlikely that the Tatmadaw would have gone into specific details. "I do not think there was a formal communication in that meeting to indicate that the coup is going to happen on a specific date," believes Tower, "but stakeholders in China would have had some careful intelligence and some fairly clear signals that something was pending."

Choudhury agrees. "I tend to believe that China knew about the coup. It is impossible that they did not. And I suspect that the leadership in Beijing were unsure whether or not it really wanted it," he told me in an online call from New Delhi. "Min Aung Hlaing has a habit of informing neighbours of decisions; he is the kind of guy who would let neighbours know, especially China and India."

That does not mean, however, that Beijing approved of the coup, according to Tower. "I do not buy the story that China gave a green light. The Chinese have had to bear much of the costs of the coup, including the shutdown in border trade for months which caused a ruckus—and some political chaos—in Yunnan," he told me. "It raised a lot of questions about whether Chinese investments in Myanmar that were agreed between Xi Jinping and President Win Myint are still viable." Win Myint is still president of the government-in-exile, the NUG, even though he is now in jail. "In addition, there is the question of instability on the border, with several incidents of gunfire coming across the border into Yunnan. That is horribly embarrassing for a so-called great power, to have a small state like Myanmar shooting bullets into Chinese houses across the border. Then there are the attacks on its gas pipeline, one of China's most important pieces of infrastructure in Myanmar. So there are a lot of ways in which China has lost as a result of the coup."

And yet, even though it may not have liked the coup, and the ensuing instability and conflict that it brought, China's focus was, in Tower's words, "to secure its interests." Its diplomatic support for the military regime came because, he believes, "it does not want Western stakeholders to get more deeply involved, and it knows that will be the outcome if the UN Security Council gets more deeply drawn into addressing the crisis. So that is something it sought to prevent." China, he adds, is not willing to "expend massive political capital in order to assist Min Aung Hlaing or any other party for that matter," but instead it will "strategically leverage" the situation in Myanmar to get "buy-in" for sealing a deal, especially with members of the Association of South-East Asian Nations (ASEAN).

That may be why China agreed to a compromise at the United Nations over the status of the current Myanmar Permanent Representative Kyaw Moe Tun, a career diplomat appointed by Aung San Suu Kyi's government who, in an electrifying speech to the General Assembly in New York, just over three weeks after the coup, declared his opposition to the coup, his support for the NLD, and his appeal for help to the world.

"We need further strongest possible action from the international community to immediately end the military coup, to stop oppressing the innocent people, to return the state power to the people and to restore the democracy," Kyaw Moe Tun told the UN on February 26, 2021. He was immediately sacked by the military regime as ambassador, but an effort was made to enable him to keep his credentials and continue to be Myanmar's accredited representative to the UN, in defiance of the junta. Later, in 2021, a debate began about whether his credentials could be renewed. In the end, a compromise was found—China agreed to a deal where he could continue, but would be lower key in his interventions, at least for a while.

"Beijing knows that the NLD is very popular in Myanmar. They witnessed the outcome of the elections. They saw the public response to China's early statements about the coup. They knew their statements had infuriated the public in Myanmar," observes Tower. "It caused a lot of anti-Chinese sentiment, and prompted attacks on Chinese infrastructure projects, assets, and Chinese nationals in Myanmar. China wanted to lessen the popular anger." In addition, the committee making the decision about Kyaw Moe Tun's credentials included other member states, including the United States. "If China wanted to make it an issue, it would have to expend a lot of political capital on something that would not bring it many benefits, and might harm its interests in the long term."

Choudhury agrees. "China realized after the coup that the military junta is increasingly isolated, both by the West but also even among ASEAN neighbours," he notes. "China understands that the junta is boxed in, which presents China with a great opportunity to exercise its leverage and secure as many concessions as possible, including completing BRI projects."

In terms of bilateral trade, China is by far Myanmar's largest trading partner, both for imports and exports. According to data from 2019, bilateral trade stands at about US$12 billion, representing a third of the total $36 billion worth of trade conducted. Since the 2021 coup, China's imports from Myanmar have only increased, rising in the first five months of 2021 to $3.38 billion, from $2.43 billion in 2020 and $2.5 billion in 2019, according to official Chinese data.[9]

China's most significant investments in Myanmar are in oil and gas, with a natural gas and oil pipeline which China constructed, running from Kyakhphyu in Rakhine State to Yunnan Province, at the cost of $4.5 billion. China has also constructed an oil terminal at Kyaukphyu, with an annual capacity of twenty-two million tons. The natural gas pipeline, according to Indian scholar Sumanth Samsani, "can account for 16.3% of China's total gas imports," while the oil pipeline provides for "4.3% of China's total oil imports."[10] In addition, China has "a complete domination" in the electricity sector in Myanmar, and has invested $2.57 billion in a liquified natural gas project at Mee Laung Gyaing, one of the largest electricity projects in the country.[11]

In total, China has invested over $21 billion of foreign direct investment in Myanmar, which makes up 28 percent of Myanmar's GDP. One of its most strategically important projects is its $1.3 billion deep-sea port at Kyaukphu, and the development of the area as a special economic zone. China has a fifty-year lease on the port, which could be extended, and, as Samsani notes, there are fears that the port could be used for military purposes, with an increasing number of People's Liberation Army naval vessels present in the Andaman Sea.[12]

In August 2021, China transferred $6 million for twenty-one projects in the Mekong-Lancang Cooperation framework and continued to expand the China-Myanmar Economic Corridor (CMEC) initiative as an umbrella for its infrastructure projects, and, although still in its early stages, the Chinese digital renminbi is being offered to Myanmar to help reduce its reliance on the U.S. dollar in trade and mitigate against the impact of international sanctions, potentially including restrictions of access to the SWIFT international payment messaging system.[13] Chinese companies are becoming more dominant in Myanmar's retail sector, too; notably, Alibaba's online platform, Shop.com.mm,[14] while Huawei is working with KBZPay to develop mobile payment platforms.

While Chinese businesses are prevalent throughout Myanmar, there is, as Sebastian Strangio notes in his book *In the Dragon's Shadow: Southeast Asia in the Chinese Century*, "a particular angst" about the alleged Chinese "takeover" of Myanmar's second-largest city and cultural and religious centre, Mandalay.[15]

Situated in the heart of Myanmar, about 450 kilometres—a day's drive—from the border with Yunnan, Mandalay today has a plethora of Chinese-owned hotels, restaurants, karaoke bars, and commercial property. "Shop signs abound in simplified Chinese, and the city's bustling jade market is frequented by snappily dressed Chinese dealers from the border town of Ruili," writes Strangio. While superficially thriving on trade with China, "Mandalay's importance to Burmese Buddhism, and its status as the one-time seat of Burma's last royal house, makes the arrival of Chinese immigrants and expats an especially sensitive issue." The potential for anti-Chinese sentiment to erupt to something much uglier is always just beneath the surface.

Few Chinese investment projects better illustrated the hostility with which they are regarded by many in Myanmar than the almost $1 billion Letpadaung copper mine, run by China's Wanbao Mining Company in partnership with the military's Myanmar Economic Holdings. In late 2012, demonstrators erupted at the mine near Monywa, in central Myanmar, and protesters gathered outside the Chinese Embassy in Yangon with banners that read: "This is our Country—Dracula China Get Out!"[16]

The project was suspended, and Aung San Suu Kyi chaired an investigation commission to assess the viability of the mine, its environmental impact, the grievances of the local community, and the police's brutal crackdown on protesters. But in the end, her report concluded that the mine should go ahead despite its unpopularity, and in government, she approved the resumption of operations at the mine.

China—together with Russia—is Myanmar's primary arms supplier. Between 2010 and 2019, Myanmar spent $1.3 billion in arms purchases from China, according to the database of the Stockholm International Peace Research Institute (SIPRI), a think tank providing data and analysis on armed conflict, military expenditure, and the arms trade. Between 2014 and 2019, China accounted for 50 percent of Myanmar's arms imports. The sales include, according to Samsani, "radars, warships, combat and trainer aircraft, armed drones, armoured vehicles, and missiles." Ninety percent of Myanmar's military transport is supplied by China.[17]

In his report to the United Nations Human Rights Council in February 2022, the UN Special Rapporteur on human rights in Myanmar, former United States congressman Tom Andrews, called out China for its arms sales to the regime.

"It should be incontrovertible that weapons used to kill civilians should no longer be transferred to Myanmar," said Andrews. "These transfers should shock the conscience. Stopping the junta's atrocity crimes begins with blocking their access to weapons. The more the world delays, the more innocent people, including children, will die in Myanmar . . . The people of Myanmar are imploring the UN to act. They deserve an up-or-down vote on a Security Council resolution that will stop the sale of weapons being used to kill them. Too many families are finding themselves in the crosshairs of weapons of war that member states are supplying. This must end."[18] Two permanent members of the UN Security Council with veto power, China and Russia, stand in the way of such a resolution, because they are the major providers of arms to the regime in Myanmar.

In addition to arms sales, China is helping Myanmar's regime intensify its surveillance systems in various ways. The Tatmadaw has reportedly acquired intelligence, surveillance, and reconnaissance (ISR) capabilities of Chinese-made unmanned aerial vehicles (UAVs) to monitor protests,[19] and the Chinese telecommunications giant Huawei is assisting the regime in Myanmar with the creation of so-called "Safe Cities." A system of 335 surveillance cameras with facial recognition technology produced by Huawei was introduced in Naypyidaw and went live in December 2020, at a cost of $2.9 million.[20] The cameras cover eight townships, and can scan vehicle number plates, according to the Naypidaw Safe City project's top advisor, Myint Swe. "Anyone with a criminal history entering Naypyidaw will be recognized. The system is able to detect and find that person," he said. "The other thing is being able to determine where a car has been just by looking at its plate number."

The same technology has been rolled out in Mandalay, Myanmar's second-largest city, which has embraced Huawei as a partner in the "Smart City Scheme," installing artificial intelligence and facial recognition equipment.[21]

Furthermore, Myanmar is turning to China for digital surveillance of the Internet. According to Lintner, at the end of 2021, it was revealed that Myanmar's regime had sought the support of Chinese Internet technicians to "develop blocking and monitoring capabilities," with the aim of intensifying Internet controls. "In essence, it means that the authorities would be able to block access to selected foreign websites and to slow down Internet traffic in and out of the country," notes Lintner. "China has every reason to watch not only Myanmar's dissidents but also the often unpredictable generals, whom they do not fully trust."[22]

Justice for Myanmar, a group that monitors the military's abuses, has revealed hundreds of pages of government documents, including official budgets, detailing the regime's plans for upgrading its surveillance technology. According to the *New York Times*, "the documents . . . catalogue tens of millions of dollars earmarked for technology that can mine phones and computers, as well as track people's live locations and listen in to their conversations."[23]

Myanmar pays an interest rate of 4.5 percent to China which, according to Samsani, "is the highest it pays to any lending country."[24] There are increasing fears that Myanmar may be unable to repay China for all the projects, resulting in growing debt dependency.

None of this is without its risks for Beijing. As Jason Tower and Priscilla Clapp, who served as the United States Chief of Mission in Myanmar from 1999 to 2002, write, "the coup and the country's chaotic state touch every aspect of Sino-Myanmar relations," presenting "mounting, unanticipated threats: an explosion of COVID-19 along the border; the risk that a multitude of new and resurgent conflicts could upend prospective projects; rising anti-Chinese sentiment among the majority of the population; and a surge in criminal activity aimed at China or organized by Chinese criminal networks."[25] Any of these developments, they argue, "would pose a challenge to Chinese investment" in Myanmar, but "together they virtually wipe out prospects for effective implementation of the two countries' overarching, grand project, the China-Myanmar Economic Corridor (CMEC)."

The role of criminal networks is significant in the China-Myanmar relationship, especially in three areas: gambling, human trafficking, and narcotics. This is most evident in China's support for the United Wa State Army (UWSA), a

20,000-strong armed organization that grew out of the now-defunct Communist Party of Burma and controls an area of northeastern Myanmar along China's border.

The UWSA is, as Bertil Lintner notes in his book *The Wa of Myanmar and China's Quest for Global Dominance*, "the largest and best-equipped military non-state actor in the Asia-Pacific region,"[26] its weaponry entirely supplied by China. This includes HN-5A Man-Portable Air Defence Systems (or MANPADS), heavy machine guns, automatic rifles, mortars, artillery, surface-to-surface free-flight missiles, armoured personnel carriers, other fighting vehicles, weaponized drones, and other "sophisticated military equipment." As Lintner observes, "this is not the kind of kit that falls off the back of a truck or could be supplied by some local PLA unit in Yunnan. The deliveries were almost certainly directed from the highest level in Beijing." In 2007, PLA advisors provided training to the UWSA in the use of 122 mm howitzers and 130 mm field guns in the Lu Fang mountain range west of Panghsang.[27]

"During the Maoist era, China wanted to export revolutionary communism. Today, their aim is economic expansion, and with it, political influence," writes Lintner.[28] "Incongruous as it may seem, it is in this grand scheme that the Wa, a little-known people living in the northeastern borderlands of Burma, have come to play a pivotal role," he continues.

The UWSA, "a trusted and useful geostrategic ally" for Beijing, provides China with a continued foothold in its backyard, leverage inside Myanmar, and a friendly de facto buffer state between China and central Myanmar. In UWSA-controlled territory, the Chinese renminbi, not the Myanmar kyat, is the only currency accepted, and cellphones and Internet connections come from Chinese servers. Chinese is more widely spoken than Burmese.[29]

Under a peace agreement with the Myanmar military, the UWSA retain control over their area and, according to Lintner, "engage in any kind of business to sustain themselves."[30] The major source of income in the remote mountains for many years was the cultivation of opium poppies, and so for more than two decades, the UWSA and its allies were Asia's main producers of opium and heroin. However, in recent years, their focus turned to production of metham-phetamines. This, notes Lintner, "led to the return of drug abuse all over China. Heroin became the drug of choice, and it was readily available not only in all Yunnanese towns such as Kunming, Ruili, and Baoshan but in all major Chinese cities."[31] Today, however, the Wa make more money from tin mining and investments in Myanmar, China, and Thailand, and are turning poppy fields into rubber plantations and tea gardens.[32]

Gambling and prostitution are also key parts of the Wa economy. Pangkham, the border town that is the UWSA's headquarters, is a thriving casino town, with hotels, karaoke bars, a bowling alley, and a twenty-four-hour casino catering predominantly to Chinese customers. Similarly, Mong La, a Myanmar border town under the control of Chinese-born Lin Mingxian and his National Democratic Alliance Army (NDAA), known as the Kokang—another splinter group from the CPB—is a notorious den of vice, to which Chinese gamblers flock. It is also, as Sebastian Strangio observes, "especially notorious for its brazen trade in endangered wildlife products, including pangolins, ivory, and tiger bone wine, all of which were sold openly at boutiques and eateries around the town. Many Chinese patrons crossed the border illegally."[33]

Chinese casino investors are now spreading throughout Myanmar, with plans underway by complex transnational networks to build three megacities in Karen State, Myanmar, as casino hubs. According to Tower and Clapp, some of these groups have "co-opted Chinese government institutions and agencies to present their activities as central to China's Belt and Road Initiative."[34]

The Wa are an almost perfect ally for China, Tower told me, because "there is no religious freedom in Wa State and the Wa could not care less about democracy or human rights," but in some aspects, the relationship is becoming an embarrassment for Xi Jinping. "On the economic front, there are growing tensions, because we see increasingly that Xi Jinping's regime is publicly embarrassed by the activities of Chinese officials working closely with transnational criminal actors," argues Tower. "The Wa are starting to feel pressure from China, and there is a Chinese campaign to call its nationals back from northern Myanmar. It is a very contentious issue."

Nevertheless, the UWSA seems ready to do China's bidding when it comes to some issues such as religion. In recent years, it appears Beijing's policies of repression are being applied across the border, particularly when it comes to the treatment of Christians.

On September 9, 2018, the UWSA—believed to be acting on China's orders—issued a statement instructing all of its military officers and administrators to "find out what the [Christian] missionaries are doing and what are their intentions."[35] It subsequently announced that all churches built after 1992 were constructed illegally and would be destroyed, and it prohibited the construction of new churches. Five churches were reportedly destroyed and fifty-two shut down. Videos emerged online which appear to show UWSA officials destroying crosses.[36] Pastors, priests, and nuns were arrested and expelled from the region, and religious schools shut down. According to Lintner, this crackdown is believed to have been prompted by "Chinese suspicion against possible influence from foreign missionaries, or that those missionaries would use the Wa Hills as a base for spreading their gospel to China."[37] It followed soon after that an ethnic Chinese pastor who is a permanent U.S. resident, John Cao, was arrested in China for illegal border crossings. He was sentenced to seven years in prison by a Chinese court.

China's tentacles spread to many of Myanmar's other ethnic groups as well, to varying degrees. The Kokang, who are ethnically Chinese and whose Myanmar National Democratic Alliance Army (MNDAA) founded by Peng Jiasheng has had a ceasefire with the Tatmadaw since soon after the MNDAA's formation in 1989, are aligned to China, as is Lin Mingxian's confusingly similarly named but distinct NDAA. To add to the complexity, Lin Mingxian is Peng Jiasheng's son-in-law, having married Peng's eldest daughter, Nang Yin.

Under the terms of their ceasefire with the Myanmar military regime, the Kokang were given autonomous control of their region, but in 2009, the regime began to pressure them to become part of Myanmar's newly formed border guard force. When they refused, the Tatmadaw launched a major offensive on the Kokang, causing the largest refugee outflow from northern Myanmar in many years. At least 30,000 people fled into China, prompting the Chinese authorities to open seven refugee camps and provide food, drinking water, shelter, and first aid. In the three-day conflict, the Myanmar military gained control of Kokang territory and forced rebel forces led by Peng Jiasheng to flee into China. A new leadership in the Kokang region was installed by the Myanmar junta, led by loyalist Bai Souqian. At least 500 people were reported killed.

China was unusually outspoken, summoning Myanmar's ambassador to Beijing to explain the regime's actions. While, as its record shows, Beijing does not normally care about human rights abuses or even humanitarian crises per se, it does care about instability on its borders, threats to its economic interests, and attacks on ethnic Chinese people. A Chinese Foreign Ministry spokesperson went as far as to say that China had "made representations about harm caused to the rights of Chinese citizens in Myanmar, restated China's position, demanded Myanmar rapidly investigate, punish law-breakers, and report the results to

China." The regime should "take prompt measures, earnestly protect the legal rights of Chinese citizens in Myanmar, and make sure similar incidents do not happen again."[38] The generals in Naypyidaw were rapped on the knuckles by the men in Zhongnanhai.

When it comes to Myanmar's other ethnic groups, which are not ethnically Chinese, Beijing's attitude is more complex. In November 2018, for example, I hosted a delegation of Kachin, Shan, and Ta'ang activists from northern Myanmar on an advocacy visit to London and Brussels, with the human rights organization I work with, Christian Solidarity Worldwide (CSW). They included the president of the Kachin Baptist Convention, a prominent and courageously outspoken pastor called Reverend Hkalam Samson; a representative of the three Catholic dioceses of northern Myanmar, Father Paul Lahpai Awng Dang; and activists representing women's organizations and civil society groups. The delegation met government ministers and senior Parliamentarians in London, and briefed European Union officials and members of the European Parliament in Brussels.

They deliberately chose to be public, give media interviews, and provide press releases about their visit—despite the risks involved, knowing that they were returning to Myanmar afterwards—because they wanted the world to pay attention.

"We are delighted to have this opportunity to speak to the international community on behalf of all the peoples of northern Burma/Myanmar, and to appeal for peace with justice," said Reverend Hkalam Samson. "We want to end decades of civil war. We want peace. But real peace can only happen through political dialogue towards a political solution, resulting in a federal democracy for Burma/Myanmar. We call on all sides, including Daw Aung San Suu Kyi and her government, the military, and all ethnic armed groups, to come to the table for a meaningful dialogue about the political future for our country. Within that, there must be justice and accountability, an end to impunity, the promotion of human rights and freedom of religion or belief and humanitarian access for all areas of conflict and displacement."[39]

Soon after the delegation's return home, the British and American ambassadors both visited Kachin State, and met Kachin political and religious leaders, including Reverend Samson and the president of the Kachin Democratic Party, Gumgrawng Awng Hkam. A week after that, the Chinese Embassy in Yangon sent an invitation to both men to meet with Chinese Ambassador Hong Liang.

Both Gumgrawng Awng Hkam and Reverend Samson welcomed the opportunity to discuss the situation in Kachin State with China's representative, but when they turned up, they were met with a reprimand and a threat. They were warned not to make close relationships with Western diplomats or they would "face serious consequences."[40]

They were also warned not to oppose China's Myitsone dam project in Kachin State, a $3.6 billion project located at the confluence of the Irrawaddy River, which President Thein Sein of Myanmar had suspended in 2011 in the face of popular protest against its environmental and social impacts. Ambassador Hong reportedly pressed the Kachin representatives to support restarting the dam project.

The Myitsone dam agreement had been signed in 2006, but as Strangio notes, "opposition was nearly universal."[41] The project, intended as the first of seven large dams along the Irrawaddy, was expected to displace more than 10,000 people and "flood an area larger than Singapore." Moreover, 90 percent of the electricity generated would be exported to Yunnan, so local people in Kachin State would not even benefit from it. It threatened to submerge a region of "profound cultural importance" to the Kachin people, the source of Kachin mythology, poetry, and songs. "It's like our lifeblood," said Mung Ra, a fifty-five-year-old Kachin Baptist pastor.[42]

The KIO/KIA—and the wider Kachin community—face a dilemma. They need to do business with China, to survive. And yet, so much of the business does not benefit ordinary local people. Instead, as Strangio notes, Beijing and Naypyididaw collude "to strip the region's rich natural resources and send them over the border." Kachin State is "like an egg . . . inside the liquid is all gone, drained by China," said Steven Naw Awng of the Kachin Development Networking Group (KDNG) in Myitkyina. "We have no benefits, and all the resources are gone."[43] Other Kachins have told me that it feels as though their land is being "raped" by China.

Moreover, the Kachins' fight for democracy and human rights puts them at odds with the Chinese regime. It is a tightrope to navigate, but it is one illustration of the dangers of becoming too dependent on an unscrupulous regime in Beijing that will then hold you to ransom.

For young women in northern Myanmar, one danger in China looms larger than all others: the risk of being trafficked and sold into slavery, into prostitution, or as a wife to a Chinese man. This particularly grotesque violation is not perpetrated directly by either of the two countries' regimes, but it is a consequence of Myanmar's economic collapse at the hands of a military dictatorship mismanaging the economy and, conversely, China's economic boom. When I was first in Kachin State in 2006, I was told that women disappear "almost every day." Since then, hundreds of cases have been documented, involving women mostly between the ages of fifteen and thirty.

Typically, women are lured with the promise of a better job in China, where wages are higher than salaries in Myanmar. But once in China, they are often taken thousands of miles, as far north as Beijing, Hunan, Shandong, and even Manchuria—to be sold into prostitution or traded as "wives" to Chinese men. Often, they are sold on by their buyers multiple times.

Those who are sold into the sex trade are often subjected to violent exploitation and grotesque treatment. I was told of a woman who had been gang-raped by ten men, before her "owner" decided he did not like her and ordered her to repay the money he had paid. When she informed him that she was unable to refund the money without a job, he arranged a job for her. Over the course of twenty-eight days, she was gang-raped every night. She eventually escaped but was chased by her captors with dogs. She wandered through the forests for five days without food or water, before reaching a town. Eventually, she found the police station and was rescued and returned to Myanmar.

In our call online from Bangkok, Jason Tower told me that he recalled seeing advertisements in Chinese newspapers for "sale of brides from Myanmar." Some of these were very explicit. "They specified the cost of a wife in a particular city in Yunnan, in renminbi. They said if you want a Myanmar wife, this is what it costs." But, he emphasized, this is not the policy of the Chinese government—though it may well be a consequence of China's decades-long one-child policy, which Xi Jinping ended in 2016.

While most trafficking cases involve women, in some instances, children have been abducted and trafficked, too. In 2008, a five-year-old boy from Laiza disappeared, and in Myitkyina, a baby was abducted and sold. In 2009, an eleven-year-old boy was taken to Yinjiang, in Yunnan Province, three hours from the border, where interested purchasers came to examine him. They found he was taller than they required, and so he was left, unsold, until eventually a woman helped him return to Myanmar.

So in its backyard, China has a neighbour that is in continued civil war after seventy-five years of conflict; has a humanitarian crisis caused by the combined effects of war, displacement, poverty, economic collapse, a coup, and COVID-19; and has challenges of narcotics trafficking, people trafficking, sexual slavery, and gambling—all of which spill over or impact its borders. What signals are sent diplomatically to other countries with a stake in the region by China's support for the military dictatorship?

In Choudhury's view, China's approach to Myanmar "is a critical factor" in the India-China relationship. "China is the dominant lens through which India views Myanmar. A lot of scholars tell the Indian government it cannot engage more broadly with Myanmar's democracy movement because that would alienate the Myanmar military, and drive the junta deeper into China's hands," he said. "India has specific interests, especially with regard to its own insurgent groups on the Myanmar border. So the dominant thinking in New Delhi is that only the Myanmar military has the strategic capability to secure that border," he explained.

But Choudhury's own view is different and more nuanced. He cites the presence of numerous ethnic armed organizations along the border and argues that the Myanmar military is allowing such instability "right under our noses." Far from being the solution, Choudhury believes the Myanmar military is "inimical to Indian security interests." For that reason, India should "diversify" its relationships, in order to strengthen its ability to "leverage influence." With China's new deep-sea port in Kyaukphyu, India needs to develop an alternative.

From a Western perspective, Andrew Heyn, former British ambassador to Myanmar from 2009 until 2013—who later served as consul-general in Hong Kong from 2016 until 2020—told me that when he arrived in Yangon he assumed that "China had access that we did not have." Until Thein Sein's reform era began in 2011, Western countries had little access to the military junta. "The agriculture minister would be rolled out to see us and he would deliver great long monologues for, literally, hours on end," Heyn recalls, "whereas the Chinese would have proper discussions, with minutes taken."

However, the dynamic in the relationship with China began to shift when Thein Sein suspended the Myitsone dam project. "I had assumed that the Chinese ambassador had been told in advance, but it seemed he had not—or if he had, it was an hour before the public announcement. That gave a sense of how the relationship was changing."

When Aung San Suu Kyi first came back into the political scene, Heyn believes "China would have been pretty spooked by the fact that someone who was so popular in the West, with such good links to the West, was poised to become the de facto head of government." In the end, however, as already noted, she developed a good relationship with Beijing. "It worked out better for both parties than they had expected. By 2020, China had a relationship with Daw Suu that was pretty functional."

Derek Mitchell, who served as United States ambassador to Myanmar from 2012 to 2016, believes the relationship between China and Myanmar is "a complicated story." Despite relying on China for diplomatic and political protection at the United Nations, an economic lifeline, and arms sales, the Tatmadaw "dislikes and distrusts China." That desire not to be overly dependent on China to the extent of becoming a satellite state of Beijing was one of the most significant incentives behind Thein Sein's reforms.

"From 2012 until about 2017, China was worried. China felt that it was losing the privileged position it had had, the free rein to exploit Myanmar, to build road and rail networks, oil and gas pipelines, to import jade and every possible mineral from the resource-rich north and west of Myanmar," Mitchell recalled. "Xi Jinping reportedly asked, 'Who lost Myanmar?'"

Aung San Suu Kyi, according to Mitchell, was initially "quite wary about China." In 2014, before she came into government, she was invited by the Chinese Communist Party to visit Beijing. The Chinese Communist Party wanted to develop a "party to party" relationship with the NLD, but she did not want that. "She was leery about it," said Mitchell. "But she was also a pragmatist. She read Kissinger's *On China*, which I had given her." And from 2017 until 2020, as the West's engagement with Myanmar receded in the wake of the Rohingya genocide, she turned increasingly to China. For Beijing, that period was "the best of all worlds—their interests were protected and the country appeared to have greater stability."

Mitchell coincided with three different Chinese ambassadors to Myanmar, and had different experiences which each of them, reflecting the changing dynamics in China's relations with Myanmar and the West.

"The first was Li Junhua, who had previously served in China's permanent mission to the UN for many years in different posts. He left soon after I arrived. Then there was Yang Houlan, who seemed scared to talk with me. When I first called on him, I suggested we explore whether there were ways we could work together to help Myanmar and keep U.S.-China tensions out of the picture," Mitchell recalled. "I reminded him that the U.S. had just dropped sanctions and were pursuing engagement, so I wanted to see if together we could help

Myanmar towards peace. He looked terrified and walked out." The third, Hong Liang, with whom Mitchell overlapped for a year, was "the most interesting." Mitchell describes him as "an early indication of wolf warrior diplomacy." Just as he had reprimanded Kachin political and religious leaders for talking with Western diplomats, Hong warned Mitchell, "Do not go to Kachin State or eastern Shan State. Respect our interests."

Heyn recalls he received similar treatment. "It was very difficult to get a sense of what the Chinese were up to," he told me. "Whereas I could talk to my American or Singaporean opposite numbers, or my Japanese opposite number openly about, for example, the peace process, I could never really have such a conversation with the Chinese ambassador. They had feet in several camps. Apart from a desire for stability, and protecting their interests, they did not have a consistent approach. They tried to have it all ways."

Most analysts do not believe China was behind the 2021 coup in Myanmar, nor even gave it the green light. Heyn believes China is "very uneasy about the coup," and Lucas Myers, writing in *Foreign Policy*, agrees. "The chaos was naturally unwelcome in Beijing, as it both threatened its long-term interests in Myanmar and harbingered a possible total meltdown and collapse that could spill over into China itself," Myers writes.

However, Beijing's calculation is always to deal with whoever is in power. "Beijing could not sit idly by and allow its interests to be harmed, so it seemingly sided with the apparent winner: the Tatmadaw," Myers concludes. "This was unlikely to have been a prearranged deal . . . Although the military did telegraph its actions beforehand, including to Chinese Foreign Minister Wang Yi, the Tatmadaw did not need Beijing's approval and is unlikely to have warned it in advance because the military remains quite wary of China . . . Instead, Beijing simply assessed that Myanmar's military is the likeliest victor and adjusted accordingly . . . China has always played this double game in Myanmar."[44]

Anna Tan, a doctoral student at the Lau China Institute at King's College London, concludes in her paper, "China and the Myanmar dilemma," that the Chinese Communist Party is "a self-interested institution" and "does not intervene in cases where it believes there are no direct risks to its domestic legitimacy, regime survival, or regional or perhaps even global influence."[45]

However, Tan argues, this does not mean that its foreign policy decisions, made out of self-interest, are always rational or far-sighted. "In the pursuit of self-interest, irrational decisions can be made and the CCP's current behaviour towards Myanmar seems to be one such occasion." The turmoil in Myanmar, she writes, "bears immense regional and, to some extent, domestic socioeconomic implications" for China. The dramatic economic contraction in Myanmar, mass poverty, and conflict are creating a failed state in Southeast Asia. "The biggest losers from this will be Myanmar's largest importers, with China topping the list," concludes Tan.

Ultimately, Beijing is complicit with some of the gravest categories of atrocity crime under international law being perpetrated in Myanmar.

By providing successive military regimes with protection at the UN, by pursuing trade and investment that sustain the regime in power, and by providing arms used to kill civilians, China is far from an innocent bystander in one of the world's longest, most brutal, and most forgotten tragedies.

As Lintner notes, without all the assistance and trade from China, "the Burmese junta would probably not have survived."[46] And, as Anders Corr argues, the regime Myanmar—along with most other genocidal regimes around the world—has "top cover from Beijing," which "supports the 'right' of other regimes to similarly repress diversity in their populations. The CCP thus exports its acceptance of genocide to the dictatorships over which it has influence."[47]

In 1993, the Chinese authorities constructed a peculiar monument in Jiegao, just across the border from Muse in Myanmar's Shan State, the main gateway for trade between the two countries. According to Strangio, "the monument depicted four Chinese figures wheeling a large circular object, eyes narrowed and chiselled faces pointed determinedly to the south. At the base of the monument were six Chinese characters that read, 'Unity, Development, Forge Ahead!'"[48] This, he explains, "symbolized" China's ambitions in Myanmar. Or, as Lintner describes, it meant "Southeast Asia here we come!"[49]

Why should any of this matter? For me, there are two reasons: personal and political.

On a personal level, China and Myanmar are the two countries into which I have invested the vast majority of my energies and emotions for much of my adult life. It was in China that I began my love of Asia, as described in the first chapter. And it has been in Myanmar where, for the past twenty years or more, I have focused much of my advocacy work, for a beautiful, benighted, diverse country that has suffered so much for too long and deserves better. From my days teaching English in Qingdao to my baptism into the Catholic Church in St. Mary's Cathedral, Yangon, by Myanmar's Cardinal Charles Maung Bo (also my friend and mentor), on Palm Sunday 2013, these two countries have been intertwined at a deeply personal level in my life. I have travelled to both countries more than fifty times each. Sadly, I have also been barred from both countries. I was deported from Myanmar not once but twice, in 2011 and again in 2012, although I made it back in between and several subsequent visits. It will be a long time before I can visit again, as Min Aung Hlaing's junta is very unlikely to grant me a visa, and I can no longer enter China in order to sneak across the Yunnan border. In 2017, as already mentioned, I was denied entry to Hong Kong, and in 2022, threatened under Hong Kong's National Security Law, so I have to assume I am banned from China. That strange symbiosis of the two countries I love deeply but can no longer visit makes them matter to me all the more.

And on a political level, what China does in Myanmar should matter to the rest of the world. If China's *modus operandi*—of complicity with atrocity crimes, aggressive pursuit of narrow self-interest with no regard to ethics or humanitarian consequences, of propping up an illegal and brutal regime which even it does not like and whose own leaders distrust Beijing, for purely utilitarian purposes—is allowed to prevail, it will change the entire world order and lead to more despots challenging or overthrowing fragile democracies. It will result in the law of the jungle replacing the international rules-based order and provide a green light that will embolden dictators everywhere, facilitating not only repression but the trafficking of narcotics and of people into slavery and prostitution. That, surely, is a reason to take what China is doing in Myanmar seriously and work out our response.

CHAPTER 11

TOTALITARIANS TOGETHER

HOW CHINA PROPS UP
NORTH KOREA

At the end of a week in China's northeastern coastal province of Liaoning, along the border with North Korea, we were enjoying our last meal together in a small inland town when we received word that the Chinese police were looking for us. Within minutes, we packed up, and, with a trusted driver who knew the roads well, we headed out of town.

The driver said we should not go to Shenyang—where we needed to be the next day to fly out—because there were checkpoints along the way. Instead, we drove to Dandong, on the North Korean border, where we had come from a few days previously. The friend I was travelling with, who had years of experience working in China with North Korean refugees, advised that we should not check into a hotel in Dandong, because we would be required to show our passports and, if the police were seriously searching for us, that could expose us. So, instead, we slept that night on the floor of a South Korean missionary couple's home. The next day, we split up—my friend returned to Seoul by ship, while I took a bus to Shenyang and flew out safely on my scheduled flight.

We learned subsequently of the reason the Chinese police were hunting us. Earlier that same day, we had stopped off at an old church building, which was an official Three-Self Patriotic Movement (TSPM) church. My friend wanted to show me the historic building, and, in particular, its antiquated heating system, but as we entered the church, the pastor—who was more like a Communist Party cadre—accosted us. Peppering us with questions about our purpose in being there, he clearly doubted our explanation that we were tourists interested in the church's old heating system. Even my friend's explanation that he and his wife live in Seoul, and we had come to this region of China because of the ethnic Korean Chinese population in the area, failed to satisfy. The pastor's suspicions did not dissipate after we left, and he telephoned the police to report on the presence of two Westerners who were clearly conducting secret Bible study meetings with the illegal, unregistered house churches in the area—an allegation that was entirely false, but, on balance, less serious than what we were actually doing.

In reality, we had spent the previous week visiting North Korean escapees in northern China. In particular, we had been deep into rural villages to meet children of North Korean women who had been trafficked into China. These children were essentially orphans, because their mothers either had been forcibly repatriated back to North Korea or had fled their abusive Chinese husbands who had bought them from brokers. These children, whose care was funded by the humanitarian charity known as HHKatakombs, which my companions ran, were living with aged grandmothers—usually the mothers of the Chinese biological fathers—who received a monthly stipend for the children's school fees and clothing.

If at any point we had been caught, we might have had a short time in a Chinese prison and then been deported, but the lives of the North Koreans would have been seriously endangered. They could have been rounded up, arrested, and forcibly repatriated to North Korea, where they would face certain torture and possible execution. We had taken care throughout the visit to be as low key, quiet, and unobtrusive as possible, and our efforts paid off. Instead of arresting North Koreans, the Chinese police merely interrogated local house church Christians about our presence. As one of our missionary partners told us, they would feel a bit of heat for a few days, but then it would blow over.

A few days before our dramatic escape from the Chinese police, I had sat on a boat on the Yalu River in Dandong and peered across the border into North Korea. The grey, bleak poverty of Sinuiju, the North Korean city on one side of the river, sat in stark contrast to the bright lights and tower blocks of Dandong. In Sinuiju, all I could see from the boat was propaganda banners praising Kim Jong-un and the regime in Pyongyang. In Dandong, there were advertising billboards promoting cosmetics, jewellery, cars, and other luxury goods. Both countries were ruled by repressive regimes with no regard whatsoever for human rights, but in one, the Orwellian nature of the dictatorship was visible for all to see, while in the other, it was hidden by the symbols of mammon.

Three years earlier, in 2010, I had travelled to Pyongyang itself, with two British Parliamentarians, Lord Alton and Baroness Cox, with the explicit purpose of trying to talk to the world's most closed, most repressive regime. The visit was part of a process which Lord Alton and Baroness Cox had begun in 2003 when they made their first visit to the "hermit kingdom." For just under a decade, they found that there were people at middle-ranking and some senior levels in the regime who clearly wanted a point of contact in the free world.

No Parliamentarian in the world is more dedicated to human rights than Lord Alton and Baroness Cox, and they did not shy away from confronting the regime with the truth about its own appalling human rights record—which a United Nations Commission of Inquiry found in 2014 to amount to "crimes against humanity." Indeed, their original visit had come about as a result of a debate in the House of Lords tabled by Lord Alton on March 13, 2003, just after the North Koreans had reopened their nuclear reactor at Yongbyon, in which he detailed the human rights atrocities committed by the regime in Pyongyang, inspired to do so by a North Korean Christian he had met a few months earlier.[1] "The threat to international security posed by North Korea may best be considered by way of pernicious actions against its own citizens," Lord Alton said. "North Korea's Stalinist dictatorship has treated its own people with unbelievable brutality and viciousness. The people are starving, the hospitals are without medicine. and a whole generation has grown up stunted and mentally retarded because of malnutrition."

The North Korean ambassador to London had responded with fury, complaining to Lord Alton and demanding a meeting. Lord Alton responded by challenging him on the fact that the regime does not allow foreign critics to visit, except in very tightly controlled circumstances. "If we invited you, would you come?" the ambassador retorted. Lord Alton said he would, on three conditions: that he and any colleagues that came with him pay their own way; that the regime should not use it for propaganda purposes; and that they be free to raise human rights concerns. Initially, the last request was impossible for the ambassador to agree to, but after consulting Pyongyang, he told Lord Alton he had an "open invitation." Lord Alton and Baroness Cox took him up on the offer a few months later, and again in 2009. The visit I joined was their third.

When I travelled with them in 2010, we flew to Beijing and on to Pyongyang. Our visit came at a historic time. A week earlier, military parades marched through Pyongyang celebrating the sixty-fifth anniversary of the founding of the Workers' Party of Korea, and the world's media had unprecedented access. Earlier in October, Kim Jong-il's son, Kim Jong-un, was made a four-star general and vice chairman of the Party's Central Military Commission at the age of twenty-seven, a clear sign that he is being prepared as the successor, to perpetuate the world's only dynastic dictatorship.

That year also marked some important anniversaries: the tenth anniversary of diplomatic relations between the United Kingdom and North Korea, and the sixtieth anniversary of the outbreak of the Korean War—in which three million Koreans died, along with thousands of American, Chinese, and other nations' troops. Over 1,000 British soldiers were killed in the Korean War, more than those killed in Iraq, Afghanistan, and the Falklands combined.

We went to North Korea at a time when tensions on the peninsula were at their highest for many years. Earlier that year, the sinking of the South Korean naval vessel the *Cheonan* led to the loss of forty-six lives. As Harvard University scholar Graham Allison observed in his book *Destined for War: Can America and China Escape Thucydides's Trap?*, that incident brought the United States and China as close as they had been for many years to a potential confrontation.

"China supported North Korea's denial of involvement. Seoul, meanwhile, insisted that Pyongyang be held accountable. Ultimately, the two Koreas and their allies stepped back from the brink," writes Allen. "But with a new set of background conditions and accelerants today, it is not clear that it would be so easy to avoid war, especially if the third parties involved were less inured to the sort of slow, grinding tensions that the Korean Peninsula has endured for decades."[2] Indeed, within forty-eight hours of our departure, North Korean soldiers opened fire across the border at the 38th parallel, the first skirmish since 2006.

Five days in North Korea was a surreal experience. At times, I felt I had walked straight into the pages of George Orwell's *1984*. Everywhere were pictures of Kim Il-sung and Kim Jong-il staring down at you, like Big Brother. And, of course, everything is thanks to either the "Great Leader" or the "Dear Leader." When film footage of father and son appeared on a big screen at a concert, followed by footage of tanks and missiles firing, we sat on our hands and refused to clap, surrounded by rows of applauding North Korean soldiers. Our minder noticed and asked why we had not joined in the applause. "Because," Lord Alton replied, "we do not think it is very nice to fire missiles off in the middle of a concert—or at any other time for that matter."

Lord Alton and Baroness Cox took every opportunity to make courteous, but firm, subtle but nevertheless clear challenges to the regime's propaganda. One day, we were taken on a tour of North Korea's "Supreme Court." Observing the noticeably uncomfortable seating arrangement for defendants, Baroness Cox asked the lawyer showing us around what that symbolized about the principle "which we have in our country" of "innocent until proven guilty." With full marks for honesty, the lawyer responded: "Oh no, in our country, when a person comes to court we do not believe they are innocent." Lord Alton then ratcheted up the conversation by raising the prison camps, the existence of which our lawyer guide denied. So we named some, notably Yodok.

"No, no, I have been to Yodok," said our lawyer guide. "There's no prison camp. It is just a village."

We pressed him, and he became irritable.

"Who told you about these 'prison camps'? Was it the South Koreans? Was it the Americans?" he demanded.

We explained that no, it was neither, but we had learned in detail about the camps from dozens of escapees whom we had met. They were also detailed in numerous human rights reports from the United Nations, Amnesty International, and Human Rights Watch, copies of which we had presented to our North Korean interlocuters in previous days.

"These people you speak of, they are liars," the lawyer said angrily. "They are criminals who have escaped from the prison camps"—which seconds earlier he claimed did not exist.

Lord Alton then raised the specific case of Shin Dong-hyuk, whom he and I both know well, who had been born in a prison camp and whose story is told in his book written with Blaine Harden, *Escape from Camp 14*.

"How can somebody be *born a* criminal?" Lord Alton asked.

The atmosphere had risen to one of the greatest moments of tension of the whole visit. We all took a deep breath. A silence ensued for what seemed like an eternity but was probably only a few seconds. None of us were quite sure what would happen next.

The lawyer broke the silence.

"Shall we continue with our tour?" he said.

Who knows what was really going through that lawyer's mind, but of one thing I am fairly certain: it was probably the only time in his life that the propaganda he had been raised on and taught to disseminate was challenged, overtly, face to face, with facts and courtesy. For that alone, the visit was worthwhile, in my view, because while we may never know the outcome, at least we gave him something to ponder in the silence of his mind, heart, and soul. Sowing small seeds of doubt that may result in questioning the whole system is often the way to bring about change. Do not underestimate the moral power of standing face to face with another man, looking him straight in the eye, and telling him you know his government is committing these violations. At least then, he knows you know and maybe, just maybe, he is given some pause for thought. I do not claim that our visit achieved that, but it was better to have tried than not.

On that visit, we also brought gifts for all our North Korean hosts. But gifts of a particular kind. Gifts designed not to flatter but to challenge. We handed out copies of Karl Popper's *The Open Society and Its Enemies*, British foreign secretary William Hague's biography of the anti-slavery campaigner William Wilberforce, and the Bible in Korean. We left our hosts in Pyongyang with plenty to think about and plenty to read.

But this book is about China, and so the question we must now turn to is what is China's relationship with the regime in North Korea?

"North Korea does not have many friends in the world. Certainly, China is one of the few, and it is its patron," argues Jung-Hoon Lee, who served as South Korea's ambassador for human rights and its inaugural ambassador for North Korean human rights. "Without China's support, the regime in North Korea would not be able to sustain itself for more than half a year. If you look at the magnitude of trade that North Korea conducts with the outside world, in terms of food imports, energy imports, and the meagre exports North Korea makes in terms of coal, iron, steel, and minerals, it is all China, and all financial transactions are conducted directly or indirectly through China. Without China, you would have either a better behaved North Korea or a collapsed North Korea. But as long as China continues its current approach, it is very difficult to see the end of the Kim regime, because China is keeping it alive."

Both Jieun Baek, a fellow at the Belfer Center at the Harvard Kennedy School and author of *North Korea's Hidden Revolution: How the Information Underground Is Transforming a Closed Society*, and Lina Yoon, Human Rights Watch's North Korea researcher, agree. They both told me that North Korea is "totally dependent on China." During the era of the Soviet Union, North Korea was able to "play

China and Russia off each other," said Baek, but since the collapse of the Soviet Union, the lifeline Pyongyang received from Moscow virtually "dried up," making it dependent on China both for political support and for basic necessities—"fuel, oil, and food aid" in particular.

Yoon goes further, claiming that between 70 and 90 percent of products sold in the markets in North Korea come from China, and 80 percent of those come from "informal trade" that avoids the customs checkpoints. "Ordinary North Koreans are totally dependent on China for everything to supply their daily needs, from cooking oil, spices, monosodium glutamate (MSG), sugar, noodles, sausages, clothes, medicine to batteries, pesticides, soap, toothpaste, pens, paper, and toilet paper," said Yoon. "China looks the other way on informal trade, because it is well aware that North Korea cannot support its people."

Bilateral trade between China and North Korea reportedly increased tenfold between 2000 and 2015, peaking in 2014 at $6.86 billion.[3] Furthermore, China is increasingly flouting international sanctions against North Korea, allowing North Korean vessels, for example, to ship coal through China's Ningbo-Zhousan area.[4] China also hosts at least 20,000 North Korean labourers, who send their earnings home, and has breached sanctions on a range of goods, including seafood and machinery.[5] China's technology giant Huawei and Chinese State-owned enterprise Panda International Information Technology are apparently secretly building North Korea's wireless network.[6]

In addition, North Korean authorities have reportedly been receiving training from China's public security apparatus. The Chinese Ministry of Public Security has shared its expertise on fighting "crime" with Pyongyang's Ministry of Social Security.[7] The transfer of surveillance technology from China to North Korea is also clearly underway.

On a more macro political level, China gives the regime in Pyongyang diplomatic protection. "If it put its mind to it, if it had the political will, China is the one country that could really influence North Korea, but it does not want to do so because it is a pawn in the larger picture of China's grand strategy in its hegemonic battle with the United States," said Ambassador Lee. North Korea plays a very useful role for Beijing, so why would China discard it?

David Slinn, who was the United Kingdom's first ambassador in Pyongyang from 2002 to 2006, agrees. "China has absolutely no interest in North Korea collapsing in its role as a very useful buffer state between the Chinese border and the Americans in South Korea. But China has had to operationalize that, to help North Korea survive," he told me in an online call from his home in Ottawa. In addition to trade, he adds, "I do not think there is much doubt that China is supplying military and security-related equipment to help ensure the regime's survival. The North Korean regime would probably have collapsed if it had not been for China's life support."

Slinn recalls that during his time in Pyongyang, "all the stuff I saw in shops was Chinese, all the foodstuffs, all the finished goods, all the consumer goods." But, in addition, he said, "China was outsourcing textile production to North Korea, and it had got its feet under the table in terms of securing natural resources in North Korea."

A British businessman once managed to visit a North Korean coal mine, looking to export equipment. According to Slinn, "he actually went down the mine, which I thought was very brave, and the North Koreans put on a good show for him. But he came back and said, 'Forget it, the Chinese have got it.' There were Chinese people there looking at these white visitors suspiciously and threateningly. China is using North Korea for its benefit."

Suzanne Scholte, who runs the North Korea Freedom Coalition based in Washington, D.C., describes the Chinese Communist Party regime as "totally complicit" in North Korea's repression. "In 2014, a United Nations Commission of Inquiry found North Korea was committing unspeakable atrocities, crimes against humanity. China is a co-conspirator in those crimes against humanity."

However, the relationship is certainly not one of equals, and nor is it without its tensions. "It is a close relationship, but also a subservient relationship," Ambassador Lee believes. Sheena Chestnut Greitens, associate professor at the Lyndon B. Johnson School of Public Affairs at the University of Texas at Austin, agrees. "It is one of the only formal alliances that China has, and that geopolitical bond is very long-lasting. But there is often friction and not always interpersonal goodwill," she told me.

Sokeel Park, South Korea country director of the human rights group Liberty in North Korea (LiNK), believes the relationship is "worse than most people would often assume" and that it is "much more complicated" than the "simplistic top-line commentary of South Korea and the United States versus North Korea and China." For example, he points out, the South Korean president meets with the Chinese president much more often than North Korea's leader, and North Korea was furious when China and South Korea normalized relations in 1992. It also should not be forgotten that China signed up to the United Nations

Security Council resolutions imposing sanctions on North Korea in response to Pyongyang's nuclear programme. "That does not seem like a healthy alliance or friendly relations, in terms of sentiment and levels of trust," Park argues.

"Of course, there is the language of friendly relations between the Korean Workers' Party and the Chinese Communist Party, and the fact that the border with China is the only meaningful, real border, because the South Korean border is the most heavily fortified and the Russian border is not very relevant, and it is true that North Korea has 100 percent reliance on China for trade and business. China is the bridgehead, or the portal, to the rest of the world," Park acknowledged. "But, ultimately, China is signing off on sanctions and refusing North Korea's most important security goals—the nuclear programme."

Park also believes the level of the relationship depends where you are in China. "If you are in Beijing, North Korea is one of fourteen neighbouring countries. But if you are in Dandong, North Korea is the outside world, the main trading partner, where there is significant economic activity," he argues. "Senior officials in the Chinese provinces bordering North Korea want to be the main gateway to North Korea."

In 2011, Slinn returned to North Korea for a month, five years after leaving his posting in Pyongyang, and found that people he talked to were "quite open about their resentment of China." On one road journey, he recalled, his vehicle happened to drive behind a large consignment of Chinese trucks provided to North Korea. "One person I talked to was quite uncharacteristically vehement in his criticism of China," Slinn recounts. "But, actually, he was more critical of his own government for agreeing to the terms that China was imposing. His line was 'we get a few trucks, they get all our minerals.' I heard that from a couple of other people, too. There was a sense of China using North Korea for its own benefit. You could almost call it the rape of the North Korean natural resources." Not dissimilar to the sentiment felt in Myanmar, the other neighbouring brutal but fragile dictatorship on China's doorstep which Beijing both props up and exploits.

After China's economic reform programme begun under Deng Xiaoping, there was an attempt by Beijing to persuade Kim Jong-il to follow the same course economically. "The Chinese took Kim Jong-il to several of their special economic zones—Shenzhen, for example—and there was quite a bit of evidence that China got excited at the prospect of North Korea going down that road," recalls Slinn. "But Kim Jong-il was very cautious on a number of levels, and that was never going to happen. The North Koreans felt they had to be careful about reform. 'Look at what happened to that nice man, Mr. Gorbachev,' was their attitude. And they were not certain what Beijing was up to." That said, he adds, "Kim Jong-il was never going to cause Beijing any problems on the political scene. So China was fairly comfortable with where North Korea was during the Kim Jong-il era."

According to Jieun Baek, there are real racist strains in the relationship, both ways. "The North Koreans are taught that they are the 'cleanest race,' and that they must protect the 'purity of their bloodline,'" she notes. "They are taught formally and socially to see the Han Chinese as 'inferior.'" That is why, she adds, North Korea forces North Korean women returning from China impregnated by Chinese men to have abortions, in order to "eliminate half-Chinese babies." Women who engage with non–North Korean men are punished. "There are a lot of social norms around the idea that North Korea is superior. Reading domestic propaganda, it is clear that North Korea does not want to be too dependent on China, and that they want to graduate to a position where they are recognized as an equal player."

At the same time, Han Chinese chauvinism is also at play. "A lot of Chinese people—in the government and among ordinary civilians—regard North Koreans as inferior, mired in poverty, in a pitiful situation," observes Baek. At the same time, Chinese society has positive views of South Korea, leading people to imitate South Korean cosmetics and fashion trends, which does not go down well in Pyongyang.

Tim Peters, an American humanitarian worker and missionary who first moved to South Korea in 1975, has been helping North Koreans since the famine and economic crisis in North Korea—known as the "Arduous March"—from 1994 to 1998. He founded Helping Hands Korea in 1996 and is one of the key activists in the "underground railroad" helping North Korean escapees out of the country, through China, Southeast Asia, and to safety in South Korea. He believes China regards North Korea as "a rump state connected to China by hundreds of miles of border" and China has "very cleverly taken hold of the key levers on the regime." He confirms the view of others, that North Korea is "economically, militarily, and diplomatically very dependent on China" and observes that "there is relatively little that North Korea can do without the tacit approval of Beijing."

One of the most significant areas of complicity by Beijing in North Korea's human rights violations is its policy of forcible repatriation of North Korean escapees, in total violation of international humanitarian norms and the principle of *non-refoulement*. Since 1996, Peters explained, "one constant has been China's adamant policy of treating all North Korean refugees as illegal economic migrants, thus refusing access to the office of the United Nations High Commissioner for Refugees (UNHCR) and forcibly repatriating North Koreans who are caught." Without exception, Scholte points out, "every single refugee who is repatriated to North Korea is imprisoned, tortured, and some are executed. According to the North Korean regime, crossing the border illegally is treason, a crime punishable by death."

North Koreans first started escaping into China in large numbers during the famine. "The early border crossers were shocked to see China's thriving economy, with electricity. They thought it was 'paradise,'" notes Scholte. "I once met a doctor who had escaped from Pyongyang into China, and he told me he was astonished to find a bowl of food for dogs outside a farmhouse in China. He said that 'dogs in China eat better than doctors in Pyongyang.'"

After the famine, more North Koreans began to flee due to political reasons, in search of freedom and not only food. In 2006, Joseph Kim—aged fifteen—escaped, crossing the border at the Tumen River, and lived in hiding in China for exactly a year. His story is told in his book, *Under the Same Sky: From Starvation in North Korea to Salvation in America*. I spoke with him one afternoon online from his office at the George W. Bush Institute in Dallas, Texas, where he is now based. We had met a few months earlier in person at a conference on North Korea at the snowy Canadian ski resort of Whistler.

"I walked for about two days to Kai San, a small village in China, where I was supposed to meet a broker who could help me find my sister. But when I reached the village, I learned that the broker had died the day before. I had made this long and dangerous journey, and now I was completely lost. It felt like I had lost everything," Joseph recalls. "The Chinese government does not recognize North Korean escapees such as myself as legitimate. If I had been caught by the Chinese authorities, I would have been sent back to North Korea without question," he added. "So I had to be very careful. When I walked on the road, even at night, if I saw a car coming from afar, I would hide until it had passed. I lived and slept in the mountains, sometimes in abandoned village houses."

Eventually, after receiving help from some churches, Joseph was introduced to the non-profit organization LiNK, and, in 2007—on February 15, exactly a year after he left North Korea—he arrived in the United States. "I remember that specifically, because one of the first meals I had when I arrived in Richmond, Virginia, with my social worker and interpreter, was pizza," he recalled. But if he had been caught in China, his fate would have been very different. "The Chinese government is very aware of the consequences faced by North Koreans who are repatriated, yet they still pursue this policy. It is a blatant human rights violation."

Timothy Cho, a close friend of mine who lives in Manchester and has stood as a Conservative Party candidate in the local council elections, spent part of his childhood living on the streets in North Korea and some of his teenage years in Chinese or North Korean prisons.

"I escaped from North Korea twice and was imprisoned four times—three times in China and once in North Korea," he told me. On his first escape, in 2004, Chinese soldiers started shooting in his direction as he ran towards the Mongolian border. "We could not run anymore when they started shooting," Timothy recalled. "There were eighteen of us North Korean refugees, and the youngest were a girl and boy aged four and six years old. I still remember their screaming and tears from the shooting."

Timothy and the seventeen others were detained first in a Manchurian prison "somewhere close to the Mongolian, Russian, and North Korean borders." From there, they were taken by bus to Tumen, a journey of three days and nights. "We were handcuffed, and our feet were shackled for the entire journey," he recalled. "North Koreans begged the Chinese police not to send us back. But instead, the Chinese police interrogated us, and passed information on to the North Koreans. The next day, I was sent back to North Korea, where I was immediately arrested and imprisoned. The experience in a North Korean prison was intense."

I have seen some of Timothy's scars from the torture he says he endured in a North Korean jail. It is a miracle that he not only survived but escaped again. On his second attempt to flee, he made it all the way to Shanghai, and found the Shanghai American School, one of the best international schools in the city. "I thought it was foreign territory, so I went in and asked them to help me. But instead, they called the police, and I was arrested and transferred to Shanghai International Prison," he recounts.

In jail in Shanghai, Timothy—like many North Korean escapees—contemplated suicide, so horrific was the prospect of being returned to North Korea. Tim Peters says such a mindset is not uncommon. "I have met North Korean women who carried razor blades with them, and who tried to slit their wrists, so terrified were they about being sent back. Others carry poison with them. The psychological stress and fear North Koreans face when they are arrested in China is severe," Peters told me.

However, Timothy was fortunate. In the last known case of a successful international intervention to help North Koreans arrested in China, diplomats were able to secure his release and deportation to South Korea, via the Philippines. Since then, China's policy has hardened and more North Koreans have been forcibly repatriated.

Jihyun Park escaped in 1998 during the Arduous March famine, after the North Korean regime stopped distributing rice. She did not say goodbye to her father, who was a loyal Party member. "I do not know when my father died," she told me. Her brother had fled before her but had been sent back. "China is not a safe country. My brother was sent back to North Korea, and I do not know whether he survived," she recalled. "He had served in the North Korean army but encountered a political problem. One night, at midnight, he was brought to our home by three army captains, beaten, bloody, and swollen. Three days later, he escaped again, because he thought he might face many years in jail."

In China, Jihyun—like many North Korean woman—was sold into slavery to a Chinese man. As Scholte told me, 90 percent of North Korean women escaping to China are trafficked and sold as "wives." The "trade" flourished especially during the time of China's one-child policy, which resulted in a shortage of women in China. Women are told by traffickers that they can find them a good job as a nanny, and they can make good money to feed their family, but instead, they are sold into slavery. "If they are not sold as wives to Chinese men, they are forced to work in brothels and in Internet pornography," Scholte said.

Sokeel Park agrees. "North Korean women are sold, escape, sold again—sold multiple times," he notes. And, according to Tim Peters, Chinese men who "buy" North Korean women often have "serious drinking problems, are violent, and sometimes share the women with others." The treatment the women face is often "extraordinarily humiliating" and the women face "a sense of powerlessness." Sometimes, when the Chinese husband dies, the family literally "discard" the North Korea wife, putting them—and often their child—out on the street. And it is not only young, attractive "mail-order brides" affected. "There are also older women who come to China and, even though they are not seen as attractive to Chinese men as brides, they are sought after to provide nursing care for ailing, elderly Chinese people," Peters explained.

The rights of children born to a Chinese father and a North Korean mother vary from province to province, according to Peters, but "as long as the North Korean woman is still in the household, and is illegal, the child has no documents and no access to education." Only if the mother is repatriated or flees without her child can the child be registered.

Jihyun Park was beaten, tortured, and reported to the Chinese police by the man who had purchased her. She gave birth to a child, but her child was stateless because she was illegal, and so she never went to hospital. "There are at least 20,000 stateless children born to North Korean mothers in China," she told me.

After five years, Jihyun was arrested and sent back to North Korea. In a harrowing account, she told me, "Ten Chinese police officers came to the house, arrested me in front of my son—who was only five years old. They handcuffed me. I said I wanted to speak to my son, but they would not let me." In the Chinese prison, in Tumen, "Chinese police forced me to take off my clothes. They searched me everywhere, including my most intimate body parts, because North Korean women hide money in their vagina, for survival."

In North Korea, she was arrested upon arrival and detained for several days for interrogation. "The North Korean officers searched my body again. Then we were put into three small rooms, with fifty or sixty people in each," she recalled. "There was only one small bowl for washing, but many women had their periods, so they needed to use towels. They were punished for doing so. We could only go to the toilet with permission. Sometimes people could not wait, and so soiled their clothes. The smell was disgusting. There was no window, no sunlight."

During the questioning, Jihyun was asked whether she had met any South Korean missionaries in China or visited a church. "I had been to a church, but I did not admit this, because it would bring about even more severe punishment," she told me. "So I only talked about being trafficked." She was sent to a labour camp, where she became seriously ill. "I had a fever, a swollen leg, and I almost died. I was released and allowed to stay in my home for three months, under close watch."

Remarkably, despite this ordeal, Jihyun crossed the border again a few months later, to find her son. "I crossed the border at midnight one night in November. I had no coat, and my whole body was freezing. I had no money and I was still ill. I knew I could die. But all I could think about was my son," she recalled. "It was a seventeen-hour journey. When I reached the area, I tried to telephone my son, but there was no answer. The phone was off. Finally, I found him, and he was very angry with me. He did not understand why I had left him when he was five years old. The family never looked after him—he was in dirty clothes, covered in blood, and they denied him food if he did not work for them. When they did feed him, they only gave him rice and soy sauce."

Eventually, in 2007, Jihyun and her son escaped across the border to Mongolia from China, to seek sanctuary in the South Korean embassy in Ulaanbaatar, walking for three days across the Gobi Desert. "We had no food, no water. It was cold, and we could not find anyone to help, but we thought we cannot die in the desert. Finally, a Korean American pastor found us and helped us," she explained. In 2008, she and her son arrived in the United Kingdom.

The lengths to which North Koreans will go to escape reflects the desperation they face. But humanitarian considerations are of no interest to the regime in Beijing, which is determined to enforce its policy of involuntary repatriation. Why?

"Several factors go into Beijing's calculus," Ambassador Lee believes. "First, China is an ally of the North Korean regime, not the North Korean people, and Kim Jong-un's regime considers those who escape as traitors and wants its friends in China to round them up and send them back. So China is heeding the demands of its ally, the Kim regime. Secondly, if China had any sense of universal human rights, even a little, then it might exercise some discretion. But the fact that it does not do so shows the total lack of ethics and morality in the Beijing regime. Thirdly, if China did allow North Koreans to take refuge in China or to pass through to a third country, they fear it could lead to an influx of North Korean escapees, which would present a major headache for Beijing."

Timothy Cho agrees. "What North Korea is most afraid of is, if there is to be any rebellion in North Korea, it would very likely be based from China," he told me. "That is why the Kim regime seeks China's co-operation in sending back refugees. And, in China, their fear is that if they do not send people back, maybe all North Koreans would escape."

In recent years, not only has China intensified its policy of forced repatriation, it has also cracked down severely on foreign missionaries and humanitarian groups providing assistance to North Korean escapees.

"In the late 1990s, there were all sorts of foreign groups, from Christian missionaries to American high school 'do-gooders' helping North Koreans in China, and they had a relative amount of space to operate," recalls Jieun Baek. "Now, under Xi Jinping, the repression is very severe. There is the almost complete prohibition of North Korean defector activity in China, combined with increased surveillance, digitalization of identity cards, biometric testing, criminalization of people 'aiding and abetting' North Koreans, and bounties placed on North Koreans. In the past, North Koreans could use the identities of dead Chinese residents when they travelled, but that does not work anymore due to the arrival of biometric tests."

Sheena Chestnut Greitens agrees. "The extensive use of facial recognition cameras means you have to have an identity card that matches your face. Buying train or plane tickets mean your faces are scanned. That has surely made it harder for North Koreans to escape through China with a fake identification," she said.

In his excellent book *Being in North Korea*, Andray Abrahamian, who helped found and run Chosun Exchange—a non-profit focused on training North Koreans in entrepreneurship and economic policy as a way of trying to help open the world's most closed country—acknowledges that defection from North Korea "has become tougher" in recent years. "Not only have both China and the DPRK[8] stepped up security at the border, but China is now implementing all sorts of high-tech security measures across the country, including facial recognition systems," he writes. "These already run in major cities and at rail hubs." Yanji, one of the key border crossing-points, is a vital hub for North Korean escapee activity. "If they ever deploy them in Yanji, they could conceivably close off the flow of illegal migrants almost entirely."[9]

Getting to the border areas is also now much more difficult, according to Baek. "China has imposed restrictions on access to the very rural border areas, and so even for Chinese citizens to go to those areas without good reason is challenging."

In Sokeel Park's view, "under Xi Jinping, controlling the border regions has become a much greater priority, and the regime has developed much greater capacity." Beijing has clearly decided, he adds, that it "does not want foreigners mucking about in the border regions."

At the same time, the crackdown on predominantly Christian-led initiatives to help North Korean escapees coincides with Xi Jinping's crackdown on the unregistered Chinese churches and religion as a whole. "It is part and parcel of the broader control in the Xi era," believes Park.

Greitens believes the crackdown on the churches in China is a key link to the intensified repression of any activity to assist North Korean escapees. "The crackdown on house churches and religion in China has definitely had an impact on the networks helping North Korean escapees," she told me.

Peter Jung, a South Korean activist and missionary who leads Justice for North Korea, agrees. "During Hu Jintao's period, the Chinese authorities were already starting to tighten up. But under Xi Jinping, particularly from 2016 to 2019, it has been a very hard time," he told me in a call from Seoul. "Xi Jinping's regime kicked out most of the missionaries. About 90 percent of the Presbyterian Church from South Korea—the biggest denomination among the churches—has been kicked out of China. Most of the underground railroad has closed."

On July 26, 2003, Jung was arrested by Chinese police at Beijing railway station and jailed for 464 days in Yangji prison, Jilin Province. Charged under China's Criminal Law Article 318 with helping illegal immigrants illegally cross the border, and making illegal passports to help North Koreans enter the South Korean Consulate, he was held in grim conditions.

"Every day from 8 a.m. until 5 p.m., I had to sit cross-legged in my prison cell, and was told not to move," he recalled. "There was no sunshine, no daylight, and I was not allowed outside. Due to a lack of vitamin D, my skin became very dry and tight. I had no access to a lawyer, no letters to my family, no calls with the South Korean Embassy. For two months, I had no money, so I had to survive on cornbread. Sleep was very difficult because there were too many prisoners in a narrow cell."

Jung recounts how he changed cells three times, being held first in a room of twenty-five prisoners, then one of thirty-five, and then finally in a cell with twelve prisoners. "After two months, friends gave me some money, so I was able to buy some little 'luxuries' from the prison shop—some food, candy, and medicine. I gave some of this to poor prisoners." His trial did not begin until a year after his arrest and took four or five months before he was finally deported to South Korea.

In 2014, Chinese security agents raided the offices in Tumen, Jilin Province, of Peter Hahn, a Korean American Christian missionary and humanitarian worker in his seventies. His charity's bank accounts were frozen and his buildings and equipment were confiscated, and he was jailed for nine months in prison in Longjing, accused of embezzlement and falsifying receipts.[10]

Canadian missionaries Julia and Kevin Garratt had a similar experience. Having lived in China off and on since 1984, from 2008 to 2014, they ran a popular coffee shop in Dandong and helped facilitate humanitarian aid to North Korea. In their moving book, *Two Tears on the Window*, the couple describe their ordeal of being arrested, detained initially under what is known as "residential surveillance at a designated location" (RSDL)—or a "black jail"—and then in prison, accused by China of espionage. They recount the pain of being separated, interrogated, handcuffed, held in leg irons, strapped into a "tiger chair" as an instrument of torture, and psychologically ill-treated for almost two years. In his trial, Kevin Garratt was found guilty of espionage and stealing State secrets and providing them to overseas entities and was sentenced to eight years in prison and then deportation. "Eight years and then deportation? I won't survive," he describes in his book. "My head spun, and the proceedings became a blur."[11] Two days later, however, he was deported back to Canada.

According to Tim Peters, "the only interruption in China's draconian policy of forced repatriation" has been as a consequence of the COVID-19 pandemic. "It was not that the leadership in Beijing underwent any epiphany, but rather that Kim Jong-un closed off the border completely early in 2020, issued shoot-on-sight orders, and refused to accept any repatriated North Koreans back," Peters told me. "It took a pandemic and a panic-stricken decision by Kim to pause China's forced repatriation policy. And Kim has not yet authorized the return of refugees."

The sealing of the border had dire economic effects on the North Korean population, resulting, according to Sokeel Park, in "poor North Koreans being priced out of food and facing deaths from starvation." In a situation he describes as "heartbreaking," there is—in the COVID-19 context—"zero immunity, zero public health capacity," he adds. Lina Yoon agrees. "People have been starving to death in North Korea since the summer of 2020," she told me. "People are dying of easily curable diseases due to lack of medicine. Half the population has iodine deficiency due to poor nutrition. The regime has taken extreme measures, requiring products arriving in North Korea to be quarantined for a month or two."

The sealing of the border has made it even more difficult, if not impossible, for North Koreans to escape. According to Cho, only forty-eight North Koreans made it out in 2021. Sokeel Park says that while from 2007 to 2011 the number of North Koreans arriving in South Korea each year was between 2,500 and 3,000, the numbers have been steadily falling since 2012, when both Xi Jinping and Kim Jong-un came to power. "There has been a buildup in physical security, an increase in border fencing, and more use of surveillance technology, on both the North Korean and Chinese sides," Park claims. "The numbers escaping dropped by 44 percent in 2012, to 1,500, and by 2019, only 1,047 escaped." Many fear Kim Jong-un may wish to keep it this way, post-COVID, and maintain a much tighter control on the border.

However, despite the dire humanitarian consequences inside North Korea, the situation presented an opportunity for those helping refugees already in China. "To my astonishment, despite the difficulties, we began to try to evacuate as many people as we could, from early 2020. We rescued more people in 2020 than any year ever—203 people, compared to 156 in 2019," Peters told me. "We helped North Koreans with disabilities who had made their way into China, and we got them safely to third countries."

Of course, the window of opportunity was limited, as the Chinese authorities locked down in the pandemic. "Chinese public health officials descended on restaurants, farms, factories where North Koreans were working, in Heilongjiang, Liaoning, and Jilin Provinces, and detained people," Peters claims. According to Suzanne Scholte, between 600 and 1,200 North Koreans are in detention in China now. "This North Korean refugee crisis could easily be solved, because, unlike any other refugees in the world, they have a place to go," Scholte argues. "Under the South Korean Constitution, they have the right to come to South Korea." But, as Peters notes, "the Chinese authorities work hand in glove with North Korean security, not only to prevent North Koreans making it to safety but allowing North Korean security agents to come to China to harass and threaten refugees and those assisting them."

Jeremiah—a pseudonym—is a Korean-born American pastor who has worked with Unification Hope Mission for many years helping to rescue North Korean refugees. He estimates that there are at least 100,000 North Korean refugees, mostly women, in China and another 150,000 children, resulting in what he calls a "quarter of a million-strong North Korean diaspora in China." All are "in danger of arrest," because they are regarded as "illegal immigrants." During the pandemic, many of them could not get vaccinated because they had no identification. China's inhumane policy is consigning hundreds of thousands of people to a dire fate—either torture, imprisonment, or execution if returned to North Korea, or slavery, insecurity, poverty, statelessness, and fear if they remain in China.

As well as the importance of the China-North Korea border in terms of an escape route out of North Korea, the border is also vital for disseminating information into North Korea. As Sokeel Park observes, "the vast majority of illegal foreign information and media going into North Korea—whether by radio or smuggled DVDs and USB sticks or other means—is coming in through the border with China." Moreover, North Koreans travelling across the border into China for trade—as they did pre-COVID—absorb more information. "The more visits they make, the more confident they become," says Park. "They might use the Internet, watch television, download material to take back inside. Not just Korean dramas, but yoga videos, postnatal care information, educational material. They are information-starved, and so they want a wide range of material. Customs officials do not stand a chance against people bringing in micro SD cards, which they can hide on the train so that it is not on their person. People carry in whole hard drives of stuff. They watch it, their family watches it, they share it with trusted friends, spread it from USB to USB. It is mind-blowing. China is massively important in terms of North Koreans being able to go and get information."

More and more North Koreans are on the Chinese telephone network, according to Park, using smartphones smuggled across the border. "They use WeChat to send photos and videos to the outside world. Without China, North Korea would have a massively reduced access to information and know much less about the outside world," Park argues. "And it does not seem like the Chinese government cares. They do not prevent North Korean access to information or mobile networks. In this particular regard, they show a benign neglect."

One area where China shows no "benign neglect" is accountability for North Korea's crimes against humanity. As Greg Scarlatoiu, executive director of Washington, D.C.-based Committee for Human Rights in North Korea, noted, "China strongly opposed the establishment of the UN Commission of Inquiry, and strongly opposes country-specific mechanisms as a matter of principle."

The China-North Korea relationship is very similar to China's relationship with Myanmar. In both relationships, there is a long history, a strong strategic and economic interest coming from Beijing, and a deep dependency on the part of the more isolated, unstable, and fragile dependent regime. Both relationships have generated human trafficking, drugs trafficking, arms sales, refugee flows, and grave atrocity crimes in violation of international laws.

Both relationships contain tension and mutual suspicion. As Daniel Wertz writes, the relationship "could be characterized as one of ostensible friendship and ideological affinity, but with tensions bubbling underneath."[12] As with the generals in Naypyidaw, North Korea's leaders have been "wary of becoming subservient to China," and so "the description of a relationship 'as close as lips and teeth' has often masked a reality of mutual—though asymmetrical—dependency as well as mutual distrust."[13]

That said, the mutual dependence is clear. "I cannot imagine North Korea can be solved without China, because China is not going to allow it to be resolved without them," former ambassador Slinn believes. "We saw how China reacted when Kim Jong-un started having his meetings with Donald Trump. All of a sudden, they upped their engagement and reached out and tried to act as a spoiler. They are the big brother, the big bear on the border, and the status quo suits them just fine."

Joseph Kim agrees. "Does China want North Korea to change? I do not think so," he said. "From China's perspective, they would not want to see a free North Korea or a unified Korea. The more North Korea is cornered and neglected by the international community, the better the value of friendship becomes between Beijing and Pyongyang."

Jihyun Park believes that, no matter what tensions they have, the two regimes are joined at the hip. "China wants the North Korean regime to survive," she told me. "Many young people in free countries do not understand or care about the value of freedom. We must teach people about Communist regimes and how they kill people and destroy people's futures. That is what the regimes in North Korea and China have in common. And if North Korea's regime collapses, the regime in China will collapse, and freedom will attain victory."

CHAPTER 12

WAKE-UP CALL

WHAT THE FREE WORLD MUST DO TO FIGHT FOR FREEDOM

On October 20, 2015, Xi Jinping addressed members of both Houses of the British Parliament in the House of Lords' Royal Gallery as part of his State visit to the United Kingdom. Earlier in the day, he had visited the Queen, arriving at Buckingham Palace in the Diamond Jubilee State Coach.

I tried to join a protest on the Mall, and as I walked across St. James' Park I was initially delighted to see thousands of people lining the famous street towards the palace, with Chinese banners. As I came closer, however, I realized that they were there not to demonstrate against the Chinese regime's leader but to welcome him. They had been bussed in by the Chinese Embassy, and completely overshadowed the small protest organized by Tibetans, Uyghurs, Falun Gong practitioners, Chinese Christians, and other Chinese activists which could not be seen behind the crowds waving Chinese flags.

As Xi's coach drove past, I tried to join the crowd in order to get a look. A Chinese man with an earpiece blocked my view by holding a big Chinese and British flag directly in front of me. "I think that is deliberate," I said to my friend. The man turned to me aggressively and said, "This is not for you." Annoyed, I pointed at the Union Jack and retorted, "But this is my country's flag." I then muttered in my limited Mandarin, under my breath but audibly enough for him to hear: "*Xi Jinping feichang feichang bu hao!*" ("Xi Jinping is very, very bad!") The man scowled threateningly.

Xi's State visit, the first by a Chinese leader to the United Kingdom in ten years, came at the height of the so-called "Golden Era" of Sino-British relations, championed by the prime minister at the time, David Cameron. It was all smiles, handshakes, and red-carpet treatment. Cameron and Xi were even pictured drinking pints of beer at an English country pub near the prime minister's country residence at Chequers. Not a single word was spoken by the government in public about China's deteriorating and grave human rights crisis. Instead, almost £40 billion worth of deals were signed, including agreements for Chinese investment in British nuclear reactors, regenerative medicine and tissue engineering research at the University of Oxford, and regeneration projects in the north of England.[1]

The only public official to say anything even mildly challenging to Xi publicly during his visit was the Speaker of the House of Commons John Bercow, who admits that by his own standards even he was "relatively understated and diplomatic." In his speech introducing Xi, Bercow made reference to the address in Westminster Hall in 2012 by Myanmar's Aung San Suu Kyi, whom he pointedly described as a "democracy champion and international symbol of the innate human right of freedom." In a veiled reference to China's repression, he added that China should aspire to be a "moral inspiration" and observed that "what China does economically, but also politically, is seen by and relevant to not merely your own citizens, it is seen by and relevant to billions more across the globe. The world will be watching and waiting expectantly on the outcome as the emerging superpower takes its new place in the world."[2]

Bercow recalls that he was "not altogether comfortable with the fact that Xi was invited," but decided to use the occasion to make two points "with perfectly adequate force" without being "rude or offensive." The first was the point about human rights, and second was that, in effect, Xi was not the first person from Asia to address the British Parliament. "David Cameron said to me afterwards that I had said what he would have liked to but could not," Bercow told me. "I thought, 'You could, if you wanted to.' If you have got to a position of power as prime minister, you could find a way of saying something about human rights and democratic institutions."

Two days later, just before the end of Xi's State visit, a member of Parliament, Fiona Bruce, tabled an Urgent Question on human rights in China, and—to the government's fury—Bercow granted it. Bruce, who was chair of the Conservative Party Human Rights Commission, asked the secretary of state for foreign and

Commonwealth affairs "if he will make a statement on human rights in China, following reports that human rights lawyer Zhang Kai imminently faces a severe prison sentence or the death penalty for defending civil liberties."

In parliamentary procedure, if an urgent question is granted by the Speaker, a minister has to respond to it, other members can contribute, and it typically becomes a short debate. Moreover, it comes at very short notice. Bruce tabled the question at about 8:30 a.m. on October 22, the Speaker approved it an hour or so later, and at 10:27 a.m., she was on her feet in the chamber asking her question. Over the course of the next half-hour, at least seventeen other members of Parliament contributed to the debate.[3]

Visibly annoyed, the Minister of State at the Foreign Office, Hugo Swire, responded: "We are in the middle of a hugely positive state visit, which my right hon. Friend the Prime Minister has said will benefit not just our nations and our peoples, but the wider world. Yesterday, the Prime Minister and my right hon. Friend the Foreign Secretary had extensive discussions with President Xi Jinping and his delegation. These discussions continue today, including when the Prime Minister hosts President Xi at Chequers. As we have made very clear, the strong relationship that we are building allows us to discuss all issues. No issue, including human rights, is off the table. The U.K.-China joint statement that we have agreed commits both sides to continuing our dialogue on human rights and the rule of law."[4]

Afterwards, Foreign Secretary Philip Hammond and government whips were incandescent that a backbench member of Parliament from the governing party would have the temerity to raise such a question while Xi Jinping was still in the country on a State visit. Hammond wrote to the Speaker complaining. But if the question had not been tabled and had the Speaker not granted it, human rights in China would not have been aired by anyone from government or Parliament publicly at all during Xi's visit. And Bercow had no regrets. "I was very clear in my mind that it was the right thing to do," he told me.

In 2016, the Conservative Party Human Rights Commission, in which I serve as deputy chair, decided to hold an enquiry into the human rights situation in China. We published a call for evidence, received over thirty written submissions, and held two hearings in Parliament, both of which lasted almost three hours, in which we heard from and questioned key witnesses. In June that year, we published our report, *The Darkest Moment: The Crackdown on Human Rights in China 2013–2016*.[5] The title came from remarks Yang Jianli, a Chinese exiled dissident, made in his evidence to us, when he said that "this is the darkest moment for Chinese human rights" since the Tiananmen massacre of 1989. Our findings were damning, and we called for action. The British government was furious. It was the final weeks of Cameron's premiership, but still the height of the "Golden Era." Many members of Parliament told us privately that they agreed with our report, but they were not willing to be associated with it publicly. David Burrowes was the only other MP besides Fiona Bruce to put his name to it, alongside a member of the House of Lords and the European Parliament.

The debate on China has moved a long way since then, in the United Kingdom and elsewhere. In 2020, the Commission held another inquiry on China and published its new report, *The Darkness Deepens*,[6] and this time, MPs were queuing up to endorse it. Cabinet ministers and Downing Street officials told me they were grateful for the report and were studying its findings, and I was told that the Foreign Secretary himself was reading it.

Four factors which came about in very quick succession were, I believe, pivotal in shifting the debate. The first was the battle over the Chinese technology company Huawei being invited into our 5G telecommunications infrastructure, at the start of 2020. The second was, of course, the COVID-19 pandemic. The third was the dramatic and rapid dismantling of Hong Kong's freedoms. And the fourth was the increasing attention which the growing body of evidence of genocide and crimes against humanity against the Uyghurs and other Muslims in western China's Xinjiang region was receiving. A fifth factor, China's so-called "wolf warrior diplomacy"—a reference to the increasing aggression of the regime's diplomats around the world—has not helped Beijing's cause. Very rapidly, we went from having a tiny handful of Parliamentarians brave enough to speak out on China to a growing parliamentary rebellion against the government's policy of kowtowing to Beijing.

One of the leaders of the rebellion on Huawei was the former Conservative Party leader and Cabinet minister Sir Iain Duncan Smith MP. Speaking to me over breakfast in Rome in November 2021, Sir Iain told me that he had been "worried" about China for some time, particularly "the growth of dependency," and had almost walked out on Xi Jinping's address to Parliament in 2015. "I nearly left the Royal Gallery, but I was a Cabinet minister at the time and I realized that would have been a major thing. But I hated the speech, the arrogance with which he lectured us and the way we were prostrating ourselves," he said. However, it was China's role in telecommunications infrastructure that catalyzed him into action. It posed, in his view, a serious threat to national security, enabling China's espionage operations.

"We started raising the alarm and trying to stop Huawei's involvement in 5G just after the General Election in 2019," he recalled. "We realized the danger—Huawei would be in the peripheral technology and that is where all the power is. It would mean they could steal anything they liked because everything goes through the antenna. Boris Johnson just did not get it. He kept saying, 'I do not know what you are on about. Our security people are saying it is okay.' I said, 'No, your security people are saying they think it is 'manageable,' which is completely different from saying it is okay.' I discovered that there was a clear division between those advising the government and the people at the Government Communications Headquarters (GCHQ) intelligence agency in Cheltenham, who did not want us to go ahead at all."

A former soldier in the Scots Guards who served in Northern Ireland and Rhodesia (now Zimbabwe), Sir Iain had then worked for telecommunications giant GEC Marconi before entering politics, so he had some understanding of the sector. He started to look into what the alternatives to Huawei were, and found that, for 5G, there were really only three companies: the Finnish company Nokia, the Swedish firm Ericsson, and the Korean group Samsung. "I was astonished," he told me.

Sir Iain worked with others in Parliament to mount a rebellion against the government's planned deal with Huawei. In January 2020, in an attempt to persuade him to back down, he was invited to a meeting with government advisors. "They gave a presentation, and they clearly thought that their smart bods would convince these stupid politicians to go along with it. To their complete astonishment, I really ripped into them, accusing them of deliberately misleading and deliberately failing to tell the government that Huawei represented a real threat," he recalled. Momentum grew behind the rebellion and eventually the government backed down and changed course. "Two months into COVID, the prime minister telephoned me and said, 'We are not going to go ahead with Huawei. You have won, and you were right.' He told me they had looked at it again and concluded that allowing Huawei into 5G 'is a really dangerous thing to do.'"

Of course, it was not only Boris Johnson's own MPs who were telling him that. The United States administration and Congress, from President Donald Trump and Secretary of State Mike Pompeo all the way through to members in both parties in the U.S. Congress were furious that the United Kingdom was even considering the deal with Huawei, as were other close allies such as Australia. Australian MPs cancelled a planned visit to the U.K. over the row, and Foreign Secretary Dominic Raab faced strong criticism during his visit to Canberra.[7] A letter from forty-two U.S. congressmen was sent warning of the "catastrophic cost" of involving Huawei,[8] senior U.S. senators wrote to Boris Johnson,[9] Pompeo urged the U.K. to reconsider,[10] and President Trump himself had a furious telephone call with Johnson.[11] Britain's role in the Five Eyes intelligence network—with the United States, Australia, Canada, and New Zealand—was called into question, with some allies suggesting they would have to review their intelligence-sharing arrangements if Huawei was in our 5G infrastructure.

The United Kingdom's U-turn on Huawei was the start of a new battle over China policy. The police brutality and the imposition of the draconian National Security Law in Hong Kong, which resulted in the rapid dismantling of the city's remaining freedoms, gained significant attention in Westminster, given the United Kingdom's historic relationship with Hong Kong and its obligations under the Sino-British Joint Declaration.

Since 2018, a growing number of Parliamentarians on all sides had been urging the British government to extend the rights of Hong Kongers who hold British National Overseas (BNO) status, to offer them a lifeline out of the city if they needed it. The BNO status had been created before the handover of Hong Kong, but in reality, it meant very little because it did not convey the right to live in the United Kingdom. It offered nothing more than a passport. Emily Lau, a leading pro-democracy politician in Hong Kong and campaigner for BNO rights, used to describe the acronym as meaning "Britain says no."[12]

Hong Kong Watch, the organization I co-founded in December 2017, had been at the forefront of this campaign, and on July 1, 2020, the day after the National Security Law was passed by Beijing's National People's Congress and came into force with immediate effect, Boris Johnson announced a generous and courageous new scheme to give Hong Kongers with BNO status the opportunity to settle in the United Kingdom and, ultimately, obtain citizenship.[13] Britain was finally saying 'yes' to up to three million people now eligible for this opportunity, and in the first year of the scheme's operation, at least 100,000 moved to Britain. Britain was finally standing up to Beijing and, needless to say, Beijing reacted with fury, vowing retaliation.

In February 2022, again because of Hong Kong Watch's advocacy, the government extended the scheme so that young people born after 1997 who have at least one parent with BNO status would be eligible to apply independently of their parents, thus offering a lifeline to many of the most vulnerable people in Hong Kong who were on the frontlines of the protests in 2019.[14]

The awakening to the China challenge in the British Parliament has been very bipartisan. Within the Conservative Party, the issue unites people on both wings: right and left, Brexiteer and Remain. In addition to Sir Iain, a leading Brexiteer considered to be on the right of his party, as well as Bob Seely, Tim Loughton, and Nusrat Ghani, other prominent voices have included Tom Tugendhat MP, now Britain's security minister and previously chair of the House of Commons Foreign Affairs Committee; former deputy prime minister Damian Green MP; and of course the last governor of Hong Kong, Lord Patten—all considered more centrist Conservatives who supported the "Remain" side in the referendum on membership of the European Union in 2016. The issue has drawn strong support from Labour politicians, too, especially Lisa Nandy MP and Stephen Kinnock MP when they served on their party's shadow foreign affairs team, and the current shadow Asia minister Catherine West MP, as well as Liberal Democrats such as Layla Moran MP and Alistair Carmichael MP.

In 2021, China sanctioned MPs Sir Iain Duncan Smith, Tom Tugendhat, Tim Loughton, Nusrat Ghani, and Neil O'Brien—as well as two members of the House of Lords, Lord Alton and Baroness Helena Kennedy KC—in retaliation for the United Kingdom's sanctioning Chinese officials and entities responsible for the Uyghur genocide. The Conservative Party Human Rights Commission and the China Research Group, which Tugendhat had formed, were also on Beijing's sanctions list. Six months later, the Speakers of both Houses of Parliament banned the Chinese ambassador to London from entering the parliamentary estate. Zheng Zeguang had been due to attend a reception in Parliament, but the Speaker of the House of Commons Sir Lindsay Hoyle said in a statement, "I do not feel it's appropriate for the ambassador for China to meet on the Commons estate and in our place of work when his country has imposed sanctions against some of our members."

Of course, the China challenge has resulted in changes, of varying degrees, across capitals throughout the free world. Nowhere more so than in the United States.

Mary Kissel, who served as senior advisor to Mike Pompeo when he was Secretary of State, played a key role behind the scenes in bringing about changes in U.S.-China policy. She believes that "the Trump administration did more to advance human rights in China than any other administration in recent history." Crucially, she explained, top policy-makers in the administration "cared an awful lot about outcomes, not gestures." When she proposed a statement to Pompeo, he would often ask, "What effect is this going to have?"

A starting point, said Kissel, was that they "spoke very honestly about the nature of the Chinese Communist Party regime." Diplomatic niceties went out of the window. "We called it totalitarian and brutal. We called it for what it was. We did it repeatedly. And that had never really been done before," she told me in an online call from New York. "That was very important, because one of the fundamentals, if you want to advance human rights, is you have to recognize what the situation is on the ground. And we did that. We changed not just Americans' view of Communist China, but the world's. We lifted the veil."

That was accompanied by action. "We imposed sanctions on top officials who committed human rights violations, issued warnings to U.S. businesses not to engage in trade with human rights violators, recognized courageous Chinese dissidents who stood for freedom, imposed visa restrictions on individuals who had committed human rights violations, sanctioned the Xinjiang Production and Construction Corps, or *Bingtuan*, and—most importantly—declared crimes against humanity and genocide in Xinjiang," recalled Kissel.

The genocide designation was especially significant and entailed a big debate before the conclusion was reached. "Secretary Pompeo is a Harvard Law School-trained attorney, so he read all the legal opinions about whether or not this constituted genocide, and he concluded that it did," Kissel said. "That was within his power, but it was a very courageous thing to do because it ran against the bureaucratic instinct of the State Department, large portions of which did not support that decision."

Former ambassador-at-large for international religious freedom Sam Brownback told me that Kissel, together with the U.S. ambassador-at-large for global women's issues Kelley Eckels Currie were the two that "drove the train" on the genocide determination and deserve a "gold star" for it. He confirms that it was a battle within the bureaucracy. "The worst legal department I have ever been around in the world is the State Department,'" Brownback said. "Every other legal department I have ever been around, you would tell them, 'Here is what I would like to try to do. Can we do it, and can you tell me how?' But the State Department's answer is always just 'No. There is no other way. We will not give you another answer.' So Mary really pushed this, and Kelly helped out and they ended up getting it through on the last day of the administration."

Within hours of Pompeo's decision, his Democrat successor, Antony Blinken, confirmed the genocide designation, a clear sign that China is the one issue that genuinely unites Republicans and Democrats in Washington, D.C. "Politics in the U.S. has turned determinably sour towards the Chinese Communist regime," Brownback said. "The Biden administration could not back away from the genocide determination without being seen as soft on China. And this is a key point—when you turn from one party to the next in the administration and maintain policy continuity, this is golden. It is what we did for years against the Soviet Union. The Republicans and Democrats both agreed that we had to confront the Soviet Union."

There may be differences in rhetoric and approach, but both parties are, according to Brownback, united in recognition of the need to "confront" Beijing. Derek Mitchell, former U.S. ambassador to Myanmar under President Barack Obama's administration and now president of the National Democratic Institute (NDI), agrees. "President Biden and Secretary Blinken believe that the defining challenge in the twenty-first century is between autocracy and democracy, and China is viewed as the most aggressive and best resourced of those challenges, and the one with the largest reach," he said. "Xi Jinping has helped to unite people in the United States, and elsewhere, and helped us to wake up to what China really is and the challenge the Chinese Communist Party really poses. There is no mask anymore. The 'wolf warrior' diplomats are doing themselves no favours; they are exacerbating the problem."

China, argues Mitchell, "has something for everybody" in terms of challenges. "It has something for the left, middle, and right. When it comes to human rights, security challenges, Taiwan, climate change—every part of the spectrum is affected by the Chinese regime's arrogance, aggression, illiberal triumphalism, and expansionism. The more Xi Jinping becomes Maoist and repressive, and expands his Orwellian State, the more his regime's actions unite the world against China."

Carolyn Bartholomew, former chief of staff to the Speaker of the House of Representatives Nancy Pelosi and former chair of the U.S.-China Economic and Security Review Commission (USCC), believes the debate has shifted so much that people previously regarded as "hawkish" outliers "are no longer outliers." Despite being a lifelong Democrat, she credits the Trump administration with "raising the visibility of the challenge," even if she did not always agree with their tactics. "The previous administration paved the way for President Biden to break away from the Clinton– and Obama–era terms of engagement with China," she told me in a call from Washington, D.C.

Perhaps one way in which the Biden administration's approach might be perceived to differ is in terms of multilateral efforts. "The Biden administration is rebuilding alliances, especially with Japan, Australia, and India," Bartholomew argues. Mitchell agrees. "The Chinese regime would love to make it about 'great power' competition between China and the United States. The more we can make it about the world versus the Chinese regime, the democratic world versus the autocratic world, and about values, the more we are able to ally ourselves with the billions of people who want a voice and want freedom. We actually care about others' freedom and sovereignty, whereas China clearly does not. Beijing's talking points mouth this 'win-win' narrative, but the world now sees China for what it is. China simply wants to get out of other countries whatever it can for its own interests."

Kissel, however, disagrees with the perception that the Trump administration did not pursue a multilateral approach. "There were many multilateral actions we took, most importantly at the United Nations," she said. "We organized a letter in Geneva with dozens of other nations to denounce the genocide of the Uyghurs, and we shared information with our partners all the time."

Kelley Eckels Currie served as the U.S. representative to the United Nations Economic and Social Council and, for four months, acting deputy ambassador to the United Nations, before she became ambassador-at-large for global women's issues. A long-time Tibet advocate, she was familiar with China's tactics, particularly how they operate within the UN, but she was surprised to find "the extent to which China had really infiltrated all of the permanent institutions of the UN," particularly the human rights and development spaces. "China is working hard through various means to shape these institutions and the normative frameworks around them," Currie told me. "From the UN Secretariat to the member state bodies like the General Assembly, the Security Council, and the Human Rights Council, to the funding bodies, programmes, and agencies, China is making inroads." They have done this particularly by "hitching the Belt and Road Initiative to the sustainable development goals (SDGs), and claiming that it is just one giant SDG-empowering machine."

The current UN Secretary-General Antonio Guterres has, Currie claims, "bought into this agenda." Or perhaps it would be more accurate to say he "was bought" into it. In 2016, China announced it would donate a billion dollars to the UN, with a payment of $20 million per year, ostensibly for peace, security, and development.[15] According to Currie, $10 million of this goes straight to the office of the secretary-general, "basically for his personal use to do whatever he wanted, with no oversight from anybody other than his office and the Chinese government."

China "co-opted" Guterres, she adds, and he thought—as many do—that co-operation with China on climate change, development, and other key issues would be successful. "It did not help that the U.S. administration was led by Donald Trump, who was the opposite of the 'Davos man' that Guterres wants to be," said Currie. "The U.S. was pulling out of the Paris Accord on climate change, pulling out of various UN agencies, demanding that the UN be financially accountable and more transparent, criticizing the waste and fraud in the system. The Chinese took total advantage of that, flattered Guterres' ego, gave him prominent roles in these Belt and Road forums, and co-opted the UN's buzzwords, claiming they were there to defend multilateralism and globalization."

The UN's Department of Economic and Social Affairs (DESA), in particular, is a "Chinese fiefdom," run by a Chinese official for many years, according to Currie. The other half of China's $20 million a year to the UN goes to this department, "for the explicit purpose of advancing the Belt and Road Initiative within the UN system." The only people who decide how these funds are spent, she adds, are the secretary-general, his chief of staff, the Chinese permanent representative to the UN, China's Ministry of Commerce and Foreign Ministry, and the auditors. "It is horrifying. It is a Chinese slush fund," she said.

Multiple UN agencies signed agreements with Chinese entities, with no transparency at all. "We were literally playing 'Whac-a-Mole' trying to uncover this stuff and do something about it. It was completely insane," Currie added. "We had to fight the UN bureaucracy, and I had my own bureaucracy to fight, too."

China has also learned to manipulate the G77 caucus of developing countries, which now has 134 members, making it the majority caucus in the General Assembly. "The G77 basically pays nothing into the system, while there are about twelve non-G77 countries that basically pay for the whole thing," she notes. "The Chinese have figured out how to manipulate the system, because they are one of the big donors, and the only major donor that caucuses with the G77. They can get their language into draft resolutions, and nobody seemed to object. They would insert Belt and Road language, and even Xi Jinping Thought into resolutions. We started to push back and object, and we had to warn partners not to think Chinese language was innocuous. It all has a very specific meaning. Even phrases such as 'win-win co-operation' and 'a shared future for all mankind' cannot be assumed to be a benign filler. We had to do a lot of educating. And we had fights all the time over resolutions and language."

The term "win-win co-operation" is an especially dangerous and "blatant" attack on the normative framework of the international human rights system, claims Currie. "The Chinese are trying to attack the whole idea that human rights attach to the individual level. They are trying to suggest that human rights can be negotiated between states," she explained. An alarming number of countries went along with the idea. "We were the only country that called a vote on that resolution, and the only country that voted against it. Seventeen other countries abstained."

Working with U.S. Ambassador to the UN Nikki Haley, Currie tried to convey the message that the United States' goal was "to make the UN actually work for the people who need it to work for them, and to make the UN great again." The U.S., she said, believed that "it matters that the UN function as an effective organization, because there are countries that rely on the UN for certain things." However, "that was not how the message was received."

One of the biggest battles Currie fought at the UN was over the plight of the Uyghurs. That was when Guterres proved to her "in spectacular fashion" that he was "truly, truly awful" and that "the Chinese own him." In 2018, she delivered a statement at the General Assembly's Third Committee (on social, humanitarian, and cultural issues), in response to the Committee on the Elimination of Racial Discrimination. "We had been looking for opportunities to bring up the situation in Xinjiang through different human rights mechanisms. I just went in, I did not ask anybody, and I delivered the statement. We had to do stuff like that," she recounted. "Then we started doing events in Geneva and New York. The real watershed was when we got the Chinese's attention and told them, 'We are serious about this, and we are going to keep bringing this up in every possible way. This is not going to go away.'"

In April that year, Dolkun Isa, president of the World Uyghur Congress, tried to attend the UN Forum on Indigenous Issues, for which China-controlled DESA is the Secretariat. "China is also the Secretariat for the NGO Committee, so China controls the accreditation of civil society participants," notes Currie. Dolkun Isa was attending as a delegate for the German NGO the Society for Threatened Peoples and came to New York with his accreditation letter.

"I went with Dolkun to the UN badge office to get his badge," Currie recalled. "I was excited. We get there, and Dolkun stands in line, and I am standing there looking at my BlackBerry, and then, suddenly, there is all sorts of consternation, and they send him somewhere else, so I asked what was going on. The UN security people were very rude, asked me who I am, and why I was there and why it was my any of my business, so I showed them my badge as an ambassador in the U.S. mission. I said I wanted to know what the problem was. They told me there was a security flag against Dolkun's name. I asked from where, and they said from the UN Security Office."

Currie sprang into action, making calls to the U.S. mission's security team and the UN Security Office. The UN claimed that there was an Interpol Red Notice, but Currie pointed out that it was "politically motivated" and had been removed two months earlier. "The secretary-general then got involved, because UN security refused to back off until they were told to by him, because they were being yelled at by the Chinese. It seems that the Chinese permanent representative was calling Guterres' office every hour. It was totally bonkers," Currie described. "The Chinese lost their minds because they did not know that the Interpol Red Notice had been revoked. We told the UN that we had given Dolkun Isa a ten-year multi-entry visa to the United States. We are not in the habit of doing that with people who we suspect of terrorism. But Guterres refused to stand up for the rights of Dolkun Isa. He was a total wet noodle the whole time. He is bought and paid for by the Chinese, and at $10 million a year, that's cheap."

Three months later, the head of Interpol at the time, a Chinese official called Meng Hongwei, disappeared—and two years later, he was sentenced to thirteen and a half years in jail in China.[16] "I am absolutely convinced there is a connection," said Currie. "I am convinced that his failure to stop that Red Notice being revoked was one of the reasons why he disappeared."

In the end, Dolkun Isa was admitted, and delivered his statement, but the Chinese reacted by trying to revoke the accreditation of the Society for Threatened Peoples. Currie would not be cowed. "I told them if they put it to a vote at the NGO Committee and won, we would bring it up at the Economic and Social Council (ECOSOC), and then at the General Assembly, and in media interviews. But I said I wanted to give them an opportunity to walk this back first, because it will not look good for them. 'I am going to give you an out here and let you walk away,' I told my Chinese counterpart. He asked what I would do if Hawaii tried to secede. I said, 'They are trying all the time, as are Texas and Puerto Rico. Let me give you a little advice. If you are going to be this prickly about everybody that does not want to be part of China, you are going to spend a lot of time doing this. And, by the way, part of being a great power is just not caring about little things. You look really insecure.'" It was, Currie adds, "such a fun conversation and one of my best meetings ever." The Chinese backed off.

One of Washington, D.C.'s most long-standing—and tireless—champions of human rights is New Jersey Republican Congressman Chris Smith, who was first elected to the House of Representatives in 1980, aged twenty-seven. His first amendment to legislation related to China was in 1984, to stop funding for forced abortions in China. He began his speech on the floor of the House on May 9, 1984, by saying, "I rise to offer this amendment in an attempt to end our complicity in and unwitting approval of the barbaric and utterly savage population policy in China that includes forced and coerced abortion."[17] His amendment passed, and his lifelong fight for freedom and human dignity began. Almost forty years later, he is still going.

Chris Smith has been one of my friends, mentors, and heroes for all the years I have known him. When I sat down with him in his office in the Rayburn Building on Capitol Hill in March 2022, he recalled all the battles he has fought over the past four decades—not only on forced abortion, but for religious freedom and the persecution of Christians, the Uyghurs, Tibet, Falun Gong, and Hong Kong. Few politicians in the free world today have as long, consistent, and robust a track record as Chris Smith. From the countless hearings he has chaired (he believes it might be as many as seventy-six), bills he has authored, and resolutions he has sponsored, he has been one of Beijing's most vocal critics for far longer than it became fashionable. And he has visited China about six times.

The world totally "misunderstood" Xi Jinping, Smith believes. "Xi is the ultimate thug," he said. But the Chinese Communist Party regime are, he adds, "bullies wherever they go."

Recognition of that fact—which Smith, together with Nancy Pelosi across the aisle, recognized years before many others did—should form the foundation for U.S. policy. That was something Pompeo and Vice President Mike Pence tried to articulate during their time in office. According to Kissel, a series of speeches by Pompeo—to the Hudson Institute, the National Governors' Association, and the Nixon Library, combined with speeches by National Security Advisor Robert O'Brien and FBI Director Chris Wray—were an attempt to expose "the nature of the regime, its ideology, and the challenges we face." These four speeches were, said Kissel, "unprecedented" and "very powerful" because they came from these key government figures "looking at Communist China's predations from different perspectives." At the Nixon Library speech, the "father" of China's democracy movement, Wei Jingsheng, was invited to attend, and on the thirtieth anniversary of the Tiananmen Square massacre, June 4, 2019, Pompeo met Tiananmen survivors in the State Department—"which was unprecedented," adds Kissel. Pompeo also made the first-ever statement calling for accountability for the 1989 massacre.

Canadian journalist Jan Wong, a third-generation Canadian Chinese, witnessed the Tiananmen Square massacre first-hand as she reported for the *Globe and Mail*. Although the Chinese Communist Party regime has tried to "erase history" in China, and more recently in Hong Kong, the record for the world cannot be wiped, she told me. "We have the books and the documentaries, and the people who were alive at the time," she notes. "You can't erase that." However, she does worry that future generations may forget.

Wong, who lived in China as a student during the Cultural Revolution and then again as a reporter in the 1980s, and returned periodically, has written two moving memoirs, *Red China Blues* and *Chinese Whispers*. On June 4, 1989, she was based in the Beijing Hotel overlooking Tiananmen Square, in a room set up as an office which she shared with the *Times* and the BBC.

In the days leading up to June 4, Wong saw ordinary people greeting soldiers, and telling them, "You are our comrades, our brothers. We love the army and the army loves the people." She had not anticipated a crackdown, at least not with the level of violence that transpired. Furthermore, before June 4, many journalists had left town. "We had been working non-stop since Mikhail Gorbachev's visit to Beijing. So some of my competitors went on vacation. We were all very tired," Wong told me. She, however, had stuck around, and saw the troops come further into the city, the mood change, and soldiers "pushed out of Beijing by the crowds."

That night, it was Wong's day off, as her newspaper had no Sunday edition, so she went swimming, out near the airport. On her way, however, she saw truckloads of soldiers coming into the city. "I decided I had better not go swimming. I had better turn around, because these did not look like the other soldiers. They looked very stern, and had boots on," Wong recalled. "That sounds ridiculous, but the other soldiers I had seen had little green canvas running shoes. This was different. It did not look good."

She headed first to various foreign media newsrooms, and then to the Square.

"It was early evening, and I went with my husband. I knew history was being made. We had to be there," she told me in an online call from her home in Toronto. "My husband was the only one who would go with me. The Square was jammed, buzzing with anticipation, rumours, tents, and stampedes."

Wong returned to the Beijing Hotel, and in the early hours of the morning witnessed from her balcony the People's Liberation Army entering the Square. "They were shooting, people were running, and people tried to rescue others. They brought out bodies on bicycle seats and pedicabs. They just ran into gunfire," she recalled. Indeed, she narrowly missed a bullet herself. "I did not realize that I was within range, on the balcony, but someone pointed out a bullet hole that went into the concrete above our heads. We could hear the gunfire."

The infamous scene of the individual who stepped in front of the tank—which became known as "Tank Man"—was witnessed by Wong from her balcony. "On Monday, June 5, my husband was on the balcony and told me, 'You had better get out here,' and so I went out on the balcony right away. The army had been running people over, and I had watched the tanks. My husband pointed to this man standing in front of a tank and said, 'Oh my God! He is going to get run over,'" she recalled. "I saw this whole dance between 'Tank Man' and the tank. He tried to stop the tank like a soccer goalie. Then he climbed onto the tank, tried to talk, then climbed down again. It was amazing and I was crying."

"Tank Man" was taken away, and no one knows where he went, who he is, or who he was taken by. But Wong believes he was rescued by protesters. "Usually, if a person is taken away by secret police, they punch you. Yet they did not hurt him. They just took him away and he melted into the crowd," Wong told me. "It took me a long time before I realized that the driver of that tank was the real hero, because he refused to run this man over."

Of all Western democracies, Canada is probably the country that has kowtowed to Beijing most, allowed Chinese Communist Party infiltration and influence to run deepest and failed to build a bipartisan consensus on the need to stand up to Xi Jinping. Unlike in Washington, D.C., and London, China policy is an issue that divides along party lines, with the incumbent Liberal Party government led by Justin Trudeau more inclined to business as usual with Beijing, while the opposition Conservatives take a more hawkish position.

The abduction and imprisonment of two Canadian citizens—Michael Kovrig and Michael Spavor—in China for almost three years, until their release in September 2021, has caused some shift in the relationship, but not as much as one might expect. Although Beijing denied it, it was clear that they were arrested in retaliation for the arrest of Huawei's Chief Financial Officer Meng Wanzhou, daughter of Huawei's founder, Ren Zhengfei, accused of violating U.S. sanctions in Iran. The "Two Michaels" as they became known were only freed after Meng herself was released from house arrest in Vancouver and returned to China.

The lesson to be learned from the case of the "Two Michaels," according to Michael Chong, a Canadian Conservative MP and shadow foreign minister, is that "we cannot give in to hostage diplomacy, because that will only further embolden the regime in Beijing." The case was, he adds, "a real wake-up call" for Canada. "To see China acting in such a malevolent way with two of our citizens really shook the establishment of this country out of its slumber on the threat China is presenting," he said.

Chong points out that there are over one hundred Canadians in detention in China today, many of them unjustly jailed. They include a Uyghur, Huseyin Celil; a Falun Gong practitioner, Sun Qian; and a Taiwanese-born winemaker, John Chang, and his wife, Allison Lu—all of whom have Canadian passports—and a Chinese pro-democracy dissident, Wang Bingzhang, who refused Canadian citizenship but whose wife and four children are Canadians.[18] "We cannot allow China to think that it can get away with this," he argues.

According to Chong, who was sanctioned by Beijing in 2021, "the senior echelons of the Liberal Party of Canada have very close business interests and significant investments in China, and there is a latent anti-Americanism in Canadian politics, so there are parts of the Canadian body politic that are reluctant to join an American-led response to China. For those two reasons, we have not had the bipartisan consensus that we have seen in other countries."

Chong, whose father came from Hong Kong, believes Canada should pursue a much tougher approach to China. "I would like to see a much more multilateral approach, in line with our democratic allies," he said. "For example, Canada should be part of the quadrilateral security dialogue between Australia, Japan, India, and the United States, which exists to counter threats that China is presenting to security in the Indo-Pacific region. Canada should have been part of the AUKUS defence pact between Australia, the United States, and the United Kingdom. And, we are unilaterally alone in not being part of the pact on Huawei. The Trudeau government should long ago have banned Huawei from Canada's telecommunications networks. It should also have issued a directive to Canada's university granting council banning partnerships with Huawei."

Chinese Communist Party infiltration in Canada is a serious concern. Kenny Chiu, a Hong Kong-born Canadian Conservative politician, lost his seat in Parliament in 2021 after just one term, and he believes Beijing played a role in his electoral defeat. He had already been sanctioned by Beijing earlier in the year due to his role on the Subcommittee on International Human Rights, and so cannot return to his birthplace. "I was targeted because I was seen by Beijing as a 'shit-stirrer.' I had been very outspoken in support of Hong Kong in Parliament, and I had tried to introduce a private member's bill in Parliament to establish transparency over foreign influence," he told me in an online call from his home in Vancouver. "It was modelled on Australia's Foreign Influence Transparency Scheme, which simply requires relationships with foreign entities to be transparent. It is a transparency bill. But Beijing spread a lot of disinformation about it among the Canadian Chinese community."

In WeChat and WhatsApp groups, and some Chinese-language media in Canada, Chiu was accused of being "anti-China." It was claimed that he "hates the Chinese" and that his bill would require all Chinese in Canada with any connections to Mainland China to register or pay a fine of up to $200,000. "That was completely fabricated, but it got repeated and amplified," he said. And the attacks were not only against him, but against his party. "Beijing wanted to destroy any chance of the Conservative Party of Canada forming a government. The message went out to the Chinese community that our leader, Erin O'Toole, was picking on China, and being used by the Americans to prevent China developing as a superpower. The regime's *Global Times* newspaper published an article warning that if the Conservatives formed a government, there would be a counterstrike against Canada."

Chiu also found himself the target of attack by a pro-Beijing radio presenter, Dr. Thomas In-sing Leung, on AM 1320, a Cantonese radio station based in his constituency of Steveston-Richmond East, in Vancouver. "Leung repeatedly attacked me on three fronts," Chiu recalled. "He accused me of interfering in Hong Kong's district council elections when I joined the international election observation mission in Hong Kong in 2019. He basically blamed the defeat of the pro-Beijing camp in those elections on the election observation mission and said that I should not be accusing foreign actors of interference in Canada when I interfered in Hong Kong's politics. That was my first sin. My second crime was to vote for a motion declaring that genocide was being committed against the Uyghurs in Xinjiang, when I have not been to Xinjiang. And my third offence, of course, was my private member's bill. He just repeated the disinformation and false accusations about it and added fuel on the fire."

At least 47 percent of the population in Chiu's constituency of Steveston-Richmond East was of ethnic Chinese descent, so stirring up hostility to someone on the grounds that he "hates the Chinese" is not difficult. In 2019, when Chiu was first elected, he won about 41.6 percent of the votes, but in 2021, he won only 33.5 percent, a decrease of 8.1 percent. He lost his seat to the Liberal Party candidate by 3,477 votes, having won it two years previously with a majority of 2,747.

In January 2022, two researchers at McGill University, Sze-Fung Lee and Benjamin Fung, published a paper concluding that Chiu's experience clearly demonstrates that "Canada remains vulnerable to the security risk constituted by foreign interference."[19]

Chong believes governments need to be able to do "two things at once": uphold democracy, freedom of expression, association, and speech, while at the same time "countering some of the subversive and coercive intimidation and influence campaigns being propagated by Beijing in our own country." That requires a co-ordinated response from central government.

"We lost a number of seats in the last election with significant Chinese communities. The evidence is that we lost those seats not because of our policies on the Communist leadership in Beijing, but because of misinformation spread by proxies on behalf of Beijing," Chong told me. "There was unprecedented meddling in our democratic process by a foreign power. The Chinese Embassy in Ottawa actually made comments during the campaign warning candidates and parties that if they took positions on China that Beijing did not like, there would be consequences. We did not have a robust plan in place to monitor the stench of disinformation that was taking place in the Chinese language, nor did we counter that misinformation. Democracies have been slow to respond to disinformation from authoritarian states or their proxies, but we are gradually starting to get our act together."

Australia is perhaps the leading democracy, besides the United States, standing up to Beijing. In recent years, it has undertaken a courageous policy shift and incurred the wrath of Xi Jinping's regime. It has taken steps to tackle Chinese Communist Party influence and infiltration—detailed in Clive Hamilton's important 2018 book, *Silent Invasion: China's Influence in Australia*—spoken out against the dismantling of Hong Kong's freedoms, and extended a lifeline to Hong Kongers wishing to leave the city. One of its leading think tanks, the Australian Strategic Policy Institute (ASPI), has published a series of groundbreaking reports about the complicity of Chinese corporations with atrocities against Uyghurs in Xinjiang Province and the use of forced labour in global supply chains in China. And it called for an international inquiry into the causes of the COVID-19 pandemic.

All of this has caused the increasingly aggressive and belligerent regime in Beijing to throw its weight around in fury. Of all the Five Eyes countries, Australia is most dependent on trade with China, with almost 40 percent of its exports going there. Australia is also strategically dependent on China for 595 different categories of goods.

China's bullying of Australia has been increasing in recent years but took on a whole new level of intensity in 2020 when it slapped an 80 percent tariff on Australian barley imports, restricted coal imports, and suspended meat imports from four of Australia's largest meat producers—in total breach of China's free trade agreement with Australia and its membership of the World Trade Organization. But the bullies in Beijing continue to flout international agreements with impunity. Australia's wine industry is the latest target, with China recently imposing crushing tariffs of over 200 percent. In December 2020, I joined an international campaign to urge people in Britain to buy only Australian wine, in solidarity with our allies. In her Mansion House speech in April 2022, the then British foreign secretary Liz Truss called for stronger alliances across the free world. "The G7 should act as an economic NATO, collectively defending our prosperity. If the economy of a partner is being targeted by an aggressive regime, we should act to support them. All for one and one for all," she said.[20]

Even the European Union, which has, until recently, been slow to stand up to Beijing, is showing signs of waking up. Some countries—such as Lithuania and the Czech Republic—have been bolder than others, but even among the most reluctant member states, there is a growing recognition of the dangers the regime in Beijing poses. The EU has imposed some sanctions against Chinese officials in response to the Uyghur genocide, prompting China to retaliate by sanctioning five members of the European Parliament, the Parliament's human rights subcommittee, an EU Council committee, and several European NGOs. European Parliament President David Sassoli said that Europe will not be China's "punching bag,"[21] and the Parliament suspended approval of the EU-China Comprehensive Agreement on Investment (CAI).[22] The EU's high representative for foreign affairs and security policy, Josep Borrell, has called China a "systemic rival" and in 2022, described an EU-China summit as "a dialogue of the deaf."[23]

The perspectives of policy-makers and advisors in two of Asia's leading democracies—Japan and South Korea—are worth paying attention to as well. In Tokyo, while the shift might not have been as strong as elsewhere, Beijing's behaviour is causing some in government, Parliament, academia, and the media to rethink.

According to Akira Igata, a lecturer at the University of Tokyo, there are two schools of thought emerging on China policy. "At the elite level, the view would be that, while they are unhappy with the way China is dealing with its own people—especially the minorities—and while they understand that China is increasingly a military threat—given its more aggressive behaviour—they also fear economic retaliation from China," he told me in an online call from Tokyo. "Many bureaucrats have been very cautious about trying not to anger China." In addition, there are some political parties in Japan, such as the Komeito (in coalition with the governing Liberal Democratic Party or LDP), who are close to Beijing. "So the manifestation of this is that those who are either afraid of China or are friends of China try to water down any policies or statements by the Japanese government towards China."

However, Igata explained, there is also "an emerging coalition of parties and stakeholders that is increasingly more vocal on human rights in China." It includes liberals who were not critical of China in the past, but who now feel the need to act, and conservatives who view China's increasing aggression with alarm.

"So you have a clash between the 'old guard,' trying to water down everything, and the new coalition, trying to push the envelope forward," notes Igata. "That is why you end up with a weird mix of new Japanese policies which are somewhat harsh, and it appears that Japan is doing something, while in reality, the position is a halfway house." For example, when Japan announced it would not send any Cabinet ministers to the Winter Olympics in Beijing in 2022, at the same time, the government said it was not "a diplomatic boycott"—and a Japanese official in the International Olympics Committee (IOC), who happens also to be a politician, did attend. "Japan was rather late to the game, too," Igata adds. "The Americans, Australians, British all came out within a couple of days, but Japan took until Christmas and couched it in a very wishy-washy way. This is the product of all the internal struggle between different factions within the bureaucracy."

A resolution on China in the Japanese legislature, known as the Diet, was passed in February 2022, but, Igata points out, it did not actually mention China. "It was supposed to be criticizing China's human rights violations, but if you look at the document itself, it talks about Xinjiang, Hong Kong, and Tibet, but the word 'China' is not there. And it is not really a statement of criticism, either, because it merely talks about how it is important for the Japanese government to look into the situation in Xinjiang and Tibet. It was called a 'censure' resolution, but the words 'criticism' or 'censure' are not there," he said. "Compared to the past, at least the Japanese Parliament decided to say something, which is a small step forward, but it did not go far enough."

A group of Japanese Parliamentarians are pushing for a Japanese version of Magnitsky sanctions legislation, known as the Human Rights Violations Sanctions Act. "But once again, there are those who are very critical of this move, and, at the moment, the government of Fumio Kishida has said that, while they are considering the possibility, they have not put it on the agenda," Igata noted. "The logic of the Japanese government is that we cannot impose sanctions because we do not have the tools to do so. But then, in response to those who argue that we should create the tools, their logic is that if we pass the law, they would then be forced by international pressure to use it, which will mean losing flexibility in diplomacy, so they do not want to have the tools."

Japan's rhetoric on Taiwan has, Igata acknowledges, become "much harsher and aggressive." Japanese politicians talk about the need to work more closely with Taiwan and to play a part if Taiwan is invaded. "But if you look at the actual policy, nothing has really changed," Igata argues. "Having said that, there is increasing realization that if war broke out over the Taiwan Strait, Japan is inevitably going to be involved because it is right there. There is no way Japan can stay aloof. We have American bases here, and China is probably going to attack those bases, which means Japan is going to be attacked. Japan seems to be moving towards a stance where they are willing to sacrifice more, work against China, work with Taiwan. But the fundamental stance still has not really changed in reality."

Perhaps one key development in Japan is the introduction of the Economic Security Promotion Act (ESPA). According to Igata, "this law allows the Japanese government to identify strategic assets that are important for Japan, and to ask companies to tell them where their supply chains lie. If the Japanese government, upon receiving reports of all the global supply chains, decided to increase the resilience of the supply chains, they could fund companies to shift their supply chains away from certain vulnerabilities." Of course, he adds, "the word 'China' does not appear once in this 130-page law, but, obviously, what the government is thinking about is whether supply chain reliance in China is too high, and the need to diversify away from it." Through this law, Igata believes, "Japan has begun to slowly decouple away from China, not just for economic security reasons but also for reasons of geopolitical risk and human rights risks."

With the election of Yoon Suk-yeol as South Korea's new president in 2022, a more robust stance towards Beijing from Seoul is expected. "We cannot turn hostile towards China because we have too much at stake—our commercial ties are too intricate and have made our businesses and our economy vulnerable," Jung-Hoon Lee, former South Korean ambassador for human rights, told me. "But the new government's approach will be significantly different from the previous administration, which was a very pro-China government. The leftist elements in Korea remain very loyal to China and anti-American. The previous president Moon Jae-in's policies were, frankly, just kowtowing to Xi Jinping, and that will change."

In 2017, South Korea accepted the United States' deployment of the Terminal High Altitude Area Defense (THAAD) missile defence system on its soil. THAAD is designed to intercept and shoot down short-, medium-, and intermediate-range ballistic missiles. Beijing was furious, and, in retaliation, expelled Lotte Mart from China. "President Moon did not protest at all. Instead, he pleaded with Xi Jinping, promising the infamous 'Three Nos.' No more THAAD deployment, no to joining the U.S. missile system, and no to any trilateral alliance between the U.S, South Korea, and Japan," recalled Ambassador Lee. "Are we a sovereign state? THAAD is a defensive weapon system; it is there because we have North Korea making missiles targeting us, threatening us, so we need a minimal level defensive capability. And Beijing is telling us what we can and cannot have to defend ourselves? It is ridiculous."

Ambassador Lee believes many Koreans are "disenchanted" with China. "When I was young, our sky was very blue. Not anymore. Every day when I wake up and I look outside, it is all grey and foggy. Scientists estimate that at least 30 percent of our pollution comes from China. Have we every protested? No, of course not," he notes. "When President Moon went to China, he waited to meet Xi, and Xi would not meet him. Then Chinese police beat up some Korean journalists covering the visit. If I was President Moon, I would have packed up and come home, or at least demanded a very, very serious apology. But he did nothing. So when it comes to the

Korean population, and especially the younger generation, they really do not like China's arrogance at all. And they do not like what they have seen happen to Hong Kong, or the Uyghurs and Tibetans."

In South Korea, when a new president is elected, they typically send a delegation to visit the United States, Japan, Russia, and China before their inauguration. "This time around, President Yoon did not send a delegation to China, Japan, or Russia, but instead to the United States and Europe. That may say something about a different approach," Lee said. "President Yoon's government may not directly antagonize China, but it will certainly be looking for ways to at least incrementally strengthen our alliances: perhaps participate in the Quad, the security alliance in the Asia-Pacific; work more closely with the United States and strengthen THAAD deployment. Those things will aggravate China, and tensions may rise, but we are a sovereign state." In the long term, Lee believes, over the next generation, South Korea will "slowly divest from China and try to be less dependent on China."

To varying degrees, thinking about the China relationship has changed in recent years in London, Washington, D.C., Ottawa, Canberra, Brussels, Tokyo, Seoul, and elsewhere. Renewed clashes between Chinese and Indian soldiers on the border of the two countries beginning on May 5, 2020, resulted in a tougher position developing in New Delhi. The behaviour of Xi Jinping's regime, with its intensifying repression at home and increasing aggression abroad, has been the primary cause of the change in attitudes towards Beijing, but the emergence of a global, more co-ordinated China human rights movement has also contributed significantly.

For many years, there have been a few excellent human rights NGOs doggedly chipping away at exposing various aspects of China's human rights record, trying to mobilize policy change. From the big organizations such as Amnesty International and Human Rights Watch, to the smaller specialist groups such as Human Rights in China, China Aid, and Citizen Power Initiatives for China, from Tibet-focused campaign organizations like the International Campaign for Tibet and Free Tibet, to religious freedom advocacy groups such as CSW, there has long been a bedrock of China human rights activism. But over the past few years, two things have happened. First, more organizations have been founded, strengthening the movement both in capacity, expertise, and visibility. Second, there has been a much greater degree of co-ordination.

In December 2017, I co-founded Hong Kong Watch, because I realized that, at the time, there was no organization dedicated to advocating for Hong Kong's freedoms and the rule of law. Trying to advocate for Hong Kong in a personal capacity, in my spare time, was no longer sustainable. The level of awareness about what was happening in Hong Kong was shockingly low, and I knew that we needed an organization that could educate, inform, and influence legislators, policy-makers, the media, and the general public. I came together with my friends Gray Sergeant, who was working for Free Tibet at the time; Aileen Calverley, a Hong Kong-born Canadian citizen living in London; Dr. Malte Kaeding, a German academic at the University of Surrey; and Johnny Patterson, a recent graduate from the University of Oxford who was doing his master's at the London School of Economics. I had known Gray for a while, Johnny had been my intern at CSW, and I met Aileen and Malte through an event we organized together on Hong Kong with the Henry Jackson Society to mark the twentieth anniversary of the handover.

Over the years since it was established, Hong Kong Watch has grown in capacity and influence. We started with Johnny working part-time while pursuing his postgraduate degree, and the rest of us volunteering in our spare time. Today, we have a team of ten employees working in London, Berlin, Washington, D.C., and Ottawa, travelling regularly to Brussels and Geneva and engaging with Parliamentarians and policy-makers as far away as Canberra and elsewhere in the Asia-Pacific. We have a group of eminent and distinguished politicians from across the spectrum who serve as the organization's patrons, and a high-quality advisory board that brings together former Hong Kong legislators and activists with experienced campaigners and policy advisors. And, we have had many successes. Even though we have lost the battle for Hong Kong's freedoms—at least for the time being—we drove the British government to provide a lifeline to Hong Kongers through its BNO scheme described earlier and have influenced Canada and Australia to do the same. We played a key role behind the scenes in mobilizing the United States to impose targeted sanctions on Beijing and Hong Kong officials, and have been at the forefront of raising awareness about ethical investment—known in the sector as environmental, social, and governance (ESG) standards—and exposed major pension funds with significant stakes in Chinese companies complicit with the regime's genocide against the Uyghurs. We have helped shape the debate, not only about Hong Kong but also about how the free world responds to China and the Chinese regime as a whole.

Since Hong Kong Watch was formed, other Hong Kong-focused groups have also been set up, including Fight for Freedom Stand With Hong Kong, the Hong Kong Liberty Team, the Hong Kong Democracy Council (HKDC), and the Committee for Freedom in Hong Kong. Each one has slightly different, though complementary, strengths and focuses, and we collaborate with them all.

The Stop Uyghur Genocide Campaign was formed in 2020, initiated by the dynamic Uyghur activist and singer Rahima Mahmut, bringing together a cross-section of campaigners from different political and religious backgrounds. It has played a leading role in driving forward campaigns to stop imports of products made by Uyghur slave labour, impose sanctions on officials in the Chinese Communist Party regime responsible for the Uyghur genocide, seeking a diplomatic boycott of the Beijing Winter Olympics and—most important—for the recognition of the atrocity crimes committed against the Uyghurs as a genocide.

In the United Kingdom, two student-based organizations have been at the forefront of the campaign. Yet Again UK, a youth-led group founded to campaign against modern-day atrocity crimes, particularly genocide, consists primarily of university students and recent graduates. Burst the Bubble is an organization with a similar mission, but founded and run by high school students. I engage with both organizations regularly, and am constantly inspired by these young people, some only sixteen or seventeen, devoting their spare time to raising awareness and mobilizing politicians into action.

One of the most significant organizations that has really changed the nature of the China debate is the Inter-Parliamentary Alliance on China (IPAC), founded by a cross-party group of Parliamentarians from around the world at the initiative of my good friend Luke de Pulford in 2020. Today, IPAC has well over 250 Parliamentarians from twenty-three different legislatures, and is a truly global and cross-party movement.

IPAC is quite unique. In all my years of human rights work, rarely have I come across as effective a body that brings together politicians of completely differing persuasions from such a broad range of jurisdictions with such positive impact in such a short space of time. Its objective, in de Pulford's words, is "to reform the approach of democratic countries towards China by using parliamentary and other campaigning techniques to shift the debate." In the short time since it was established, it has already begun to do that.

It came about, de Pulford explained, after discussions with "various politicians about the need for a cross-party, international group of legislators to work together on China," but it only really "got going" when he and Sir Iain Duncan Smith started discussing it. "We agreed strongly that the rules-based and human rights order was coming under heavy pressure, which needed a united response," said de Pulford. "We agreed that legislators had a key role to play in holding governments to account for their China policy, and that co-ordinated action could help reframe the China debate." Initially, they begun building the network through the Five Eyes countries, and then they expanded to Japan and India, and across Europe and Africa. "We were clear that the initiative had to avoid party politics, and had to be owned by the politicians themselves, so we drew up a constitution, and developed criteria."

The model is based on the principle of having two co-chairs per legislature: one from the governing party and one from the major opposition party, with "sufficient standing within their respective parties to be influential," according to de Pulford. "They needed to have a history of cross-party collaboration and the willingness to 'lean in' to the project. We found that it was an idea whose time had come. It was not hard to recruit members."

Sir Iain Duncan Smith agrees. The Labour peer and prominent human rights barrister Baroness Helena Kennedy KC joined him as co-chair of the United Kingdom group, Republican Senator Marco Rubio and Democrat Senator Bob Menendez came on board in Washington, D.C., Liberal Irwin Cotler and Conservative MP Garnett Genuis led the Canadian group, and German Green Party politician Reinhard Bütikofer joined Slovakian Conservative Miriam Lexmann to co-chair the group in the European Parliament. "I was very clear from the word 'go' that this had to be left and right," recalls Sir Iain. "Once we started, we realized that there were a lot of others out there that had actually reached the same conclusions that we had. The evidence about the Uyghurs had helped enormously to focus people's minds, and then when China moved on Hong Kong, that sent alarm bells ringing everywhere. This regime is trashing international agreements, and that brought us all together, as rather strange bedfellows from the left and right of politics around the world."

IPAC has already had a significant impact. It played a leading role in pushing governments around the world to impose a diplomatic boycott of the 2022 Beijing Winter Olympics, tabling motions and debates in eleven different legislatures. "Many doubted that diplomatic boycotts would be possible, but through the persistence of the network, seven countries eventually announced them," notes de Pulford. IPAC has also advanced the goal of recognition of the atrocities against the Uyghurs as a genocide. Its Parliamentarians tabled legislative motions recognizing the atrocities, and seven different legislatures have now adopted them. This, in de

Pulford's view, means there is "considerable pressure upon governments as a result."

In the United Kingdom, IPAC members led a "genocide amendment" campaign, and almost defeated the government on it. The amendment, introduced in early 2021 to the Trade Bill, would have empowered the High Court of England and Wales to determine genocide if a case was brought to them, with a requirement that the government review any trade agreements with countries where genocide is proven. Although it did not pass, it did result in some major policy concessions for the government, forcing a shift of U.K. policy on the Uyghurs.

"IPAC members were also critical to securing the suspension of extradition agreements with Hong Kong, in collaboration with Hong Kong Watch," adds de Pulford. And, in addition to highlighting China's human rights record, IPAC has also been at the forefront of campaigning against China's economic coercion and arguing the case for reducing dependency, especially in areas of critical infrastructure. "This has seen some movement with companies such as Huawei and Hikvision."

In addition to its policy and legislative successes, IPAC provides an element of solidarity for politicians who might otherwise be lone voices. "In many emerging economies, dependency on China is so heavy that Parliamentarians raising concerns about it are often isolated and ignored," de Pulford said. "IPAC offers these voices the implied credibility of a global network of senior Parliamentarians, and this emboldens them, making them harder to ignore. As a result, we have seen a major advance in countries like Lithuania and New Zealand, which were previously not nearly as vocal as they are now." Four of IPAC's former co-chairs have been promoted to ministerial positions, including Czech Parliamentarian Jan Lipavsky, who is now the Czech foreign minister. "This has obvious connotations for policy development in those places, and is a credit to the influence of the IPAC network."

In the future, de Pulford hopes that IPAC will expand into Belt and Road countries, and, he believes, in light of China's support for Vladimir Putin's invasion of Ukraine, "there is a pressing need to admit Ukraine into the network." The group also has more work to do to develop proposals for reducing strategic dependency.

Hong Kong activist Chung Ching Kwong, who now works for IPAC, believes we have seen much greater co-ordination among activists from the different communities in recent years. "It is very, very important that we form an alliance of victims of the Chinese Communist Party," she told me. "None of these issues—Hong

Kong, Taiwan, the Uyghurs, Tibet, or the persecution of Chinese dissidents is a stand-alone cause. It all stems from one thing, the Chinese Communist Party's authoritarian regime. We all represent different dimensions of the same problem. Standing together sends a very important message, that there is a huge group of victims that you cannot ignore. And none of us would say no to the idea of a democratic China in which we could be free from our suffering, so that is why solidarity among the different groups is so important."

This chapter has looked at what has been done. Now let us ask the following question: What more should the free world be doing to address China's human rights crisis and the increasing threat which the Chinese Communist Party regime poses to our own freedoms, too?

The first thing that should be done is to better understand the nature, and scale, of the challenge. Levels of understanding of China are shockingly low. While the foreign policy community in Washington, D.C., and Canberra is streets ahead of anywhere else, insiders bemoan the shortage of China experts within the beltway. And as two recent books—Isaac Stone Fish's *America Second: How America's Elites Are Making China Stronger* and Josh Rogan's *Chaos Under Heaven: Trump, Xi and the Battle for the 21st Century*—make clear, the Chinese Communist Party's penetration of the key spheres of influence in the United States, from Capitol Hill to Wall Street, from Harvard and Yale to Hollywood and Silicon Valley, is deep and dangerous.

If Washington, D.C., still has further to go, think how far behind London, Brussels, and Ottawa are. Charles Parton, a former British diplomat who specializes in China, believes in the case of London, the problem is "a lack of attention." The government, he argues, "has neither the structures, the personnel, or the political direction" to comprehensively deal with the challenge. It is a matter of "resources, both financial and people." It is an issue, Parton fears, that the British government has not "grasped."

The National Security Council should form a working group on China, he suggests. "How often has the National Security Council met on China? How actively does it pursue the issues? There should be meetings right across Whitehall to ensure that a cross-departmental policy is drawn up and implemented," Parton argues. "The U.K. does not have a China policy. There are rudiments of policies, but no strategy, and it is ever-changing. But China is not going away."

Rush Doshi, founding director of the Brookings China Institute, sets outs the Chinese regime's intentions in his superb book, *The Long Game: China's*

Grand Strategy to Displace American Order. Through a careful analysis of Chinese Communist Party documents and speeches, Doshi builds up a clear picture of the regime's goals. "Politically, Beijing would project leadership over global governance and international institutions, split Western alliances, and advance autocratic norms at the expense of liberal ones," he writes. "Economically, it would weaken the advantages that underwrite US hegemony and seize the commanding heights of the 'fourth industrial revolution' from artificial intelligence to quantum computing, with the United States declining into a 'deindustrialized, English-speaking version of a Latin American republic . . . Militarily, the People's Liberation Army (PLA) would field a world-class force with bases around the world that could defend China's interests in most regions and even in most domains like space, the poles, and the deep sea."[24] In other words, writes Doshi, "China's ambitions are not limited to Taiwan or dominating the Indo-Pacific," but instead focused on "the global order and its future." Doshi's research and analysis should be taken seriously. China, he claims, poses a challenge "unlike any" we have faced before.[25]

Elizabeth Economy, whose book *The World According to China* should also be required reading, agrees. "Xi's ambition, as his words and deeds over the past decade suggest, is to reorder the world order," she writes.[26] "His call for 'the great rejuvenation of the Chinese nation' envisions a China that has gained centrality on the global stage: it has reclaimed contested territory, assumed a position of preeminence in the Asia-Pacific, ensured that other countries have aligned their political, economic, and security interests with its own, provided the world's technological infrastructure for the 21st century, and embedded its norms, values, and standards in international law." We must not let him succeed. But in order to stop him, we must better understand him and the system over which he prevails and rid ourselves of any idea that there is anything benevolent or benign about it.

Chinese artist Badiucao understands the dangers of the Chinese Communist Party better than most. Based in Australia, he comes from a family of artists in Shanghai. His grandparents were pioneering filmmakers who were persecuted during the Hundred Flowers Movement. "My family's tragic history played a very significant role in shaping my understanding of China," he told me in an online call from his home in Melbourne. Since 2011, he has used his art for political activism purposes, drawing cartoons and paintings depicting China's human rights crisis, and speaking up for the Uyghurs, Tibet, and Hong Kong as well as the crackdown on dissent in Mainland China. In 2021 and early 2022, he developed a campaign using his art as posters protesting against the Beijing Winter Olympics. "It provided an opportunity to highlight China's dark side—or real side—in which the regime has committed so many human rights violations against its own people," he said. "It also proved how important art can be in a social movement, to deliver a hard message in a playful, satirical way."

But as a consequence, Badiucao has become a target for the long arm of Beijing. He has received death threats, cyberattacks, and regular harassment. "When I was in Italy for exhibitions in 2021, the Chinese Embassy in Rome wrote a threatening letter to the mayor of Brescia urging him to cancel the exhibition, warning that China would cancel all other cultural programmes between China and Italy if they did not," he told me. "Then the local Chinese community, which is manipulated and controlled by the regime, organized a savage campaign on WeChat, and sent people to my events to disturb them. I even received death threats during my stay in Italy. People came up to me and said, 'There are a lot of Mafia members in Italy, and they could kill you at any minute. You should just leave.'" These, he adds, are "things I have to face on a daily basis, but the threats peak every time I have major events like an exhibition or a global campaign."

Badiucao believes the free world should tackle the issue of the Chinese government's control of overseas Chinese communities, particularly Chinese students abroad. "Organizations like the Chinese Students and Scholars Association (CSSA) and the Confucius Institutes are monitoring students and threatening people. Western society must understand this very clearly and work out a way to unplug these groups," he said. Action should also be taken to stop the regime's control in the Chinese-language digital space. "China's propaganda is so sophisticated, and it is intertwined with apps that Chinese people use daily, such as WeChat, TikTok, and Douyin. These are not just entertainment or communication apps. The Chinese government has a hundred percent control of them. If you post something about the Tiananmen massacre on WeChat, it will be deleted very quickly, your account will be frozen, and possibly your family in China will be in trouble. Why would a democratic society tolerate such a threat to free speech? The West should tell these companies that if they want to have a market in the West, they must uphold the principles of freedom of expression. If they censor on behalf of the Chinese government, they should not be allowed to operate in the free world."

Yang Jianli, a Chinese dissident in exile in Washington, D.C., runs Citizen Power Initiatives for China. The son of a Communist Party official, Yang himself joined the Party and was promoted to the middle ranks of the hierarchy. "Xi

Jinping was just one level up from me at the time," he told me. "They even called me a rising star in the system." But he became disillusioned and, in 1986, moved to the United States to study at the University of California, Berkeley. "As a Party official, I was supposed to report to the Chinese Embassy, but I chose not to do so. Ever since I set foot in the United States, I have never visited the Chinese Embassy." In 1989, Yang saw the pro-democracy movement in Tiananmen Square developing and decided to return to China to participate. In the early hours of June, 4 Yang and his colleagues cycled into the Square. "We saw the troops open fire, and we saw many people killed," he told me, in an emotional online call. "It was so hard to believe. I saw tanks moving at high speed, tear gas, machine gunfire, and I heard so much screaming. That was what propelled me into becoming an activist."

Yang managed to return to San Francisco. "I cried all the way from Beijing to San Francisco," he told me. A few days later, he was invited to testify to the United States Congress, and he then organized demonstrations and embarked on his advocacy work. But in 2002, he decided to return to China on a visit, to help advise laid-off workers involved in a labour rights protest in Liaoning Province, in northeast China. He ended up being arrested at Kunming airport, and spent five years in prison in China, including at least fifteen months in solitary confinement.

Informed by his inside knowledge of the Communist Party and his experiences in prison, Yang has ideas for what could be done. But his starting point is to recognize the gravity of the situation. "Even in my darkest moments, on the morning of June 4, 1989, when I witnessed the tanks crushing students to death on the streets of Beijing, and the fifteen months I spent in solitary confinement in prison in China, I never imagined that the Chinese Communist Party's tyranny would continue unabated until today," he said. "Many people ask, 'What should we do?' I propose that we change our way of thinking. First, we should identify the necessary conditions for the dictatorship to shift in the direction of greater freedom and dignity for its people. And second, we must do everything possible to make these necessary conditions a reality."

Yang identifies four conditions for change. "No. 1, the people must be strongly discontented with the political status quo, and demand change. Democracy must be homegrown," he told me. "No. 2, as a consequence, a viable democratic opposition arises. Discontent is not enough—it must be translated into a viable democratic opposition. A lot of opposition groups in the past thirty years have arisen, but none of them turned out to be viable. No. 3, a rift must occur within the leadership of the Chinese Communist Party regime. And No. 4, the international community must believe that China's democratic opposition is viable, and recognize it and support it. These four conditions must be met if we are to have a chance of changing China."

Civil society space in China under Xi Jinping has been "squeezed to zero," according to Yang. So the question facing us is how to help people in China "recreate" civil society space.

The first thing to do, Yang argues, is to address Internet freedom. "If we can do something to help people in China communicate more freely, and use the Internet as an organizational tool, then we will see something grow from there," he believes. "If we can bring Chinese civil society activists together with technology experts, funders, and policy-makers, that could really help. But we need the willpower and vision to do it."

In the process of researching this book, I have interviewed more than eighty people and read more than forty books on China. I have not yet counted the number of reports, papers, opinion editorials, and newspaper articles I have also read, highlighted, and filed—many of which I kept in a pile on the bed in my spare room, ready to be quoted from and referenced. In the end, I could use only a fraction of them, because if I had quoted from them all, this book would have turned into an encyclopaedia. As a result of all this material, however, ten recommendations have crystalized in my mind as an action plan going forward. These ten points are by no means exhaustive, but they provide the foundations for what the free world might—and should—do.

The ten ideas can be grouped into three thematic "clusters": the first basket is ending impunity, ensuring accountability, and applying punitive consequences for the regime's behaviour; the second is providing lifelines for those who need to escape, and empowering dissent, within and beyond China's borders; the third is around defending and strengthening our own freedoms and values, and the international rules-based order.

In the first cluster, I believe we must impose targeted sanctions against those responsible for grave violations of human rights. That means Magnitsky–style sanctions against individual officials in Beijing, Xinjiang, Tibet, and Hong Kong, which have already begun but which must be continued. But it also means sanctions against commercial entities complicit with the Chinese Communist Party regime's tools of repression and surveillance. "Money is the most important thing to Chinese Communist Party officials," Tiananmen protest leader Wang

Dan told me. "They will only get nervous if they are hit economically. Western countries must act in unison, ban Chinese Communist Party officials and their families from immigrating, and freezing their property and assets abroad." Wei Jingsheng, the father of China's democracy movement, agrees. "Sanctions are a must," he said.

In addition, however difficult it may be to achieve, we should pursue international justice and accountability mechanisms for atrocity crimes and grave violations of international treaties. Easier said than done, given that China cannot be brought to either the International Criminal Court or the International Court of Justice, because it would veto such a referral, and finding a government with the political will to work to set up an ad hoc tribunal will be a challenge. But legal minds should put their heads together to work out a creative way of bringing the regime to justice. The two independent tribunals discussed in this book—the China Tribunal into forced organ harvesting and the Uyghur Tribunal—provide the foundations for justice and accountability.

There must also be an international inquiry into the causes of COVID-19. As Wei Jingsheng told me in a call from his home in Washington, D.C., "If China does not allow an independent investigation, it shows that it has something to hide and will create new disasters in the future."

In the second basket, we should do more to provide rapid, fast-tracked pathways for Uyghurs, Hong Kongers, Tibetans, Chinese dissidents, Chinese Christians, and Falun Gong practitioners to find sanctuary and a platform in the free world. That means not only lifeboat schemes and better asylum processes, but also more overt recognition and support. Margaret Thatcher and Ronald Reagan used to meet with Soviet dissidents, and George W. Bush met with several Burmese and North Korean exiled activists. Western political leaders should make a point of meeting Uyghur, Tibetan, and Hong Kong activists, and Chinese dissidents, unashamedly.

World leaders should resume contact with His Holiness the Dalai Lama, and high-level parliamentary and ministerial visits to Taiwan should increase. Mary Kissel told me that she made a point of ensuring that whenever the Trump administration talked about Taiwan, the word "democracy" would be there. "We used various phrases when we talked about Taiwan, such as 'force for good in the world,' 'thriving democracy,' and 'vibrant economy,'" she said. "Putting in the word 'democracy' every time we talked about Taiwan was very important, because it distinguishes Taiwan from Communist China implicitly. Taiwan represents what China could be—prosperous and free."

Pompeo also ramped up interactions with Taipei. "Not only did we sell Taiwan more weapons than any other administration in recent memory, and promoted a science and technology dialogue with Taiwan, and advocated for Taiwan to be a member of the World Health Assembly, but we advocated for the broadest possible unofficial relationship with Taiwan," recalled Kissel. "Until then, the State Department controlled who could talk to Taiwanese officials in Washington, D.C., but Secretary Pompeo issued a memo to eliminate all restrictions on interactions with the Taiwanese. The State Department has unofficial relations with all kinds of bodies. For instance, we have an unofficial relationship with Amnesty International. There is no one telling State Department officials they cannot have lunch with Amnesty International. So if we wanted closer cooperation with Taiwan, which we did, we could not have that if we could not talk to them. That is why it was an important move."

There should be investment, as Yang Jianli proposed, in circumventing, or breaking down, the Great Firewall of China, enhancing Internet freedom, and finding other ways to support civil society—without, of course, unduly endangering them.

In the third grouping, the free world must absolutely diversify supply chains; reduce strategic dependency on China; divest from unethical investments; ensure that Beijing is in no doubt about our intentions to defend Taiwan; and defend academic freedom in our universities by reducing financial dependence on Chinese funding and extracting the Chinese Communist Party's Confucius Institutes from our own institutions, tackling the Chinese regime's influence and infiltration operations, and strengthening the alliances among democracies.

Some of our major pension funds in the United Kingdom, the United States, Canada, Australia, New Zealand, Japan, and Korea and across Europe have significant investments in Chinese companies directly involved in, and complicit with, the genocide of the Uyghurs and the growth of the surveillance State in China. In 2021, Hong Kong Watch published a new report, *ESG, China and Human Rights: Why the time has come for investors to act*, which found that "more money is being invested in China by Western pension funds, sovereign wealth funds, and other institutional investors than ever before."[27]

The growing presence of Chinese equities in funds run by firms like BlackRock, the world's largest asset manager, means that pretty much every pension fund has serious shares in Chinese equities. For example, the U.K. Universities Superannuation Scheme (USS) is the largest private pension scheme in the country in terms of assets, covering all university staff. Of all the global holdings (not only those in emerging markets) in the British USS—one of the largest pension funds in Britain—Tencent is the second-largest stock and Alibaba is the fifth-largest stock. Given that £25 billion is invested in publicly listed equities, this means, the fund is investing hundreds of millions of pounds into the two firms. The fund also has more than £100 million invested in China Construction Bank.

There are a number of reasons to be concerned by this. First, little attention has been paid to the human rights record of Chinese technology firms. Investments in Tencent and Alibaba are problematic because Chinese technology companies of their size cannot divorce themselves from the Chinese State, which is increasingly using a mixture of surveillance and technology to oppress and target minorities within its borders. Alibaba has produced facial recognition software that has been used by the Chinese government to target Uyghurs, and has helped construct the surveillance State and prison camps in which over a million Uyghurs are currently detained. It has also developed a privately run social credit application, Sesame Credit, which may be absorbed into the Chinese State's dystopian social credit system. WeChat, owned by Tencent, has been accused by Human Rights Watch of censoring and putting its users under surveillance on behalf of the Chinese State. Other Chinese technology firms raise similar alarm bells.

But it is not only human rights that should concern us. Institutional investment in China has national security implications. Chinese State-owned banks are the largest bankroller of Chinese State-owned enterprises, which, in turn, have spent the last decade buying up a substantial amount of strategic infrastructure in the West, as well as being the largest lenders to the Belt and Road Initiative, which has been accused of exploiting developing nations and being used as a tool for "debt diplomacy." These firms, in turn, fund Chinese State-owned enterprises like the China National Oil Corporation, China General Nuclear Power Group, or Beijing Construction Engineering Group, which have been blacklisted by the United States. Greater scrutiny is needed.

Finally, questions should be asked of the safety of international institutional investment in China at a time when Xi Jinping is conducting a regulatory crackdown. The rule of law is non-existent in China. One day, firms have the support of the Communist Party; the next, they can find they are charged with corruption—this is the lesson of Desmond Shum's bombshell book about the inner workings of the Communist Party, *Red Roulette*. There are no guarantees that what appear shrewd investments now will not go sour in the next regulatory crackdown.

It is time to ask our pension fund providers to stop increasing their China allocations. Financier George Soros has written in both the *Financial Times* and the *Wall Street Journal* criticizing BlackRock, arguing that "pouring billions of dollars into China now is a tragic mistake."[28] Xi Jinping, Soros notes, "regards all Chinese companies as instruments of a one-party state" and investors buying into that "are facing a rude awakening."[29] Leading British financier Baroness Helena Morrissey has called on investors to withdraw from China.[30] And Matt Pottinger, former U.S. deputy national security advisor, has called out "the naked hypocrisy" of investment funds that claim to further "environmental, social, and governance" goals while investing in Chinese companies "that feature atrocious records in all three categories."[31]

Moreover, despite China's remarkable economic growth hitherto, there are increasing reasons to be concerned about the risks of doing business with China going forward. Xi Jinping appears to have embarked on a campaign against private enterprise, reining in companies and individual entrepreneurs whom he fears have become too powerful.[32] The role of the Communist Party in the private sector, the denunciations of "big capitalists," the disappearance of entrepreneurs such as Jack Ma or film stars like Fan Bingbing all speak of a dangerous investment environment.[33] And the crisis in the property sector, with the near collapse of real estate giant Evergrande, suggest deep-seated problems. The founder and chair of one of Asia's largest private equity investors, Wejian Shan, whose group PAG manages more than $50 billion, has said he is diversifying away from China because the regime's policies have caused a "deep economic crisis."[34]

Charles Parton believes we should not have Chinese investment in our critical national infrastructure, and we should "properly defend ourselves" against increasing espionage. The chief of Britain's Secret Intelligence Service (SIS), Richard Moore, highlighted this in a speech in November 2021, in which he described China as "the single greatest priority" for MI6. "The fact remains that China is an authoritarian state, with different values from ours. This is reflected in the threats we see emanating from the Chinese state," he said. "The Chinese Intelligence Services are highly capable and continue to conduct large-scale espionage operations against the U.K. and our allies. This includes targeting those working in government, industries, or on research of particular interest to the Chinese state. They also monitor and attempt to exercise undue influence over the Chinese diaspora."[35]

Understanding the way China's United Front Work Department operates is essential. In 2014, Xi Jinping described it as one of the Communist Party's "magic weapons," the body that co-ordinates the regime's foreign influence operations throughout the business, political, academic, cultural, and media spheres and among the Chinese diaspora. As New Zealand scholar Anne-Marie Brady writes, "even more than his predecessors, Xi Jinping has led a massive expansion of efforts to shape foreign public opinion in order to influence the decision-making of foreign governments and societies . . . Political influence activities in the Xi era draw heavily on the approaches set in the Mao years and the policies of Deng, Jiang, and Hu, but take them to a new level of ambition."[36]

The recent exposure of a British Chinese lawyer, Christine Lee, as a United Front agent for China should be a wake-up call. For years, she operated at the heart of British politics, with access to senior politicians in all major political parties. In 2022, MI5 blew the whistle on her, exposing her work as a spy for Beijing. As Parton argues in two papers—one published in 2019 by the Royal United Services Institute (RUSI)[37] and one in 2020 by King's College London[38]—the British government, and other governments, too, need to investigate China's United Front activity and develop a strategy for countering it.

Perhaps, most important of all, we should strengthen alliances among democracies. President Biden has started this work, with the Summit for Democracy in 2021; Boris Johnson called for a "D-10" group of the world's ten leading democracies; and Britain's new prime minister, Liz Truss, has talked of a "network of liberty." But there is a need to do more. If countries act together in, for example, imposing sanctions, it becomes much more difficult for China to retaliate effectively. When countries act unilaterally, China is able to pick them off, play them off one another, and create divisions. To defend freedom, the free world needs to form its own United Front to counter Beijing's.

One vital thing we should do, and I am passionate about doing, is to make it loudly, repeatedly, and abundantly clear that this is not about being anti-China, or anti-Chinese—but rather anti-authoritarianism. As I hope this book has made clear, I am deeply pro-China. I love China and its people and culture. It is the brutal regime that represses those people that I love that I detest.

Badiucao believes this is a "very, very important" message. "If the West or the so-called 'free world' really wants to help the Chinese people and potentially move China in a better direction, then every critic of the Chinese government must understand the importance of distinguishing between the Chinese Communist

Party and the people of China," he told me. "And the best way to help the Chinese people to change China is to empower the overseas Chinese population." That does not mean, he added, "blindly supporting anyone with a Chinese background," because we must be alert to the Chinese regime's attempts at infiltration—and we must also counter Beijing's narrative that criticism of the Party is akin to racism. "The Chinese government describes my art as anti-China racism, which is ridiculous," said Badiucao. Striking the right balance—between countering genuine racism while at the same time being critical of the regime in Beijing—is vital. "I do not think it is very hard. People with knowledge and a moral compass should not have difficulty telling whether criticism is against the government or against ordinary people," he argues.

As Michael Chong told me, we need to do two things. "We must acknowledge that the Chinese people are part of an ancient civilization that dates back millennia, that has contributed greatly to the progress of humanity, through paper, gunpowder, calligraphy, and so many other things. Chinese civilization has provided much of the advances of humanity and is something to be celebrated," he emphasized. "And we need to denounce anti-Asian hate and discrimination, wherever we see it. We must condemn people who use the threats that the Communist leadership in Beijing is presenting to us as an excuse for bigoted and racist views about people of Asian descent. Our quarrel is not with the Chinese people. Our quarrel is with the Communist Party leadership in Beijing and the threats they present to the international rules-based order, through their gross violations of human rights. If we do not counter the threats from Beijing, either we are going to abandon our fellow citizens of Asian descent targeted for their race, or we are going to fail to counter those threats to our democracy."

Chong is right, and those principles apply not only in Ottawa and across Canada, but in the United Kingdom and the United States, and across Australia, Europe, and beyond. This is a fight for freedom, one which is most intense within China's borders but which, due to the behaviour of the regime in Beijing, does not stop at China's borders.

"You have to consider what Xi Jinping himself has said," Mary Kissel points out. "He speaks often of a struggle with the West. He is steeped in Marxist-Leninist doctrine. He has made it very clear that he believes he is in a struggle with us." She notes that it may not be "entirely analogous to the Cold War with the Soviet Union"—in many ways, it is "far more dangerous and advanced," because China is so interconnected with the global economy, deeply embedded in our own societies, and has "co-opted" a lobby spread across Wall Street, Hollywood, and Silicon Valley. "It is a very insidious, sophisticated challenge. They are inside the gates, in the United States, Britain, Canada, Australia, New Zealand, all over the world. So it is a very different problem from the one we faced during the Cold War with the Soviet Union." But it is essential that we confront it and, argues Kissel, to remember that "our system is better, and we need to have the confidence to say that and believe it."

The last governor of Hong Kong, Chris Patten, reflected to me in a conversation in 2021 about Xi Jinping's speech in which he had said that he wanted China to be regarded by the rest of the world as "loveable, credible, and respected."[39] Lord Patten laughed at the idea. "Is the Chinese Communist Party seen as 'loveable'? Not in Tibet, not in Xinjiang, not in Hong Kong. Is what the Chinese regime says 'credible'? Not when they refuse to give an open reckoning on how coronavirus began, and keep preventing others doing so. Is it respected? Not when it sticks to the international rule book except when it suits it. China has been throwing its weight around in the South China Sea, despite commitments that Xi Jinping made not to do so. Credible, loveable, respected? I think not." Or, as the 2021 U.S.-China Economic and Security Review Commission report puts it, the Chinese Communist Party regime "is a long-term, consequential, menacing adversary determined to end the economic and political freedoms that have served as the foundation for security and prosperity for billions of people."[40]

Ian Williams, in his excellent book *Every Breath You Take: China's New Tyranny*, argues that "China bullies because it can, and because it has been able to get away with it." He is exactly right. For too long, we have kowtowed to Beijing, and that has emboldened the regime in its aggression. "Too often its targets back down, offering words of contrition, rather like payment of tribute in imperial times," writes Williams. What is now called for, he adds, is "a recognition of what China has become under Xi Jinping: an aggressive and expansionary power which not only represses its own people but is now the biggest threat to Western democracies, their like-minded allies, and to democratic values in general. Xi's is an aggressive nationalist regime, sustained by technology—a digital totalitarian state. Standing up to Xi, asserting liberal democratic values, and becoming less economically dependent on China are moral and practical imperatives."[41]

As Wu'erkaixi told me, "Congressman Chris Smith said on the thirtieth anniversary of the Tiananmen Square massacre that 'In between the tank and the Tank Man, you have to choose one side. There is no middle way; there is no in between.' Today, with more than a million Uyghurs in concentration camps, a pandemic that hit the whole world, the dismantling of Hong Kong's freedoms, threats to Taiwan increasing, we need to end what the foreign policy establishment calls 'strategic ambiguity' and introduce 'strategic clarity.' That clarity is the answer to the question of what the free world should do. Stand clear and tell Beijing there is a red line."

The goal, as dissident Xu Zhiyong puts it in his powerful book *To Build a Free China: A Citizen's Journey*, is "a free China with democracy and rule of law, a just and prosperous civil society, and a new national spirit of 'Freedom, Justice, and Love.'" If we can help the peoples of China—and Hong Kong, Tibet, and East Turkistan—achieve that, the world will be a better, more peaceful, and safer place.

ACKNOWLEDGMENTS

Writing a book on China is a mammoth task. The size of the country, the scope of its history, the scale of its influence, the nature of its ruling Communist Party regime, and the severity of the challenges it poses to its own people and to the rest of the world are enormous.

Even limiting the scope of a book to the human rights violations perpetrated by the Chinese Communist Party regime, the complicity of that regime with atrocities in neighbouring countries, and the threats that the regime poses to freedom itself would still leave a massive task for any author foolhardy enough to attempt it.

In writing this book, I have drawn extensively on my own experiences, knowledge, reflections, and materials in my files. But even though I have been in and around China since I was eighteen years old, it was always inconceivable to think that I could fulfill this task entirely on my own. The subject is too vast, and I suffer from the fact that I have not been able to travel to China for several years (the decision of the regime in Beijing). Furthermore—and most important— what matters in this account of the human rights crisis in China is not my voice but the voices of those who have suffered first-hand: Uyghurs, Tibetans, Chinese Christians, Falun Gong practitioners, Hong Kongers, Mainland Chinese dissidents, and human rights defenders. Also important are those among China's neighbours—especially in Taiwan, Myanmar, and North Korea—who have suffered, directly or indirectly, at the hands of the Chinese regime. In addition, there were many gaps in my knowledge that could be filled only by experts with far greater insights and inside knowledge: policy-makers, diplomats, and academics.

I have, therefore, conducted over eighty interviews for this book, and I'm deeply indebted to every single individual who graciously and generously made time to talk with me. There are some who wish to remain anonymous, for obvious security reasons, and I wish to respect their anonymity. They know who they are, and I hope they know I am grateful. Among those who can be named, I am profoundly thankful to the following:

Chinese exiled dissidents Wei Jingsheng, Wang Dan, Wu'erkaixi, Yang Jianli, Teng Biao, and the artist Badiucao—all of whom spared time to share their experiences of the past, especially the Tiananmen Square massacre, and their thoughts for the future. In addition, Ai Weiwei and Ma Jian, whom I did not interview for this book but have had the privilege of meeting and talking with and whose insights inspire me, also deserve recognition.

Dolkun Isa, Rahima Mahmut, Nury Turkel, Rushan Abbas, Enver Tohti, and Wu'erkaixi provided first-hand stories, insights, and analysis for the chapter on the Uyghurs, and Louisa Greve provided valuable analysis. I am also deeply indebted to both Dr. Joanne Smith Finley and Louisa Greve for reading the draft chapter and providing detailed, extensive, and extremely helpful suggested amendments.

For the chapter on Tibet, Tenzin Choekyi, Wangden Kyab, Tsering Dawa, Nyima Lhamo, Senator Con Di Nino, MP Tim Loughton, Lord Alton of Liverpool, and Ambassador Sam Brownback provided very valuable insights. John Jones of Free Tibet provided helpful background information and advice, and, along with the interviewees and other Tibet experts, he reviewed the draft chapter. Most significantly, His Holiness the Dalai Lama was gracious enough to answer some questions and to permit me to quote him, as I do in the chapter, from our personal correspondence.

Bob Fu of China Aid and my colleagues at Christian Solidarity Worldwide provided invaluable insights for the chapter on the persecution of Christians.

For the chapter on forced organ harvesting, I am grateful to Anastasia Lin, Ethan Gutmann, David Matas, and Matthew Robertson for their insights and inspiration, and to many Falun Gong practitioners whom I have been privileged to come to know. And I would like especially to pay tribute to my friend, mentor, and hero, former Canadian Parliamentarian and Cabinet minister who served in many positions, including as secretary of state for Asia-Pacific, David Kilgour. I spoke to David for and about this book just a few months before he sadly died in April 2022. He was a patron of Hong Kong Watch, a constant source of inspiration, and someone whom I, along with many others in the human rights movement across the world, will profoundly miss.

I am deeply grateful to Nathan Law, both for writing the foreword to this book and for sparing time to be interviewed. Former Hong Kong legislators Ted Hui and Dennis Kwok, now in exile, as well as Alex Chow, Chung Ching Kwong, Ray Wong, Joey Siu, Jim Wong, Ed Chin, Finn Lau, Catherine Li, former district councillor Kawai Lee, and Pastor Roy Chan were very generous with their time for the chapter on Hong Kong, as were several other Hong Kongers, including lawyers, journalists, and activists who do not wish to be named. Distinguished journalists Stephen Vines, a former presenter on the public service broadcaster RTHK; Mark Clifford, former editor of the *South China Morning Post*; Chris Wong, a former TVB news anchor; and several former *Apple Daily* and *Ming Pao* reporters provided valuable insights. I was also privileged to know and talk with several of Hong Kong's most prominent pro-democracy activists in recent years, but many of those I could call my friends are now in jail or keeping a low profile, and I do not want to add to their difficulties by naming them. They know I am thinking of them, campaigning for them, and praying for them every day.

For the chapter on Myanmar (Burma), I am grateful to Jason Tower, former United States ambassador Derek Mitchell, former United Kingdom ambassador Andrew Heyn, Anna Tan, and Angshuman Choudhury, among others, and for the chapter on North Korea, the insights provided by Tim Peters, Suzanne Scholte, Greg Scarlatoiu, Sokeel Park, Jieun Baek, Peter Jung, former United Kingdom ambassador to Pyongyang David Slinn, North Korean escapees Timothy Cho, Jihyun Park, and Joseph Kim, and others who do not wish to be named are greatly appreciated.

For the chapter on Taiwan, I am deeply grateful to the spokesperson for the president of Taiwan, Kolas Yotaka; former Taiwanese diplomat Vincent Chao; the leader of the Sunflower Movement, Lin Fei-fan; the vice president of the Taiwan Foundation for Democracy, Dr. Ketty Chen; Taiwan scholar Ian Easton; my friend and colleague Gray Sergeant; and others for their advice.

In addition, many China experts in the worlds of academia, journalism, advocacy, and policy-making have graciously agreed to speak with me, including Jerome Cohen, Charles Parton, Akira Igata, Jan Wong, Joanne Chiu, Nicola Macbean, Peter Dahlin, Peter Mattis, and Peter Humphrey. I am also deeply grateful to Dimon Liu.

I am profoundly appreciative of British Parliamentarians such as the last governor of Hong Kong, Lord Patten; Sir Iain Duncan Smith MP; Tim Loughton MP; Lord Alton; former Speaker of the House of Commons John

Bercow. In Canada, I'm grateful to many former and current politicians, including Senator Con Di Nino, Michael Chong, Kenny Chiu, Garnett Genuis, Irwin Cotler, Senator Leo Housakos, Jenny Kwan, and, before his death, David Kilgour, as well as others who have either been directly interviewed for this book or inspired me in its writing. I also offer thanks to U.S. Congressman Chris Smith; the chair of the U.S.- China Economic and Security Review Commission, Carolyn Bartholomew; former U.S. ambassador-at-large for international religious freedom Sam Brownback; former U.S. ambassador-at-large for global women's issues Kelley Currie; and Mary Kissel, former senior advisor to Secretary of State Mike Pompeo for their insights and time.

Finally, among the many brave people who have helped me with this book, I want to thank Angela Gui, whose father, Gui Minhai, was abducted by the Chinese regime in Thailand and then jailed in China. Angela, whom I am proud to call a friend, shared her reflections on her real and raw personal journey as it intertwined with China's fight for freedom.

These interviews would never have made it into the book without the help of John Stackhouse, Max Darby, and Tom Webster, who spent many hours transcribing them. To them, I am profoundly grateful. John Stackhouse also deserves commending for sharing many sources of information, assisting with research, and providing insights on various aspects of the book.

My colleagues at Hong Kong Watch, especially Johnny Patterson and Sam Goodman, provided support, both by offering wisdom, research, and insight and by giving me space to write and feedback on what I had written. I am also deeply grateful to the trustees of Hong Kong Watch, Gray Sergeant, Aileen Calverley, and Dr. Malte Kaeding, for their partnership in our advocacy for Hong Kong and their encouragement of this book. And I also want to thank my colleagues in Christian Solidarity Worldwide, with whom I have worked in different capacities for almost three decades. They inspired me into human rights advocacy and have encouraged, supported, equipped, mentored, and developed me throughout this work, and I owe them such gratitude.

Laura Harth, Perseus, Luke de Pulford, and other friends also reviewed various chapters, and I am very appreciative of their help.

To anyone I have inadvertently failed to acknowledge, I apologize. Just as the subject matter is vast, the number of people who helped me in various ways is similarly large. To everyone who helped, directly or indirectly, thank you.

And a special thank you to my excellent editors, my publisher, Optimum

Publishing International, and its managing director, Dean Baxendale: thank you for taking me on, for being allies in the cause, and for your friendship, guidance, support, and wise counsel throughout the process of producing this book and all related initiatives.

Together, let us work for freedom for all the peoples of China. In modern online-speak, let's #FightForFreedom.

NOTES

INTRODUCTION

1. *Hong Kong Free Press*, "UK Conservative Party Member 'Assaulted by Chinese State TV Reporter' at Conference," October 2018, https://www.youtube.com/watch?v=J9bd04kkGbg&t=22s.
2. Alvin Lum, "Threatening Letters Sent from Hong Kong Make British Human Rights Activist 'More Determined' to Speak Up for City," South China Morning Post, 13 July 2018, https://www.scmp.com/news/hong-kong/politics/article/2155147/threatening-letters-sent-hong-kong-make-british-human-rights.
3. Joseph Loconte, "Chinese Intimidation Comes to Benedict Rogers' Mailbox," *Washington Examiner*, 23 July 2018, https://www.washingtonexaminer.com/weekly-standard/chinese-intimidation-comes-to-benedict-rogerss-mailbox.
4. Hong Kong Watch, "Hong Kong Watch Co-Founder and CEO Benedict Rogers Threatened under National Security Law," 14 March 2022, https://www.hongkongwatch.org/all-posts/2022/3/14/hong-kong-watch-co-founder-and-ceo-benedict-rogers-threatened-under-national-security-law.
5. Henry Zeffman, "Hong Kong Threatens British Human Rights Activist," *Times* (London), 14 March 2022, https://www.thetimes.co.uk/article/hong-kong-threatens-british-human-rights-activist-3k5zvjdfk.
6. James Landale, "Hong Kong: Briton Accused of Jeopardising China's Security," BBC News, 14 March 2022, https://www.bbc.co.uk/news/uk-60732949.

CHAPTER 1: FROM DUMPLINGS WITH EVERYTHING TO ALICE IN WONDERLAND

1. *Economist*, "China Has Built the World's Largest Bullet Train Network," 13 January 2017, https://www.economist.com/china/2017/01/13/china-has-built-the-worlds-largest-bullet-train-network.
2. *Economist*, "China Will Soon Open a New Stretch of Rail across Tibet," 3 June 2021, https://www.economist.com/china/2021/06/03/china-will-soon-open-a-new-stretch-of-rail-across-tibet.

CHAPTER 3: CHINA'S CRACKDOWN AFTER A DECADE OF OPENING

1. Blake Hounshell, Charter 08, *Foreign Policy*, 8 October 2010, https://foreignpolicy.com/2010/10/08/charter-08/.

2. *Financial Times*, "'Western Values' Forbidden in Chinese Universities," 30 January 2015, https://www.ft.com/content/95f3f866-a87e-11e4-bd17-00144feab7de.

3. UN OHCHR, "UN Human Rights Chief Says China's New Security Law Is Too Broad, Too Vague," 7 July 2015, https://www.ohchr.org/en/NewsEvents/Pages/DisplayNews.aspx?NewsID=16210&LangID=E

4. *Guardian*, "China Passes Law Imposing Security Controls on Foreign NGOs," 28 April 2016, https://www.theguardian.com/world/2016/apr/28/china-passes-law-imposing-security-controls-on-foreign-ngos.

5. Charles Parton, "Engineering the Soul of China," *Standpoint*, August/September 2020.

6. The Conservative Party Human Rights Commission, *The Darkness Deepens: The Crackdown on Human Rights in China 2016–2020*, p. 9, https://conservativepartyhumanrightscommission.co.uk/wp-content/uploads/2021/01/CPHRC-China-Report.pdf.

7. Ibid., p. 37.

8. Ibid., p. 37.

9. CSW, "China: Commentary by detained human rights lawyer," 16 October 2017, https://www.csw.org.uk/2017/10/16/press/3758/article.htm.

10. Grace Gao, "Truth Is Power and I Will Keep Speaking It Until My Father Is Free," International Service for Human Rights, October 2016.

11. The Conservative Party Human Rights Commission, *The Darkest Moment: The Crackdown on Human Rights 2013–2016*, p. 26, https://conservativepartyhumanrightscommission.co.uk/wp-content/uploads/2020/03/CPHRC_China_Human_Rights_Report_Final.pdf.

12. Ibid., p. 26.

13. *Hong Kong Free Press*, "Wife of Activist Barred from Leaving China Dies in US after 15 Years Apart," 11 January 2022, https://hongkongfp.com/2022/01/11/wife-of-activist-barred-from-leaving-china-dies-in-us-after-15-years-apart/.

14. The Conservative Party Human Rights Commission, *The Darkness Deepens: The Crackdown on Human Rights in China 2016–2020*, p. 32, https://conservativepartyhumanrightscommission.co.uk/wp-content/uploads/2021/01/CPHRC-China-Report.pdf.

15. Ibid.

16. Kris Cheng, "'My Ordeal Haunts Me': UK Regulator Must Ban Chinese State TV, Says Man Who Appeared in 'Forced Confession,'" *Hong Kong Free Press*, 23 November 2018, https://hongkongfp.com/2018/11/23/ordeal-haunts-uk-regulator-must-ban-chinese-state-tv-says-man-appeared-forced-confession/.

17. Alex Hern "Chinese State Broadcaster Loses UK Licence after Ofcom Ruling," *Guardian*, 4 February 2021, https://www.theguardian.com/world/2021/feb/04/chinese-news-network-cgtn-loses-uk-licence-after-ofcom-ruling.

18. University of Southampton, "Early and Combined Interventions Crucial in Tackling Covid-19 Spread in China," 11 March 2020, https://www.southampton.ac.uk/news/2020/03/covid-19-china.page.

19. The Henry Jackson Society, "Coronavirus Compensation? Assessing China's Potential Culpability and Avenues of Legal Response," April 2020, https://henryjacksonsociety.org/publications/coronaviruscompensation/.

20. Andrew Green, "Li Wenliang—Obituary," *Lancet*, 18 February 2020, https://www.thelancet.com/journals/lancet/article/PIIS0140-6736(20)30382-2/fulltext.

21. Lily Kuo, "Coronavirus: Wuhan Doctor Speaks Out against Authorities," *Guardian*, 11 March 2020, https://www.theguardian.com/world/2020/mar/11/coronavirus-wuhan-doctor-ai-fen-speaks-out-against-authorities.

22. CSW, "Fears for Health of Christian Activist on Hunger Strike in Detention," 13 October 2020, https://www.csw.org.uk/2020/10/13/press/4848/article.htm.

23. Ibid.

CHAPTER 4: CHRISTIANITY UNDER FIRE

1. Bob Whyte, *Unfinished Encounter: China and Christianity* (Fount Paperbacks, 1988), p. 216.

2. Tony Lambert, *The Resurrection of the Chinese Church*, 1994, OMF IHQ, p. 18.

3. Bob Whyte, *Unfinished Encounter: China and Christianity*, (London: Collins Fount Paperbacks, 1988), p. 292.

4. Tony Lambert, *The Resurrection of the Chinese Church*, OMF IHQ, p. 63.

5. Human Rights Watch, *Freedom of Religion in China*, 1992, p. 5.

6. Tony Lambert, *The Resurrection of the Chinese Church*, p. 61.

7. Human Rights Watch, *Freedom of Religion in China*, p. 2.

8. *Hong Kong Free Press*, "Religious Groups 'Must Adhere to the Leadership of the Communist Party'—Pres. Xi Jinping," 24 April 2016, https://hongkongfp.com/2016/04/24/religious-groups-must-adhere-to-the-leadership-of-the-communist-party-pres-xi-jinping/.

9. UCANews, "Chinese Communist Party Issues Warning to Members Harboring Religious Beliefs," 25 May 2015, https://www.ucanews.com/news/chinese-communist-party-issues-warning-to-members-harboring-religious-beliefs/73667#.

10. The Conservative Party Human Rights Commission, *The Darkest Moment: The Crackdown on Human Rights in China 2013–2016*, p. 37, https://conservativepartyhumanrightscommission.co.uk/wp-content/uploads/2020/03/CPHRC_China_Human_Rights_Report_Final.pdf.

11. Ibid., p. 37.

12. Liao Yiwu, "A Brainwashing War: An Appeal for the Poet-Preacher Wang Yi," China Change, 4 March 2019, https://chinachange.org/2019/03/05/a--brainwashing-war-an-appeal-for-the-poet-preacher-wang-yi/.

13. Ibid.

14. The Foreign Correspondents' Club, Hong Kong, "Religious Freedom: Global Threats and the World's Response," 8 March 2019, https://www.fcchk.org/event/club-breakfast-religious-freedom-global-threats-and-the-worlds-response/.

15. CBN News, "Letter from a Chengdu Jail by Wang Yi," 16 December 2018,

https://www1.cbn.com/cbnnews/cwn/2018/december/early-rain-church-releases-letter-written-by-pastor-arrested-by-chinese-authorities.

16. Wang Yi, "My Declaration of Faithful Disobedience," China Partnership, 12 December 2018, https://www.chinapartnership.org/blog/2018/12/my-declaration-of-faithful-disobedience.

17. The Conservative Party Human Rights Commission, *The Darkness Deepens: The Crackdown on Human Rights in China 2016–2020*, p. 25, https://conservativepartyhumanrightscommission.co.uk/wp-content/uploads/2021/01/CPHRC-China-Report.pdf.

18. CSW, "Church Leaders Facing Terrorism and National Security Charges," 26 July 2021, https://www.csw.org.uk/2021/07/26/press/5359/article.htm.

19. CSW, "Chinese Christian Couple Sentenced," 1 March 2016, https://www.csw.org.uk/2016/03/01/press/3000/article.htm.

20. The Conservative Party Human Rights Commission, *The Darkest Moment: The Crackdown on Human Rights in China 2013–2016*, p. 38, https://conservativepartyhumanrightscommission.co.uk/wp-content/uploads/2020/03/CPHRC_China_Human_Rights_Report_Final.pdf.

21. Ibid., p. 39.

22. The Conservative Party Human Rights Commission, *The Darkness Deepens: The Crackdown on Human Rights in China 2016–2020*, p. 26, https://conservativepartyhumanrightscommission.co.uk/wp-content/uploads/2021/01/CPHRC-China-Report.pdf.

23. CSW, Exclusive Briefing on Targeting of House Churches amid the Covid-19 Pandemic, 21 September 2020, https://www.csw.org.uk/2020/09/21/press/4814/article.htm.

24. CSW, *China Voices*—a quarterly update, January–March 2021.

25. CSW, China: Shenzhen Holy Reformed Church, August 2021, https://www.csw.org.uk/2021/08/13/report/5371/article.htm.

26. Zhang Chunhua, "Christian Pastors Told to Preach in Sermons Confidence in the Party and Xi Jinping," *Bitter Winter*, 21 December 2021, https://bitterwinter.org/three-self-church-preaching-confidence-in-ccp/.

27. Xia Qiao, "New Directives on Sinicisation of Religion: 'Love the Party, Love Socialism,'" *Bitter Winter*, 24 March 2022, https://bitterwinter.org/new-directives-on-sinicization-of-religion-love-the-party-love-socialism/.

28. Pope Francis, *Let Us Dream: The Path to a Better Future* (Simon & Schuster, 2020), p. 12.

29. Cardinal Charles Bo, "The Chinese Regime and Its Moral Culpability for Covid-19," UCANews, 1 April 2020, https://www.ucanews.com/news/the-chinese-regime-and-its-moral-culpability-for-covid-19/87609.

30. Cardinal Bo, "Cardinal Bo Urges Prayer Octave for China," GlobalPrayerforChina.org, 7 May 2021, https://globalprayerforchina.org/cardinal-bo-urges-prayer-octave-for-china/.

31. *Catholic News Agency*, "Report: Chinese Government Imprisoning More Priests, Bishops," 19 September 2020, https://www.catholicnewsagency.com/news/45889/report-chinese-government-imprisoning-more-priests-

bishops%C2%A0.

32. Tom Lantos, "Religious Freedom in China: The Case of Bishop James Su Zhimin," Human Rights Commission, 30 July, 2020, https://humanrightscommission.house.gov/events/hearings/religious-freedom-china-case-bishop-james-su-zhimin.

33. Michael R. Pompeo, "China's Catholics and the Church's Moral Witness," *First Things*, 18 September 2020, https://www.firstthings.com/web-exclusives/2020/09/chinas-catholics-and-the-churchs-moral-witness.

34. *Catholic Herald*, "'China Is the Best Implementer of Catholic Social Doctrine,' says Vatican bishop," 6 February 2018, https://catholicherald.co.uk/china-is-the-best-implementer-of-catholic-social-doctrine-says-vatican-bishop/.

35. *Guardian*, "Vatican Defends Inviting Chinese Ex-Minister to Organ Trafficking Talks," 6 February 2017, https://www.theguardian.com/world/2017/feb/06/vatican-defends-inviting-chinese-ex-minister-huang-jiefu-to-organ-trafficking-talks.

36. *Daily Telegraph*, "Hong Kong Churches Face Christmas under Beijing's Shadow," 29 December 2020, https://www.telegraph.co.uk/news/2020/12/29/hong-kong-churches-face-christmas-beijings-shadow/.

37. *Guardian*, "Hong Kong Police Raid Church Hours after Pastor Said HSBC Froze Accounts," 8 December 2020, https://www.theguardian.com/world/2020/dec/08/hong-kong-church-pastor-says-hsbc-froze-personal-and-charity-bank-accounts.

38. *Catholic News Agency*, "Hong Kong Cardinal Warns Priests to 'Watch Your Language' in Homilies," 1 September 2020, https://www.catholicnewsagency.com/news/45680/hong-kong-cardinal-warns-priests-to-watch-your-language-in-homilies.

39. Benedict Rogers, "Hong Kong's New Bishop Faces Delicate Balancing Act," *UCA News*, 4 December 2021, https://www.ucanews.com/news/hong-kongs-new-bishop-faces-delicate-balancing-act/95231.

40. *AsiaNews*, "Bishop Chow: My Hong Kong Has Hope in Young People," 30 January 2022, https://www.asianews.it/news-en/Bishop-Chow:-My-Hong-Kong-has-hope-in-young-people-55030.html.

41. Congressman Chris Smith, quoted in W. Grigg's article "For the Sake of Their Faith," *New American*, 17 March 1997.

42. Mary Wang, *The Chinese Church That Will Not Die* (Hodder & Stoughton, 1971), p. 159.

CHAPTER 5: TIBET

1. Central Tibetan Administration, "International Support Groups Meet in Dharamsala to Deal with Critical Situation in Tibet," 16 November 2012, https://tibet.net/international-support-groups-meet-in-dharamsala-to-deal-with-critical-situation-in-tibet/.

2. Sam Van Schaik, *Tibet: A History* (Yale University Press, 2011), p. 208.

3. Ibid., p. 209.
4. Ibid., p. 208.
5. Ibid., p. 210.
6. Ibid., p. 214.
7. Ibid., p. 215.
8. Ibid., p. 215.
9. Ibid., p. 215.
10. Ibid., p. 218.
11. The Dalai Lama, *Freedom in Exile* (Abacus, 1998), p. 98.
12. Ibid., pp. 108–109.
13. Ibid., p. 121.
14. Ibid., p. 1.
15. Michael van Walt van Praag and Mike Boltjes, *Tibet Brief 20/20* (Outskirts Press, 2020), p. v.
16. Ibid., p. v.
17. Ibid., p. vi.
18. International Commission of Jurists, "The Question of Tibet and the Rule of Law," 1959, http://www.icj.org/wp-content/uploads/1959/01/Tibet-rule-of-law-report-1959-eng.pdf, and "Summary of a Report on Tibet: Submitted to the ICJ by Shri Purshottam Trikamdas," 5 June, 1959, https://www.icj.org/summary-of-a-report-on-tibet-submitted-to-the-international-commission-of-jurists-by-shri-purshottam-trikamdas-senior-advocate-supreme-court-of-india/.
19. The Dalai Lama, p. 136.
20. Van Schaik., p. xv.
21. The Conservative Party Human Rights Commission, *The Darkness Deepens: The Crackdown on Human Rights in China 2016–2020,* p. 65, https://conservativepartyhumanrightscommission.co.uk/wp-content/uploads/2021/01/CPHRC-China-Report.pdf.
22. Ibid., p. 65.
23. Human Rights Watch, "'Prosecute Them With Awesome Power': China's Crackdown on Tengdro Monastery and Restrictions on Communications in Tibet,"July 2021, https://www.hrw.org/report/2021/07/06/prosecute-them-awesome-power/chinas-crackdown-tengdro-monastery-and-restrictions.
24. Human Rights Watch, "'They Say We Should Be Grateful': Mass Rehousing and Relocation Programs in Tibetan Areas of China," June 2013, https://www.hrw.org/report/2013/06/27/they-say-we-should-be-grateful/mass-rehousing-and-relocation-programs-tibetan.
25. Human Rights Watch, "China's Bilingual Education Policy in Tibet," March 2020, https://www.hrw.org/report/2020/03/04/chinas-bilingual-education-policy-tibet/tibetan-medium-schooling-under-threat.
26. Ibid.
27. Ibid.
28. Tibet Action Institute, "Separated from Their Families, Hidden from the World: China's Vast System of Colonial Boarding Schools Inside Tibet," 2021, https://tibetaction.net/embargoed/.

29. Tibetan Centre for Human Rights and Democracy, "Surveillance and Censorship in Tibet," 2020, https://tchrd.org/new-report-mass-surveillance-and-censorship-conceal-widespread-human-rights-violations-in-tibet/.

30. The Conservative Party Human Rights Commission, *The Darkness Deepens: The Crackdown on Human Rights in China 2016–2020*, p. 65, https://conservativepartyhumanrightscommission.co.uk/wp-content/uploads/2021/01/CPHRC-China-Report.pdf.

31. International Campaign for Tibet, "Party Above Buddhism: China's Surveillance and Control of Tibetan Monasteries and Nunneries," March 2021, https://savetibet.org/party-above-buddhism/.

32. Ibid.

33. Tibet Watch, "An Interview with Nyima Lhamo," October 2016

34. Tibet Watch, "An Interview with Nyima Lhamo," 2016, https://www.tibetwatch.org/s/an_interview_with_nyima_lhamo-3aaw.pdf.

35. The Conservative Party Human Rights Commission, *The Darkness Deepens: The Crackdown on Human Rights in China 2016–2020*, p. 66, https://conservativepartyhumanrightscommission.co.uk/wp-content/uploads/2021/01/CPHRC-China-Report.pdf.

36. Ibid., pp. 66–67.

37. Free Tibet, "19 Year-Old Tibetan Monk Tenzin Nyima Dies from Injuries after Police Detention," 22 January 2021, https://freetibet.org/news-media/na/19-year-old-tibetan-monk-tenzin-nyima-dies-injuries-after-police-detention.

38. Human Rights Watch, "China: Tibetan Tour Guide Dies from His Injuries," 16 February 2021, https://www.hrw.org/news/2021/02/16/china-tibetan-tour-guide-dies-prison-injuries.

39. Alexander Norman, *The Dalai Lama: The Biography* (Rider, 2020), p. xiii.

40. Central Tibetan Administration, "Sikyong Penpa Tsering Completes 100 Days in Office: Exclusive Interview with Tibet TV," 4 September 2021, https://tibet.net/sikyong-penpa-tsering-completes-100-days-in-office-exclusive-interview-with-tibet-news-bureau/.

41. Tenzin Dorjee, "Divide, Depoliticize, and Demobilize: China's Strategies for Controlling the Tibetan Diaspora," Jamestown Foundation *China Brief*, 21, no. 18 (September 24, 2021), p. 27.

42. University of Aberdeen and the Scottish Centre for Himalayan Research, "Climate Change on the Third Pole: Causes, Processes and Consequence," January 2021, https://www.abdn.ac.uk/the-north/news/15518/.

43. The Dalai Lama, p. 262.

44. The Conservative Party Human Rights Commission, *The Darkness Deepens: The Crackdown on Human Rights in China 2016–2020*, p. 65, https://conservativepartyhumanrightscommission.co.uk/wp-content/uploads/2021/01/CPHRC-China-Report.pdf.

45. The Dalai Lama, p. 295.

46. The Dalai Lama, p. 290.

CHAPTER 6: UYGHUR GENOCIDE

1. Gene Bunin, "From Camps to Prisons: Xinjiang's Next Great Human Rights Catastrophe," The Art of Life in Chinese Central Asia, 5 October 2019, https://livingotherwise.com/2019/10/05/from-camps-to-prisons-xinjiangs-next-great-human-rights-catastrophe-by-gene-a-bunin/.
2. James Millward, *Eurasian Crossroads: A History of Xinjiang* (C. Hurst & Co., 2021), p. 77.
3. Sean Roberts, *The War on the Uyghurs: China's Campaign against Xinjiang's Muslims* (Princeton University Press, 2020), p. 27.
4. See https://east-turkistan.net/first-east-turkistan-republic-1933-1934/.
5. Michael Sheridan, "Revolt Stirs Among China's Nuclear Ghosts," *Sunday Times*, April 19, 2009, https://www.thetimes.co.uk/article/revolt-stirs-among-chinas-nuclear-ghosts-s2s9lw3vzn6.
6. *Death on the Silk Road*: see https://www.youtube.com/watch?v=-PRb8Xcdxp8.
7. Tom Cliff, "Xinjiang Today: Wang Zhen Rides Again?," *Made in China Journal*, 17 May 2018, https://madeinchinajournal.com/2018/05/17/xinjiang-today-wang-zhen-rides-again-2/.
8. Hasan Karrar, *The New Silk Road Diplomacy* (UBC Press, 2009), p. 78.
9. Andrew Nathan and Perry Link, *The Tiananmen Papers* (Abacus, 2001), p. 477.
10. Colin Mackerras, *China's Ethnic Minorities and Globalisation* (RoutledgeCurzon, 2003), p. 38.
11. Ibid., p. 28.
12. Uyghur Human Rights Project, "The Bingtuan: China's Paramilitary Colonizing Force in East Turkistan," p. 7, https://docs.uhrp.org/pdf/bingtuan.pdf.
13. Ethan Gutmann, *The Slaughter: Mass Killings, Organ Harvesting, and China's Secret Solution to Its Dissident Problem* (Prometheus, 2014), p. 22.
14. Radio Free Asia, "Uyghurs Still Push for Accountability 25 Years after Ghulja Massacre," 13 February 2022, https://www.rfa.org/english/news/uyghur/ghulja-massacre-02112022175649.html.
15. Sean Roberts, p. 55.
16. Gardner Bovingdon, *The Uyghurs: Strangers in Their Own Land* (New York: Columbia University Press, 2010), p. 127.
17. Amnesty International, "People's Republic of China: Gross Violations of Human Rights in the Uighur Autonomous Region," April 1999, https://www.amnesty.org/en/wp-content/uploads/2021/06/asa170181999en.pdf.
18. Ibid., p. 127.
19. Sean Roberts, p. 55.
20. Ondrej Klimes and Joanne Smith Finley, "China's Neo-Totalitarian Turn and Genocide in Xinjiang," *Society and Space*, 7 December 2020, https://www.societyandspace.org/articles/chinas-neo-totalitarian-turn-and-genocide-in-xinjiang.
21. Amnesty International, "Rebiya Kadeer's Personal Account of Gulja after the Massacre on 5 February 1997," 2007, https://www.amnesty.org/en/wp-

content/uploads/2021/07/asa170012007en.pdf.

22. Joanne Smith Finley, "Securitisation, Insecurity and Conflict in Contemporary Xinjiang: Has PRC Counter-Terrorism Evolved into State Terror?," Central Asian Survey, 11 March 2019, https://www.tandfonline.com/doi/full/10.1080/02634937.2019.1586348.

23. Pablo A. Rodríguez-Merino, "Old 'Counter-Revolution,' New 'Terrorism': Historicizing the Framing of Violence in Xinjiang by the Chinese State," Central Asian Survey, 2019, pp. 27–45, https://www.tandfonline.com/doi/abs/10.1080/02634937.2018.1496066.

24. Sean Roberts, p. 77.

25. James Millward, "Introduction: Does the 2009 Urumchi Violence Mark a Turning Point?," Central Asian Survey, 30 March 2010, https://www.tandfonline.com/doi/abs/10.1080/02634930903577128.

26. Yufan Hao and Weihua Lua, "Xinjiang: Increasing Pain in the Heart of China's Borderland" Journal of Contemporary China, 21, no. 74 (2012), pp. 205–225, https://www.tandfonline.com/doi/abs/10.1080/10670564.2012.635927?scroll=top&needAccess=true&journalCode=cjcc20.

27. Sean Roberts, p. 161.

28. For more on police recruitment, see Adrian Zenz and James Leibold, "Securitizing Xinjiang: Police Recruitment, Informal Policing and Ethnic Minority Co-optation," China Quarterly 242 (June 2020), https://www.cambridge.org/core/journals/china-quarterly/article/abs/securitizing-xinjiang-police-recruitment-informal-policing-and-ethnic-minority-cooptation/FEEC613414AA33A0353949F9B791E733. For an analysis of security spending, see Adrian Zenz, "China's Domestic Security Spending: An Analysis of Available Data," China Brief 18, no. 4 (March 2018), https://jamestown.org/program/chinas-domestic-security-spending-analysis-available-data/.

29. Joanne Smith Finley, "The Wang Lixiong Prophecy: 'Palestinianisation' in Xinjiang and the Consequences of Chinese State Securitization of Religion," Central Asian Survey, 13 November 2018, https://www.tandfonline.com/doi/full/10.1080/02634937.2018.1534802?scroll=top&needAccess=true.

30. Tom Lantos Human Rights Commission: United States Congress, "Ilham Tohti," https://humanrightscommission.house.gov/defending-freedom-project/prisoners-by-country/China/Ilham%20Tohti.

31. Uyghur Human Rights Project, "The Bingtuan: China's Paramilitary Colonizing Force in East Turkistan," p. 11.

32. Ilham Tohti, We Uyghurs Have No Say: An Imprisoned Writer Speaks (Verso Books, 2022), https://www.versobooks.com/books/3895-we-uyghurs-have-no-say?msclkid=8551edaeafe011ecbba37b07a1527f79.

33. The Conservative Party Human Rights Commission, The Darkness Deepens: The Crackdown on Human Rights in China 2016–2020, p. 56, https://conservativepartyhumanrightscommission.co.uk/wp-content/uploads/2021/01/CPHRC-China-Report.pdf.

34. Ibid., p. 56.

35. Human Rights Watch, "China: Visiting Officials Occupy Homes in Muslim Region," 13 May, 2018, https://www.hrw.org/news/2018/05/13/china-visiting-officials-occupy-homes-muslim-region.

36. Geoffrey Cain, *The Perfect Police State: An Undercover Odyssey into China's Terrifying Surveillance Dystopia of the Future* (PublicAffairs, 2021), p. 1.

37. Adrian Zenz and James Leibold, "Chen Quanguo: The Strongman Behind Beijing's Securitization Strategy in Tibet and Xinjiang," *China Brief* 17, no. 12 (September 2017), https://jamestown.org/program/chen-quanguo-the-strongman-behind-beijings-securitization-strategy-in-tibet-and-xinjiang/.

38. Adrian Zenz, "The Karakax List: Dissecting the Anatomy of Beijing's Internment Drive in Xinjiang," *Journal of Political Risk* 8, no. 2 (February 2020), jpolrisk.com/karakax/ and Uyghur Human Rights Project, "'Ideological Transformation': Records of Mass Detention from Qaraqash, Hotan," 18 February 2020, https://uhrp.org/report/ideological-transformation-records-mass-detention-qaraqash-hotan-html/.

39 Adrian Zenz, "The Xinjiang Police Files: Re-Education Camp Security and Political Paranoia in the Xinjiang Uyghur Autonomous Region," *Journal of the European Association of Chinese Studies* 3 (2022), https://journals.univie.ac.at/index.php/jeacs/article/view/7336.

40. The Laogai Research Foundation, "Laogai Handbook 2005–2006," (Washington, D.C., 2006), https://web.archive.org/web/20080527202338/http://www.laogai.org/news2/book/handbook05-06.pdf.

41 See supporting evidence from Xinjiang's own police computers: Zenz, "The Xinjiang Police Files."

42 Adrian Zenz wrote a key academic paper that became the foundation for the UN's 2018 statement that there were credible reports of over one million Uyghurs in camps. See Adrian Zenz, "New Evidence for China's Political Re-Education Campaign in Xinjiang," *China Brief* 18, no. 10 (May 2018), https://jamestown.org/program/evidence-for-chinas-political-re-education-campaign-in-xinjiang/.

43. See https://www.youtube.com/watch?v=cI8bJO-to8I&t=9s.

44. DW, "Xinjiang Footage Sheds New Light on Uyghur Detention Camps," 22 November 2021, https://www.dw.com/en/xinjiang-footage-sheds-new-light-on-uyghur-detention-camps/a-59880898.

45. Associated Press, "Room for 10,000: Inside China's Largest Detention Center," 22 July 2021, https://apnews.com/article/business-religion-china-only-on-ap-f89c20645e69208a416c64d229c072de.

46. Ibid.

47. Darren Byler, *In the Camps: Life in China's High-Tech Penal Colony* (Atlantic Books, 2022), p. 12. Byler's book draws on Zenz's work. See, for example, Adrian Zenz, "Brainwashing, Police Guards and Coercive Internment: Evidence from Chinese Government Documents about the Nature and Extent of Xinjiang's 'Vocational Training Internment Camps,'" Journal of Political Risk 7, no. 7 (July 2019), https://www.jpolrisk.com/brainwashing-police-guards-and-coercive-internment-evidence-from-chinese-government-

documents-about-the-nature-and-extent-of-xinjiangs-vocational-training-internment-camps/. In 2019, Zenz told the Irish Times that the camps were probably the "largest incarceration of an ethno-religious minority since the Holocaust." See Colm Keena, "Mass Internment of Uighur People in Camps Laid Bare in Leaked Documents," Irish Times, 24 November 2019, https://www.irishtimes.com/news/world/asia-pacific/china-cables-the-largest-incarceration-of-a-minority-since-the-holocaust-1.4089726.

48. Congressional-Executive Commission on China, "Hearing: The Communist Party's Crackdown on Religion in China, November 28, 2018: Testimony of Mihrigul Tursun," https://www.cecc.gov/sites/chinacommission.house.gov/files/documents/REVISED_Mihrigul%20Tursun%20Testimony%20for%20CECC%20Hearing%2011-28-18_0.pdf.

49. *Bitter Winter*, "Mihray Erkin: The Senseless Killing of a Uyghur Young Girl," 2021, bitterwinter.org/mihrab-erkin-the-senseless-killing-of-a-uyghur-young-girl.

50. BBC, "Their Goal Is to Destroy Everyone: Uighur Camp Detainees Allege Systematic Rape," 2 February 2021, https://www.bbc.co.uk/news/world-asia-china-55794071.

51. Al Jazeera, "Exposed: China's Surveillance of Muslim Uighurs," 1 February 2019, https://www.aljazeera.com/features/2019/2/1/exposed-chinas-surveillance-of-muslim-uighurs.

52. Tom Cheshire, "Uyghurs Tortured and Beaten to Death in Xinjiang, Former Chinese Police Officer Reveals," *Sky News*, 11 October 2021, www.news.sky.com/story/Uyghurs-tortured-and-beaten-to-death-in-re-education-camps-in-xinjiang-former-chinese-police-officer-reveals-12431122.

53. Ibid.

54. Ibid.

55. Australian Strategic Policy Institute (ASPI), "Uyghurs for Sale," 2020, https://www.aspi.org.au/report/uyghurs-sale.

56. The Conservative Party Human Rights Commission, *The Darkness Deepens: The Crackdown on Human Rights in China 2016–2020*, p. 47, https://conservativepartyhumanrightscommission.co.uk/wp-content/uploads/2021/01/CPHRC-China-Report.pdf.

57 Zenz disputes this figure and has critiqued the ASPI report in his own work. His recent research estimates that between 2 and 2.5 million Uyghurs are at risk of being subjected to forced labour. Adrian Zenz, "Unemployment Monitoring and Early Warning: New Trends in Xinjiang's Coercive Labor Placement Systems," *China Brief* 22, no. 11, https://jamestown.org/program/unemployment-monitoring-and-early-warning-new-trends-in-xinjiangs-coercive-labor-placement-systems/.

58. *The Darkness Deepens*, p. 47.

59. Ibid., p. 48. See also Adrian Zenz, "Coercive Labor and Forced Displacement in Xinjiang's Cross-Regional Labor Transfer Program," Jamestown Foundation, 2 March 2021, https://jamestown.org/program/coercive-labor-and-forced-displacement-in-xinjiangs-cross-regional-labor-transfer-program/.

60. *Guardian*, "'Virtually Entire' Fashion Industry Complicit in Uighur Forced Labour, Say Rights Groups," 23 July 2020, https://www.theguardian.com/global-development/2020/jul/23/virtually-entire-fashion-industry-complicit-in-uighur-forced-labour-say-rights-groups-china. The key research report on forced labour in cotton, which was the basis for the US import ban on Xinjiang cotton, is Adrian Zenz, "Coercive Labor in Xinjiang: Labor Transfer and the Mobilization of Ethnic Minorities to Pick Cotton," New Lines Institute for Strategy and Policy, 14 December 2020, https://newlinesinstitute.org/china/coercive-labor-in-xinjiang-labor-transfer-and-the-mobilization-of-ethnic-minorities-to-pick-cotton/.

61. Adrian Zenz, "Public Security Minister's Speech Describes Xi Jinping's Direction of Mass Detentions in Xinjiang," *ChinaFile*, 24 May 2022, https://www.chinafile.com/reporting-opinion/features/public-security-ministers-speech-describes-xi-jinpings-direction-of-mass.

62. Amy Qin, "In China's Crackdown on Muslims, Children Have Not Been Spared," *New York Times,* 28 December 2019, https://www.nytimes.com/2019/12/28/world/asia/china-xinjiang-children-boarding-schools.html. By 2018, that figure had increased to nearly 900,000. Adrian Zenz, "Parent-Child Separation in Yarkand County, Kashgar: Evidence from Local Government Spreadsheets about the Fate of Thousands of Students with One or Both Parents in Internment Camps," *Medium*, 15 October 2020, https://adrianzenz.medium.com/story-45d07b25bcad.

63. Emily Feng, "Uighur Kids Recall Physical and Mental Torment at Chinese Boarding Schools in Xinjiang," WBUR, 3 February 2022, https://www.wbur.org/npr/1073793823/china-uyghur-children-xinjiang-boarding-school.

64. Rian Thum, "The Spatial Cleansing of Xinjiang: Mazar Desecration in Context," *Made in China Journal*, 24 August 2020, https://madeinchinajournal.com/2020/08/24/the-spatial-cleansing-of-xinjiang-mazar-desecration-in-context/.

65. The Conservative Party Human Rights Commission, *The Darkness Deepens: The Crackdown on Human Rights in China 2016–2020*, p. 27, https://conservativepartyhumanrightscommission.co.uk/wp-content/uploads/2021/01/CPHRC-China-Report.pdf.

66. Ibid., p. 28.

67. Joanne Smith Finley, "Now We Don't Talk Anymore: Inside the 'Cleansing' of Xinjiang," *ChinaFile*, 28 December 2018, https://www.chinafile.com/reporting-opinion/viewpoint/now-we-dont-talk-anymore.

68. The Conservative Party Human Rights Commission, *The Darkness Deepens: The Crackdown on Human Rights in China 2016–2020*, p. 28, https://conservativepartyhumanrightscommission.co.uk/wp-content/uploads/2021/01/CPHRC-China-Report.pdf.

69. Adrian Zenz, "Sterilisations, IUDs, and Mandatory Birth Control: The CCP's Campaign to Suppress Uyghur Birth Rates in Xinjiang," Jamestown Foundation and the Inter-Parliamentary Alliance on China (IPAC), *China Brief*, 20, no. 12, 15 July 2015, https://jamestown.org/program/sterilizations-

iuds-and-mandatory-birth-control-the-ccps-campaign-to-suppress-uyghur-birth-rates-in-xinjiang/.

70. Emma Murphy, "Uighur Doctor Tells ITV News of Disturbing Testimonies of 'Forced Abortions and Removal of Wombs in China,'" ITV, 2 September 2020, https://www.itv.com/news/2020-09-02/uighur-doctor-tells-itv-news-of-disturbing-testimonies-of-forced-abortions-and-removal-of-wombs.

71. Uyghur Tribunal Judgment, 2021, https://uyghurtribunal.com/wp-content/uploads/2021/12/Uyghur-Tribunal-Summary-Judgment-9th-Dec-21.pdf.

72. Ethan Gutmann, *The Slaughter* (2014), p. 9.

73. Ethan Gutmann, "A Personal Note to the British Foreign Office," International Coalition to End Transplant Abuse in China, Westminster Statement, September 11, 2019, https://endtransplantabuse.org/a-personal-note-to-the-british-foreign-office-ethan-gutmann/.

74. Ethan Gutmann, "The Nine Points Memo: China's Forced Organ Harvesting in Xinjiang/East Turkistan," International Coalition to End Transplant Abuse in China, December 2020, https://endtransplantabuse.org/wp-content/uploads/2021/01/Chinas-Forced-Organ-Harvesting-from-Uyghurs-Memo-EthanGutmann_ETAC_12Dec2020.pdf.

75. Taiwan News, "Saudis Allegedly Buy 'Halal Organs' from 'Slaughtered' Xinjiang Muslims," taiwannews.com.tw/en/news/3862578.

76. Jonathan Manthorpe, *Claws of the Panda: Beijing's Campaign of Influence and Intimidation in Canada* (Cormorant Books, 2019), p. 13.

77. Amnesty International, "Uyghur Jailed for 15 Years in Secret Trial," 2020, https://www.amnesty.org.uk/urgent-actions/uyghur-jailed-15-years-secret-trial.

78. Joseph Torigian, "What Xi Jinping Learned—and Didn't Learn—from His Father About Xinjiang," *The Diplomat*, 26 November 2019, https://thediplomat.com/2019/11/what-xi-jinping-learned-and-didnt-learn-from-his-father-about-xinjiang/.

79. David Shambaugh, *China's Leaders from Mao to Now* (Polity Press, 2021), p. 292.

80. Elizabeth Economy, *The World According to China* (Polity Press, 2022), p. 93.

81. Rush Doshi, *The Long Game: China's Grand Strategy to Displace American Order* (Oxford University Press, 2021), p. 161.

82. Uyghur Human Rights Project, "International Responses to the Uyghur Crisis," https://uhrp.org/responses/.

83. CNBC, "U.S. Bans Imports from China's Xinjiang Region, Citing Human Rights Abuses," 23 December, 2021, https://www.cnbc.com/2021/12/23/us-bans-imports-from-chinas-xinjiang-region-citing-uyghur-forced-labor.html.

84. *Washington Post*, "China Has Launched a Massive Campaign of Cultural Extermination against the Uighurs," 7 January 2019, https://www.washingtonpost.com/opinions/global-opinions/china-has-launched-a-massive-campaign-of-cultural-extermination-against-the-uighurs/2019/01/07/efe03c9c-12a4-11e9-b6ad-9cfd62dbb0a8_story.html.

85. U.S. State Department, "Determination of the Secretary of State on Atrocities

in Xinjiang," 19 January 2021, https://2017-2021.state.gov/determination-of-the-secretary-of-state-on-atrocities-in-xinjiang/index.html.

86. Uyghur Tribunal, see www.uyghurtribunal.com.

87. David Tobin, "Peering In to China's Decision-Making: What Are the 'Xinjiang Papers,'" RUSI, 16 December 2021, https://www.itv.com/news/2021-06-09/family-members-of-uyghur-tribunal-witnesses-put-up-by-china-to-rebut-their-relatives-claims. See also Adrian Zenz, "The Xinjiang Papers: An Introduction," Uyghur Tribunal, 27 November 2021, https://uyghurtribunal.com/wp-content/uploads/2021/11/The-Xinjiang-Papers-An-Introduction-1.pdf.

88. *Guardian*, "Leaked Papers Link Xinjiang Crackdown with China Leadership," 29 November 2021, https://www.theguardian.com/world/2021/nov/29/leaked-papers-link-xinjiang-crackdown-with-china-leadership.

89. Adrian Zenz, "Public Security Minister's Speech Describes Xi Jinping's Direction of Mass Detentions in Xinjiang," *ChinaFile*, 24 May 2022, https://www.chinafile.com/reporting-opinion/features/public-security-ministers-speech-describes-xi-jinpings-direction-of-mass.

CHAPTER 7: A CRIMINAL STATE

1. Caroline Davies, "Miss World Canada 'Barred from Entering China' for Pageant," *Guardian*, 26 November 2015, https://www.theguardian.com/world/2015/nov/26/canada-miss-world-china-stopped-pageant-anastasia-lin.

2. Oxford Union debate, 26 February 2016, https://www.youtube.com/watch?v=vhbP8ACPiVk&t=3s.

3. The Conservative Party Human Rights Commission, *The Darkest Moment: The Crackdown on Human Rights in China 2013–2016*, June 2016, p. 45, https://conservativepartyhumanrightscommission.co.uk/wp-content/uploads/2020/03/CPHRC_China_Human_Rights_Report_Final.pdf.

4. Ibid., p. 45.

5. Julie Keith, "Experience: I Found a Cry for Help Hidden in My Halloween Decorations," *Guardian*, 30 October 2020, https://www.theguardian.com/lifeandstyle/2020/oct/30/experience-i-found-a-cry-for-help-hidden-in-my-halloween-decorations?CMP=share_btn_fb&fbclid=IwAR1I3tT6TiyzZNdEBwKVEE3xpBa2_Y6u7NNod8aTD-RtZHrEmXEvgT_02vc.

6. *Oregonian*, "Halloween Decorations Carry Haunting Message of Forced Labor," 23 December 2012, https://www.oregonlive.com/happy-valley/2012/12/halloween_decorations_carry_ha.html?fbclid=IwAR2UYZTAOGP54pWApaXXSfwNS6QCRAtNfRdmPbqIyv2TMOnsY6kuwP-1RlA.

7. Jon Kelly, "The SOS in My Halloween Decorations," BBC, 29 October 2018, https://www.bbc.co.uk/news/stories-45976946.

8. Julie Keith, "Experience: I Found a Cry for Help Hidden in My Halloween Decorations," *Guardian*, 30 October 2020, https://www.theguardian.com/lifeandstyle/2020/oct/30/experience-i-found-a-cry-

for-help-hidden-in-my-halloween-decorations?CMP=share_btn_
fb&fbclid=IwAR1I3tT6TiyzZNdEBwKVEE3xpBa2_Y6u7NNod8aTD-
RtZHrEmXEvgT_02vc.

9. Ibid.

10. Ethan Gutmann, "The Anatomy of Mass Murder: China's Unfinished Harvest
    of Prisoners of Conscience," Congressional-Executive Commission on China,
    18 September, 2015, https://www.cecc.gov/sites/chinacommission.house.gov/
    files/CECC%20Hearing%20-%20Human%20Rights%20Abuses%20-%20
    18Sept15%20-%20Ethan%20Gutmann.pdf.

11. European Parliament resolution, 11 December 2013, https://www.europarl.
    europa.eu/doceo/document/RC-7-2013-0562_EN.html?redirect.

12. United States House of Representatives, H.Res.343, 2015, https://www.
    congress.gov/bill/114th-congress/house-resolution/343/text.

13. *Epoch Times*, "Prominent Transplant Ethicist Supports Investigation into
    Organ Sourcing in China," 20 September 2016, https://www.theepochtimes.
    com/prominent-transplant-ethicist-supports-investigation-into-organ-
    sourcing-in-china_2159364.html.

14. Didi Kirsten Tatlow, "Chinese Claim That World Accepts Its Organ
    Transplant System Is Rebutted," *New York Times*, 19 August 2016, https://
    www.nytimes.com/2016/08/20/world/asia/china-hong-kong-organ-
    transplants.html.

15. U.S. House of Representatives Foreign Affairs Committee Joint Sub-
    Committee hearing, chaired by Congressman Christopher Smith, 23 June
    2016, https://docs.house.gov/meetings/FA/FA16/20160623/105116/HHRG-
    114-FA16-20160623-SD006.pdf.

16. NTDTV, Interview with Yu Xinhui, see https://www.youtube.com/
    watch?v=jfkxshiw08I.

17. The Conservative Party Human Rights Commission, "Forced
    Organ Harvesting in China," September 2016, https://
    conservativepartyhumanrightscommission.co.uk/wp-content/
    uploads/2020/03/CPHRC_ORGAN_HARVESTING_REPORT.pdf.

18. Benedict Rogers, "The Nightmare of Human Organ Harvesting in China,"
    Wall Street Journal, 5 February 2019, https://www.wsj.com/articles/the-
    nightmare-of-human-organ-harvesting-in-china-11549411056.

19. The Conservative Party Human Rights Commission, "Forced
    Organ Harvesting in China," September 2016, https://
    conservativepartyhumanrightscommission.co.uk/wp-content/
    uploads/2020/03/CPHRC_ORGAN_HARVESTING_REPORT.pdf.

20. China Tribunal, see www.chinatribunal.com.

CHAPTER 8: BROKEN PROMISES, SHATTERED DREAMS

1. *Hong Kong Free Press*, "'A Death Knell for Rule of Law and Human Rights':
    25 Int'l Figures Condemn Jailing of Hong Kong Democracy Activists," 18

August 2017, https://hongkongfp.com/2017/08/18/death-knell-rule-law-human-rights-16-intl-figures-condemn-jailing-democratic-activists/.

2. Joshua Wong, *Unfree Speech: The Threat to Global Democracy And Why We Must Act, Now* (Penguin Random House, 2020), p. 243.

3. Ibid., p. 247.

4. Chris Patten, "What China Promised Hong Kong," *Washington Post*, 3 October 2014, https://www.washingtonpost.com/opinions/chris-patten-with-hong-kong-chinas-honor-is-at-stake/2014/10/02/ebc4e9b2-4a5f-11e4-a046-120a8a855cca_story.html.

5. House of Commons Select Committee on Foreign Affairs, Tenth Report, Hong Kong, 2000, https://publications.parliament.uk/pa/cm199900/cmselect/cmfaff/574/57402.htm.

6. Mark Clifford, *Today Hong Kong, Tomorrow the World* (St. Martin's Press, 2022), p. 21.

7. BBC, "Hong Kong Democracy 'Referendum' Draws Nearly 800,000," 30 June 2014, https://www.bbc.co.uk/news/world-asia-china-28076566.

8. *Financial Times*, "Hong Kong Democracy Activists Vent Their Anger against Beijing," 1 September 2014, https://www.ft.com/content/e57acc96-30e9-11e4-b2fd-00144feabdc0.

9. Martin Lee, "Who Will Stand with Hong Kong?," *New York Times*, 3 October 2014, https://www.nytimes.com/2014/10/04/opinion/martin-lee-hong-kongs-great-test.html.

10. Alan Wong, "Lawyers Defend Hong Kong Rule of Law in Show of Unity against Beijing," *New York Times*, 27 June 2014, https://sinosphere.blogs.nytimes.com/2014/06/27/lawyers-defend-hong-kong-rule-of-law-in-show-of-unity-against-beijing/.

11. *Wall Street Journal*, "A Hong Kong Judge's Warning," 21 April 2016, https://www.wsj.com/articles/a-hong-kong-judges-warning-1461280717.

12. Benedict Rogers, "The Sinister Aftermath of the Hong Kong Crackdown," Conservativehome.com, 6 January 2015, https://www.conservativehome.com/thecolumnists/2015/01/benedict-rogers-the-sinister-aftermath-of-the-hong-kong-crackdown.html.

13. *South China Morning Post* "Gloomy Verdict: Hong Kong Appeal Judge Says Courts Face 'Grave Challenges' in Years Ahead," 18 April 2016, https://www.scmp.com/news/hong-kong/article/1936964/gloomy-verdict-hong-kong-appeal-judge-says-courts-face-grave.

14. Gov.uk, "Six-Monthly Report on Hong Kong, July to December 2015," 11 February 2016, https://www.gov.uk/government/publications/six-monthly-report-on-hong-kong-july-to-december-2015.

15. The Conservative Party Human Rights Commission, *The Darkness Deepens: The Crackdown on Human Rights in China 2016–2020*, 2021, https://conservativepartyhumanrightscommission.co.uk/wp-content/uploads/2021/01/CPHRC-China-Report.pdf.

16. Ibid.

17. Hong Kong Watch, "In the Firing Line: The Crackdown on Media Freedom

in Hong Kong," 2022, p. 9, www.hongkongwatch.org.

18. Ibid., p. 10.

19. *Hong Kong Free Press*, "Hong Kong Riot Police Target Journalists during Sunday Unrest as Reporter Shot in the Eye with Projectile," 30 September 2019, https://hongkongfp.com/2019/09/30/hong-kong-riot-police-target-journalists-sunday-unrest-reporter-shot-eye-projectile/.

20. Dr. Darren Mann, "International Humanitarian Norms Are Violated in Hong Kong," *Lancet*, 21 November 2019, https://www.thelancet.com/journals/lancet/article/PIIS0140-6736(19)32909-5/fulltext.

21. The Conservative Party Human Rights Commission, *The Darkness Deepens: The Crackdown on Human Rights in China 2016–2020*, 2021, https://conservativepartyhumanrightscommission.co.uk/.

22. Mandates of the Special Rapporteur on the Right of Everyone to the Enjoyment of the Highest Attainable Standard of Physical and Mental Health; the Working Group on Arbitrary Detention; the Special Rapporteur on the Rights to Freedom of Peaceful Assembly and of Association and the Special Rapporteur on the Right to Privacy, 19 February 2020, https://spcommreports.ohchr.org/TMResultsBase/DownLoadPublicCommunicationFile?gId=25054.

23. Mandates of the Special Rapporteur on the Implications for Human Rights of the Environmentally Sound Management and Disposal of Hazardous Substances and Wastes and the Special Rapporteur on the Rights to Freedom of Peaceful Assembly and Association, 29 January 2020, https://spcommreports.ohchr.org/TMResultsBase/DownLoadPublicCommunicationFile?gId=25048.

24. The Conservative Party Human Rights Commission, *The Darkness Deepens: The Crackdown on Human Rights in China 2016–2020*, 2021, https://conservativepartyhumanrightscommission.co.uk/.

25. Ibid.

26. Stephen Vines, *Defying the Dragon: Hong Kong and the World's Largest Dictatorship* (C. Hurst & Co., 2021), p. 136.

27. Hong Kong Watch, "In the Firing Line: The Crackdown on Media Freedom in Hong Kong," 2022, p. 15, www.hongkongwatch.org.

28. Reporters Without Borders, Press Freedom Index 2022, https://rsf.org/en/country/hong-kong.

29. Ibid.

30. "Foreign Secretary Supports the Withdrawal of Serving UK Judges from the Hong Kong Court of Final Appeal," 30 March 2022, https://www.gov.uk/government/news/foreign-secretary-supports-the-withdrawal-of-serving-uk-judges-from-the-hong-kong-court-of-final-appeal.

CHAPTER 9: THE THREATS TO TAIWAN

1. Office of the President of the Republic of China (Taiwan), "President Tsai Attends Opening of a Civil Society Dialogue on Securing Religious Freedom in the Indo-Pacific Region," 11 March 2019, https://english.president.gov.tw/

NEWS/5654/religious%20freedom.

2. *Taiwan Today*, "Taiwan Makes US$1 Million Commitment to US State Department's International Religious Freedom Fund," 13 March 2019, https://taiwantoday.tw/news.php?unit=2,6,10,15,18&post=151220.
3. Reuters, "China Releases Jailed Taiwanese Activist, Sends Him Home," 15 April 2022, https://www.reuters.com/world/asia-pacific/china-releases-jailed-taiwanese-activist-sends-him-home-2022-04-15/.
4. Benedict Rogers, "Beijing's Chilling Imprisonment of a Taiwanese Critic," *Wall Street Journal*, 31 March 2019, https://www.wsj.com/articles/beijings-chilling-imprisonment-of-a-taiwanese-critic-11554057567?mod=article_inline.
5. *Wall Street Journal*, "China Shows Its Real Self with Li Ming-che," 2 April 2019, https://www.wsj.com/articles/china-shows-its-real-self-with-li-ming-che-11554241428?fbclid=IwAR0wE5y5gb6ZNNAlVjUa80BEn8yDsdyfJQBpSv4Oz2rZU-c8AJFbJisMq8U.
6. Office of the President of the Republic of China (Taiwan), "President Tsai Attends Taiwan International Religious Freedom Forum," 30 May 2019, https://english.president.gov.tw/News/5745.
7. *Taiwan News*, "Taiwan International Religious Forum Slams Organ Harvesting and Uyghur Repression by China," 1 June 2019, https://www.taiwannews.com.tw/en/news/3715328.
8. Taiwan International Religious Freedom Forum, "Declaration on Uyghur Religious Freedom," http://tirff.org/taiwan-declaration.html.
9. *Taiwan News*, "Dalai Lama Sends Message of Support for Taiwan and Religious Freedom," 30 May 2019, https://www.taiwannews.com.tw/en/news/3714225.
10. *Taiwan News*, "Beijing Angered by Taiwan President's Meeting with Tiananmen Square Activists," 30 May 2019, https://www.taiwannews.com.tw/en/news/3713461.
11. Brendan Taylor, *Dangerous Decade: Taiwan's Security and Crisis Management*, The International Institute for Strategic Studies, (Routledge, 2019), p. 18.
12. Ibid., p. 18.
13. Richard C. Bush, "Taiwan's democracy and the China challenge," Brookings Institute, 22 January 2021, https://www.brookings.edu/articles/taiwans-democracy-and-the-china-challenge/.
14. Ibid.
15. *Taipei Times*, "Anti-Media Monopoly Explained," 4 February 2013, https://www.taipeitimes.com/News/editorials/archives/2013/02/04/2003554169.
16. Ian Rowen, "Inside Taiwan's Sunflower Movement: Twenty-Four Days in a Student-Occupied Parliament, and the Future of the Region," *Journal of Asian Studies*, 74, no. 1 (February 2015): pp. 5–21, https://www.cambridge.org/core/journals/journal-of-asian-studies/article/inside-taiwans-sunflower-movement-twentyfour-days-in-a-studentoccupied-parliament-and-the-future-of-the-region/DB4A7B57538A6F06DC6C8CF0058C8040.
17. Ibid.

18. Ibid.
19. Ibid.
20. Ibid.
21. Ming-sho Ho, "The Road to Mainstream Politics: How Taiwan's Sunflower Movement Activists Became Politicians," Carnegie Endowment for International Peace, 24 October 2019, https://carnegieeurope.eu/2019/10/24/road-to-mainstream-politics-how-taiwan-s-sunflower-movement-activists-became-politicians-pub-80150.
22. Ian Rowen, p. 8.
23. Ibid., p. 11.
24. Ibid., p. 13.
25. Ibid., p. 14.
26. Ibid., p. 16.
27. Ming-sho Ho, "The Activist Legacy of Taiwan's Sunflower Movement," Carnegie Endowment for International Peace, 2 August 2018, https://carnegieendowment.org/2018/08/02/activist-legacy-of-taiwan-s-sunflower-movement-pub-76966.
28. Ming-sho Ho, "The Road to Mainstream Politics: How Taiwan's Sunflower Movement Activists Became Politicians," 24 October 2019, Carnegie Endowment for International Peace, https://carnegieeurope.eu/2019/10/24/road-to-mainstream-politics-how-taiwan-s-sunflower-movement-activists-became-politicians-pub-80150.
29. Ian Rowen, p. 1.
30. *Taipei Times*, "Interview: China Seeking Win with Information Warfare: Professor," 22 April 2019, http://www.taipeitimes.com/News/taiwan/archives/2019/04/22/2003713841.
31. *New Bloom*, "Fighting Fake News and Disinformation in Taiwan: An Interview with Puma Shen," 6 January 2020, https://newbloommag.net/2020/01/06/puma-shen-interview/.
32. *Guardian*, "John Cena 'Very Sorry' for Saying Taiwan Is a Country," 25 May 2021, https://www.theguardian.com/world/2021/may/26/john-cena-very-sorry-for-saying-taiwan-is-a-country.
33. *Hong Kong Free Press*, "Hong Kong Journalist Who Challenged WHO Official Quits RTHK," 13 April 2021, https://hongkongfp.com/2021/04/13/journalist-yvonne-tong-quits-rthk-source/.
34. Safeguard Defenders, "China's Hunt for Taiwanese Overseas," 30 November 2021, https://safeguarddefenders.com/en/blog/new-investigation-exposes-prc-hunting-taiwanese-overseas.
35. *Financial Times*, "Taiwan Fights Back Against Beijing's Airline Pressure," 18 June 2018, https://www.ft.com/content/e28a51ce-7081-11e8-852d-d8b934ff5ffa.
36. *Taiwan Today*, "Tsai Lauds Taiwan's Democracy, Calls for Like-Minded Countries to Defend Shared Values," 25 June 2018, https://taiwantoday.tw/news.php?unit=2&post=136758.
37. AFP, "Interview: Taiwan Pres. Tsai Ing-wen Urges World to Stand Up to

China and Reaffirm Democratic Values," *Hong Kong Free Press*, https://hongkongfp.com/2018/06/26/interview-taiwan-pres-tsai-ing-wen-urges-world-stand-china-reaffirm-democratic-values/.

38. *South China Morning Post*, "'I Am Taiwanese': Czech Senate President Channels JFK in Show of Support for Island," 1 September 2020, https://www.scmp.com/news/china/diplomacy/article/3099782/i-am-taiwanese-czech-senate-president-channels-jfk-show.

39. European Parliament, "Chair's and Vice-Chair's Message of 20 August 2020 to Ambassador Zhang Ming," https://www.europarl.europa.eu/delegations/en/d-cn/documents/communiques

40. Hansard, "UK-Taiwan Friendship and Co-operation," 10 February 2022, https://hansard.parliament.uk/Commons/2022-02-10/debates/64A09D24-D41C-4974-ABCE-1C3785CD4C16/UK-TaiwanFriendshipAndCo-Operation.

41. *Al Jazeera*, "United States Should Recognize 'Free' Taiwan, Mike Pompeo Says," 4 March 2022, https://www.aljazeera.com/news/2022/3/4/us-should-recognise-free-taiwan-pompeo-says.

42. *Taiwan News*, "Lithuanian Rum Sells Out within Hour at Taiwan Liquor Stores," 1 February 2022, https://www.taiwannews.com.tw/en/news/4428174#:~:text=In%20December%2C%20Taiwan%20purchased%20the,its%20warming%20relations%20with%20Taiwan.

43. Brendan Taylor, *Dangerous Decade*, p. 29.

44. BBC, "Xi Jinping Says Taiwan 'Must and Will Be' Reunited with China," 2 January 2019, https://www.bbc.co.uk/news/world-asia-china-46733174.

45. *Guardian*, "China Sends Largest Incursion of War Planes into Taiwan Defence Zone Since October," 24 January 2022, https://www.theguardian.com/world/2022/jan/24/china-sends-largest-incursion-of-warplanes-into-taiwan-defence-zone-since-october.

46. Howard Mustoe and Helen Cahill, "Taiwan Holds Its Breath as China Ramps Up Firepower," *Daily Telegraph*, 28 March 2022, https://www.telegraph.co.uk/business/2022/03/27/taiwan-holds-breath-china-takes-us-global-arms-race/.

47. Ho Ming-sho, "The Activist Legacy of Taiwan's Sunflower Movement," Carnegie Endowment for International Peace," 2 August 2018, https://carnegieendowment.org/2018/08/02/activist-legacy-of-taiwan-s-sunflower-movement-pub-76966.

48. Mainland Affairs Council, Republic of China (Taiwan), "Mainstream Public Voice Support: Taiwan's Option Is to Become Stronger, More United, and More Determined to Defend Itself," MAC Press Release No.010, 9 September 2021, https://www.mac.gov.tw/en/News_Content.aspx?n=A921D-FB2651FF92F&sms=37838322A6DA5E79&s=49B5B3D25A7D8E9A.

49. Brendan Taylor, *Dangerous Decade*, p. 20.

50. Gray Sergeant, "Supporting Taiwan: A Calling for Global Britain," The Henry Jackson Society, July 2021, https://henryjacksonsociety.org/publications/taiwan-global-britain/.

CHAPTER 10: IN CHINA'S BACKYARD

1. Bertil Lintner, "China and Myanmar: No Interference?," *Irrawaddy*, 21 March 2021, https://www.irrawaddy.com/opinion/guest-column/china-myanmar-no-interference.html
2. Ibid.
3. Ibid.
4. Jason Tower, "China's High-Stakes Calculations in Myanmar," US Institute of Peace, 7 April 2021, https://www.usip.org/publications/2021/04/chinas-high-stakes-calculations-myanmar.
5. Ibid.
6. AP, "China to Back Military-Ruled Myanmar Regardless of Situation," 2 April 2022, https://apnews.com/article/wang-yi-aung-san-suu-kyi-china-myanmar-diplomacy-d68de69436c1462f647f6475b6315c92.
7. Jason Tower, "China's High-Stakes Calculations in Myanmar."
8. Ibid.
9. *Financial Times*, "China Bolsters Ties with Myanmar Junta Despite International Condemnation," 23 June 2021, https://www.ft.com/content/ca43da4c-4287-4de6-ad8a-57a2a32fe7f3.
10. Sumanth Samsani, "Understanding the Relations between Myanmar and China," Observer Research Foundation, 26 April 2021, https://www.orfonline.org/expert-speak/understanding-the-relations-between-myanmar-and-china/.
11. Ibid.
12. Ibid.
13. Amara Thiha, "Revisiting the China-Myanmar Economic Corridor After the Coup," *Diplomat*, 11 April 2022, https://thediplomat.com/2022/04/revisiting-the-china-myanmar-economic-corridor-after-the-coup/.
14. Ibid.
15. Sebastian Strangio, *In the Dragon's Shadow: Southeast Asia in the Chinese Century* (Yale University Press, 2020), p. 156.
16. Ibid., p. 149.
17. Sumanth Samsani, "Understanding the Relations between Myanmar and China."
18. UN News, "Stop Weapons Supply to Myanmar, Rights Expert Urges," 22 February 2022, https://news.un.org/en/story/2022/02/1112422#:~:text=Weapons%20exports%20to%20the%20military,had%20been%20used%20against%20civilians.
19. Center for Strategic and International Studies, "Tatmadaw Deploys Chinese-Made UAVs," 6 May 2021, https://www.csis.org/analysis/tatmadaw-deploys-chinese-made-uavs#:~:text=Reports%20suggest%20that%20the%20military,surveillance%20in%20northern%20Rakhine%20State.
20. Myanmar Now, "Hundreds of Huawei CCTV Cameras with Facial Recognition Go Live in Naypyitaw," 15 December 2020, https://www.myanmar-now.org/en/news/hundreds-of-huawei-cctv-cameras-with-facial-recognition-go-live-in-naypyitaw#:~:text=Hundreds%20of%20Huawei%20CCTV%20cameras%20with%20facial%20recognition%20go%20live%20

in%20Naypyitaw,-Hundreds%20of%20Huawei&text=A%20system%20of%20 335%20surveillance,4bn%20kyat%20(%242.9m).

21. *Irrawaddy*, "Amid Int'l Espionage Concerns, Mandalay to Embrace Huawei for 'Safe City' Project," 19 June 2019, https://www.irrawaddy.com/opinion/ analysis/amid-intl-espionage-concerns-mandalay-embrace-huawei- safe-city-project.html#:~:text=The%20public%20has%20questioned%20 whether,looking%20to%20access%20citizens'%20data.

22. Bertil Lintner, "Myanmar Junta Turns to China for Help Policing Internet Use," *Irrawaddy*, 22 February 2022, https://www.irrawaddy.com/opinion/guest- column/myanmar-junta-turns-to-china-for-help-policing-internet-use.html.

23. Hannah Beech, "Myanmar's Military Deploys Digital Arsenal of Repression in Crackdown," *New York Times*, 1 March 2021, https://www.nytimes. com/2021/03/01/world/asia/myanmar-coup-military-surveillance.html.

24. Sumanth Samsani, "Understanding the Relations between Myanmar and China."

25. Jason Tower and Priscilla Clapp, "Chaos in Myanmar Is China's Nightmare," US Institute for Peace, 28 May 2021, https://www.usip.org/ publications/2021/05/chaos-myanmar-chinas-nightmare.

26. Bertil Lintner, *The Wa of Myanmar and China's Quest for Global Dominance* (Silkworm Books, 2021), p. 1.

27. Ibid., p. 136.

28. Ibid., p. 2.

29. Ibid., p. 8.

30. Ibid., p. 3.

31. Ibid., p. 132.

32. Ibid., p. 123.

33. Sebastian Strangio, *In the Dragon's Shadow: Southeast Asia in the Chinese Century*, p. 164.

34. Jason Tower and Priscilla Clapp, "Myanmar's Casino Cities: The Role of China and Transnational Criminal Networks," US Institute of Peace, 27 July 2020, https://www.usip.org/publications/2020/07/myanmars-casino-cities- role-china-and-transnational-criminal-networks.

35. Lintner, p. 208.

36. CSW, "United Wa State Army Continues Crackdown on Christians," 18 October 2018, https://www.csw.org.uk/2018/10/18/press/4124/article.htm.

37. Lintner, p. 208.

38. Reuters, "China Raps Myanmar after Recent Border Unrest," 25 September 2009, https://www.reuters.com/article/idINIndia-42703120090925.

39. CSW, "Northern Burma Delegation Calls for Action," 20 November 2018, https://www.csw.org.uk/2018/11/20/press/4162/article.htm.

40. *Irrawaddy*, "Analysis: Behind the Threats and Warnings of Chinese Ambassador's Kachin Visit," 9 January 2019, https://www.irrawaddy.com/ news/burma/analysis-behind-threats-warnings-chinese-ambassadors-kachin- visit.html.

41. Sebastian Strangio, *In the Dragon's Shadow: Southeast Asia in the Chinese Century*, p. 143.

42. Ibid., p. 143.
43. Ibid., p. 149.
44. Lucas Myers, "China Is Hedging Its Bets in Myanmar," *Foreign Policy*, 10 September 2021, https://foreignpolicy.com/2021/09/10/china-myanmar-coup-national-league-for-democracy/.
45. Anna Tan, "China and the Myanmar Dilemma," Lau China Institute, King's College London, Policy Series 2021, https://www.kcl.ac.uk/lci/assets/lci-policy-paper-china-and-the-myanmar-dilemma.pdf.
46. Lintner, p. 190.
47. Anders Corr, "China's Other Genocide: Against the Rohingya in Burma," 24 March 2022, https://www.theepochtimes.com/chinas-other-genocide-against-the-rohingya-in-burma_4352629.html.
48. Strangio, p. 150.
49. Lintner, p. 189.

CHAPTER 11: TOTALITARIANS TOGETHER

1. Hansard, "North Korea," 13 March 2003, https://hansard.parliament.uk/Lords/2003-03-13/debates/aaa7bab0-7d92-48d9-890c-b692be56a62b/NorthKorea.
2. Graham Allen, *Destined for War: Can America and China Escape Thucydides's Trap?* (Scribe, 2017), p. 176.
3. Eleanor Albert, "The China-North Korea Relationship," The Council on Foreign Relations, 25 June 2019, https://www.cfr.org/backgrounder/china-north-korea-relationship.
4. *Wall Street Journal*, "Covert Chinese Trade with North Korea Moves into the Open," 7 December 2020, https://www.wsj.com/articles/covert-chinese-trade-with-north-korea-moves-into-the-open-11607345372.
5. Ibid.
6. *Washington Post*, "Leaked Documents Reveal Huawei's Secret Operations to Build North Korea's Wireless Network," 22 July 2019, https://www.washingtonpost.com/world/national-security/leaked-documents-reveal-huaweis-secret-operations-to-build-north-koreas-wireless-network/2019/07/22/583430fe-8d12-11e9-adf3-f70f78c156e8_story.html.
7. *Diplomat*, "North Korea's Public Security Gets Lessons from China," 5 August 2021, https://thediplomat.com/2021/08/north-koreas-public-security-gets-lessons-from-china/.
8. Democratic People's Republic of Korea, the official name for North Korea
9. Andray Abrahamian, *Being in North Korea* (Walter H. Shorenstein Asia-Pacific Research Center, 2020), p. 152.
10. Tim Peters, "Beset from Within, Beleaguered from Without: North Korea's Catacombs in an Era of Extermination," *Freedom of Belief & Christian Mission*, Regnum Edinburgh Centenary Series, 28, p. 8.
11. Julia and Kevin Garratt, *Two Tears on the Window* (First Choice Books, 2018), p. 260.

12. Daniel Wertz, "Issue Brief: China-North Korea Relations," National Committee on North Korea, November 2019, https://www.ncnk.org/resources/briefing-papers/all-briefing-papers/china-north-korea-relations.

13. Ibid.

CHAPTER 12: WAKE-UP CALL

1. Gov.uk, "Chinese State Visit: Up to £40 Billion Deals Agreed," 23 October 2015, https://www.gov.uk/government/news/chinese-state-visit-up-to-40-billion-deals-agreed

2. *Daily Mail*, "John Bercow Takes a Second Swipe at China," 20 October 2015, https://www.dailymail.co.uk/news/article-3280895/Bercow-takes-extraordinary-swipe-state-visit-Communist-Chinese-President-hails-great-democracy-India.html.

3. *Guardian*, "Minister Ordered to Address Chinese Human Rights Issue in Commons," 22 October 2015, https://www.theguardian.com/uk-news/2015/oct/22/minister-ordered-address-chinese-human-rights-issue-commons.

4. Hansard, China (Human Rights), 22 October 2015, https://hansard.parliament.uk/commons/2015-10-22/debates/cb69cdb6-6527-428c-9f81-41c3c28d6793/CommonsChamber.

5. The Conservative Party Human Rights Commission, *The Darkest Moment: The Crackdown on Human Rights in China 2013–2016*, 2016, https://conservativepartyhumanrightscommission.co.uk/reports.

6. The Conservative Party Human Rights Commission, *The Darkness Deepens: The Crackdown on Human Rights in China 2016–2020*, 2021, https://conservativepartyhumanrightscommission.co.uk/reports.

7. BBC, "Huawei Row: Australian MPs Cancel UK Trip amid Tensions over Leak," 15 February 2020, https://www.bbc.co.uk/news/world-australia-51513886.

8. *Daily Mail*, "US Congressmen Send Letter to MPs Warning Britain of the 'Catastrophic Cost' of Allowing Chinese Firm Huawei to Build the UK's 5G Networks," 2 February 2020, https://www.dailymail.co.uk/news/article-7957085/US-congress-warn-MPs-cost-allowing-Huawei-build-UKs-5G-networks.html.

9. Senator Marco Rubio, "Rubio, Cotton, Cornyn Urge Members of the United Kingdom's National Security Council to Reject Huawei in 5G Infrastructure," 27 January 2020, https://www.rubio.senate.gov/public/index.cfm/2020/1/rubio-cotton-cornyn-urge-members-of-united-kingdom-s-national-security-council-to-reject-huawei-in-5g-infrastructure.

10. BBC, "Huawei: Pompeo Urges UK to 'Relook' at Decision Ahead of UK Visit," 30 January 2020, https://www.bbc.co.uk/news/uk-politics-51290646.

11. *Hill*, "Trump 'Apoplectic' in Phone Call with UK's Johnson about Huawei Decision: Report," 6 February 2020, https://thehill.com/homenews/administration/481869-trump-apoplectic-in-phone-call-with-uks-johnson-about-huawei-decision/.

12. *Politico*, "Hong Kong Activists Urge UK to Give Ex-Colony's Residents Real Citizenship," 23 November 2019, https://www.politico.eu/article/hong-kong-activists-urge-uk-on-residents-citizenship/.

13. BBC, "Hong Kong: UK Makes Citizenship Offer to Residents," 1 July 2020, https://www.bbc.co.uk/news/uk-politics-53246899.

14. *South China Morning Post*, "Britain Plans Extension of BN(O) Visa Scheme to Allow Hong Kongers Aged 18 to 24 to Apply Independently of Parents," 24 February 2022, https://www.scmp.com/news/hong-kong/society/article/3168295/emigration-wave-continues-about-100000-hongkongers-apply-bno.

15. Reuters, "China Takes First Step in $1 Billion Pledge to UN to Fund Peace, Development," 6 May 2016, https://www.reuters.com/article/us-china-un-idUSKCN0XX1YI.

16. BBC, "Meng Hongwei: China Sentences Ex-Interpol Chief to 13 Years in Jail," 21 January 2020, https://www.bbc.co.uk/news/world-asia-china-51185838.

17. Congressional Record—House, 9 May 1984, H.R.5119, p. 11604.

18. *Toronto Star*, "The 'Forgotten' Canadians Detained in China," 20 December 2018, https://www.thestar.com/vancouver/2018/12/20/the-forgotten-canadians-detained-in-china.html.

19. *Policy Options*, "Misinformation and Chines Interference in Canada's Affairs," 4 January 2022, https://policyoptions.irpp.org/magazines/january-2022/misinformation-and-chinese-interference-in-canadas-affairs/.

20. Gov.uk, "The Return of Geopolitics: Foreign Secretary's Mansion House Speech at the Lord Mayor's 2022 Easter Banquet," 27 April 2022, https://www.gov.uk/government/speeches/foreign-secretarys-mansion-house-speech-at-the-lord-mayors-easter-banquet-the-return-of-geopolitics.

21. *Politico*, "David Sassoli to China: Europe Is No 'Punching Bag'," 23 March 2021, https://www.politico.eu/article/david-sassoli-to-china-europe-is-not-a-punching-ball/.

22. European Parliament, "MEPs Refuse Any Agreement with China Whilst Sanctions Are in Place," 20 May 2021, https://www.europarl.europa.eu/news/en/press-room/20210517IPR04123/meps-refuse-any-agreement-with-china-whilst-sanctions-are-in-place.

23. European Parliament, "EU China Summit Was a 'Dialogue of the Deaf'," 5 April 2022, https://www.youtube.com/watch?v=JyskvN7VNpo.

24. Rush Doshi, *The Long Game: China's Grand Strategy to Displace American Order* (Oxford University Press, 2021), p. 5.

25. Ibid., p. 6.

26. Elizabeth Economy, *The World According to China*, (Polity Press, 2022), p. 2.

27. Hong Kong Watch, "New Report: ESG, China and Human Rights," 2021, https://www.hongkongwatch.org/all-posts/2021/9/22/new-report-esg-china-and-human-rights-why-the-time-has-come-for-investors-to-act.

28. George Soros, "BlackRock's China Blunder," *Wall Street Journal*, 6 September 2021, https://www.wsj.com/articles/blackrock-larry-fink-china-hkex-sse-authoritarianism-xi-jinping-term-limits-human-rights-ant-didi-global-

national-security-11630938728.

29. George Soros, "Investors in Xi's China Face a Rude Awakening," *Financial Times*, 30 August 2021, https://www.ft.com/content/ecf7de34-e595-4814-9cbd-4a5119187330.

30. *Times*, "Helena Morrissey Calls on Investors to Ditch China Because of Rights Abuse," 5 October 2021, https://www.thetimes.co.uk/article/helena-morrissey-calls-on-investors-to-ditch-china-because-of-rights-abuse-rtfnwvmtq.

31. Matt Pottinger, "Beijing's American Hustle: How Chinese Grand Strategy Exploits US Power," *Foreign Affairs*, September/October 2021, https://www.foreignaffairs.com/articles/asia/2021-08-23/beijings-american-hustle.

32. *Wall Street Journal*, "Xi Jinping Aims to Rein in Chinese Capitalism, Hew to Mao's Socialist Vision," 20 September 2021, https://www.wsj.com/articles/xi-jinping-aims-to-rein-in-chinese-capitalism-hew-to-maos-socialist-vision-11632150725.

33. *Financial Times*, "The Chinese Control Revolution: The Maoist Echoes of Xi's Power Play," 5 September 2021, https://www.ft.com/content/bacf9b6a-326b-4aa9-a8f6-2456921e61ec.

34. *Financial Times*, "China in 'Deep Crisis', Says Hong Kong Private Equity Chief," 28 April 2022, https://www.ft.com/content/6bf52409-fe31-4f57-ae24-f2bd9146a698.

35. Gov.uk, "C's Speech to the International Institute for Strategic Studies," 30 November 2021, https://www.gov.uk/government/speeches/cs-speech-to-the-international-institute-for-strategic-studies.

36. Anne-Marie Brady, "Magic Weapons: China's Political Influence Activities under Xi Jinping," Wilson Center, 18 September 2017, https://www.wilsoncenter.org/article/magic-weapons-chinas-political-influence-activities-under-xi-jinping.

37. Charles Parton, "China-UK Relations: Where to Draw the Border Between Influence and Interference," RUSI, 20 February 2019, https://www.rusi.org/explore-our-research/publications/occasional-papers/china-uk-relations-where-draw-border-between-influence-and-interference.

38. Charles Parton, "Towards a UK Strategy and Policies for Relations with China," King's College London, June 2020, https://www.kcl.ac.uk/policy-institute/assets/towards-a-uk-strategy-and-policies-for-relations-with-china.pdf.

39. BBC, "Xi Jinping Calls for More 'Loveable' Image for China in Bid to Make Friends," 2 June 2021, https://www.bbc.co.uk/news/world-asia-china-57327177.

40. U.S.-China Economic and Security Review Commission, "2021 Annual Report to Congress," https://www.uscc.gov/annual-report/2021-annual-report-congress.

41. Ian Williams, *Every Breath You Take: China's New Tyranny* (Birlinn, 2021), p. 283.

INDEX